WJEC/Eduqas A Level Law

Book 1

Sara Davies • Karen Phillips • Louisa Draper-Walters

Published in 2018 by Illuminate Publishing Ltd
PO Box 1160, Cheltenham, Gloucestershire GL50 9RW

Orders: Please visit www.illuminatepublishing.com
or email sales@illuminatepublishing.com.

British Library Cataloguing in Publication Data.

A catalogue record for this book is available from the British Library.

ISBN 978-1-911208-45-7

Printed by Standartu Spaustuvė, Lithuania

03.18

The publisher's policy is to use papers that are natural, renewable and recyclable products made from wood grown in sustainable forests. The logging and manufacturing processes are expected to conform to the environmental regulations of the country of origin.

Editor: Julia Sandford-Cooke (WordFire Communications)
Design and layout: Kamae Design
Cover design: Kamae Design
Cover image: arosoft / Shutterstock.com

Acknowledgements
Crown copyright information is reproduced with the permission of the Controller of HMSO and the Queen's Printer for Scotland.

Dedication
In memory of Dr Pauline O'Hara, who was an inspiration to us and many Law students.

Contents

Introduction

How to use this book

The contents of this textbook are designed to guide you through the WJEC or Eduqas Law specification and lead you to success in the subject. It has been written by senior examiners who have pinpointed what is required of candidates, in terms of content, to achieve the highest marks. In addition, common errors have been identified, and support and advice given in how to avoid these errors, which will help lead to success in your AS/A Level examination. It contains a range of specimen exam questions for each specification, along with sample answers and examiner commentaries.

The book covers:

- Eduqas AS Level components 1 and 2
- Eduqas A Level components 1, 2 and 3
- WJEC AS Level units 1 and 2
- WJEC A Level units 3 and 4.

This textbook covers the knowledge content that is required for each topic within the various specifications. There is also a selection of learning features throughout the topics.

Key terms: Important legal terms are emboldened in the main text and accompanied by a definition in the margin. They have also been compiled into a glossary at the end of the book for ease of reference.

Grade Boost: This gives you an insight into the examiner's mind and provides advice on things you should include to achieve the higher marks.

Stretch and Challenge: These activities provide opportunities to research a topic further and give you advice on wider reading. These are usually additional cases, current affairs or areas under reform, knowledge of which should really impress your examiner.

Cases and Key Cases: Examples of cases are highlighted to clarify the points of law they illustrate.

Exam Skills: This gives advice and guidance on how to prepare for your exams.

Summary: At the end of each topic there is a handy summary to help you structure your revision.

The **Exam practice and techniques** section provides you with both an opportunity to practise your own examination skills and an insight into the quality of answer that is expected to achieve a high grade. This section shows you examples of responses relating to higher and middle mark bands. A detailed commentary explains how the candidates achieved their marks, and key tips suggest how these answers can be improved. The marks that would have been given to a candidate are split into the Assessment Objectives, so you can see how the exam answer has been marked.

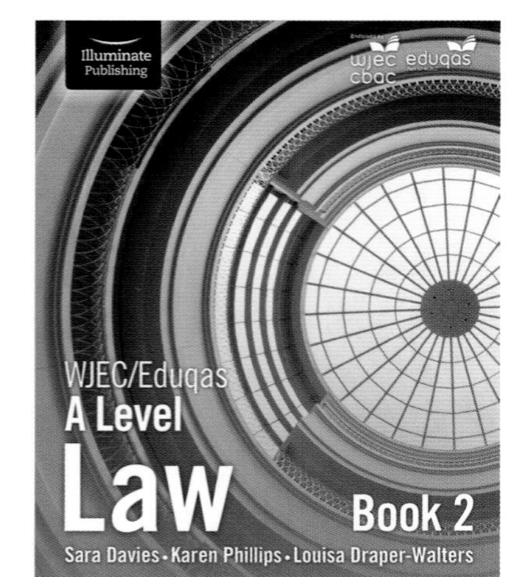

AS/A Level qualifications

The book is intended to support you in AS and **some** of the A Level study for both Eduqas and WJEC. Additional content required for A Level specifications for both Eduqas and WJEC can be found in Book 2 (ISBN 978 1 911208 46 4).

The content coverage section below explains exactly what can be found in each book. References to the WJEC specifications are represented by the letter W and references to the Eduqas specifications are represented by the letter E. Content that is **only** relevant to specific parts of either the Eduqas or WJEC specifications is colour coded in both the main text and the topic overview tables.

WJEC

WJEC only (purple)

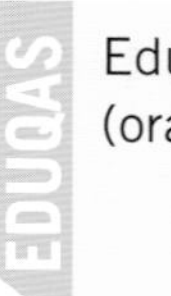

Eduqas AS only (orange)

EDUQAS A-LEVEL

Eduqas A Level only (blue)

Book 1	Book 2
Law making, the Nature of Law and the Welsh and English Legal Systems **E1.1.1 W1.1** Law making Law reform **E1.1.2 W1.2** Delegated legislation **E1.1.3 W1.3** Statutory interpretation **E1.1.4 W1.4** Judicial precedent **E1.2.1 W1.5** Civil courts **E1.2.2 W1.6** Criminal process Juries **E1.2.3 W1.7** Legal personnel: Barristers and solicitors Judiciary Magistrates **E1.2.4 W1.8** Access to justice and funding **Law of Contract** **E2.1.1 W3.6** Rules of contract **E2.1.2 W3.7** Essential requirements of a contract **E2.1.3 E2.1.5 W3.10** Discharge of contract **E2.1.4 E2.1.6 W3.11** Remedies: Contract **Law of Tort** **E2.2.1 W2.1** Rules of tort **E2.2.2 W2.2** Liability in negligence **E2.2.3 W2.3** Occupier's liability **E2.2.4 E2.2.7 W2.4** Remedies: Tort **Criminal Law** **E2.3.1 W3.12** Rules of criminal law **E2.3.2 W3.13** General elements of criminal liability **E2.3.3 W3.14** Offences against the person **Human Rights Law** **E2.4.1 E 2.4.2 W3.1** Rules, theory and protection of human rights law **E2.4.3 W3.2** Specific provisions of the ECHR **E2.4.5 E2.4.6 W3.5** Reform of human rights **E2.4.4 W3.3** Restrictions of the ECHR	**Law of Contract** **E2.1.3 W3.8** Express and implied terms **E2.1.4 W3.9** Misrepresentation and economic duress **Law of Tort** **E2.2.4** Torts connected to land **E2.2.5** Vicarious liability **E2.2.6** Defences: Tort **Criminal Law** **E2.3.3 W3.14** Fatal offences against the person **E2.3.4 W3.15** Property offences **E2.3.5 E2.3.6 W3.16 W3.17** Capacity and necessity defences **E2.3.7 W3.17** Preliminary offences of attempt

Which qualification are you studying for?

You may be studying for either Eduqas qualifications or WJEC qualifications. This book covers the examination requirements for both. Most of the content is very similar in all the specifications, and the questions and mark schemes only differ slightly.
For more information, look at the examination guidance section of this book and the examination papers and mark schemes of the qualification for which you are studying and discuss them with your teacher.

WJEC AS/A Level examination content

Wales

In Wales, most candidates will be studying for the WJEC AS in their first year followed by the A Level in their second year. In most cases, AS exams will be sat at the end of the first year and these will be combined with the A Level exams sat at the end of the second year to achieve the full A Level qualification. For the full WJEC specification content, go to www.wjec.co.uk.

- The AS is less challenging and worth 40% of the full A Level qualification.
- The AS is a stepping stone to the full A Level qualification, so ideas introduced at AS will be developed on the full A Level papers.
- A full WJEC A Level has four units or examinations. This content is covered across both books 1 and 2.
- A WJEC AS Level has two units or examinations. This textbook includes enough topics to help you prepare for the exams.

<table>
<tr><th></th><th>Unit 1</th><th>Unit 2</th><th>Unit 3</th><th>Unit 4</th></tr>
<tr><th rowspan="3">WJEC AS Level</th><td>The Nature of Law and the Welsh and English Legal Systems</td><td>The Law of Tort</td><td>n/a</td><td>n/a</td></tr>
<tr><td>80 marks available (25% of full A Level qualification)</td><td>60 marks available (15% of full A Level qualification)</td><td>n/a</td><td>n/a</td></tr>
<tr><td>1 hour and 45 minutes</td><td>1 hour and 30 minutes</td><td>n/a</td><td>n/a</td></tr>
<tr><th rowspan="3">WJEC A Level</th><td colspan="2" rowspan="3">Units 1 and 2, above, plus units 3 and 4</td><td>The Practice of Substantive Law</td><td>Substantive Law Perspectives</td></tr>
<tr><td>100 marks available (30% of full A Level qualification)</td><td>100 marks available (30% of full A Level qualification)</td></tr>
<tr><td>1 hour and 45 minutes</td><td>2 hours</td></tr>
</table>

The overall weightings are 40% for AS and 60% for A Level.

- **Unit 1:** The Nature of Law and the Welsh and English Legal Systems (25%).
- **Unit 2:** The Law of Tort (15%).
- **Unit 3:** The Practice of Substantive Law (30%).
- **Unit 4:** Substantive Law Perspectives (30%).

Key terms and legal authority

Students often say that studying law is like learning a whole new language. In fact, you will need to become familiar with some Latin terms, such as *ratio decidendi*. If you are to get into the top mark bands, you need to use appropriate legal terminology. Key terms are highlighted throughout the book. Many of the shorter exam questions will require you to explain the meaning of a term, or describe a concept. Extended-response essays should always start with an explanation of the key term in the question. The rest of your answer should focus on ideas and debates related to that key term.

In order to support the points you make, you should include legal authority. This can be a case, statute or legislation, for example ***Donoghue v Stevenson (1932)*** or ***s1 Theft Act 1968***.

Eduqas AS/A Level examination content

England

In England, most candidates will be studying for the Eduqas AS or A Level. For the full Eduqas specification content, go to www.eduqas.co.uk.

The Eduqas AS Level is half of the content of the full A Level but is equally challenging as the full A Level.

- A full Eduqas A Level has three components or examinations. This content is covered over both books 1 and 2.
- A full Eduqas AS Level has two components or examinations. This textbook includes enough topics to help you prepare for the exams.

	Component 1	Component 2	Component 3
Eduqas AS Level	The Nature of Law and the English legal System	Understanding Substantive Law	n/a
	60 marks available (50% of qualification)	60 marks available (50% of qualification)	n/a
	1 hour and 30 minutes	1 hour and 30 minutes	n/a
Eduqas A Level	The nature of Law and the English Legal System	Substantive Law in Practice	Perspectives of Substantive Law
	50 marks available (25% of qualification)	75 marks available (37.5% of qualification)	75 marks available (37.5% of qualification)
	1 hour and 30 minutes	2 hours and 15 minutes	2 hours and 15 minutes

AS Level Law with Eduqas is a stand-alone qualification and is weighted at 40% of the overall A Level. Each component is worth 50% of the qualification.

A Level Law with Eduqas is a linear course and the components are weighted as follows:

- **Component 1:** 25%.
- **Component 2:** 37.5%.
- **Component 3:** 37.5%.

Assessment in Eduqas and WJEC Law

Assessment is covered in more detail in the examination section at the end of this book. However, before you start to study, it will help you to understand the Assessment Objectives that you are being tested on. These consist of the following:

- **Assessment Objective 1 (AO1):** Describing what you know.
- **Assessment Objective 2 (AO2):** Applying your knowledge.
- **Assessment Objective 3 (AO3):** Analysing/evaluating this knowledge.

All mark schemes offer marks for the different skills and examiners are trained to look for and recognise them.

- **AO1:** You must demonstrate knowledge and understanding of legal rules and principles.
- **AO2:** You must apply legal rules and principles to given scenarios in order to present a legal argument using appropriate legal terminology.
- **AO3:** You must analyse and evaluate legal rules, principles, concepts and issues.

THE NATURE OF LAW AND THE WELSH AND ENGLISH LEGAL SYSTEMS

Law making

Spec reference	Key content	Assessment Objectives	Where does this topic feature on each specification/ exam?
WJEC AS/A Level 1.1: Law making **Eduqas AS Level 1.1.1:** Parliamentary and European law making **Eduqas A Level 1.1.1:** Parliamentary and European law making	• Historical context of law making in Wales and the United Kingdom, including parliamentary sovereignty, separation of powers and the rule of law; Royal Prerogative • Parliamentary law making including Green and White Papers; the legislative process; the composition and role of Parliament. Concept and application of parliamentary sovereignty • The legislative process in Wales and the UK; Welsh legislature law making: the composition and role of Parliament and the Welsh legislature • The Devolution Settlement in Wales including the role of the Supreme Court • The UK Constitution including sovereignty, separation of powers and the rule of law; Royal Prerogative • European Union law including the institutions of the European Union; the sources of European Law • The impact of European Union law on the law of Wales and England	**AO1** Demonstrate knowledge and understanding of legal rules and principles **AO2** Apply legal rules and principles to given scenarios in order to present a legal argument using appropriate legal terminology	**WJEC AS/A Level:** Unit 1 Section A **Eduqas AS Level:** Component 1 Section A **Eduqas A-Level:** Component 1 Section A

'Sources of law' refers to the way in which our law comes into existence.

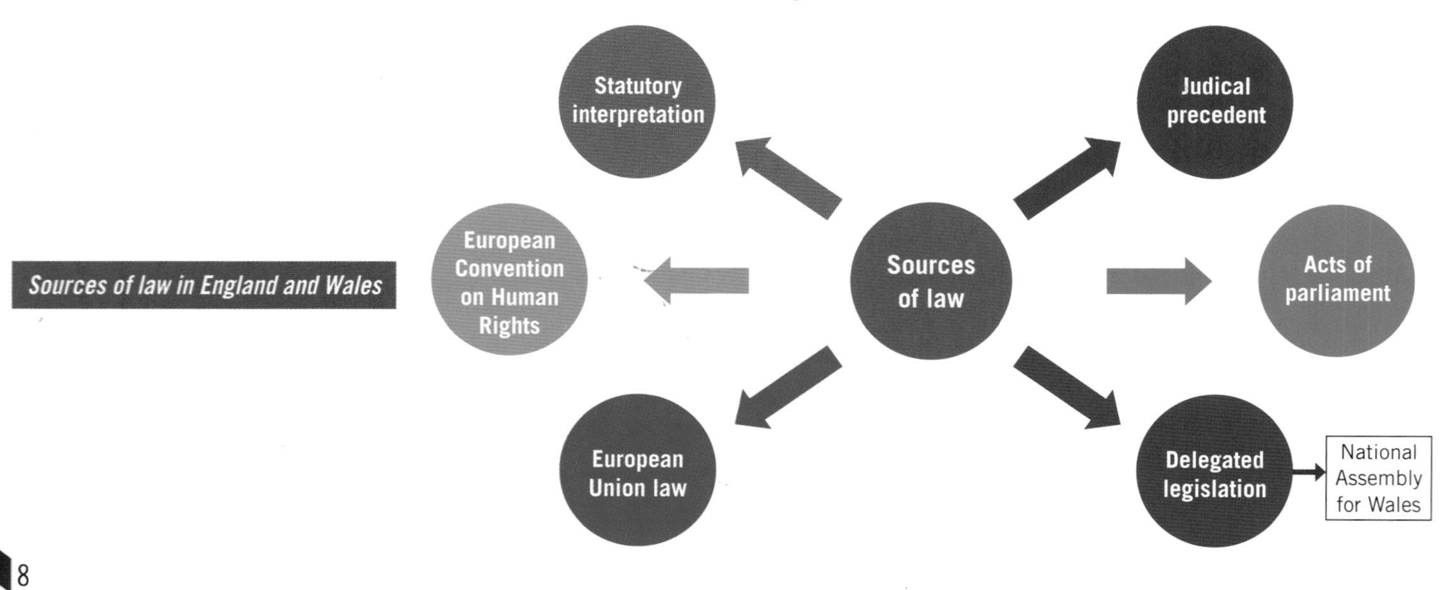

Sources of law in England and Wales

Acts of Parliament

Most of our law comes from the UK Parliament, which passes hundreds of laws every year. Parliament is made up of three institutions.

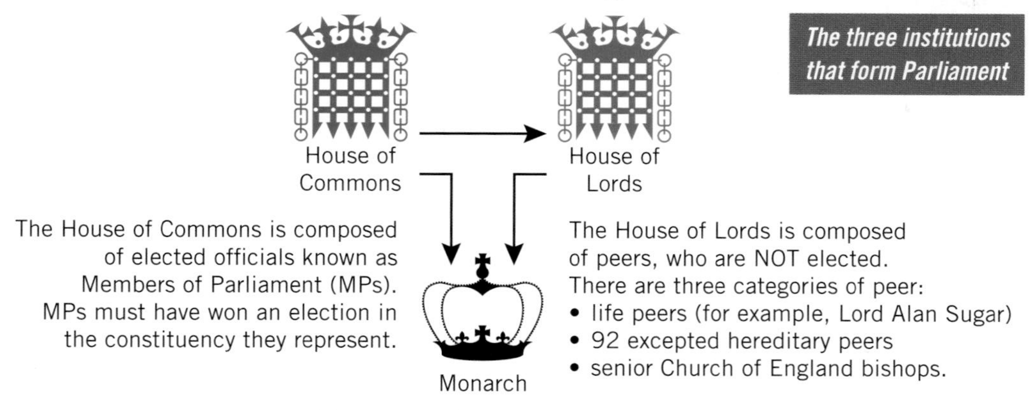

The UK Parliament is based at the Palace of Westminster in London so is sometimes referred to as 'the Westminster Parliament' or simply 'Westminster'. It consists of two debating chambers: the House of Commons and the House of Lords. The third element of the UK Parliament is the monarch, who is the head of state. The role of the monarch is hereditary: it normally passes from the present monarch to their eldest child when the reigning monarch dies.

All three parts of the UK Parliament must approve Acts of Parliament before they can become law.

Green and White Papers

The first stage is often to consult relevant people via a Green and/or White Paper.

Green Papers

This is an intention to change the law and outlines the format this change could take. It is published on the Internet for the public to comment on and copies are also distributed to interested parties. These individuals will then comment and put forward suggestions on the proposal.

White Papers

Parliament will then publish a White Paper, which is a positive proposal on the format the new law will take. It often includes changes as a response to the opinions of the interested parties. There is then a further chance for consultation before the final Bill enters Parliament for consideration.

Bills

All Acts of Parliament begin life as Bills, which is a draft law or a proposal for a change in the law. There are three types of Bill: Public Bills, Private Members' Bills and Private Bills.

Public Bills

A Public Bill involves matters of public policy that will affect the whole country or a large section of it. These Bills will sometimes reflect the manifesto of the government in power at the time. Most government Bills are in this category. Examples include:

- ***Children and Social Work Act 2017***
- ***Juries Act 1974***
- ***Finance Act 2017***.

GRADE BOOST

Public Bills currently being considered by Parliament can be found at www.parliament.uk/business/bills-and-legislation.
Recent legislation can be found at www.legislation.gov.uk/ukpga

Private Members' Bills

These Bills are sponsored by individual MPs. At each parliamentary session, 20 members are chosen from a ballot to take their turn in presenting their Bills to Parliament. Relatively few Private Members' Bills become law, and the time available for debating them is very short. As they tend to cover issues that the individual MP is interested in, they also rarely reflect the government's general agenda. Examples of Private Members' Bills that have become law are:

- ***Abortion Act 1967***
- ***Marriage Act 1994.***

Private Bills

A Private Bill is a law that is designed to affect only individual people or corporations. Examples include:

- ***University College London Act 1996***
- ***Whitehaven Harbour Act 2007.***

Legislative process

When a Bill is prepared, it is first presented to the UK Parliament and then has to go through a specific process before it officially becomes law.

How a Bill progresses through Parliament (Source: www.parliament.uk/about/how/laws/flash-passage-bill. Crown Copyright)

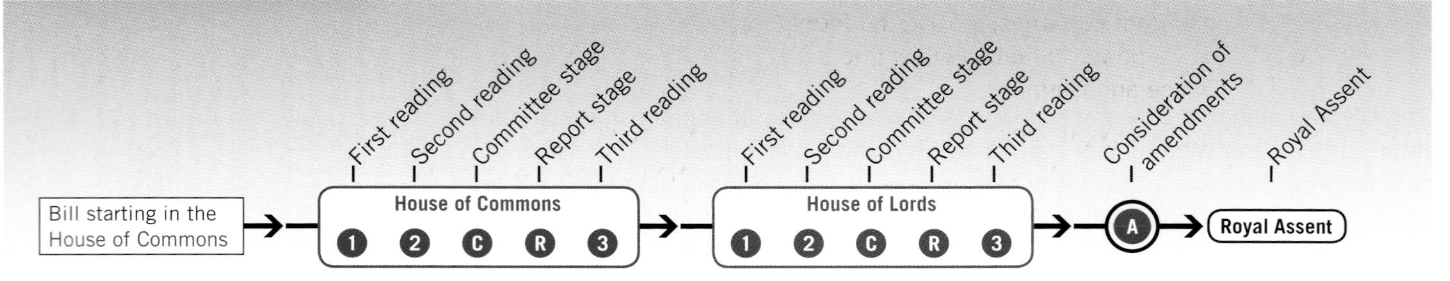

The House of Commons can use powers under the ***Parliament Acts 1911*** and ***1949*** to make a law without the consent of the **House of Lords**. This rarely happens but is an available option if the House of Lords cannot reach an agreement. An example of the House of Commons using this power was when they passed the ***Hunting Act 2004***, which outlawed the hunting of wild animals using dogs.

KEY TERMINOLOGY

House of Lords: the name of the Upper House in Parliament, which is the legislative chamber. Confusion arose before the establishment of the Supreme Court, as the highest appeal court was also called the House of Lords.

First reading

The title of the prepared Bill is read to the House of Commons. This is called the first reading, and acts as notification of the proposed measure.

Second reading

This is the first opportunity for MPs to debate the main principles of the Bill. At the end of the debate, the House of Commons votes on whether the legislation should proceed.

Committee stage

This is a detailed examination of the Bill where every clause is agreed to, changed or removed, taking into account the points made during the debates at the first and second readings.

Report stage

The committee will then report back to the House of Commons, and any proposed amendments are debated and voted upon.

Third reading

This is a final chance for the House of Commons to debate the contents of a Bill but no amendments can be made at this stage. There is simply a vote on whether to accept or reject the legislation as it stands.

House of Lords

The Bill then goes to the House of Lords, where it travels through a similar process of three readings. If the House of Lords alters anything, the Bill returns to the Commons for consideration. This is known as 'ping pong'.

Royal Assent

In the majority of cases, agreement between the Lords and the Commons is reached and the Bill is then presented for Royal Assent. Technically, the Queen must give her consent to all legislation before it can become law but, in practice, that consent is never refused and is always granted.

The Bill is now an Act of Parliament and becomes law, though most Acts do not take effect the moment the Queen gives her consent, but instead on a specified future date. This is known as 'commencement'.

The UK constitution

The United Kingdom does not have a written constitution. This means that it has no single legal document which sets out the fundamental laws outlining how the state works. Unlike in most other countries, there is no formal regulation of the organisation and distribution of state power. Countries which do have a written constitution include the USA, France and Germany.

We therefore rely on three key principles to underpin the UK's unwritten constitution:

1. **parliamentary sovereignty** **2.** the rule of law **3.** separation of powers.

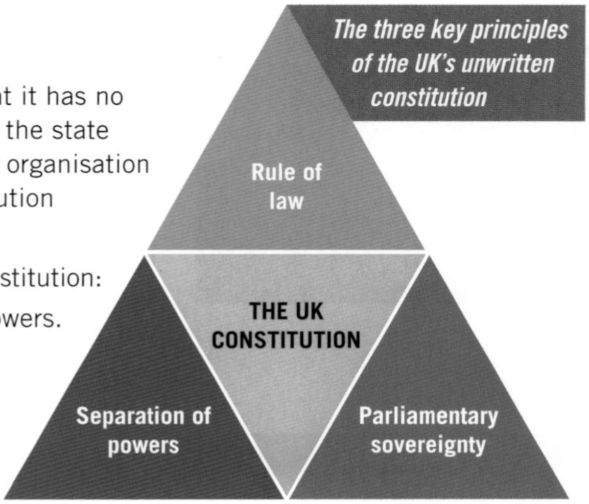

The three key principles of the UK's unwritten constitution

Rule of law

THE UK CONSTITUTION

Separation of powers

Parliamentary sovereignty

Parliamentary sovereignty

In its most simple form, sovereignty is the principle of absolute and unlimited power. An **Act of Parliament** can completely overrule any **custom**, **judicial precedent**, **delegated legislation** or previous Act of Parliament. This is because MPs are elected by the voters in their constituency in a democratic process so each MP is participating in the legislative process on behalf of those voters.

Dicey's theory of parliamentary sovereignty

AV Dicey was a famous Oxford scholar and his traditional view has three main points that explain the concept of parliamentary sovereignty.

1. Parliament is sovereign and can make or unmake any law on any subject without legal constraints

This means that Parliament is the highest source of English law and has the right to make or unmake any law, and to override or set aside any existing legislation. So, if Parliament decided that all dog owners also had to own a cat, there might be a public outcry, but the laws would still be valid and the courts would be obliged to uphold them.

The reason for this power is that Parliament is democratically elected and therefore has the upper hand when making the laws that every citizen has to follow.

2. No Parliament can bind another

An Act of Parliament passed by a previous Parliament can be repealed by the next Parliament. No Act of Parliament is entrenched like the American Bill of Rights.

3. No Act can be challenged by a court nor its validity questioned

This means that, even if it were alleged that an Act has been passed by fraudulent means, it has to be upheld by the courts anyway. It cannot be overruled by another 'arm' of the state. The only way to challenge the action of ministers, or any other law makers, is through **judicial review**, which is dealt with by the Queen's Bench Division of the High Court.

KEY TERMINOLOGY

parliamentary sovereignty: Dicey's principle that Parliament has absolute and unlimited power, and that an Act of Parliament overrules any other source of law.
Act of Parliament (statute): a source of primary legislation that comes from the UK legislature.
custom: rules of behaviour which develop in a community without being deliberately invented.
judicial precedent (case law): a source of law where past judges' decisions create law for future judges to follow.
delegated legislation (secondary or subordinate legislation): law created by a body other than Parliament but with the authority of Parliament, as laid down in primary legislation.

Threats to Dicey's theory

Dicey's theory of parliamentary sovereignty is a little out of date, and does not reflect our current legal position because there are three significant erosions of parliamentary sovereignty.

1. Membership of the European Union

European Union (EU) law overrides any UK law made before or after the UK joined the EU in 1972. However, since the 2016 Brexit referendum result, it remains to be seen how EU law will continue to influence the UK.

2. Human Rights Act 1998

The ***Human Rights Act 1998*** made it a legal requirement that all public authorities must behave in a way that does not infringe our human rights. This means that under ***s3*** judges have to interpret every Act of Parliament in a way that upholds human rights. If the law abuses human rights, they have to declare it incompatible under ***s4*** and send the law back to Parliament to change.

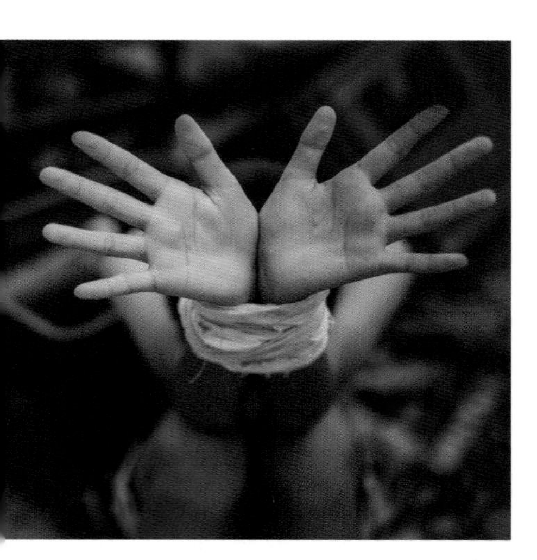

3. Devolution

There have been changes to our constitution through **devolution**. The formation of the Welsh Government, Northern Ireland Assembly and the Scottish Parliament have had an impact on parliamentary sovereignty.

Rule of law

Dicey was also responsible for the second theory that underpins the UK's unwritten constitution. He said that the concept of the **rule of law** has three components:

1. No sanction without breach

No one should be punished unless they have broken a law. This means that there should be proper legal procedure and that all law should be public and cannot be secret. In principle, no law should have **retrospective effect**; that is, a new law should not apply to past events.

In our legal system actions of, and decisions by, government ministers can be challenged by judicial review. This element of the rule of law ensures that the state does not have wide discretionary powers to make arbitrary decisions.

2. One law should govern everyone

This means that everybody (including the government) is equal before the law. Dicey's idea was that court proceedings, the judicial mechanisms controlling society would apply to the citizen and to the government and public bodies. However, some institutions of the state, such as the police, are given more powers than citizens to enable the state to function.

3. Rights of individuals are secured by decisions of judges

This engages with the idea of judicial precedent, which is that the highest courts can make a decision in a case which has to be followed by the lower courts. In this way, no new legal principles are created. Although most modern laws are created by Acts of Parliament and delegated legislation, judicial decisions do still create law.

Problems with Dicey's theory

Dicey's theory conflicts with the principle of parliamentary supremacy. This is the acknowledgement that Parliament has the right to make or unmake any law, including granting arbitrary power to the state. This is exactly the sort of arbitrary power that the rule of law seeks to forbid.

Dicey also considered equality before the law. This is often compromised because the cost of taking legal cases to court is very high and so may not be accessible to everyone.

KEY TERMINOLOGY

judicial review: the process of challenging the legality of a decision, action or failure to act by a public body such as a government department or court.
devolution: the transference of power from central government to regional or local government (e.g. the formation of the Welsh Government, the Northern Ireland Assembly and the Scottish Parliament).
rule of law: the state should govern its citizens in accordance with rules that have been agreed upon.

GRADE BOOST

Other theorists who have developed modern interpretations of the rule of law include Lord Bingham and Joseph Raz.

Breaches of the rule of law

There have been many allegations in which the rule of law was alleged to have been breached. Here are some examples:

- **John Hemming MP**: Mr Hemming disclosed the name of a famous footballer subject to an injunction by using parliamentary privilege.
- **Prisoners' vote**: Conservative MPs proposed to ignore a ruling by the European Court of Human Rights (ECtHR) that gave UK prisoners the right to vote.
- **Abu Qatada**: The ***Human Rights Act 1998*** protects people from torture, and Abu Qatada would have been tortured or received an unfair trial for terrorist crimes that he had allegedly committed if he had been deported to his home country of Jordan. In 2013, Abu Qatada left the UK after Jordan signed a treaty promising not to use evidence obtained by torture.

Upholding the rule of law

There are also examples which show judges upholding the rule of law:

- ***The Constitutional Reform Act 2005***: This Act recognised the rule of law and the importance of the independence of the judiciary.
- ***Section 1 Constitutional Reform Act 2005***: this states that the Act does not adversely affect 'the constitutional principle of the rule of law or the Lord Chancellor's existing constitutional role in relation to that principle'.
- ***Section 17(1) Constitutional Reform Act 2005***: this outlines the oath to be taken by the Lord Chancellor to respect the rule of law and defend the independence of the judiciary. This is significant because this is the first time that the rule of law was recognised as a central issue in a statutory provision.

GRADE BOOST

Research these examples, which show judges upholding the rule of law:

- The ***Belmarsh Prisoners*** case
- ***Black Spider Memos*** case
- ***Al Rawi and others v Security Service and others***

KEY TERMINOLOGY

separation of powers: state power is separated into three types, Executive, judicial and legislative, with each type exercised by different bodies or people.
Executive: the government.

Separation of powers

Montesquieu was an 18th century French philosopher. His theory stated that the only way to safeguard the liberty of citizens is to keep the three arms of the state separate. This theory requires that individuals should not be members of more than one arm of the state, but in reality there is some overlap and we are increasingly seeing a fusion of the arms, rather than a separation.

The Prime Minister and their cabinet make up the **Executive**, but they are also members of Parliament who sit in the legislature. The Executive is also influential on the legislative agenda, as proposed policies are often part of the government's manifesto. This may reflect a particular political viewpoint, as the Executive is usually formed by the party that won the most seats in the House of Commons at a general election. This is deemed acceptable however, as the Executive is formed in a democratic way, having been elected by the public.

For a long time, there was also considerable overlap between the judiciary and the legislature. This is because the House of Lords was a legislative debating chamber as well as being the highest appeal court of the UK. This was deemed unsatisfactory because it goes against the theory of the separation of powers whereby the legislature has to be kept separate from the judiciary. As a result, the ***Constitutional Reform Act 2005*** created the UK Supreme Court, which is the highest appeal court in the United Kingdom, thus removing the most senior court from the legislature.

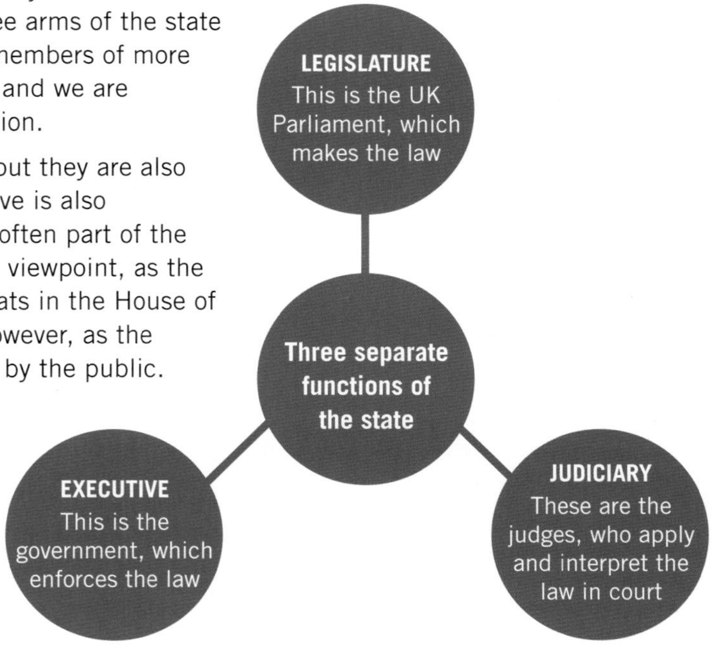

LEGISLATURE
This is the UK Parliament, which makes the law

Three separate functions of the state

EXECUTIVE
This is the government, which enforces the law

JUDICIARY
These are the judges, who apply and interpret the law in court

Montesquieu's theory states that there are three functions of the state and that these should be kept separate

WJEC

The devolution settlement

In 1998, the ***Government of Wales Act*** created a legislature for Wales, called the National Assembly for Wales, which allowed ministers to create secondary legislation in around ten areas. The ***Government of Wales Act 2006*** increased the Assembly's power by allowing it to make laws in 20 areas with the approval of the UK Parliament, and also allowed for the creation of the Welsh Government (the Executive of Wales).

Following a referendum in 2011, Wales voted to increase the Assembly's powers further so that Wales can now make its own primary legislation within a number of key specific areas, such as education and health.

This means that the laws passed in the Westminster Parliament still apply in Wales but certain subject areas are now transferred to the Welsh Government, which is based in the Senedd in Cardiff.

The Welsh Assembly

The Welsh Assembly is the legislature for Wales and includes 60 Assembly Members (AMs), one for each constituency shown on the map. The AMs are representatives from all different political parties.

MAs scrutinise proposed legislation being put forward in the Westminster Parliament when legislation is being debated.

The Welsh Government

The Welsh Government is different to the Welsh Assembly because it is the Executive, made up of representatives from the single party that holds the majority of seats in the Welsh Assembly. Its role is to implement the laws made through the legislative process. The leader of the Welsh Government is known as the First Minister.

This structure also upholds the theory of the separation of powers in Wales.

Law-making powers in Wales

The National Assembly of Wales can pass laws on all subjects in 20 devolved areas, without needing the agreement of the UK Parliament. The 20 devolved areas are contained in ***Schedule 5*** of the ***Government of Wales Act 2006***. The devolved areas are:

1. agriculture, fisheries, forestry and rural development
2. ancient monuments and historical buildings
3. culture
4. economic development
5. education and training
6. environment
7. fire and rescue services
8. food
9. health and health services
10. highways and transport
11. housing
12. local government
13. National Assembly for Wales
14. public administration
15. social welfare
16. sport and recreation
17. tourism
18. town and country planning
19. water and flood defences
20. Welsh language.

As with the UK Parliament, proposed laws are called Bills and enacted laws are called Acts. Once a Bill has been passed by the Assembly and given Royal Assent, it becomes an Act of the Assembly.

STRETCH AND CHALLENGE

Watch this video on 20 years of devolution. What are the biggest successes of devolution?
http://www.walesonline.co.uk/news/politics/seven-ways-devolution-changed-wales-13630066

The future for Wales

The Wales Act 2017 is an Act of the Parliament of the United Kingdom that sets out amendments to the ***Government of Wales Act 2006*** and devolves further powers to Wales. The legislation is based on the proposals of the St David's Day Agreement. The Act gives extra powers to the National Assembly for Wales and the Welsh Government:

- The ability to amend sections of the ***Government of Wales Act 2006*** that relate to the operation of the National Assembly of Wales and the Welsh Government, including control of its electoral system.
- Legislative control over areas such as road signs, speed limits, onshore oil and gas extraction, harbours, rail franchising, consumer advocacy and advice, among others.
- Management of Ofcom (the communications regulator) in Wales.
- Recognition that the National Assembly for Wales and the Welsh Government are permanent parts of the UK's constitutional arrangements, with a referendum required before either can be abolished.

The Act also recognised that there is a body of Welsh law and it established the position of President of Welsh Tribunals, although it does not change the single England and Wales jurisdiction.

In September 2017, First Minister Carwyn Jones established the **Commission on Justice for Wales**, covering courts, probation, prisons and youth justice. The aim of the Commission is 'to develop a distinct Welsh justice system, which improves people's access to justice, reduces crime and promotes rehabilitation'. The Commission is chaired by the outgoing Lord Chief Justice, Lord Thomas, and he will review the idea of a separate Welsh legal system.

Who is your Assembly Member? What political party do they represent?

GRADE BOOST

Read this article, which outlines the provisions of the ***Wales Act 2017***, due to come into force in 2018: http://www.walesonline.co.uk/news/politics/wales-bill-now-law-heres-12532956

GRADE BOOST

In November 2017, Lord Thomas of Cwmgiedd delivered a lecture in Cardiff University entitled 'The Past and the Future of Law in Wales'. Read a transcript of the lecture at http://sites.cardiff.ac.uk/wgc/2017/11/15/the-past-and-the-future-of-the-law-in-wales-lord-thomas-lecture-now-online

The European Union (EU)

The UK voted to leave the EU in the referendum on 23 June 2016. This has become known as **Brexit**. To leave the EU, the UK invoked an agreement called ***Article 50*** of the ***Lisbon Treaty***, which gave the country and the EU two years to agree the terms of the split. Until then, the UK remains one of the 28 member states of the EU and is affected by its law in exactly the same way.

KEY TERMINOLOGY

Brexit: the common name given to Britain's exit from the European Union and is widely used by the media when referring to issues surrounding the negotiations.

EU institutions

The UK joined the EU on 1 January 1973 by passing the ***European Communities Act 1972***. Each of the current 28 member states remain as independent sovereign states but agree to recognise the supremacy of the European Union law created by the institutions of the EU. They have also delegated some of their decision-making powers to the EU institutions. The latest addition, and the 28th member state of the EU is Croatia, which joined in July 2013.

There are five key institutions.

Brexit is ongoing, so the UK is still affected by EU law

European Parliament

The European Parliament is the directly elected arm of the EU, and is its main law-making body, along with the Commission and the Council of the European Union. The Parliament currently has 751 Members of the European Parliament (MEPs), from all 28 EU countries. They are elected every five years by the citizens of the member states. MEPs are not grouped by nationality but broadly according to their political affiliation.

The number of MEPs reflects the populations of member states and is decided according to a system of degressive proportionality. This means that MEPs from more populous countries will each represent more people than those from smaller countries. For example, the UK has 73 MEPs, Germany, which has a larger population, has 96 and the small state of Cyprus has just 6.

The European Parliament has three main roles:

1. **Legislative**: passing EU laws in conjunction with the Council of the European Union (see below), based on proposals put forward by the European Commission.
2. **Supervisory**: supervising all other EU institutions, and electing the President of the European Commission.
3. **Budgetary**: managing the EU budget, along with the Council.

European Commission

The Commission is the Executive arm of the European Union, and its main job is to manage the day-to-day running of the EU, as well as proposing legislation. The Commission is known as the 'Guardian of the Treaties' and ensures that all member states comply with their EU obligations. If they do not, the Commission can take action against them in the Court of Justice of the European Union (CJEU).

There are 28 members of the Commission, one for each member state, although they represent the interests of the EU as a whole rather than their own state. They also represent the EU internationally, negotiating agreements between the EU and other countries.

The Council of the European Union

The Council of the European Union is the main decision-making body of the EU and is its legislative arm. Its membership varies according to the topic under discussion. For example, if the topic is environmental issues, the environment minister from each state will attend.

Council ministers represent national interests by balancing the role of the Commission. They approve the budget jointly with the European Parliament.

The European Council

The European Council became an official institution after the Treaty of Lisbon in 2009. It consists of the heads of the member states, together with its president. The European Council meets every six months, or more often if the Council president requires. The meetings are known as summits and are used to set out overall EU policy.

The Court of Justice of the European Union

The CJEU is based in Luxembourg. It ensures that EU legislation is applied and interpreted consistently throughout the member states and that they uphold their EU obligations.

There is one judge from each member state assisted by eight advocates general. Cases can be brought to the CJEU by businesses, individuals and EU institutions. It has the power to issue sanctions and settle disputes but does not follow a system of precedent, instead deciding cases by a majority. For the sake of efficiency, the CJEU rarely sits as a full court with 28 judges present. It generally sits as a 'Grand Chamber' of just 13 judges or in chambers of five or three judges. Since 1988, the CJEU has been assisted by a Court of First Instance to help it cope with the large number of cases brought before it.

The CJEU has two main functions:

1. **Judicial**: The CJEU hears cases to decide whether member states have failed to fulfil their treaty obligations. These actions are usually started by the European Commission, although they can also be started by another member state. If they are found to be at fault, the accused member state must change their practice at once. If they don't comply, the court may impose a fine on the member state.

Tachographs: Commission v UK (1979)
The UK was not enforcing the EU regulation that stipulated road vehicles used for the carriage of goods (such as lorries) had to have tachographs fitted (devices that record information about driving time, speed and distance). The UK had to fulfil its EU obligation and make it compulsory for these road users to fit tachographs.

2. **Supervisory**: This is known as the preliminary ruling procedure. It helps to ensure that EU law is consistently applied in all member states. The power is given in ***Article 267*** of the ***Treaty of the Functioning of the EU***. This procedure allows a national court to ask for advice on the interpretation and validity of EU law. The preliminary ruling will help the court come to a decision in the national case.

The case of ***Bulmer v Bollinger (1974)*** laid down guidelines as to where national courts should refer questions to the CJEU. Generally, only the highest court in the member state should refer questions to the CJEU, under the principle that member states should first exhaust their own national appeal process to see if they can reach a conclusion.

The guidelines state that a referral should only be made where a ruling by the CJEU is necessary to enable the member state's court (for example, the English court) to give judgement in the case; that is, the ruling would be conclusive. The courts should also take into account:

- whether the CJEU has already made a judgement on the meaning of EU law
- whether the point is clear
- the circumstances of the case, for example, the length of time that may elapse before a ruling is given
- possible overloading of the CJEU
- the expense of taking it to the CJEU in relation to the wishes of the parties.

Sources of EU law

EU sources of law are either primary or secondary, and have **horizontal and vertical direct effect.**

- **Horizontal direct effect** is where an individual wishes to enforce an EU law against another individual or private company.
- **Vertical direct effect** is where an individual wishes to enforce an EU law against the state, or against 'emanations of the state' such as public bodies or authorities.

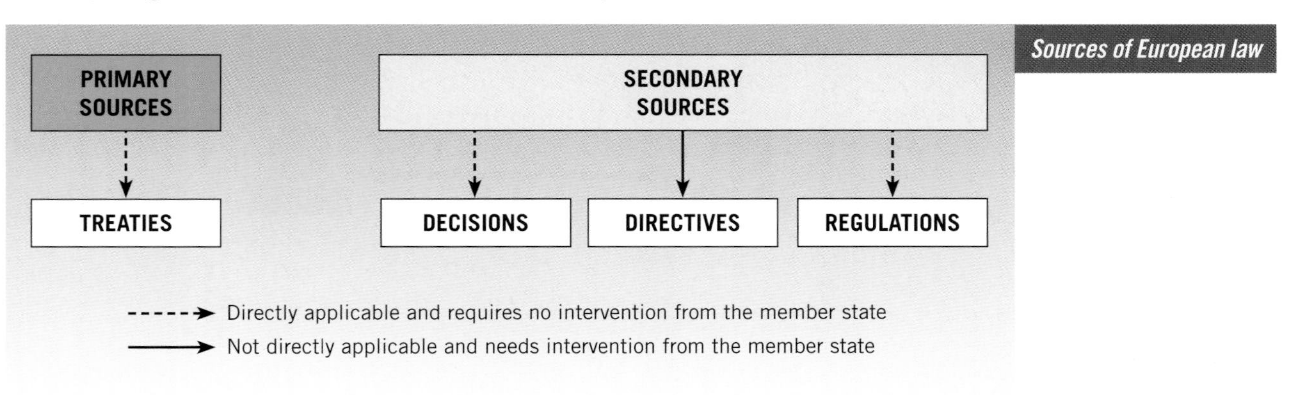

Sources of European law

KEY TERMINOLOGY

direct effect: allows individuals from EU member states to rely upon EU law in their own national courts, without having to take the case to the European courts.
held: decided; the decision of the court.

Primary sources: treaties

The primary sources of EU law are treaties, the most important being the ***Treaty of Rome***, which established the European Union. The ***Lisbon Treaty*** is also important for the purposes of Brexit.

Treaties are agreements between all 28 member states and are the highest source of EU law. Treaties set out basic principles of EU law and the aims of the EU overall.

Provisions of treaties are called articles and outline the general principles of EU law rather than giving detailed, technical rules. The application and interpretation of the articles is left to the CJEU.

Treaty provisions have both horizontal and vertical **direct effect**, which means that individuals can rely on the provisions before a national or European court, even if their member state has not implemented the legislation.

- Horizontal direct effect example case: ***Macarthys Ltd v Smith (1980)***.
- Vertical direct effect example case: ***Van Gend en Loos (1963)***.

Secondary sources: regulations

Secondary sources of EU law are passed by the institutions of the EU under ***Article 288*** of the ***Treaty on the Functioning of the European Union***.

Regulations are 'binding in every respect and directly applicable in each member state'. This means that they do not need to be adopted by the member state to become law because they apply directly with no intervention from the legislative process of the member state.

Tachographs: Commission v UK (1979)
An EU regulation required tachographs, mechanical recording equipment to be installed in vehicles used for the carriage of goods, such as lorries. The UK government decided not to implement the regulation, but left it to lorry owners to decide whether or not to install the equipment. The CJEU **held** *that member states have no discretion in the case of regulations and that* ***Article 288*** *was explicit in that all regulations automatically become law in all member states. They could not pick and choose which regulations they would implement.*

- Horizontal direct effect example case: ***Antonio Munoz v Frumar Ltd (2002)***.
- Vertical direct effect example case: ***Leonesio v Italian Ministry of Agriculture (1972)***.

Direct effect of treaties and regulations

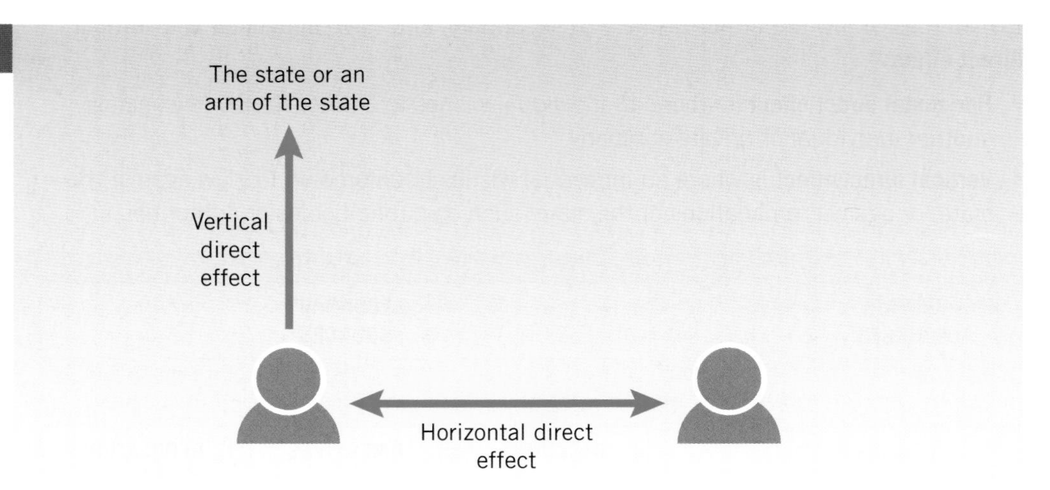

Secondary sources: decisions

Decisions are made by the European Commission against member states, corporations or individuals. These are only binding on those to whom the decisions are directed.

Secondary sources: directives

Directives are the main way in which harmonisation of laws within member states is reached. Directives are formal instructions that require member states to change their national laws within a stated period of time to give effect to the directive and achieve a particular result.

Directives are binding, but the manner of implementation is left to the discretion of the member states. This means that member states will pass their own laws, either by statute (written laws that have been passed by a legislative body in that state) or delegated legislation to bring directives into effect.

Directives can cover many topics, including company laws, banking, insurance, health and safety of workers, equal rights, consumer law and social security. Directives have vertical direct effect only.

- Vertical direct effect example cases: ***Marshall v Southampton Health Authority (1986); Van Duyn v Home Office (1974)***
- Horizontal direct effect **does not apply to directives.** Example case: ***Duke v GEC Reliance (1982).***

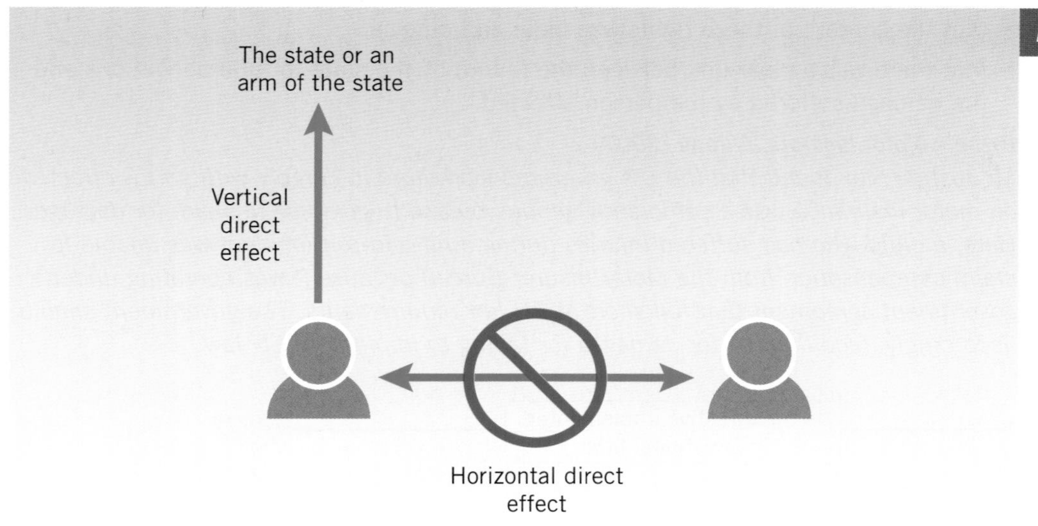

Direct effect of directives

Overcoming the problem of no horizontal direct effect for directives

Certain steps have been taken by the CJEU to overcome the problem of directives having 'no horizontal direct effect'. These include the following:

- Providing a **wide definition of 'the state' or 'emanations of the state'**. For example, in ***Foster v British Gas (1990)***, the central question was whether British Gas, which was going to be privatised, was an 'emanation of the state'. The CJEU held that it was subject to a degree of state control and providing a public service. Therefore, Foster could rely on the ***Equal Treatment Directive*** against British Gas as an emanation of the state.

- **Interpreting national law in conformity with EU law**. This uses the purposive approach to interpretation, which means that courts look for the purpose of the legislation before interpreting its words. This leads to the indirect effect principle, as laid down in the case of ***Marleasing (1990)***. Here, Spanish company law conflicted with an EU directive. National courts were required by the CJEU to interpret law 'in every way possible' to reflect the text and aims of a directive. Such interpretation gives way, indirectly, to horizontal direct effect by enabling individuals to sue a private body. This is also known as **the Von Colson principle** after the case where this technique was used.
- **The Francovich principle** allowed individuals the right to compensation from their state if it fails to implement EU law.

Francovich v Italy (1991)

A directive required member states to set up a scheme to ensure that employees received their outstanding wages if their employer had gone into liquidation. The Italian government did not set up such a scheme, so when Francovich's employer became insolvent he lost his wages and there was no scheme to compensate him. The CJEU held that Francovich had a right to compensation from the Italian government for failing to implement the directive.

This right to compensation would be recognised, provided that three criteria were satisfied:

- that the purpose of the directive was to grant such rights to individual citizens
- that the content of those rights was clear and precise
- that there was a clear link between the failure by the state to fulfil obligations and the damage suffered by the person affected.

Byrne v Motor Insurers' Bureau (2007)

Mr Justice Flax found that the UK government's failure to comply with an EC directive on motor insurance was a sufficiently serious breach to give rise to claim for damages. Here, a child who had suffered injuries during a hit-and-run incident was unable to claim compensation from the Motor Insurer Bureau because it was operating under a government agreement that fell short of EU law requirements. The government should, accordingly, face liability for damages for failing to implement EU law.

Direct effect of EU directives

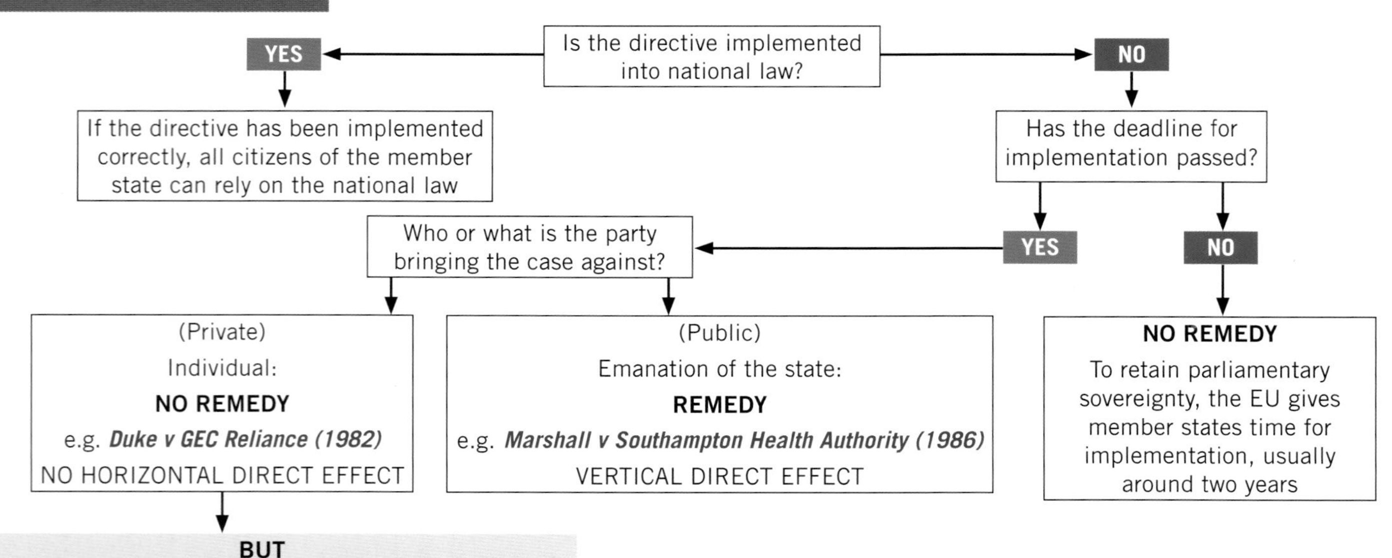

The impact of EU law on the law of the United Kingdom

It is often argued that membership of the European Union has led to an erosion of parliamentary sovereignty and that, by joining the EU in 1973, the UK gave away powers to allow it to determine its own affairs. Therefore, it can be claimed that the direct effect and the **direct applicability** of EU laws in domestic law has eroded sovereignty of member states. The supremacy of EU law and the decline of parliamentary sovereignty has been confirmed by a number of decisions made by the CJEU.

KEY TERMINOLOGY

direct applicability: when a piece of EU legislation is automatically binding and becomes part of a member state's law as soon as it is passed by the EU.

Costa v ENEL (1964)

It was held that, in the event of a conflict between national law and EU law, EU law prevails.

R v Secretary of State for Transport ex p Factortame (1991)

*A UK national law, the **Merchant Shipping Act 1988**, restricted opportunities for foreign fishermen to register their ships in the UK, thus preventing them from fishing in UK waters. The fishermen applied to the European Court, as this appeared to be a contravention of an article of the **Treaty of Rome**.*

The court held that the ***Merchant Shipping Act 1988*** did not comply with EU law and the Act should be suspended. This marked the first time that a national law was in clear breach of EU law and so the UK had to accept that, in such a situation, EU law would take precedence.

There is no doubt that the passing of the ***European Communities Act 1972*** did result in a loss of sovereignty. However, it happened willingly and Parliament has always been able to withdraw from the EU if it so wished and regain full sovereignty.

Bulmer v Bollinger (1974)

Lord Denning said in his case report: 'Our sovereignty has been taken away by the European Court of Justice ... courts must no longer enforce our national laws. They must enforce community law ... no longer is European law an incoming tide flowing up the estuaries of England. It is like a tidal wave bringing down our sea walls and flowing inland over our fields and houses – to the dismay of all.'

The UK has now chosen to leave the EU and ***Article 50*** has been triggered, despite a legal challenge by Gina Miller. Ms Miller had appealed to the Supreme Court, arguing that the government could not invoke ***Article 50*** of the ***Lisbon Treaty*** without seeking approval from Parliament. She won and Theresa May had to seek approval, which was successful. This demonstrates the sovereignty of Parliament, and the process will ultimately lead to the United Kingdom no longer being part of the EU.

The European Union (Withdrawal) Bill 2017–2019 is making its way through the legislative process. Using a reliable news source, keep up to date with its progress.

GRADE BOOST

This is a really useful BBC article about Brexit and what it means for the UK: www.bbc.co.uk/news/uk-politics-32810887

Exam Skills

When applying the law relating to EU sources of law, it is useful to think about the **IDA** acronym. This can be used for any topic where there is an AO2 element to the question that requires you to apply the law.

I: Identify the area of law concerned
What is the source of EU law? Who are the parties concerned?

D: Describe the area of law concerned
Describe the usual effect of that source of law. Is it direct applicability, horizontal direct effect or vertical direct effect?

A: Apply the law to the scenario
Apply the effect to the parties in the scenario. Make sure you use case law to support your application.

Summary: Law making

- **Sources of law:** UK has an unwritten constitution, so it is based on three principles:
  1. **Parliamentary sovereignty** (Dicey): Parliament is supreme with absolute and unlimited power. Threats: EU, ***Human Rights Act 1998***, devolution
  2. **Rule of law** (Dicey): no sanction without breach, one law should govern everyone, rights are secured by decisions of judges
     Examples of breaches: ***John Hemming MP, prisoners' vote, Abu Qatada***
     Promotion: ***Constitutional Reform Act 2005, Black Spider Memos***
  4. **Separation of powers** (Montesquieu): three functions of the state should remain separate:
     - **Legislature**: UK Parliament makes the law
     - **Executive**: UK government enforces the law
     - **Judiciary**: judges apply and interpret the law
- **UK Parliament:** Legislative arm of the United Kingdom
- Three elements:
  1. House of Commons **2.** House of Lords **3.** Monarch
- All three must agree on a Bill before it becomes an Act, subject to the exceptions in the ***Parliament Acts 1911*** and ***1949***
- Three types of Bill can result in an Act of Parliament:
  - Public Bill
  - Private Members' Bill
  - Private Bill
- All potential Acts have to go through the legislative process: five stages in the House of Commons, five stages in the House of Lords and Royal Assent
- **Devolution settlement in Wales**
- **Legislature**: National Assembly for Wales makes the laws (Acts of the Assembly)
- 60 Assembly Members (AMs)
- **Executive**: Welsh Government enforces the law, led by First Minister
- ***Government of Wales Act 1998*** devolved powers to make secondary legislation in nine areas
- ***Government of Wales Act 2006*** devolved powers to make secondary legislation in 20 areas, including health, transport, education and the environment
- **2011 referendum** increased powers for the National Assembly to make primary legislation in the 20 devolved areas
- ***Wales Act 2017*** secured the future for Welsh devolution

WJEC

- **European Union (EU) institutions**
- The UK became a member of the EU following the ***European Communities Act 1972*** but voted to leave in a referendum on 23 June 2016 (Brexit)
- Five key institutions:
  1. **European Parliament**: legislative, supervisory and budgetary roles
  2. **European Commission**: Executive of the EU, 'Guardian of the Treaties', represents interests of EU as a whole, ensures member states comply with EU obligations
  3. **Council of the EU**: legislature of the EU and ministers represent national interests in the area being discussed
  4. **European Council**: established in 2009 under ***Treaty of Lisbon*** and is made up of heads of member states
  5. **Court of Justice of the European Union (CJEU)**: ensures EU legislation is applied consistently in the member states. It has two roles:
     - **Judicial**: hears cases where member states have failed to fulfil treaty obligations
     - **Supervisory**: hears preliminary rulings under ***Article 267***
- **Sources of EU law**
- Primary sources: **treaties**:
  - Horizontal direct effect: ***Macarthys Ltd v Smith (1980)***
  - Vertical direct effect: ***Van Gend en Loos (1963)***
- Secondary sources: **regulations**:
  - Horizontal direct effect: ***Antonio Munoz v Frumar Ltd (2002)***
  - Vertical direct effect: ***Leonesio v Italian Ministry of Agriculture (1972)***
- Secondary sources: **directives**:
  - No horizontal direct effect: ***Duke v GEC Reliance (1982)***
  - Vertical direct effect: ***Marshall v Southampton Health Authority (1986)***
- Secondary sources: **decisions**:
  - Binding on those to whom they are directed only

Law reform

Spec reference	Key content	Assessment Objectives	Where does this topic feature on each specification/exam?
WJEC AS/A Level **1.1:** Law making **Eduqas AS Level** **1.1.1:** Parliamentary and European law making **Eduqas A Level** **1.1.1:** Parliamentary and European law making	• The influences on Parliament; the advantages and disadvantages of influences on law making • Law reform; role of official law reform agencies, including the Law Commission and the role of pressure groups and judicial influences	**AO1** Demonstrate knowledge and understanding of legal rules and principles **AO2** Apply legal rules and principles to given scenarios in order to present a legal argument using appropriate legal terminology	**WJEC AS/A Level:** Unit 1 Section A **Eduqas AS Level:** Component 1 Section A **Eduqas A Level:** Component 1 Section A

Judicial change

The law does not, and cannot, stand still. It needs to keep up with society's changing attitudes and respond to events and media pressure.

Most legislation in the English and Welsh legal systems stands still until it is repealed. Where it is clear that the law is no longer reflective of society's needs, there are a number of ways in which it can be reformed and a number of agencies that can put pressure on the government to change the law.

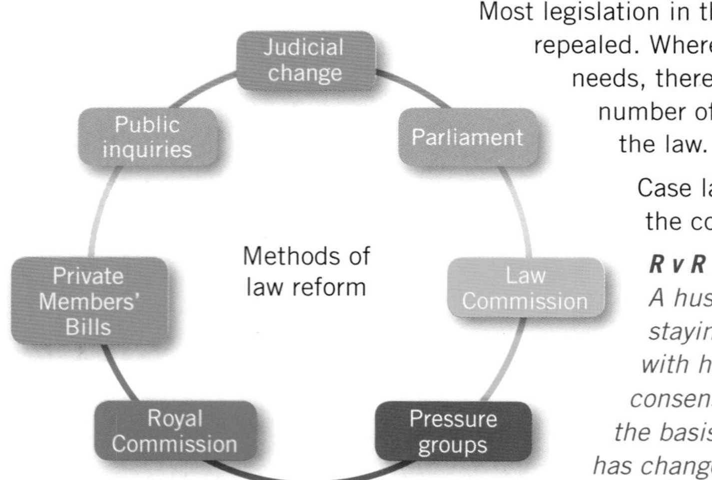

There are many channels that can be used to reform the law

Case law can bring about some reform through the development of the common law, also known as judicial precedent.

R v R (1991)
A husband broke into the house where his estranged wife was staying with her mother and forced her to have non-consensual sex with him. The House of Lords declared that a husband who has non-consensual sexual intercourse with his wife can be guilty of rape on the basis that the status of women, and particularly of married women, has changed out of all recognition in various ways. As a result, the ***Sexual Offences Act*** *was amended to reflect the fact that non-consensual intercourse is rape regardless of marital status.*

Ghaidan v Godin-Mendoza (2004)
Here the court held that homosexuals living in a long-term loving relationship should enjoy the same tenancy rights as heterosexual couples.

There are several reasons why judicial law making is rare, and why it should not regularly happen.

1. Courts can only deal with cases that are brought to them so they are unable to enter into wide-ranging law reform.
2. The parties involved in cases often do not have the money or interest to pursue the reform.
3. Judges are usually unable to consult experts or commission research. They will be wary of reforming the law without this specific knowledge, as their decision will have future influence.

4. Judges are unable to make changes where the doctrine of precedent applies, which inhibits any radical reforms.
5. A precedent change is retrospective (that is, they cover something that has already happened), whereas parliamentary reforms are prospective (they take effect only from the day they come into force).
6. Judges are unelected so it is often argued that their constitutional position is not to reform the law. The theory of separation of powers shows this.

However, judges are skilful at identifying issues to Parliament. Within their judgements, they are willing to point to areas of difficulty with a view to raising the profile of such issues and attracting the attention of Parliament to get reforms.

Judicial precedent is one way of reforming laws

Parliamentary change

The government of the day has control over what ideas enter Parliament, even though they are often influenced by other bodies.

Much legislation reflects the political ideas of the government that is in power when the Act is passed. Such legislation may start as a political commitment in the manifesto of a political party. The government of the day will set out their legislative agenda in the Queen's Speech on the first day of a parliamentary session.

Parliamentary law reform happens in four ways

Repeal

- Old and obsolete laws are removed.
- Out-of-date laws will often stay on the statute books for a long time before they are repealed.

Creation

- Completely new laws are created, either in response to public demand or because of pressure from another group.
- Existing provisions can also be adapted to meet new needs.

Consolidation

- When a statute is created, problems may appear over time and new legislation may be enacted to amend it.
- It brings together successive statutes on the same subject.

Codification

- Where a particular area of law has developed over time, a large body of case law and statute can make the law confusing.
- Codification brings together all the rules into one statute to increase certainty.

A number of circumstances may provide the stimulus for a new Act of Parliament:

1. Events

Unexpected events can lead to an urgent need for law reform that the government may not have foreseen. For example, the attacks of 9/11 led to a tightening of the UK's terrorist laws through the creation of the ***Anti-Terrorism, Crime and Security Act 2001***.

The famous red briefcase is said to contain the Budget recommendations

2. The Budget

Each year, the Chancellor of the Exchequer presents a budget statement to MPs in the House of Commons. Once the budget is agreed, a Finance Bill is presented to Parliament and will make its way through Parliament to give effect to the changes. Government expenditure changes in line with the needs of the country and so this law needs to be passed every year.

STRETCH AND CHALLENGE

Clare's Law: Research the law introduced as a result of a campaign by the father of Clare Wood, who was murdered by her ex-partner in 2009. A good starting point is www.bbc.co.uk/news/uk-politics-26488011

3. The media

Through the media, issues of public concern can be highlighted. Newspapers in particular will often push a particular cause. For example, the *Daily Mail* will often run headlines on immigration and asylum issues to try to achieve greater immigration controls and the *Sun* has consistently campaigned against what it sees as the growing influence of the EU on British life.

Sarah's Law

An excellent example of media influence was the campaign run by the *News of the World* in 2000 following the murder of Sarah Payne by a known paedophile. The subsequent law change ('Sarah's Law') was included in ***s327 Criminal Justice Act 2003***, which places a duty on authorities to consider the disclosure of information about convicted sex offenders to parents in an area, if they consider that the offender presents a risk of serious harm to their children.

4. Law reform agencies

There are several formal agencies of law reform that put pressure on Parliament to change the law. They include:

- the Law Commission
- pressure groups
- Royal Commissions
- public inquiries.

5. Public opinion

If they feel strongly about an issue, members of the public can make their feelings known by writing to their MP or visiting their MP's surgery in their constituency. If the MP agrees, they can introduce the proposal to Parliament via a Private Members' Bill.

The ***Dangerous Dogs Act 1991*** was introduced because of public concern about dangerous dogs. The legislation was swiftly passed and is often criticised.

6. European Convention on Human Rights (ECHR)

Changes prompted by the requirements of ECHR can also prompt parliamentary law reform.

Goodwin v UK (2002)

This case illustrated the inequalities in the law regarding transsexual rights. As a result of this case being heard in the European Court of Human Rights ((ECtHR), the UK Parliament passed the ***Gender Recognition Act 2004****.*

Pressure groups

Pressure groups are those organisations that seek to influence the direction of law and policy on the basis of the views and opinions of their members.

If a pressure group begins to reflect the opinions of many members of the public, it can put a lot of pressure on Parliament. Remember that a pressure group cannot create law but can heavily influence Parliament. Parliament will also consult pressure groups to seek their views on law proposals.

There are two types of pressure groups:

1. Interest groups

These are sometimes also called 'sectional', 'protective' or 'functional' groups and represent a particular section of society, such as workers, employers, consumers, ethnic or religious groups, trade unions, business corporations, trade associations or professional bodies. Specific examples include the British Medical Association (BMA), the Law Society, the National Union of Teachers (NUT), the Confederation of British Industry (CBI) and the Trades Union Congress (TUC).

There are a few things to note about interest groups:

- They are concerned with the interests of their members.
- Membership of these groups is limited to those in a particular occupation, career or economic position.
- Members can be motivated by self-interest.
- Interest groups tend to be influential in the development of the law and are often consulted by Parliament in the early stages of law development.

2. Cause groups

These are sometimes called 'promotional', 'attitude' or 'issue' groups and are based on shared attitudes or values, rather than the common interests of their members. They seek to advance various causes ranging from charity activities, poverty reduction, education and the environment to human rights, international development and peace. Specific examples include the Worldwide Fund for Nature (WWF), Amnesty International, Shelter, the Royal Society for the Protection of Birds (RSPB) and the Electoral Reform Society.

There are a few things to note about cause groups:

- They seek to advance particular ideals or principles.
- Membership is open to all.
- Members are motivated by moral issues.

Occupy London set up an anti-capitalist protest camp outside St Paul's Cathedral in London but, due to its illegal status, an injunction was issued and bailiffs were used to remove the camp and protesters

The role of pressure groups as influential bodies

Pressure groups use a variety of tactics, including:

- letter writing
- protest marches
- lobbying MPs
- organising petitions
- gaining publicity and media attention
- attracting celebrities to support their campaign.

Some groups are more effective than others; size obviously helps, but other factors such as sheer persistence and headline grabbing can be very productive. Some groups use direct action, which in some cases can be illegal, such as violence or occupying land.

The role of pressure groups as consultative bodies

Pressure groups also have a role as a consultative body. When an idea for a new law is proposed, Parliament may wish to begin with a consultation before it is presented to Parliament. This consultation can take the form of a Green Paper and White Paper (see page 9).

How effective are pressure groups?

Pressure groups can be effective and influential.

✓ They enhance democracy and encourage ordinary people to engage in politics.

✓ They facilitate public discussion on key issues.

✓ Their specialist knowledge can inform governments.

✓ They make political parties more responsive to the public.

✓ They enhance freedom of expression under ***Article 10*** and freedom of assembly and protest under ***Article 11***.

✓ They raise public awareness and educate the public on key issues.

✓ They often conduct their own specialist research, which can highlight important issues.

However, there are a few reasons why pressure groups should be regarded with care.

✗ They only provide a one-sided view of an issue.

✗ If the group is small, their views can be distorted and not based on any substantial research.

STRETCH AND CHALLENGE

Research some key pressure groups, for example Fathers 4 Justice, Greenpeace, Shelter Cymru, National Union of Students, Amnesty International, Age UK, Friends of the Earth, Liberty, or No Dash for Gas. Find out:

- their objectives
- their methods
- any successful attempts at law change.

✗ They are undemocratic in the sense that they are not elected but can still influence the government.

✗ Some groups advocate the use of direct action, which can be illegal.

Law Commission

The Law Commission is the only full-time law reform body in the United Kingdom. It is an independent commission that comprises five members drawn from the judiciary, the legal profession and legal academics. The chairperson is a High Court judge. Members are appointed for a five-year term and are assisted by legally qualified civil servants and research assistants who are often law graduates.

The Law Commission was set up under the ***Law Commission Act 1965***, and ***s3*** of that Act states that its role is to:

'keep under review all the law ... with a view to its systematic development and reform, including in particular the codification of such law, elimination and anomalies, the repeal of obsolete and unnecessary enactments, the reduction of the number of separate enactments, the simplification and modernisation of the law'.

The Law Commission looks into laws and then seeks opinion on the possible reforms. The consultation paper will describe the current law, set out the problems and look at the options for reform. Then the Law Commission will draw up positive proposals for reform in a report, which will also set out the research that led to the conclusions. Often there will be a draft Bill attached to the report. This may then go to Parliament.

The Law Commission's law reform process

Research → Consultation → Report of recommendations → Draft Bill → Parliament

The Law Commission can reform law in the same four ways as Parliament: by repeal, consolidation, codification and creation.

The ***Law Commission Act 2009*** is the most recent piece of legislation passed in relation to the Law Commission, to try to improve its success in reforming the law.

- It requires that the Lord Chancellor tells Parliament each year whether the government has decided to implement any of the previous year's Law Commission proposals and, if not, why not. This aims to hold ministers to account.
- It also introduced a new parliamentary procedure which reduces the time and resources required to implement non-controversial Law Commission Bills.
- The Act also sets out how the Law Commission and government departments should work together and a protocol has been agreed that the Law Commission will not take on a project without an undertaking from the relevant government minister that there is a serious intention to reform the law in that area.

Success of the Law Commission

1965–1975

The Law Commission was initially successful in reforming small areas of law. Its first 20 reform programmes were enacted within an average of two years, and included the ***Unfair Contract Terms Act 1977***, ***Supply of Goods and Services Act 1982*** and ***Occupiers' Liability Act 1984***.

Within ten years, it had a success rate of 85 per cent of its proposals for reform being enacted. Its reports led to the repeal of 2,000 obsolete statutes and partial repeal of thousands of others.

1975–2000

During this period, some academics argued that the process of law reform had stalled.

- In the 10–15 years from the late 1970s, only 50 per cent of its proposals became law.
- The rate hit an all-time low in 1990 when none of its proposed reforms was enacted.

- In 1992, there was a backlog of 36 Bills which Parliament had failed to consider.
- The lack of success during this period was put down to lack of parliamentary time and an apparent disinterest by Parliament in technical law reform.

One area highlighted by the Law Commission in 1989 was the need for criminal law to be codified. The government has failed to respond to the idea that the UK should mirror other jurisdictions where there is a single criminal code but there has been no sign of progress in implementing these changes.

2003: Halliday Review

This review found that the main problem with law reform was the inability of government departments to accept reform proposals and create an opportunity for discussion in Parliament. In some cases, the delay in implementing the Law Commission reports was significant.

For example, the review found that the Law Commission's proposal for reform of the landlord's right of distress on the tenant's property was contained in its report on 'distress for rent', published in 1991. It took 16 years for those proposals to become part of the ***Tribunals, Courts and Enforcement Act 2007***. Key factors in this delay can be traced to political issues, personnel changes and staffing.

The amount of annual legislation increased not only in numbers but also in length, adding further burdens to an already busy Parliament. Everyone from the Prime Minister and MPs to government departments sought to find a slot in which to introduce their legislation ideas.

Present day

In 2008, the Law Commission announced it would no longer seek to codify the criminal law but instead concentrate on simplifying specific areas of the criminal law, rather than repealing big chunks. Acts that have incorporated criminal law reform recommendations include:

- ***Criminal Justice Act 2003***
- ***Domestic Violence, Crimes and Victims Act 2003***
- ***Fraud Act 2006***
- ***Serious Crime Act 2007***
- ***Coroners and Justice Act 2009.***

Since the ***Law Commission Act 2009***, there have been annual reports to Parliament by the Lord Chancellor, resulting in varying levels of success. Implementation rates have improved, although there are still reports waiting to be made law. The Law Commission's Annual Report of 2011–2012 showed that 15 reports awaited implementation.

The government rejects around one in six of the Law Commission's reports.

Advisory committees

These are temporary law reform bodies. They are set up to research, consult and propose laws on a particular issue or to investigate where the law needs to be reformed following a tragedy or big event, such as the Hillsborough disaster, the Brixton Riots, or because of advances in science and technology that need to be reflected in the law.

Royal Commissions

These are temporary committees, set up by the government to investigate and report on one specific area of law. Once the report has been published, the Royal Commission is disbanded. Royal Commissions returned to popularity in the 1990s after not being used at all while Margaret Thatcher was Prime Minister. Examples include:

- **Phillips Commission:** resulted in the ***Police and Criminal Evidence Act 1984***, which is key act for police powers and accountability

GRADE BOOST

It is always good practice in an exam to show recent knowledge and an awareness of current issues. Here are some ideas in relation to the Law Commission:

1. The Law Commission recently published a report recommending reform of the ***Offences Against the Person Act 1861*** (www.lawcom.gov.uk/project/offences-against-the-person). Summarise its main findings.
2. The Law Commission recently published a report recommending changes to the law surrounding wills (www.lawcom.gov.uk/project/wills). Summarise its proposals.
3. One of the biggest successes of the Law Commission in recent years has been changes to offences surrounding jury conduct during trials. These changes have been included in the ***Criminal Justice and Courts Act 2015***.

STRETCH AND CHALLENGE

In order to keep on top of the progress of Law Commission proposals, it is a good idea to read the annual reports published by the Lord Chancellor's office, required by the ***Law Commission Act 2009***. You can read the reports in full at www.gov.uk/government/collections/implementation-of-the-law-commission-proposals. Using these and other knowledge, evaluate how successful the Law Commission has been since the implementation of the ***Law Commission Act 2009***.

- **Runciman Commission:** established the Criminal Cases Review Commission, which investigates possible miscarriages of justice and can recommend a retrial at the Court of Appeal.

Public inquiries

These are set up, usually as a response to a significant event, and will examine options for changing the law as a result of some failing by the government or the current law. Examples include:

- **Stephen Lawrence Inquiry:** concluded that the Metropolitan Police had been **institutionally racist** in its handling of the murder of black teenager Stephen Lawrence. Some recommendations were implemented, such as the requirement for a Racial Equality Scheme in all police forces.
- **Bloody Sunday Inquiry**: British soldiers were found to have shot dead unarmed and already injured civilians in Ireland.
- **Leveson Inquiry**: looked at the culture, practice and ethics of the press after allegations of the press invading the privacy of celebrities using tactics such as telephone hacking.

KEY TERMINOLOGY

institutional racism: a public or private body's operation or policies and procedure are deemed to be racist.

STRETCH AND CHALLENGE

The Grenfell Tower Inquiry is a highly publicised inquiry into the Grenfell Tower fire. Make a list of the priorities for the inquiry. This link may help: www.grenfelltowerinquiry.org.uk/news/prime-minister-announces-inquiry-terms-reference

Other ad hoc committees

Other temporary committees are set up at the request of a particular government minister to investigate, and produce a report about, specific areas of law. Examples include:

- **Auld Report**: investigated the workings of the criminal justice system. Recommendations from this report resulted in the ***Criminal Justice Act 2003***.
- **Woolf Report**: investigated the civil procedure system. Its recommendations resulted in one of the biggest changes to civil procedure in the form of the ***Access to Justice Act 1999***.

Law reform in Wales

WJEC

There are particular influences on law reform in Wales.

Welsh Language Society / Cymdeithas yr Iaith Gymraeg

This is a direct-action pressure group in Wales which campaigns for the rights of Welsh people to use the Welsh language in every aspect of their lives.

It has contributed to the passing of various Welsh Language Acts to increase opportunities to learn and use the Welsh language. These Acts also created the role of the Welsh Language Commissioner and the Welsh TV channel, S4C.

Yes for Wales / Ie dros Gymru

This is a pressure group that wants increased devolution in Wales, possibly even a fully independent Wales.

Cymuned

This Welsh community pressure group was established in 2001 and campaigns on behalf of Welsh-speaking and rural communities, which it perceives to be under threat due to demographic changes.

What are the problems with law reform bodies?

- The Law Commission is the only full-time law reform body. So much law reform needs to happen that it may be that it is not big enough to cope with the demand.
- There is no obligation for the government to consult permanent law reform bodies, or to set up Royal Commissions or other committees.
- Governments also have no obligation to follow any recommendations made by law reform bodies, and are able to reject them entirely. Even where general proposals are implemented, the detailed proposals are often ignored or radically altered.
- Even where proposals are implemented, there may be insufficient funding to put them into practice.
- Legal professionals, such as judges and barristers, contribute to the consultation documents and their strong influence on any type of reform can defeat proposals even before they reach an official report or get to Parliament.
- The temporary committees are disbanded after they have produced their report, and take no part in the rest of the law-making process, so this can be a waste of expertise.
- There is no single ministerial department responsible for law reform, so ministers are unlikely to make law reform their priority.

Summary: Law reform

- **Judicial change:** Judges can bring about law reform through judicial precedent
- Examples: ***R v R (1991), Ghaidan v Godin-Mendoza (2004)***
- Judicial law making is rare because of constitutional position and judges not being elected to make laws
- **Parliamentary change:** main way to reform law, usually to reflect government manifesto or a political agenda
- Changes can be made in one of four ways:
  - **Repeal**: Take old and obsolete laws off the statute books
  - **Create**: Make completely new laws
  - **Consolidate**: Bring together successive statutes on the same subject
  - **Codify**: Bring together all the rules into one statute to increase certainty
- Influences on Parliament are media pressure, the annual Budget, significant events, recommendations from law reform agencies, public opinion and the ***European Convention on Human Rights***
- Two types of **pressure groups**:
  - **Interest groups**: a particular section of society, e.g. the British Medical Association, National Union of Teachers
  - **Cause groups:** a shared attitude or value, e.g. Amnesty International, Fathers 4 Justice
- Pressure groups sometimes use illegal methods to attract attention, and are not always successful in forcing change
- They are good at highlighting issues that Parliament may decide needs debate
- **Law Commission:** Role under ***s3 Law Commission Act 1965*** is to 'keep under review all the law'
- The only full-time law reform body
- Puts draft Bills before Parliament after a period of research and consultation
- ***Law Commission Act 2009*** puts an obligation on the Lord Chancellor to report to Parliament whether the government has decided to implement any of the previous year's Law Commission proposals
- Successful at first, less so in the 1980s and 1990s, then more success since the 2009 Act
- **Advisory committees:** Temporary committees set up to review a particular area of law, e.g. Royal Commissions, public inquiries and ad hoc committees

Delegated legislation

Spec reference	Key content	Assessment Objectives	Where does this topic feature on each specification/exam?
WJEC AS/A Level **1.2:** Delegated legislation **Eduqas AS Level** **1.1.2:** Delegated legislation **Eduqas A Level** **1.1.2:** Delegated legislation	• Sources of delegated legislation including types of delegated legislation in Wales and the UK: Statutory Instruments, byelaws, orders in council • Controls on delegated legislation including judicial review, positive affirmation and negative affirmation, and the role of the parliamentary committees that scrutinise delegated legislation • Reasons for the use of delegated legislation and advantages and disadvantages of delegated legislation • Role of devolved legislatures; the Devolution Settlement in Wales, including the role of the Supreme Court	**AO1** Demonstrate knowledge and understanding of legal rules and principles **AO2** Apply legal rules and principles to given scenarios in order to present a legal argument using appropriate legal terminology	**Eduqas AS Level:** Component 1 Section A **Eduqas A Level:** Component 1 Section A **WJEC AS/A Level:** Unit 1 Section A

What is delegated legislation?

Delegated, sometimes called **secondary or subordinate**, **legislation** is a law made by a body other than Parliament but with authority given to it by Parliament. Parliament normally passes an enabling (or parent) Act to delegate the authority to make law to the other body, which has to stay within the terms and conditions set out in the enabling Act. If the enabling body does not, any law it makes may be declared *ultra vires* (void, see page 35). Delegated legislation is often used to 'flesh out' a piece of legislation or make changes to an Act where it is not practical to pass a new Act. It can also be used for technical reasons such as changing the amount of a fine.

The *Legislative and Regulatory Reform Act 2006* allows ministers to issue Statutory Instruments to amend existing **primary legislation**. These are known as **legislative reform orders**. This is controversial as it is seen as shifting power from the elected Parliament to the Executive.

KEY TERMINOLOGY

delegated (secondary or subordinate) legislation: law created by a body other than Parliament, but with the authority of Parliament laid down in primary legislation.
primary legislation: law made by the legislature, which in the UK is Parliament. Acts of Parliament are primary legislation.
legislative reform order: a Statutory Instrument which can amend an Act of Parliament without the need for a parliamentary Bill.

Forms of delegated legislation

There are four main forms of delegated legislation:

Statutory Instruments

These are made by government departments and make up most of the 3,000 or so pieces of delegated legislation passed each year. They are normally drafted by the legal office of the relevant government department, which will consult with interested bodies and parties. They are made via either **affirmative resolution** or **negative resolution** (see page 35) as part of the parliamentary controls on delegated legislation.

Byelaws

Byelaws are made by local authorities, public corporations and companies and usually concern local issues or matters relating to their area of responsibility. For example, county councils make byelaws that affect the whole county, while district or town councils only make byelaws for their particular area. The laws are made with awareness of the needs of that area. A local council may introduce a byelaw banning dogs from its beaches during certain months or imposing fines for littering.

The proposed byelaw must be advertised to allow local people to view and comment on it. They are accompanied by some sanction or penalty for their non-observance.

Orders in council

These are generally made in times of emergency (under the ***Emergency Powers Act 1920*** and the ***Civil Contingencies Act 2004: the 'enabling Acts'***) and have to be approved by the Privy Council (a committee of the monarch's senior advisors) and signed by the Queen. They can also be used to amend law and to give effect to EU law. For example, ***The Misuse of Drugs Act 1971 (Modification) (No. 2) Order 2003*** downgraded cannabis from a Class B to a Class C drug.

Devolution

This is the process of transferring power from central government to regional or local government (e.g. the Scottish Parliament, the Welsh Government and the Northern Ireland Assembly).

Following devolution, the Welsh Government initially only had the power to make secondary legislation (then called Assembly Orders) on certain matters such as education and agriculture. This power has since been increased. The Scottish Parliament has greater power than the Welsh Government.

The Senedd (Welsh Assembly building) in Cardiff

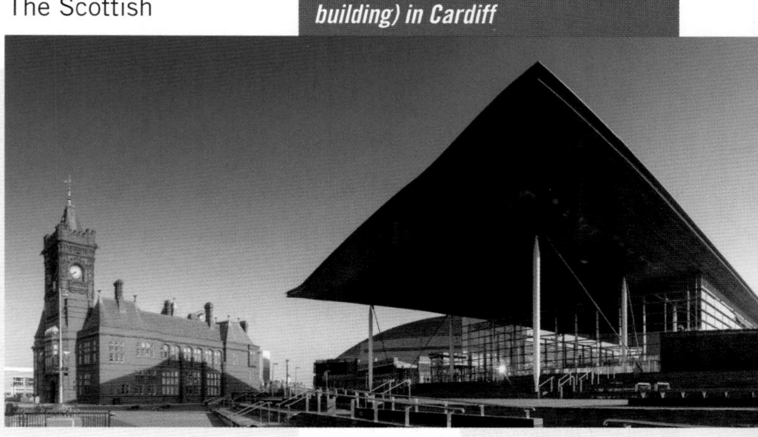

WJEC

Delegated legislation in Wales

In 1998, the ***Government of Wales Act*** established the Welsh Assembly (now known as the Welsh Government). The same Act created the National Assembly for Wales as a single corporate body. This provided the Assembly with the right to create secondary legislation; there are 60 Assembly Members (AMs). Parliament delegated 20 areas of law-making powers to Wales, for example health, education and social services. Issues outside these 20 devolved areas are still governed by Parliament (for example defence and foreign policy).

The effects of the *Government of Wales Act 2006*

In 2006, the ***Government of Wales Act 2006*** was passed in the Westminster Parliament and transferred power to the Welsh Assembly to make its own laws (primary legislation) within a number of specific areas, such as education and health. This meant that the laws passed in the Westminster Parliament still apply to Wales but certain subject areas are now transferred to the Welsh Government.

Until 2010, the Welsh Government had to seek approval from Parliament for all the laws it passed. This created some conflict; for example, Parliament refused to let Wales pass the opt-out donor scheme.

The effects of the 2011 referendum

On 3 March 2011, a referendum took place in Wales asking whether the Welsh Assembly should be allowed to pass its own legislation. The outcome of the referendum meant that the 20 devolved fields no longer needed further approval from the Westminster Parliament in order to create new laws.

It also means that the terminology has changed. Instead of using the phrase 'measures', the Welsh Assembly considers new legislation in the form of a Bill, which, if passed, will become a statute (an 'Act'). This means that the Welsh Assembly has gained additional powers and reflects the same law-making process as carried out in the Westminster Parliament.

It also has the power to create **subordinate** (or 'delegated') **legislation**. The Assembly scrutinises subordinate legislation drawn up by the Welsh ministers under powers delegated by an Act or Measure of the Assembly or by an Act of Parliament. Subordinate legislation includes orders, regulations, rules and schemes as well as statutory guidance and local orders.

Legislative Competence Orders are no longer necessary, as these were requests to the UK Parliament to allow the Assembly to make laws in new subjects within the 20 devolved areas.

The laws passed by the Welsh Assembly are specific to Wales and those making the laws are democratically elected. For example, free prescriptions and the organ donation presumed consent scheme only applies to people in Wales.

The Silk Commission and the Wales Acts

The Commission on Devolution in Wales – also known as the **Silk Commission** – was established by the UK government in 2011 to look at the future of the devolution settlement in Wales. It recommended the transferring of further powers such as tax raising, and the ***Wales Act 2014*** made some provision for this.

The ***Wales Act 2017*** is an Act of the Parliament of the United Kingdom. It sets out amendments to the ***Government of Wales Act 2006*** and devolves further powers to Wales. The legislation is based on the proposals of the St David's Day Agreement which were not included in the ***Wales Act 2014***.

One of the most important provisions is that the Act moved Wales from a conferred matters model to a **reserved matters model**, which is used in Scotland under the ***Scotland Act 1998***. The Act repealed the provision of the ***Wales Act 2014*** for a referendum in Wales on devolution of income tax. A conferred powers model is where the Assembly has only the powers conferred on it by the UK Parliament, whereas a reserved powers model would allow the Assembly to legislate on any matter provided that the matter in question has not been expressly reserved from its competence.

The role of the Supreme Court in devolution

The Supreme Court, established in 2009, is the United Kingdom's final court of appeal for civil cases. It also rules on devolution cases where it is required to interpret devolution statutes in order to clarify the legal and constitutional meaning of the UK's devolution settlements.

The Supreme Court is an important source of judgements relating to devolution

The relevant devolution statute outlies the 'legislative competence' (legal competence) of each legislature, for example, the ***Scotland Act 1998***, the ***Northern Ireland Act 1998*** and the ***Government of Wales Act 2006***. These Acts also enable the Supreme Court to rule that primary legislation, made by each of the devolved legislatures, is outside their legislative competence. This was demonstrated in the case of ***Agricultural Sector (Wales) Bill***, where the UK government had challenged the legality of a National Assembly for Wales Bill on the basis that Bill went beyond the powers specified in the ***Government of Wales Act 2006***.

The Supreme Court ruled that the Bill was within the Assembly's legislative competence.

Control of delegated legislation

A huge amount of delegated legislation is passed each year by non-elected individuals and bodies. For that reason, it is important that the passing of this legislation is controlled. There are two types of control – parliamentary and judicial.

Parliamentary controls

There are several ways in which Parliament controls delegated legislation.

Affirmative resolution

This is where the Statutory Instrument has to be laid before both Houses of Parliament and they must expressly approve the measure. Where used, this is an effective control.

Negative resolution

This is where the Statutory Instrument is published but no debate or vote takes place. It may be annulled by a resolution of either House of Parliament.

About two-thirds of Statutory Instruments are passed via negative resolution and therefore are not actually considered before Parliament. They merely become law on a future specified date and so afford limited control over the delegated authority.

Super-affirmative procedure

This is sometimes required to oversee legislative reform orders issued under the ***Legislative and Regulatory Reform Act 2006***. The super-affirmative procedure provides Parliament with more power to scrutinise the proposed delegated legislation. Reports must be produced and each House of Parliament must expressly approve the order before it can be made.

Consultation

Many enabling Acts require consultation with interested parties or those who will be affected by the delegated legislation. Consultation is an effective control but not all enabling Acts require consultation, which limits its usefulness. The enabling Act itself is a form of control as it sets the parameters and procedures for the delegated power.

Joint Committee on Statutory Instruments (JCSI)

All Statutory Instruments are subject to review by the JCSI, which reports to the House of Commons or House of Lords on any Statutory Instrument which it identifies as needing special consideration and could cause problems. Its control is limited by the fact that it can only make recommendations to the Houses of Parliament rather than compel them to take on board their suggestions.

Judicial controls

A Statutory Instrument can be challenged by someone who has been directly affected the law. The process for challenge is called judicial review and takes place in the Queen's Bench Division of the High Court. The person making the challenge asks the judge to review the legislation and decide whether it is ultra vires ('beyond powers'). If so, the delegated legislation will be declared void (without legal force or binding effect).

Procedural ultra vires

This is where the procedures laid down in the enabling Act for making the Statutory Instrument have not been followed (e.g. consultation was required but not carried out).

Agricultural Horticultural and Forestry Industry Training Board v Aylesbury Mushrooms Ltd (1972)

The enabling Act required interested parties to be consulted before making the law. They were not and therefore the correct procedure had not been followed. The delegated legislation was therefore declared as procedurally ultra vires.

GRADE BOOST

Give a case for each of these judicial challenges:
- **Procedural ultra vires**
- **Substantive ultra vires**
- Unreasonableness

KEY TERMINOLOGY

procedural ultra vires: where the procedures laid down in an enabling Act for making a Statutory Instrument have not been followed (e.g. consultation was required but not carried out). Literal meaning: 'beyond the powers'.
substantive ultra vires: where delegated legislation goes beyond what Parliament intended.

Substantive ultra vires

This is where the delegated legislation goes beyond what Parliament intended.

Customs and Excise v Cure and Deeley Ltd (1962)

The Customs and Excise Commissioners tried to impose a tax and decide the amount to be collected but this went beyond the power conferred by Parliament.

Unreasonableness

The delegated legislation can be challenged as being unreasonable if the person making it has taken into account matters which they ought not to have done or not taken into account matters which they ought to have done. Even if that test is passed, it still needs to be proved that it is a decision that no reasonable body could have come to.

Associated Provincial Picture Houses Ltd v Wednesbury Corporation (1947)

A cinema was allowed to open on a Sunday but its licence barred under 15s from attending. The cinema challenged on the grounds that it was unreasonable but the courts disagreed.

unreasonable

STRETCH AND CHALLENGE

Look around your local area and see if you can spot any byelaws, for example banning ball games in the park. Make a list or take a picture on your phone. Why are these byelaws made at a local level?

When considering parliamentary controls, be aware of the ***Legislative and Regulatory Reform Act 2006***. This gives the government wide powers to make delegated legislation. It allows ministers to issue Statutory Instruments to amend legislation. The Act is controversial because it is seen to be an 'enabling' Act that removes the constitutional restriction on the Executive introducing and altering laws without assent or scrutiny by Parliament.

Exam Skills

Exam questions on delegated legislation may require you to **explain** an aspect of the topic or you may be required to **apply** the law (e.g. the controls that could be used) to a hypothetical example to reach a conclusion.

Advantages and disadvantages of delegated legislation

ADVANTAGES	DISADVANTAGES
Flexibility: Delegated legislation is often used to amend existing legislation. It is easier to use delegated legislation than to pass a new Act of Parliament.	**Lack of control:** Most Statutory Instruments are passed using the negative resolution procedure. This is a loose control of delegated legislation. In addition, if consultation is not required, it is not carried out and so is also a limited control.
Time: Parliament does not have time to debate and pass all the laws needed to run the country effectively. It barely has time for the 70 Acts per year it does pass.	**Undemocratic:** It is often argued that laws should be made by those elected to do so. Delegated legislation is made by unelected individuals/bodies.
Speed: It is far quicker to introduce a piece of delegated legislation than a full Act of Parliament. Orders in Council can be used in an emergency when a law is needed very quickly.	**Sub-delegation:** The power to make the delegated legislation is often sub-delegated to those not given the original authority to pass law, for example, from a government minister to a department and then to a group of experts. This further distances it from the democratic process.
Expertise: Delegated legislation is made by specialised government departments who have experts in the relevant field. MPs would not have that technical expertise.	**Volume:** So much delegated legislation (about 30,000 SIs) is made each year that laws can be difficult to find and keep up with.
Local knowledge: Byelaws are made by local authorities who are familiar with the needs of their local area and people. Parliament does not have the same local awareness.	

Summary: Delegated legislation

- Parliament delegates power to make law to another person/body
- Power delegated by an enabling Act
- Main forms of delegated legislation are:
  - Statutory Instruments made via either affirmative resolution or negative resolution
  - byelaws
  - orders in council
  - laws made by devolved legislatures
- **Devolution:** in Wales: ***Government of Wales Acts 1998, 2006, Wales Act 2014, Silk Commission, Wales Act 2***
- Role of Supreme Court in devolution e.g. ***Agricultural Sector (Wales) Bill***
- Control of delegated legislation: parliamentary:
  - Affirmative resolution
  - Consultation
  - Negative resolution
  - Joint Committee on Statutory Instruments (JCSI)
- Control of delegated legislation (judicial):
  - Procedural ultra vires
  - Substantive ultra vires
  - Unreasonableness
- **Advantages:**
  - Flexibility
  - Time
  - Speed
  - Expertise
  - Local knowledge
- **Disadvantages:**
  - Lack of control
  - Undemocratic
  - Sub-delegation
  - Volume

Statutory interpretation

Spec reference	Key content	Assessment Objectives	Where does this topic feature on each specification/exam?
WJEC AS/A Level 1.3: Statutory interpretation **Eduqas AS Level 1.1.3:** Statutory interpretation **Eduqas A Level 1.1.3:** Statutory interpretation	• Statutory interpretation, including the various rules of statutory interpretation, including the literal rule, golden rule, mischief rule, purposive approach • The impact of the Human Rights Act 1998 and European Union law on statutory interpretation • The use of intrinsic and extrinsic aids	**AO1** Demonstrate knowledge and understanding of legal rules and principles **AO2** Apply legal rules and principles to given scenarios in order to present a legal argument using appropriate legal terminology	**WJEC AS/A Level:** Unit 1 Section A **Eduqas AS Level:** Component 1 Section A **Eduqas A Level:** Component 1 Section A

What is a statute?

This is a law made by Parliament, otherwise known as an Act of Parliament. It is primary legislation and is the highest source of law.

What is statutory interpretation?

Parliament makes the law and judges apply it. In doing this, they create precedents for future cases to follow. Statutory interpretation is the procedure by which a judge works out the meaning of words in an Act of Parliament and how this applies to the facts of the case before them. In most cases, the meaning of statutes is clear and a judge's role is simply to determine how this law applies to the facts of the case before them.

However, occasionally words require interpreting. There are a number of reasons why judges need to interpret statutes.

The Supreme Court is the final court of appeal for all United Kingdom civil cases, and criminal cases from England, Wales and Northern Ireland

1. **A broad term is used.** This may be deliberate if it covers more than one possibility and to allow the judge some flexibility. The judge still has to decide the meaning to be applied to the case before them. An example is the word 'type' in the ***Dangerous Dogs Act 1991***, which means dogs of the 'type' known as the pit bull terrier, which the court held to include not only pedigree pit bull terriers but also dogs with a substantial number of characteristics of pit bulls. The Act was also interpreted in ***Brock v DPP (1993)***.
2. **Changes in the use of language.** Language use changes over time, for example 'gay'. The issue of how language has changed was also the subject of the interpretation in ***Cheeseman v DPP (1990)***.
3. **Ambiguous words.** Some words have more than one meaning and the judge has to decide which meaning applies, for example 'bar' or 'wind' are words with more than one meaning.
4. **A drafting or other error.** An error in the drafting of a statute may not have been picked up during the Bill stage.
5. **New developments.** Changes in technology can sometimes mean that an older Act of Parliament does not seem to cover a modern situation, for example ***Royal College of Nursing v DHSS (1981)***, when subsequent medical methods and advances may not have been foreseen at the time of passing the Act.

Approaches to statutory interpretation

Judges use four different rules or 'approaches' when dealing with a statute that requires interpretation. They are free to use any of the four approaches in combination with the other aids to interpretation discussed in this section.

Literal rule

The judge will give the words contained in the statute their ordinary and plain meaning even if this causes an absurd result. Many people think this should be the first rule applied by judges in the interpretation of an unclear statute.

Whiteley v Chappel (1968)

In this case, it was an offence to 'impersonate anyone entitled to vote' at an election. The defendant had pretended to be a dead person and taken their vote. He was found not guilty of the offence as the judge interpreted the word 'entitled' literally. As a dead person is no longer 'entitled' to vote, the defendant had done nothing wrong.

Golden rule

If the literal rule causes an absurd result, the judge can take a more flexible approach to rectify the absurdity. Courts can take either a narrow or a wide interpretation considering the statute as a whole. With both the golden and literal rules, judges use **internal (intrinsic) aids** (anything within the Act itself, such as its titles and headings; see page 40).

Adler v George (1964)

S3 Official Secrets Act 1920 *states that it is an offence to obstruct a member of the armed forces 'in the vicinity of' a 'prohibited place'. The defendant in the case had obstructed an officer in an army base (a 'prohibited place') and argued that the natural meaning of 'in the vicinity of' means in the surrounding area or 'near to' and not directly within. Had the judge applied the literal rule, he could have escaped prosecution but the judge used the golden rule to reasonably assume the statute to include both within and around the prohibited place.*

Mischief rule

Laid down in ***Heydon's Case (1584)*** and allows the judge to look for the 'mischief' or problem the statute in question was passed to remedy. It directs the judge to use **external (extrinsic) aids** (elements beyond the Act, such as case law) and look for Parliament's intention in passing the Act.

Elliot v Grey (1960)

It is an offence under the ***Road Traffic Act 1930*** *to 'use' an uninsured car on the road. In this case, a broken-down car was parked on the road but could not be 'used' because its wheels were off the ground and its battery had been removed. The judge decided that the* ***Road Traffic Act 1930*** *was passed to remedy this type of hazard and, even though the car could not be 'used' on the road, it was indeed a hazard to other road users.*

Purposive approach

This is similar to the mischief rule in that it looks for the intention or aim of the Act. This approach has become more common since the UK joined the EU, due in part to the different way that European laws are drafted. While our laws are more wordy and suit a literal interpretation, EU laws are more vaguely written, requiring the judge to construct a meaning. Lord Denning was a supporter of the use of the purposive approach and giving judges more discretion when interpreting Acts. Judges look for the 'purpose' of the Act or, as Lord Denning said, the 'spirit of the legislation'.

GRADE BOOST

When answering a question on statutory interpretation, it is important to apply all four rules and give a case example for each. Other aids to interpretation may also be needed to give a complete answer to a problem scenario style question.

GRADE BOOST

Think of some further examples of each of the reasons why judges may need to interpret statutes.

Magor and St Mellons Rural District Council v Newport Corporation (1950)

Lord Denning, sitting in the Court of Appeal, stated 'we sit here to find out the intention of Parliament and of ministers and carry it out, and we do this better by filling in the gaps and making sense of the enactment than by opening it up to destructive analysis'.

Lord Simmons criticised this approach when the case was appealed at the House of Lords, calling this approach 'a naked usurpation of the legislative function under the thin disguise of interpretation'. He suggested that 'if a gap is disclosed, the remedy lies in an amending Act'.

STRETCH AND CHALLENGE

Think of an advantage and disadvantage for each of the four rules, to help you to consider how to evaluate them. Here are some examples.

- **Literal rule**
  Advantage: Respects parliamentary sovereignty.
  Disadvantage: Can cause absurd results.
- **Golden rule**
  Advantage: Gives judges discretion and puts right absurdities caused by literal rule.
  Disadvantage: Judges given power to interpret what is constitutionally the role of the legislator.
- **Mischief rule**
  Advantage: The most flexible of the rules and allows judges flexibility when dealing with statutes.
  Disadvantage: This approach was developed when parliamentary supremacy was not fully established and common law was the primary source of law. It is felt that the mischief rule gives too much power to the unelected judiciary to interpret the 'will of Parliament'.
- **Purposive approach**
  Advantage: Flexible and seeks the purpose or reason why the Act was passed.
  Disadvantage: Described by Lord Simonds as 'a naked usurpation of the judicial function, under the thin disguise of interpretation'.

Aids to interpretation

As well as the four main approaches to statutory interpretation, a judge can use other aids to help determine the meaning of a statute. These can also be divided into internal (intrinsic) aids and external (extrinsic) aids.

Presumptions

These may be regarded as intrinsic, as it refers to presumptions of the Act itself, but they can also be seen as neither intrinsic nor extrinsic. The court will start with the presumption that certain points are applicable in all statutes, unless explicitly stated otherwise. Some of the main presumptions are:

- statutes do not change the common law
- mens rea ('guilty mind') is required in criminal cases
- the Crown is not bound by any statute
- statutes do not apply retrospectively.

Internal (intrinsic) aids

Intrinsic aids are found within the Act itself. Examples are:

- the long title to the Act
- preamble: normally states the aim of the Act and intended scope
- headings
- schedules
- interpretation sections.

Rules of language

Judges can use other words in the statute to help give meaning to specific words that require interpretation.

Ejusdem generis

This means 'of the same kind'. Where general words follow a list of specific words, the general words are limited to the same kind/class/nature as the specific words.

Powell v Kempton (1899)

A statute stated that it was an offence to use a 'house, office, room or other place for betting'. The defendant was using a ring at a racecourse. The court held that the general term 'other place' had to include other indoor places because the specific words in the list were indoor places and so the defendant was found not guilty.

Expressio unius est exclusio alterius

This means 'express mention of one thing is the exclusion of all others'.

R v Inhabitants of Sedgley (1831)

In this case, it was held that, due to the fact the statute stated 'lands, houses and coalmines' specifically in the Act, this excluded application to other types of mine.

Noscitur a sociis

This means 'a word is known by the company it keeps'. Words in a statute must be read in context of the other words around them.

Muir v Keay (1875)

A statute required the licensing of all venues that provided 'public refreshment, resort and entertainment'. Defendant argued his café did not fall within the Act because he did not provide entertainment. Court held the word 'entertainment' in the Act referred to refreshment houses, receptions and accommodation of the public, not musical entertainment and therefore did include the defendant's café.

GRADE BOOST

Look carefully at what the question is asking. Some exam questions ask for all the aids available to judges, whereas others focus on just one or two types of aid such as Hansard. Remember to include as many case examples as you can, not just for the rules of interpretation but the other aids too.
Be prepared to discuss ***sections 3 and 4 Human Rights Act 1998*** in a statutory interpretation question and the implications for statutory interpretation of these sections.

STRETCH AND CHALLENGE

Try to think of your own hypothetical example for each of the rules of language.

External (extrinsic) aids

With both the mischief and purposive approach, the judge is directed to use external or extrinsic aids. These are found outside of the Act and include:

- dictionaries and textbooks
- reports, for example from the Law Commission
- historical setting
- treaties
- previous case law.

Hansard

Perhaps the external aid that has caused the most problems is Hansard, the daily record of parliamentary debate during the passage of legislation. Some argue that it acts as a good indicator of Parliament's intention; however, over the years its use has been subject to limitations.

Traditionally, judges were not allowed to consult Hansard to assist them in the interpretation of statutes to reinforce the separation of powers. Lord Denning disagreed with this approach and said in the case of ***Davis v Johnson (1979)*** that: 'Some may say, and indeed have said, that judges should not pay any attention to what is said in Parliament. They should grope about in the dark for the meaning of an Act without switching on the light. I do not accede to this view ....' The House of Lords disagreed with him and held that the prohibition on using Hansard should stand. However, the key case of ***Pepper v Hart (1993)*** finally permitted the use of Hansard, albeit in limited circumstances. This was confirmed in the case of ***Three Rivers District Council v Bank of England (No. 2) (1996)***.

Wilson v Secretary of State for Trade and Industry (2003)
The House of Lords stated that Hansard could be used to look for the meanings of words but not to read the general debates to look for Parliament's intention. The House of Lords was also of the opinion that the statements of one or two ministers in a debate did not necessarily represent the intention of Parliament. Therefore, the Wilson case has restricted the use of Hansard so that only statements made by an MP or other promoter of legislation can be looked at by the court, and other statements recorded in Hansard must be ignored.

Human Rights Act 1998 (HRA)

The ***HRA*** incorporates into UK law the ***European Convention on Human Rights***. Under ***s3 HRA***, courts are required 'so far as it is possible to do so, primary and subordinate legislation must be read and given effect in a way which is compatible with convention rights'. If the statute cannot be interpreted to be compatible then the court can issue a **declaration of incompatibility** under ***s4***. This asks the government to change the law to bring it in line with the convention. They can use the **fast-track procedure** to make amendments quickly but there has to be a 'compelling reason' to do so and, under ***s10(2)***, the issuing of a declaration of incompatibility is not necessarily a compelling reason. ***Section 2*** also requires judges to take into account any previous decision of the European Court of Human Rights (ECtHR) though they are not bound by it.

GRADE BOOST

Make sure you cite ***ss3 and 4 Human Rights Act 1998*** and understand how they apply to this topic. In addition, be sure to know some cases on the use of Hansard. Examiners are looking for a range of case law and an understanding of how the law has evolved.

STRETCH AND CHALLENGE

Research and find the case of ***Ghaidan v Godin-Mendoza (2004)*** regarding the issue of human rights when interpreting statutes. What happened in the case and how did human rights apply? What is the current approach regarding interpreting statutes compatibly with human rights?

KEY TERMINOLOGY

declaration of incompatibility: issued under ***s4 Human Rights Act 1998***, this gives senior judges the power to question the compatibility of legislation with human rights. The declaration is sent to Parliament. It does not allow judges to strike out laws.

Summary: Statutory interpretation

- Judges sometimes need to **interpret** Acts of Parliament (statutes) due to:
  - Ambiguous terms
  - Broad terms
  - Changes in the use of language
  - Error
- Judges can use four **approaches** to interpretation:
  - Literal rule: ***Whiteley v Chappel (1968)***
  - Golden rule: ***Adler v George (1964)***
  - Mischief rule: ***Elliot v Grey (1960)***
  - Purposive approach: ***Magor and St Mellon's Rural district Council v Newport Corporation (1950)***
- Judges use other '**aids**' to help them interpret statutes
- **Intrinsic aids:**
  - The long title to the Act
  - Preamble
  - Headings
  - Schedules
  - Interpretation sections
- **Extrinsic aids:**
  - Dictionaries and textbooks
  - Reports e.g. from the Law Commission
  - Historical setting
  - Treaties
  - Hansard
  - Previous case law: ***Pepper v Hart (1993)***, ***Three Rivers (1996)***, ***Wilson (2003)***
  - **Rules of language:** *ejusdem generis, noscitur a sociis, expressio unius est exclusio alterius*
  - Presumptions
- **The Human Rights Act 1998 (HRA)**
  - ***Section 2***: Judges must 'take into account' precedents of the ECtHR (persuasive precedent only)
  - ***Section 3***: Interpret statutes compatibly 'so far as possible'
  - ***Section 4***: Declaration of incompatibility
  - ***Section 10***: Parliament can change an incompatible law using a fast-track procedure if there is a compelling reason

Exam Skills

Exam questions on statutory interpretation may require you to 'explain' an aspect of the topic or you may be required to 'apply' the rules to a hypothetical example to reach a conclusion.

Use the following table as a guide on how to approach the rules of statutory interpretation.

Literal rule	**Golden rule**
Explain the rule Give a case example Advantage Disadvantage APPLY to the scenario	Explain the rule Give a case example Advantage Disadvantage APPLY to the scenario
Mischief rule	**Purposive approach**
Explain the rule Give a case example Advantage Disadvantage APPLY to the scenario	Explain the rule Give a case example Advantage Disadvantage APPLY to the scenario
Intrinsic aids and extrinsic aids	**CONCLUSION**
Identify and explain some intrinsic and extrinsic aids and apply them	Decide which rule you would apply

Judicial precedent

Spec reference	Key content	Assessment Objectives	Where does this topic feature on each specification/exam?
WJEC AS/A Level 1.4: Judicial precedent **Eduqas AS Level 1.1.4:** Judicial precedent **Eduqas A Level 1.1.4:** Judicial precedent	• Judicial precedent including the doctrine of precedent, identification of *ratio decidendi* and *obiter dicta* and types of precedent to include persuasive and binding • The hierarchy of the courts in Wales and England including the Supreme Court • Avoidance techniques to include overruling, reversing and distinguishing • Advantages and disadvantages of precedent • Use of the Practice Statement 1966 and the exceptions in Young v Bristol Aeroplane Company	**AO1** Demonstrate knowledge and understanding of legal rules and principles **AO2** Apply legal rules and principles to given scenarios in order to present a legal argument using appropriate legal terminology	**WJEC AS/A Level:** Unit 1 Section A **Eduqas AS Level:** Component 1 Section A **Eduqas A Level:** Component 1 Section A

Elements of precedent

The English legal system is a common law system. This means that much of the law has been developed over time by the courts, through cases. The basis of this system of precedent is the principle of ***stare decisis***. This requires a later court to use the same reasoning as an earlier court where the two cases raise the same legal issues, which in turn ensures a just process.

1. The court hierarchy

This establishes which decisions are binding on which courts. Decisions of higher courts are binding on lower courts.

Court of Justice of the European Union (CJEU)

Decisions from this court on European matters bind all English courts on matters of EU law. The CJEU is not bound by its own decisions. (This will remain the situation until the UK leaves the EU.)

↓

Supreme Court

The highest appeal court on civil and criminal matters, the Supreme Court binds all other English courts. It was bound by its own decisions as the House of Lords until 1966 (see House of Lords 1966 Practice Statement on page 46).

Court of Appeal

It has criminal and civil divisions that do not bind each other. The Supreme Court, and the old House of Lords, bind both divisions. The Criminal Division is not usually bound by its previous decisions.

High Court

The High Court consists of the divisional courts: Queen's Bench Division (criminal appeals and judicial review), Chancery Division and Family Division, and the ordinary High Court. The Court of Appeal, the Supreme Court and the old House of Lords binds the High Court.

Crown Court

All the courts above bind this court. Decisions from the Crown Court do not form **binding precedent** but can form **persuasive precedent**; they are not bound by their previous decisions.

Magistrates' and county courts

Bound by the High Court, Court of Appeal, old House of Lords and Supreme Court. They do not produce precedents; they are not bound by their previous decisions.

European Court of Human Rights (ECtHR)

Under ***s2 Human Rights Act 1998***, English courts must take account decisions from the ECtHR but they are not bound by them.

KEY TERMINOLOGY

stare decisis: to stand by the previous decisions.
binding precedent: a previous decision that has to be followed.
persuasive precedent: previous decision that does not have to be followed.
original precedent: a decision in a case where there is no previous legal decision or law for the judge to use.
retrospective effect: laws that operate affecting acts done before they were passed.

2. Accurate law reporting

This allows legal principles to be collated, identified and accessed. The earliest form of law reporting was in year books from around 1272. Modern reporting dates from the Council on Law Reporting, established in 1865. There are also private series of reports, for example the All England Law Reports (All ER), as well as reporting in journals (such as the *New Law Journal*) and newspapers (such as *The Times*). More recent innovations include online systems (such as LEXIS), and the Internet.

3. The binding element

The judgement contains four elements:

- Statement of material (relevant) facts.
- Statement of legal principle(s) relevant to the decision (the ***ratio decidendi***: 'the reason for the decision').
- Discussion of legal principles raised in argument but not relevant to the decision (***obiter dicta***: 'things said by the way').
- The decision or verdict.

The binding element in future cases is the *ratio decidendi*. This is the part of the judgement that future judges, depending on their position in the court hierarchy, have to follow. The *obiter dicta*, while never binding, may have strong persuasive force. This is known as **persuasive precedent**, and it particularly persuasive if it comes from the higher courts like the Court of Appeal, the Supreme Court and the old House of Lords.

Other forms of persuasive authority include:

- decisions of other common law jurisdictions (especially from Australia, Canada and New Zealand)
- decisions of the Privy Council: see ***Attorney General for Jersey v Holley (2005)***
- writing of legal academics.

KEY TERMINOLOGY

ratio decidendi: 'the reason for the decision'. This is the binding element of precedent, which must be followed.
obiter dicta: 'things said by the way'. This is not binding and is only persuasive.

4. Flexibility and certainty

The system of binding precedent, sometimes referred to as the doctrine of **judicial precedent**, does create the certainty needed to allow people to plan and lawyers to advise. It also creates flexibility, as precedent enables the common law to develop.

How judicial precedent works

Normally judges will **follow** an earlier precedent. The other options of **overruling**, **reversing**, **distinguishing** and **departing** are means of avoiding having to follow a difficult precedent.

- **Following**: if the facts are similar, the precedent set by the earlier court is followed.
- **Overruling**: higher courts can overrule lower courts.
- **Distinguishing**: where a lower court points to material differences that justify the application of different principles.
- **Departing**: where, in certain circumstances, a court can depart from its previous decision.
- **Reverse**: on appeal, a higher court may change the decision of a lower court.

KEY TERMINOLOGY

per incuriam: 'made by mistake'. Before the 1966 Practice Statement this was the only situation in which the House of Lords could depart from its previous decisions.

EDUQAS A LEVEL

House of Lords Practice Statement 1966

Until 1966, the House of Lords was bound by its own previous decisions (see ***London Street Tramways v LCC (1898)***) unless the decision had been made ***per incuriam*** (by mistake). In 1966, the House of Lords issued the **Practice Statement**. This stated that the House of Lords will normally be bound by its previous decisions but may depart, as well as on the grounds of *per incuriam*, when it is right to do so.

The following cases show where the House of Lords departed from previous decisions:

Case	Significance regarding the Practice Statement
Conway v Rimmer (1968)	This first use of the Practice Statement only involved technical law on discovery of documents.
Herrington v British Railways Board (1972)	The first major use of the Practice Statement, on the duty of care owed to child trespassers.
Anderton v Ryan (1985)	This precedent was overruled in ***R v Shivpuri (1987)***.
Rondel v Worsley (1969)	This precedent was overruled in ***Hall v Simons (2000)***.
R v Caldwell (1981)	The Practice Statement was later used in ***R v G and another (2003)*** to overrule the decision in Caldwell on recklessness in criminal law.
R v R (1991)	This set a new precedent for the law on rape within marriage, overruling a precedent set hundreds of years before.
Pepper v Hart (1993)	The Practice Statement was used to allow the courts to look at Hansard for the purpose of statutory interpretation.
Austin v London Borough of Southwark (2010)	The Supreme Court stated that the Practice Statement applied to it.

Court of Appeal (Civil Division)

While normally bound by its own previous decisions, it can depart from such decisions if any of the exceptions established in ***Young v Bristol Aeroplane Co (1944)*** and ***R (on the application of Kadhim) v Brent London Borough Housing Benefit Review Board (2001)*** apply. It can depart when:

- the previous decision was made *per incuriam*
- there are two previous conflicting decisions
- there is a later, conflicting, House of Lords decision
- a proposition of law was assumed to exist by an earlier court and was not subject to argument or consideration by that court.

The Court of Appeal (Criminal Division) is also not bound to follow its previous decisions where, in the previous case, the law was misapplied or misunderstood resulting in a conviction (***R v Taylor (1950)***); extra flexibility is given to the Criminal Division because it deals with the liberty of the citizen.

The Privy Council

The **Privy Council** is the final appeal court for Commonwealth countries. The general rule is that decisions of the Privy Council do not bind English courts but its decisions do have strong persuasive authority.

R v James and Karimi (2006)

The Court of Appeal applied the Privy Council's judgement in ***Attorney General for Jersey v Holley (2005)*** *rather than the House of Lords' judgement in* ***R v Smith (Morgan) (2001)***.

KEY TERMINOLOGY

Privy Council: the final appeal court for most Commonwealth countries.

Judges as law makers

Are judges making law, or are they simply interpreting existing law? Should judges make law or should this be left to Parliament? The following cases clearly support the view that judges do make law.

Airedale NHS Trust v Bland (1993)

The House of Lords stated that this case raised wholly moral and social issues that should be left to Parliament to legislate for; nevertheless they had no option but to give a decision.

R v Dica (2004)

The Court of Appeal overruled a previous decision, and held that a defendant could be criminally liable for recklessly infecting another person with HIV. The court gave this decision despite Parliament refusing to introduce legislation to impose such liability.

Kleinwort Benson Ltd v Lincoln City Council (1998)

In this case, the House of Lords changed a long-standing rule regarding contract law, despite the Law Commission's recommendations that this rule should be changed by Parliament.

Director of Public Prosecutions (DPP) v Jones (1999)

The House of Lords concluded that statutory highway laws replaced unrealistic restrictions on the public.

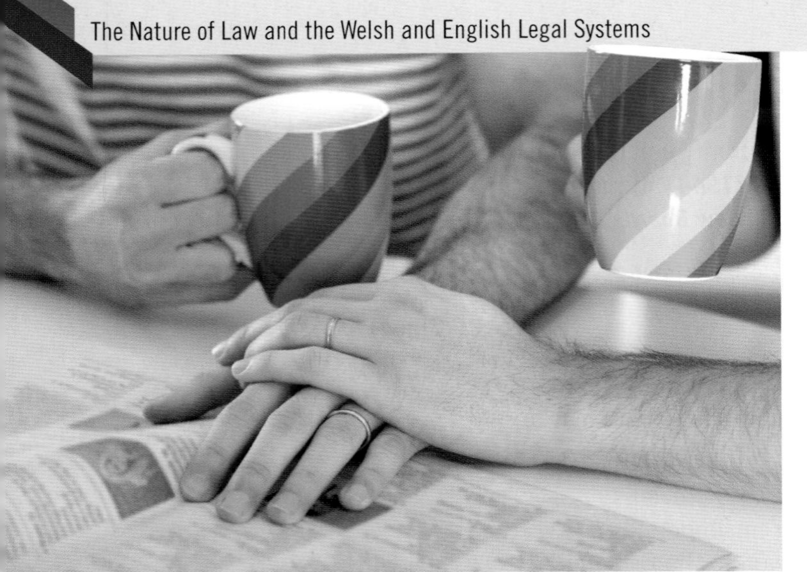

Fitzpatrick v Sterling Housing Association Ltd (2000) allowed same-sex partners to establish a familial link for the purposes of the Rent Act 1977

Fitzpatrick v Sterling Housing Association Ltd (2000)
House of Lords held that same-sex partners could establish a familial link for the purposes of the ***Rent Act 1977****, overruling the Court of Appeal's decision that this should be left to Parliament to determine.*

Gillick v West Norfolk and Wisbech Area Health Authority (1985)
The House of Lords, faced with no lead from Parliament on the issue in this case, held that a girl under 16 could be given contraceptive services without her parents' consent, if she is mature enough to make up her own mind.

Donoghue v Stevenson (1932)
In this famous case Lord Aitken developed the law of negligence, that is the principle that those who harm others should pay compensation for damage done.

R v R (1991)
The House of Lords established that rape within marriage was a crime, overruling a precedent set hundreds of years before, and after pleas from the House of Lords for several years to Parliament to change the law in this area.

Simmons v Castle (2012)
The Court of Appeal stated in this case that judges should change the law if Parliament intended then to do so, and a failure to do so would be a breach of faith. This case concerned changes to the ***Legal Aid, Sentencing and Punishment of Offenders Act 2012****.*

GRADE BOOST

In the exam you are often required to apply the principles of precedent to a scenario-type question, so you must fully understand how it works and be able to apply the principles with supporting legal authority.
It is also important that you are up to date with the functions of the Supreme Court and recent cases decided there. Decisions of the Supreme Court can be found on the website of the Supreme Court (www.supremecourt.uk/decided-cases).

Advantages and disadvantages of judicial precedent

Advantages	Disadvantages
A just system: Like cases will be treated the same.	**Developments contingent on accidents of litigation**: Case law only changes if someone is determined enough to pursue a case through the courts.
Impartial system: Treating like cases in similar ways promotes impartiality.	**Retrospective effect:** Unlike legislation, case law applies to events which took place before the case came to court (see ***SW v UK (1996)***; ***R v C (2004)***).
Practical rules: Case law is always responding to real-life situations. As a result, there is a large body of detailed rules that give more information than statutes.	**Complex**: While case law gives us detailed practical rules it also means that there are thousands of cases, and identifying relevant principles and the *ratio decidendi* can be difficult and time consuming.
Certainty: Claimants can be advised that like cases will be treated in a similar way and not by random decisions of judges.	**Rigid**: Depending on the place of the court in the hierarchy, precedent can be very rigid, as lower courts are bound to follow decisions of higher courts even where they think the decision is bad or wrong.
Flexibility: Case law can change quickly to meet changes in society.	**Undemocratic**: Judges are not elected and should therefore not be changing or creating laws, unlike Parliament that has been elected to do so.

The Supreme Court and precedent

The *Constitutional Reform Act 2005* established the Supreme Court to replace the House of Lords. The aim was to achieve a complete separation between the United Kingdom's senior judges and the Upper House of Parliament, which is also called the House of Lords, emphasising the independence of the law lords and removing them from the legislature.

In August 2009, the justices moved out of the House of Lords (where they sat as the Appellate Committee of the House of Lords) into their own building. They sat for the first time as the Supreme Court in October 2009.

The Supreme Court is highest appeal court in the UK. It also took over from the Privy Council the role of hearing cases concerned with the devolution of Wales, Scotland and Northern Ireland. The impact of Supreme Court decisions extends far beyond the parties involved in a case, shaping society and affecting our everyday lives. However, the Supreme Court does not have the power to strike out legislation.

STRETCH AND CHALLENGE

- Research the two cases of ***Balfour v Balfour (1919)*** and ***Merritt v Merritt (1971)*** to see how distinguishing works in practice.
- Research the following cases and debate the effect of ***S2 Human Rights Act 1998*** on judicial precedent:
  - ***Morris v UK (2002)***
  - ***R v Boyd (2002)***
  - ***R v Horncastle (2009)***
  - ***Al-Khawaja and Thaery v UK (2009)***
  - ***Kay v Lambeth London BC (2006)***
  - ***Manchester City Council v Pinnock (No.2) (2011).***

Summary: Judicial Precedent

- Precedent is based on **stare decisis** ('let the decision stand')
- Courts must follow precedents set by courts **higher in the hierarchy**
- The **Supreme Court** is usually bound by its own decisions, but since the 1966 Practice Statement the Supreme Court can depart from a previous decision where it is right to do so
- The **Court of Appeal (Civil Division)** is bound by its previous decisions, unless any of the exceptions in Young's case apply
- ***Ratio decidendi*** is the reason for the decision and creates a binding precedent for future cases
- ***Obiter dicta*** ('things said by the way'). It is the rest of the judgment and does not create a binding precedent
- Judges in later cases do not have to follow precedent if they can use an avoidance technique: **distinguish; overrule, reverse**
- **Advantages of precedent:** creates certainty; flexibility; consistency; saves time
- **Disadvantages of precedent:** can be rigid, complex and slow

Civil courts

Spec reference	Key content	Assessment Objectives	Where does this topic feature on each specification/exam?
WJEC AS/A Level 1.5: Civil courts **Eduqas AS Level 1.2.1:** Civil courts **Eduqas A Level 1.2.1:** Civil courts	• Civil courts: structure, powers and appellate functions including the use of juries in civil cases: their selection, their limited role in civil cases and criticisms of use • Civil process • Tribunals, arbitration and alternative dispute resolution including their advantages and disadvantages • Development, role and control of tribunals including examples of the different types of tribunals • Arbitration within and outside the court system • Alternative dispute resolution including arbitration, mediation, conciliation and negotiation.	**AO1** Demonstrate knowledge and understanding of legal rules and principles **AO3** Analyse and evaluate legal rules, principles, concepts and issues	**WJEC AS/A Level**: Unit 1 Section B **Eduqas AS Level:** Component 1 Section B **Eduqas A Level:** Component 1 Section B

Civil process, structure, courts and appeals

The civil justice system is used to settle disputes between private individuals or organisations. The person bringing the action is called the **claimant** (or the **plaintiff** in cases before 1 April 1999) and the person defending the action is known as the **defendant.** The case has to be proved **on the balance of probabilities** (the standard of proof) and the burden to prove the case is on the claimant. The claimant is normally seeking some form of **remedy**, which could be the payment of compensation or an injunction. Often, these cases are **settled out of court.**

KEY TERMINOLOGY

claimant: the person bringing the action. Before 1 April 1999, this person was known as the plaintiff.
defendant: the person defending the action (e.g. the person accused of a crime).

The civil court hierarchy

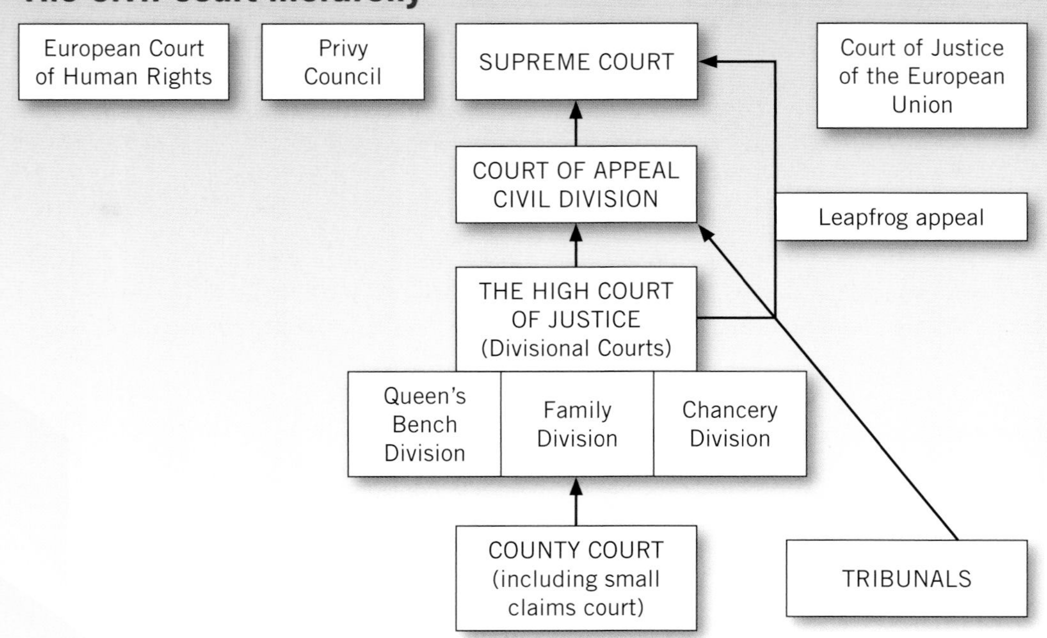

Civil court structure

The county court and the High Court are the two **first instance civil courts**, which means that civil cases are started in one of these courts.

Since the implementation of reforms proposed by **Lord Woolf** in the mid-1990s, civil cases fall into three categories, called **tracks**. The allocation of a case to a particular track determines where it will be tried and the process under which it is dealt with.

- **The small claims track** (cases up to £10,000 or £1,000 for personal injury): tried in the small claims court.
- **The fast track** (cases between £10,000 and £25,000): tried in the county court.
- **The multi-track** (cases above £25,000): tried in either the county court or the High Court.

County court

County courts have jurisdiction over:

- claims under contract and tort
- cases for the recovery of land
- disputes over partnerships, trusts and inheritance up to a value of £30,000.

High Court

All civil cases not dealt with in the county court are dealt with in the High Court. Cases in the High Court are organised according to case type and are heard in one of the three separate courts, called divisions. Each division has separate functions and differing jurisdictions. The three divisions are:

- Queen's Bench Division
- Chancery Division
- Family Division.

Appeals in civil law

High Court

Each division of the High Court has an appellate division called a **divisional court** (e.g. the Queen's Bench Divisional Court). A first instance case in a High Court division is heard by a single judge, whereas an appeal case in a divisional court is heard by three judges. The divisional courts hear appeals from the county court. The Queen's Bench Divisional Court can also hear appeals from the (criminal) magistrates' court and Crown Court as well as conducting judicial review proceedings.

Court of Appeal Civil Division

The head of this division is called the **Master of the Rolls.** The Court of Appeal (Civil Division) hears appeals from the three divisions of the High Court, divisional courts and county courts. It also hears appeals from the Tribunal Service. Usually, a minimum of three judges will sit, although this can increase to five. All appeals need 'leave to appeal' (permission).

Supreme Court

The Supreme Court replaced the House of Lords as the top of the hierarchy of English courts, providing a second level of appeal. There are 12 judges, with at least one from Scotland and one from Northern Ireland. They must sit as an uneven panel, so three, five, seven, nine (or, in rare cases, such as ruling on Brexit) judges can hear an appeal. A case will only be heard in this court if leave to appeal is granted, either by the Supreme Court or by the court against whose decision the appeal is being sought (usually the Court of Appeal). The court hears only 50 cases on average every year. Permission to appeal is only granted if the case is certified as involving a **point of law of general public importance.** From a decision of the Court of Appeal, there is further appeal to the Supreme Court, but only if the Supreme Court or Court of Appeal gives permission to appeal.

KEY TERMINOLOGY

first instance (trial court): a court in which the first hearing of a case takes place. It is distinguished from an appellate court, which hears appeal cases.

GRADE BOOST

- Find out some features of each of the three tracks. How do they try to remedy the three main problems Woolf found of cost, delay and complexity?
- Find out about Money Claim Online.

Leapfrog appeals

These go directly from the High Court to the Supreme Court ('leapfrogging' over the Court of Appeal). They can only be made on the granting of a certificate by the High Court judge and where the case involves a point of law of general public importance which either concerns the interpretation of a statute or involves a binding precedent of the Court of Appeal or Supreme Court which the trial judge must follow. In addition, the Supreme Court must give permission to appeal.

Civil appeal process

Either party to a dispute may make an appeal. Permission to appeal will be granted where the appeal has a realistic chance of success or where there is a compelling reason why the appeal should be heard. Appeals are generally made to the next level of judge in the court hierarchy.

STRETCH AND CHALLENGE

Find more out about the civil appeals process. This is another area that can be examined and it is important to understand the appeal routes and what can happen as a result of an appeal.

Civil procedure before the 1999 reforms

Before the **Woolf reforms** in April 1999, there were two separate sets of civil procedure, depending on where the case commenced. Cases in the High Court used the 'White Book' and cases in the county court used the 'Green Book' (these are the rules of civil procedure and practice, and had either a white cover or a green cover). There were also different procedures for commencing a case. A case in the county court was started with a **summons**, but a case in the High Court was started with a **writ.** The system could be confusing for plaintiffs because of the differing rules of procedure and evidence.

Lord Woolf was tasked with reforming the civil justice system. This culminated in 'Access to Justice: Final Report', which was published in 1996 and soon became known as the **Woolf Report**. He concluded that the civil justice system of the time had some key flaws:

- **Expensive**: His report found that costs often exceeded the amount in dispute.
- **Delays**: Cases took an average of three–five years to reach the trial stage.
- **Complex**: With differing procedures for the county and High courts, litigants found the system complex. As a result, more lawyers would be hired, increasing costs for plaintiffs.
- **Adversarial**: There was an emphasis on exploiting the system rather than cooperation between parties.
- **Unjust:** There was an imbalance of power between the wealthy represented party and the underrepresented party. This was a particular problem with out-of-court settlements, with one party under pressure to settle more than the other.
- **Emphasis on oral evidence**: Most evidence did not need to be presented orally and could have been pre-assessed by the judge. This made trials slow and inefficient and led to an increase in costs, with expert witnesses having high fees.

As a result of the findings of the Woolf Report, the main recommendations were put into effect in the ***Civil Procedure Rules 1998***, which came into force in April 1999. They represent one of the biggest reforms of the civil justice system, with some people questioning whether such wide reforms were needed. ***Rule 1.1(2)*** states:

> *Dealing with a case justly includes, so far as is practicable –*
> *(a) ensuring that the parties are on an equal footing;*
> *(b) saving expense;*
> *(c) dealing with the case in ways which are proportionate –*
> *(i) to the amount of money involved; (ii) to the importance of the case; (iii) to the complexity of the issues; and (iv) to the financial position of each party;*
> *(d) ensuring that it is dealt with expeditiously and fairly; and*
> *(e) allotting to it an appropriate share of the court's resources, while taking into account the need to allot resources to other cases.*

The Woolf reforms

Several significant changes were made as a result of the ***Civil Procedure Rules 1998***.

Simplified procedure

The overriding aim of this reform was to provide a common procedural code for the county and High courts. Some terminology was changed to make it more accessible for claimants (previously plaintiffs).

Pre-action protocols

One of the biggest themes of the reforms was to encourage parties to cooperate. Pre-action protocols are designed to encourage parties to exchange information as early as possible, be in contact with each other and cooperate over the exchange of information. Their overall aim was to encourage parties to settle out of court, reducing costs and delay.

Case management

One of the most important reforms has been judges becoming the managers of cases, with proactive powers to set timetables and sanction parties that do not cooperate. The overall aim of this reform was to pass the management of the case to the court and not the parties, to improve efficiency and reduce costs.

Alternative dispute resolution (ADR)

Parties can postpone proceedings for one month to attempt to settle the case using ADR (see page 55). Courts should also actively promote its use. However, in ***Halsey v Milton Keynes General NHS Trust (2004)***, the Court of Appeal said the courts cannot force parties to ADR as it might be against ***Article 6 European Convention on Human Rights*** (the right to a fair trial).

The three tracks

- **The small claims track** (cases up to £10,000 or £1,000 for personal injury): tried in the small claims court.
- **The fast track** (cases between £10,000 and £25,000): tried in the county court.
- **The multi-track** (cases above £25,000): tried in either the county court or the High Court.

Sanctions

The overriding aim of the reforms was to ensure that cases are as efficient and cost effective as possible. With judges taking on the role of case managers, they have been given powers to issue sanctions where parties do not follow the timetables they set or delay unnecessarily. Two main sanctions are:

- adverse award of costs
- order for a case to be struck out (in part or full).

In ***Biguzzi v Rank Leisure plc (1999)*** it was held that striking out a case would only happen if it was proportional and there were other options available to deal with delay. In ***UCB Halifax (SW) Ltd (1999)*** however, it was stressed that a lax approach should not be used for serious cases and courts should use the new powers available to them.

Civil procedure

The civil procedure

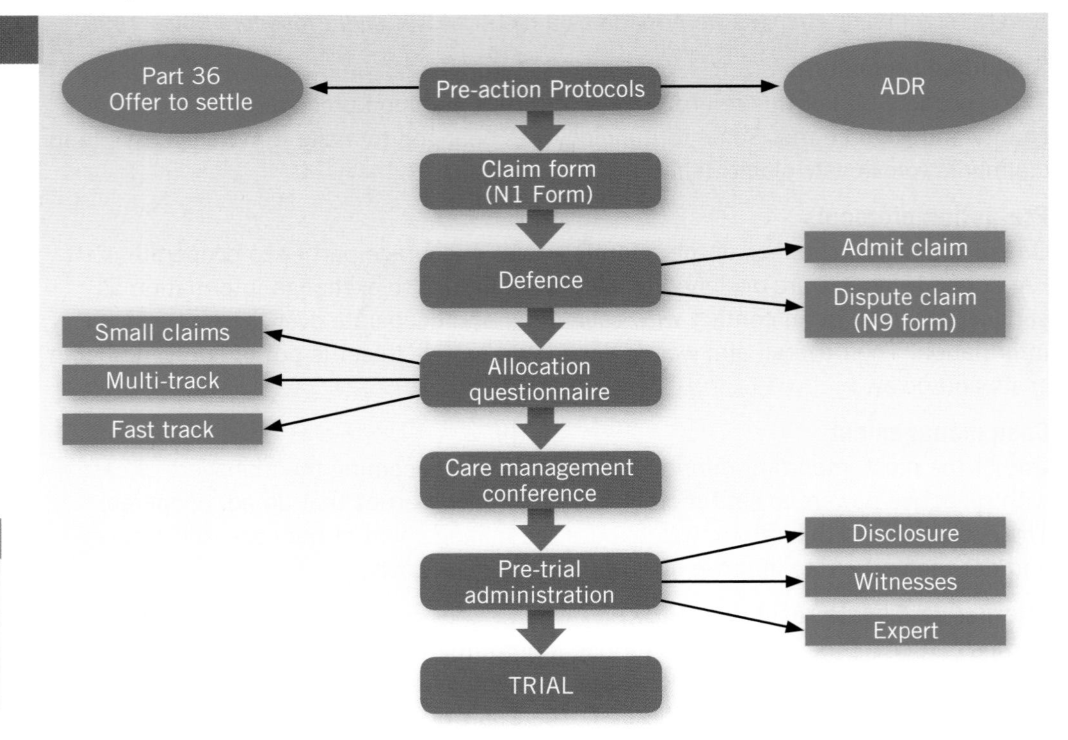

KEY TERMINOLOGY

disclosure: the obligation on both defence and prosecution to disclose all relevant evidence to the other side.

Exam Skills

This topic could feature on Section B of WJEC AS Law, Eduqas component 1 AS and A Level. It is likely to be examined in a similar way to the WJEC 'old' specification LA1.

Part a) questions will require you to **explain** an aspect of the topic covering AO1 skills.

Part b) questions require you to **analyse and evaluate** an aspect of the topic covering AO3 skills.

Though the marks and timing allocations are different, it would be a good idea to look back over legacy LA1 papers on the WJEC website.

WJEC

Juries in civil cases

Juries are used in less than 1 per cent of civil cases. They decide whether or not the claimant has proved their case 'on the balance of probabilities' (the standard of proof) and they also decide the amount of damages the defendant should pay the claimant if they decide in favour of the claimant.

Parties have the right to jury trial only in the following cases, according to ***s69 Senior Courts Act 1981*** for High Court cases and ***s66 County Courts Act 1984*** for cases in the county court:

- False imprisonment
- Malicious prosecution
- Fraud.

s11 of the Defamation Act 2013 removed the presumption of a trial by jury for defamation cases. Defamation cases are therefore tried without a jury unless the court orders otherwise.

Why are juries used rarely in civil cases?

- They tend to award excessive damages.
- They do not have to give reasons for their decisions.
- Excessive cost.

Juries in personal injury cases

In personal injury civil cases in the Queen's Bench Division of the High Court, the parties can apply to the judge for a jury trial but it is rarely granted. The Court of Appeal in the case of ***Ward v James (1966)*** laid down guidelines for personal injury cases, which, in effect, stopped the use of juries for personal injury cases. They said that personal injury cases should normally be tried by a judge sitting alone, because such cases involve assessing compensatory damages that need to relate to conventional scales of damages, with which the judge will be familiar.

Singh v London Underground (1990) and ***H v Ministry of Defence (1991)*** show how the courts have proved reluctant use juries in personal injury cases.

GRADE BOOST

A further case demonstrating the reluctance to use juries in personal injury cases is ***Singh v London Underground (1990)***. The request was refused on the basis it involved wide issues and technical points.

Exam Skills

Juries have three roles – in the criminal, civil and coroner's courts. You need be familiar with all aspects of a jury's role as you could both be asked a question on the role of the jury (requiring you to explain all three roles) or asked about just one of the jury's roles. The other roles are covered within the topic of criminal process on page 62.

Alternative dispute resolution (ADR)

Reasons for ADR

ADR is a method of resolving issues out of court. Court action (**litigation**) is not always the most appropriate means of resolving a dispute because of the:

- complexity of legal procedures
- delay it causes in resolution
- cost of court action
- intimidating atmosphere of the courts
- public nature of court action
- adversarial nature of court action, which can result in a deterioration of the relationship between the parties.

ADR is encouraged by ***Part 1*** of the ***Civil Procedure Rules 1998***, where it is part of a judge's role in **active case management** (where the judge plays an active role in resolving the case) to encourage ADR where appropriate. ADR is only used in civil cases; this is because, in criminal cases, there is too much at risk to justify an alternative to the criminal justice system. ADR has grown in popularity over the last 50 years, and is now increasingly seen as a compulsory step in the process rather than an alternative. Indeed, some parties have been 'punished' with an **adverse costs order** (where one party pays the other's costs) for refusing to cooperate in a method of ADR.

GRADE BOOST

Civil Procedure Rules (CPR) 1998, which were introduced following Lord Woolf's Report, require active case management and include 'encouraging parties to use an ADR procedure if the court considers it to be appropriate'. ***Rule 26.4*** allows judges to stay (i.e. suspend) court proceedings where they feel that ADR should be attempted. The judge can make this decision with or without the agreement of the parties.
Under ***Rule 44.5*** of ***CPR***, if a court believes that a case could have been more effectively settled via ADR it can punish the party who insisted on a court hearing by penalising them in costs. So, for example, even if a claimant wins the case, they might not have their costs paid by the losing party.
The application of this rule is demonstrated in the case of ***Dunnett v Railtrack (2002)***.

GRADE BOOST

The ***Halsey and Steel cases (2004)*** are also important. Research the Court of Appeal judgement in this case.

Forms of ADR

TYPE OF ADR	DESCRIPTION
ARBITRATION Commonly used in commercial and contract cases, and most notably in high-profile sports cases. 	This is the most formal method and is **adjudicative** (disputes are resolved through a neutral third party who has the authority to bind the parties to the terms of a decision). The parties agree to let an independent arbitrator make a **binding** decision. Many contracts include a ***Scott v Avery*** clause to agree pre-contractually to arbitrate in the event of a dispute. The decision of the arbitrator is called an 'award'. There can be a hearing but many cases are conducted using 'paper arbitration', when parties submit their arguments and evidence in writing to the arbitrator as opposed to making oral submissions at a hearing. An award can be appealed only on the basis of serious irregularity in the proceedings or on a point of law (***s65 Arbitration Act 1996***). The ***European Directive on Alternative Dispute Resolution*** (which came into force in July 2015), requires all EU countries to have ADR available for consumer disputes. It also requires ADR providers to meet certain standards.
MEDIATION Commonly used in family disputes or any area where a relationship needs to be maintained. 	The parties are encouraged to come to their own settlement with the help of a neutral third party or mediator who acts as a go-between. The mediator's role is to facilitate rather than to actively shape the outcome. The Ministry of Justice funds the **Civil Mediation Online Directory**. Individuals can search the directory for a mediation provider that is local to them; and the cost of mediation is based on a fixed fee, depending on the value of the dispute. Not automatically binding unless contract is drawn up.
CONCILIATION Commonly used in industrial disputes. 	The third party plays a more active role in the proceedings to push towards a settlement.
NEGOTIATION Used in most cases at the outset of a dispute. 	Resolving the dispute between the parties themselves; can involve solicitors. Can be completed using letters, email, phone, meeting, etc. At its most basic, involves returning faulty goods to a shop; at its most complex, it involves solicitors and settlement offers being exchanged.

LEGAL AUTHORITY/EXAMPLE	ADVANTAGES	DISADVANTAGES
• ***Arbitration Act 1996*** • Institute of Arbitrators • ***Scott v Avery*** • The ***European Directive on Alternative Dispute Resolution***	• The parties have discretion over the choice of arbitrator via the **Institute of Arbitrators**. • The hearing procedure is left to the discretion of the parties; they can choose the venue, date, number of witnesses etc. • There is rarely any publicity. • The award is **binding** and can be enforced by the courts. • The arbitrator is an expert in the field.	• Public funding is not available, so one party may have an advantage from the outset. • Appeals are restricted in the arbitration process. • Parties may feel they do not get their 'day in court'. • If a legal point arises, there is not always a legal professional in the hearing.
• ***Dunnett v Railtrack*** • ***Halsey v Milton Keynes NHS Trust*** • Neighbour disputes • Mediation in **divorce cases:** under ***s10 Child and Families Act 2014***, in most cases involving a dispute over finances or children, the parties will be required to attend a **Mediation Information and Assessment Meeting (MIAM)** • **Small Claims Mediation Service** • **Court of Appeal Mediation Scheme** • Online dispute resolution is available (e.g. www.mediate.com/odr) • **Centre for Effective Dispute Resolution (CEDR):** commercial mediators	• A private and confidential process. • The parties enter into mediation voluntarily. • Quick, cost effective and accessible. • A good chance that the parties can maintain a relationship. • CEDR reports 80% of cases are settled at mediation.	• The dispute may end up going to court anyway if mediation fails, resulting in greater costs. • Increasingly seen as a compulsory step in the process. • Where parties are forced into mediation, there is a half-hearted commitment, decreasing the chances of success.
• **Advisory, Conciliation and Arbitration Service (ACAS)** • Early conciliation via ACAS	• A cheaper option than litigation. • A private and confidential process. • ACAS adopts a 'prevention rather than cure' approach to dispute resolution. • Process identifies and clarifies the main issues in the dispute. • Conciliator plays an active role.	• Heavily relies on the skills of the conciliator. • The dispute may go to court anyway if conciliation fails, resulting in greater costs.
N/A	• Completely private. • Quick resolution, maintaining relationships. • Relatively informal method of resolution.	• Involving solicitors can make the process costly. • Offers are often exchanged and are not agreed until the day of court, wasting time and money. • People see it as a 'halfway house', and think that they are not receiving as much as if they had gone to court.

GRADE BOOST

When an examination question asks you about the ***Civil Procedure Rules*** or ***CPR*** remember to talk about ALL the Woolf Reforms, not just ADR. It is a common mistake for students to only discuss ADR in a civil procedure question. In preparation for the examination, it is worth mentioning any recent cases you have researched that have involved ACAS, as it is always impressive to show examiners your knowledge of current affairs. Also make sure that you mention all relevant sections of the ***Arbitration Act 1996***.

STRETCH AND CHALLENGE

Mediation Information and Assessment Meetings (MIAMs) require all divorcing couples attend compulsory mediation. Do you think this will cause resentment about the system, or encourage people to be more amicable in their disputes? Will it eventually replace solicitors?

Exam Skills

This topic could feature on Section B of WJEC AS Law, Eduqas component 1 AS and A Level. It is likely to be examined in a similar way to the WJEC 'old' specification LA1.

Part a) questions will require you to **explain** an aspect of the topic covering AO1 skills.

Part b) questions require you to **analyse and evaluate** an aspect of the topic covering AO3 skills. Though the mark and timing allocations are different, it would be a good idea to look back over legacy LA1 papers on the WJEC website.

Tribunals

Tribunals are an important part of the legal system and act as specialist courts for disputes in specialised areas, mainly welfare and social rights. For example, employment disputes are often resolved using a tribunal, as are immigration and social security disputes.

Tribunals are frequently seen as another alternative to the courts, but the biggest difference is that, if the case fails at the tribunal stage, there is no redress to the courts, whereas if any other form of ADR fails, the parties still get the option of going to court to resolve their dispute.

There are three different types of tribunal:

- **Administrative**: these deal with disputes between individuals and the state over rights contained in social welfare legislation, such as social security, immigration and land.
- **Domestic**: these are internal tribunals used for disputes within private bodies, such as the Law Society and the General Medical Council.
- **Employment**: these are the most common use of tribunals, and deal with disputes between employees and employers over rights under employment legislation.

Tribunals date back to the birth of the welfare state and were established to give people a way of making sure their rights were enforced. When they were first introduced, there were more than 70 different tribunals, all with different procedures and administration. This led to over-complication and many users felt intimidated and confused by the system.

History of tribunals

1957: Franks Committee recommended that tribunal procedures should be an example of **'openness, fairness** and **impartiality'**. The recommendations were implemented in the ***Tribunals and Inquiries Act 1958***.

1958: Council on Tribunals was set up to supervise and review tribunal procedures. The Council would deal with complaints and submit recommendations for improvement. However, some people regarded it as a 'watchdog with no teeth', meaning it had very little power to make changes.

2000: Sir Andrew Leggatt: **'Tribunals for Users – One System, One Service'**. This report marked a radical reform of the tribunal system, since Leggatt reported that tribunals lacked independence, coherence and were not user friendly.

LEGGATT RECOMMENDATION	DETAILS
A single Tribunal Service to be responsible for the administration of all tribunals.	This makes the Tribunal Service independent of its government department. The support that it gives to tribunals is unified both in procedure and administration.
Tribunals should be organised into divisions grouping together similar tribunals.	The divisions that were created are Education, Financial, Health and Social Services, Immigration, Land and Valuation, Social Security and Pensions, Transport, Regulatory and Employment. Each division is headed by a registrar who takes on case management duties in line with the ***Civil Procedure Rules (CPR)***.
The system should be user friendly.	Users are encouraged to bring their own cases without legal representation. Written judgements should be given in plain English. Information about procedures, venues etc. should be made freely available.
Single route of appeal.	Each division has a corresponding appeal tribunal, and only then will there be a redress to the Court of Appeal.

2007: ***Tribunals, Courts and Enforcement Act*** formalised and implemented most of Leggatt's reforms and contributed to the most radical shake up of the tribunal system seen for many years.

Tribunals, Courts and Enforcement Act 2007

This Act implemented many of Leggatt's reforms. In particular, ***Part 1*** established a **Tribunal Service** that unified all the procedures and created a new structure that addressed many of Leggatt's concerns. There are now only two tribunals: the First Tier Tribunal and the Upper Tribunal, within which are **chambers**, or groups of tribunals with similar jurisdictions. The Upper Tribunal has the power to conduct a **judicial review** of a case which has been heard in the First Tier Tribunal, minimising the need for the courts to get involved in the case. All members are appointed by the **Judicial Appointments Commission**, and are thus recognised as judges, which increases the status of tribunals. Further appeal from the Upper Tribunal is available to the Court of Appeal, but this is rare because of the well-structured system.

The whole system is headed by the **Senior President of Tribunals** who is responsible for assigning judges to the chambers, looking after their general welfare and helping with any issues. The president has the power to issue **practice directions** in order to help tribunal judges maintain a unified procedure across all the chambers.

KEY TERMINOLOGY

lay (person): someone who is not legally qualified.
First Tier Tribunal: part of the legal system that aims to settle the 'first instance' stage of legal disputes. It is split into seven chambers or specialist areas.
Upper Tribunal: hears appeals from the First Tier Tribunal, and in some complex cases will act within a first instance jurisdiction.

Composition

Cases in the First Tier Tribunal are heard by a **tribunal judge**. Also, for some types of case, two specialist non-legal, members sit with the judge to make the decision. These specialist members have expertise in the particular field of the tribunal, such as social care or housing. In employment tribunals there are also two **lay** members. These will usually be a person representing both the employer and employee. This gives them a clear understanding of employment issues.

<table>
<tr><th colspan="7">COURT OF APPEAL</th></tr>
<tr><th colspan="7">UPPER TRIBUNAL</th></tr>
<tr><td>Administrative Appeals Chamber</td><td colspan="2">Tax and Chancery Chamber</td><td colspan="2">Lands Chamber</td><td colspan="2">Asylum and Immigration Chamber</td></tr>
<tr><th colspan="7">FIRST TIER TRIBUNAL</th></tr>
<tr><td>Social Entitlement Chamber</td><td>Health, Education and Social Care Chamber</td><td>War Pensions and Armed Forces Compensation Chamber</td><td>General Regulatory Chamber</td><td>Taxation Chamber</td><td>Land, Property and Housing Chamber</td><td>Asylum and Immigration Chamber</td></tr>
</table>

The Employment Tribunal operates separately from the First Tier tribunals.

The Council on Tribunals has now been replaced by the **Administrative Justice and Tribunals Council**, which is much more powerful in terms of reviewing the system, keeping it under control and advising the government on future reforms of the Tribunal Service. Tribunals are overseen by Her Majesty's Court and Tribunal Service.

GRADE BOOST

When you are writing an essay on tribunals, make sure you include a little about the history of the tribunal system. More importantly, you need to show your knowledge of the current system and be able to cite the ***Tribunals, Courts and Enforcement Act 2007*** and its provisions.
Be prepared to talk about tribunals both as a topic in its own right, and as a form of ADR.

Employment tribunals

Employment tribunals are not included in the structure because it was felt that the types of disputes dealt with by employment tribunals were very different from the other tribunals, and so the employment tribunal and the employment appeals tribunal remain distinct from the structure. From July 2013, fees are charged for both employment tribunals and employment appeal tribunals.

Advantages and Disadvantages of tribunals

Advantages

✓ **Speed**: There is a duty on the tribunal judges to take on case management duties, so they are able to impose strict timetables to ensure that most cases can be heard within one day.

✓ **Cost**: Parties are encouraged to take their own cases without the need for representation. This has been made even easier with the availability of application forms online and a more transparent Tribunal Service since the reforms.

✓ **Expertise**: At least one member of the tribunal will be an expert in the relevant field, so this will save time explaining complex technicalities to a judge in court.

✓ **Informality**: Tribunals are much less formal than a court hearing, though they are more formal than other methods of ADR. The parties benefit from a private hearing and have the chance to maintain a relationship after the case is over.

✓ **Independence**: Because of the involvement of the Judicial Appointments Commission in appointing tribunal judges, the tribunal system is more transparent, independent and fair. The unified set of procedures and rules minimises the risk of inconsistencies between tribunals.

Disadvantages

✗ **Lack of funding**: Legal funding is available for some disputes; for example, a trade union may pay for your case if you are a member. However, funding is not always available, which can be detrimental to a person taking on a big company that has the benefit of expensive representation. In addition, fees for claims in the employment tribunal or employment appeal tribunal may prevent some people from pursuing a claim.

✗ **Delay**: If the case is complex, there can be a delay in getting it heard.

✗ **Intimidated parties**: Parties may still feel intimidated and daunted at the prospect of taking a case to 'court', particularly without the comfort of having a legal representative.

✗ **Lack of precedent**: Tribunals do not operate a strict system of precedent, so the outcome of cases can be unpredictable.

Exam Skills

This topic could feature on Section B of WJEC AS Law, Eduqas component 1 AS and A Level. It is likely to be examined in a similar way to the WJEC 'old' specification LA1.

Part a) questions will require you to **explain** an aspect of the topic covering AO1 skills.

Part b) questions require you to **analyse and evaluate** an aspect of the topic covering AO3 skills. Though the marking and timing allocations are different, it would be a good idea to look back over legacy LA1 papers on the WJEC website.

Summary: Civil courts

- Civil justice settles disputes between private individuals and companies
- Cases are claimant versus defendant; the claimant is seeking a **remedy**
- Case depends on the standard of proof (balance of probabilities)
- First instance courts are the **county** and **High courts**
- High Court has three divisions: **Queen's Bench, Family and Chancery**
- Three tracks for civil hearings:
  - small claims
  - fast track
  - multi-track
- **Appeals** happen at High Court Divisional Courts, Court of Appeal and Supreme Court
- All appeals need **leave to appeal**
- Leapfrog appeals go straight from the High Court to the Supreme Court
- Lord Woolf's 'Access to Justice: Final Report' (1996) identified key flaws in the justice system:
  - Expensive
  - Complex
  - Unjust
  - Delays
  - Adversarial
  - Emphasis on oral evidence
- **Woolf Report's** main recommendations were put into effect in the ***Civil Procedure Rules (CPR) 1998***. Main reforms:
  - Case management
  - Increased ADR
  - Pre-action protocols
  - Three tracks
  - Sanctions
- **Juries in civil cases:** Less than 1% of civil cases use juries
- Juries decide for or against the claimant and amount of damages
- ***s69 Senior Courts Act 1981*** and ***s66 County Courts Act 1984*** state that cases in the county court can allow for jury trial in cases of false imprisonment, malicious prosecution and fraud
- Juries are no longer used in defamation cases (***s11 Defamation Act 2013***)
- Juries are rarely used in personal injury cases: see ***Ward v James (1966)***
- **Alternative dispute resolution (ADR):** Alternative to litigation. Encourages settlements out of court
- Four main methods of ADR:
  - **Arbitration**: Binding decision. ***Arbitration Act 1996***. ***Scott v Avery*** arbitration clause
  - **Mediation**: Facilitative third party e.g. MIAMs, Small Claims Mediation
  - **Conciliation**: Active third party e.g. ACAS, early conciliation
  - **Negotiation**: With or without lawyers; phone, email, letter, meeting
- **Tribunals:** Specialist 'courts': an alternative to courts but the only avenue for some cases
- **Three types**: administrative, domestic, employment
- **Franks Committee** report recommended openness, fairness, impartiality
- **Leggatt** report led to ***Tribunals, Courts and Enforcement Act 2007***, which introduced:
  - First Tier
  - Upper Tier
  - appeals to Court of Appeal
  - tribunal judges
- Organised by **Her Majesty's Courts and Tribunal Service**
- Overseen by **Administrative Justice and Tribunals Council**
- Employment tribunals now charge **a fee**
- **Advantages**: Cost, expertise, speed, independence
- **Disadvantages**: Lack of funding, lack of precedent, delay, intimidated parties

Criminal process

Spec reference	Key content	Assessment Objectives	Where does this topic feature on each specification/exam?
WJEC AS/A Level **1.6:** Criminal process **3.12:** Criminal law **Eduqas AS Level** **1.2.2:** Criminal process **Eduqas A Level** **1.2.2:** Criminal process	• Criminal courts: structure, powers and appellate functions; powers of the Magistrates' Courts and Crown Court; Court of Appeal guidelines for bringing appeals • Crown Prosecution Service: powers and duties • Bail: police and court; problems • General principles of sentencing of adults and youths under appropriate legislation; theories and objectives of sentencing	**AO1** Demonstrate knowledge and understanding of legal rules and principles **AO3** Analyse and evaluate legal rules, principles and issues.	**WJEC AS/A Level:** Unit 1 Section B **Eduqas AS Level:** Component 1 Section B **Eduqas A Level:** Component 1 Section B

Introduction

The law lists many criminal offences to which a suspect can plead guilty or not guilty, but the procedure that follows arrest varies depending on the **classification of offence** that has been committed. Remember that, throughout the process, the suspects are **innocent until proven guilty** and at all times their ***Article 6 ECHR*** **right to a fair trial** should be upheld, and the courts have a duty under the ***Human Rights Act 1998*** to make sure this happens.

In terms of criminal procedure, every case has an initial hearing in the magistrates court, even if it is only for the official passing over to the Crown Court. This is known as the **early administrative hearing**. The ***Criminal Procedure Rules 2013*** govern the pretrial and trial process in England and Wales.

There are three categories of offence in the English and Welsh legal system:

Category of offence	Place of trial	Examples of offence
Summary	Magistrates' court	• Driving without a licence • Taking a vehicle without consent • Common assault
Triable either way	Magistrates' court **or** Crown Court (the defendant chooses)	• Theft • Assault occasioning actual bodily harm • Obtaining property by deception
Indictable	Crown Court	• Murder • Manslaughter • Rape • Robbery

KEY TERMINOLOGY

early administrative hearing: the first appearance at magistrates' court for all defendants suspected of a summary or indictable offence. This hearing considers legal funding, bail and legal representation.

pre-sentence report: a report that helps the court to decide whether there are any factors in the defendant's history which may affect the sentencing.

Summary offences

Early administrative hearing at magistrates' court deals with administration such as:

- whether defendant should be bailed or remanded in custody
- what legal funding provisions are in place
- **pre-sentence reports**

PLEAD GUILTY → **Sentencing** at magistrates' court

PLEAD NOT GUILTY → **Summary trial** at magistrates' court

Process for summary offences

Indictable offences

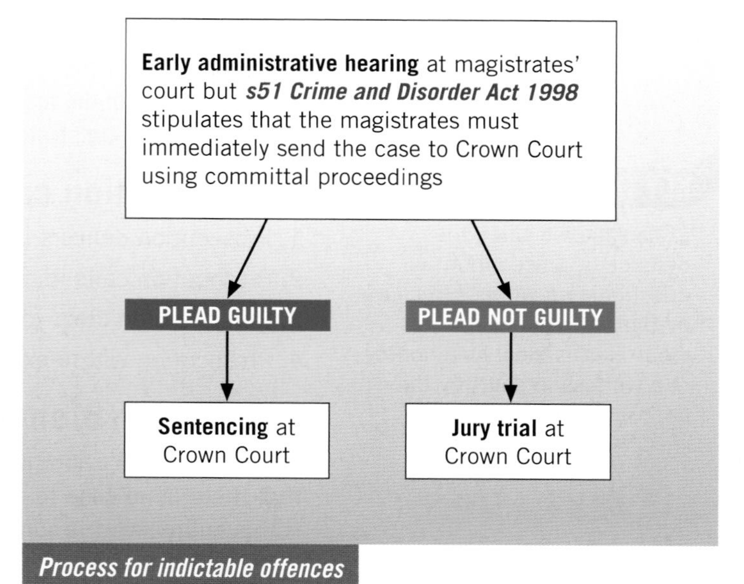

Process for indictable offences

Triable either way offences

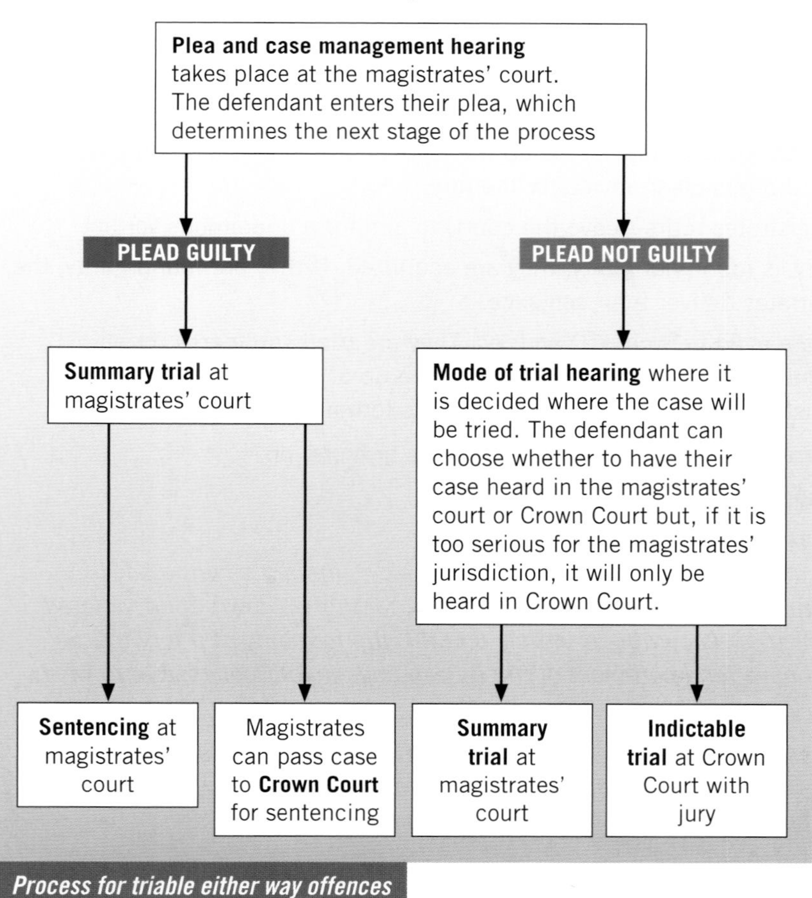

Process for triable either way offences

STRETCH AND CHALLENGE

In triable either way offences, the defendant has the option to choose whether or not they wish to have a trial by jury. Research the implications of choosing a trial by jury, and the arguments for and against abolishing the right to choose a trial by jury.

GRADE BOOST

Remember that magistrates have limited sentencing powers; they can sentence up to a one-year custodial sentence and (**usually**) a £5,000 fine.

STRETCH AND CHALLENGE

s85 Legal Aid, Sentencing and Punishment of Offenders Act 2012 changed the maximum fine available for seven offences that can still be tried summarily by magistrates. Research these and explain if you think the law is justified in allowing magistrates to impose an unlimited fine in these cases?

The trial process

In both the magistrates' and Crown courts, the **burden of proof** lies with the prosecution who have to prove **beyond reasonable doubt** that the defendant is guilty.

The procedure in the magistrates' and Crown courts is essentially the same. However, there is **no jury in the magistrates' court**, and the magistrates are guided on the law by their clerk, as magistrates are not legally qualified.

KEY TERMINOLOGY

examination in chief: the defence or prosecution questioning a witness in court by their own counsel.
cross-examination: questioning of a witness in court by the opposing counsel.

1. Prosecution case

1. Prosecution delivers its **opening speech** to outline facts.
2. Prosecution calls its witnesses to support its case and conducts **examination in chief**.
3. Defence then **cross-examines** those witnesses.
4. Prosecution will **re-examine** those witnesses if necessary.

2. Determination of whether there is a case

When the prosecution has presented all its evidence, the defence can then submit that there is no case to answer; that is, there is not enough evidence to prosecute. If this submission is successful, a verdict of not guilty will be directed.

3. Defence case

1. Defence calls its witnesses to support its case and conducts examination in chief.
2. Prosecution then **cross-examines** those witnesses.

4. Closing speeches

1. Both sides make closing speeches to the jury or magistrates. The prosecution goes first so that the defence has the last say.
2. If in the Crown Court, the judge sums up the legal and factual issues which should be balanced and offers clear advice for the jury.
3. The jury or magistrates retire (leave the court) to aim for a unanimous verdict.
4. If the defendant is found not guilty, they are acquitted. If they are found guilty, the judge or magistrates deliver their **sentence**.

KEY TERMINOLOGY

sentence: the punishment given to someone who has been convicted of an offence. It can be imprisonment, a community sentence or a suspended sentence or discharge.
charge: the decision that a suspect should stand trial for an alleged offence.

Young offenders are aged between 10 and 17. They are tried summarily for all offences in the youth court. The youth court is made up of specially trained and experienced magistrates and sits in private with less formality unless:

- the offence carries a possible penalty of 14 years or more; or
- the young person is **charged** jointly with an adult.

Thompson and Venables v UK (1999)
*The European Court of Human Rights (ECtHR) upheld complaints by the boys convicted of the murder of Jamie Bulger that their trial in the Crown Court violated their right to a fair trial. According to **Article 6 ECHR**, the formality of a jury trial in open court would have rendered most of the proceedings incomprehensible to them.*

The ECtHR ruled that the trial of a young person should be held in a courtroom in which everyone is on the same level and the defendants should be permitted to sit with their family. Wigs and gowns should not be worn and public and press attendance should be restricted if necessary.

The Old Bailey is probably the most famous Crown Court, and is also known as the Central Criminal Court

Role of the Crown Court

The Crown Court hears serious, indictable cases such as rape, murder, manslaughter and robbery. ***The Courts Act 1971*** established the Crown Court but its jurisdiction is now contained in the ***Supreme Court Act 1981***.

Trials in the Crown Court are heard before a judge and a jury. Although the Crown Court is always described as singular, there are 77 court centres across England and Wales, for example in large towns.

The Crown Court has four basic duties:

1. To try serious, indictable criminal offences such as murder, rape and robbery. Where the defendant pleads guilty, there will be no need for a jury; the judge will sentence.
2. To carry out jury trials for the most serious offences, where the defendant has pleaded not guilty.
3. To hear appeals from magistrates' courts; these will usually be summary offences.
4. To sentence defendants from the magistrates' court where the defendant has had their trial there but the magistrates have passed the case to the Crown Court to sentence because a sentence greater than their powers is required.

Criminal appeals

Criminal cases, in the first instance, are heard either in the **magistrates' court** or the **Crown Court**. After several high-profile miscarriages of justice, the appeal system was reformed significantly under the ***Criminal Appeal Act 1995***.

Appeals from magistrates' courts

Following a trial in the magistrates' court, two routes of appeal are open to a defendant, depending on what basis they want to appeal.

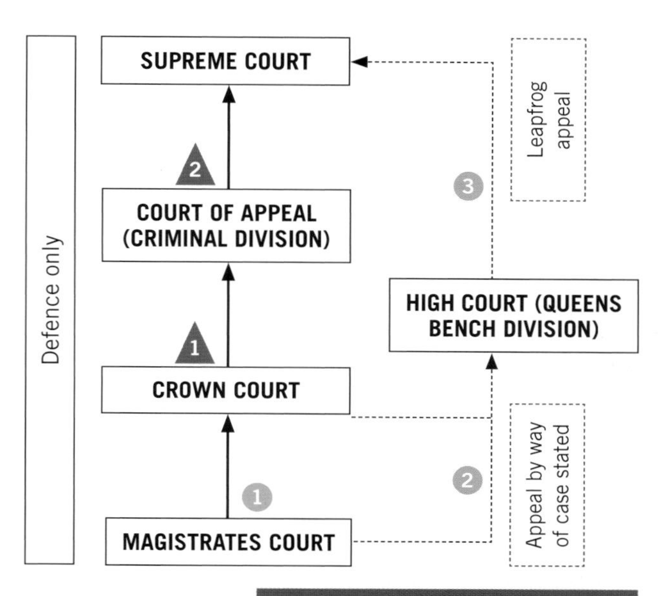

Hierarchy and appeal routes of the criminal courts

1. If the defendant wishes to appeal against conviction or sentence, they can appeal to the Crown Court as of right. This **automatic right of appeal** is open to the **defence** only if they pleaded not guilty. The appeal must be lodged within 28 days of the case finishing.
   - **Appeal against conviction**: the procedure is the same as in the magistrates' court but is heard by a judge sitting with two magistrates.
   - **Appeal against sentence**: the prosecution read out the facts and the defence can put forward mitigating factors relating to the offence or the offender. The Crown Court can then impose any sentence which the magistrates could have given.
2. If they wish to appeal by way of **case stated**, they must appeal to the **Divisional Court of the Queen's Bench Division** of the High Court. This method can be used by the **defence** against a conviction, or by the **prosecution** if the defendant has been acquitted. This appeal route is based on a mistake having been made in the application of the law. This route of appeal is not used very often. The divisional court can either allow or dismiss the appeal. They can also re-order a hearing before a new bench of magistrates.
3. A further appeal from the High Court is available to the **Supreme Court** but this will only happen if the matter is one of **public importance**.

C v Director of Public Prosecutions (DPP) (1994)

This case considered the issue of children having criminal responsibility. It was held that it was not to be presumed that children aged between 10 and 14 knew the difference between right and wrong, and therefore criminal activity will not always result in prosecution. The Divisional Court of the Queen's Bench Division had wanted to change the law so that it was always presumed that a child aged 10–14 knew the difference between right and wrong, but the Supreme Court held that they were bound by precedent and were not at liberty to change the law.

KEY TERMINOLOGY

conviction: the defendant has been found guilty and the case will proceed to the sentencing stage.
case stated: appeals on the grounds that there has been an error of law or the magistrates have acted out of their jurisdiction. Can be used by both the prosecution and defence.

Appeals from the Crown Court

1 By the defence

Appeals from the **Crown Court** to the **Court of Appeal (Criminal Division)** are the most common route of appeal by the **defence** against conviction and/or sentence. However, the defendant must have **leave to appeal**; and a request must be made within 28 days of the defendant being convicted. If leave is granted, the Court of Appeal have the following powers available to them:

- Allow the appeal, so the conviction will be quashed (rejected as invalid).
- Dismiss the appeal, so the conviction will stand.
- Decrease the sentence given.
- Reduce the conviction to a lesser offence (such as murder to manslaughter).
- Order a retrial in front of a new jury at the Crown Court.

2 By the prosecution

Appeals by the prosecution against an **acquittal** are rare, and can only be done with the permission of the **Attorney General**, who can:

1. refer a point of law to the Court of Appeal; or
2. can apply for leave against an **unduly lenient** sentence.

In 2016, 146 cases out of 190 applications had their sentences increased after the Court of Appeal found the sentences unduly lenient.

A further appeal from the **Court of Appeal** (Criminal Division) to the **Supreme Court** is extremely rare but is available to the **prosecution** and **defence**. Leave to appeal is rarely granted and then only on legal points of **'general public importance'**.

Leave to appeal

This is permission to appeal by a Court of Appeal judge; the rules for granting leave to appeal are contained in the ***Criminal Appeal Act 1995*** where it is stated that the Court of Appeal shall:

1. allow an appeal against conviction if they think that the conviction is unsafe
2. dismiss such an appeal in any other case.

Common examples of this are misdirections by the judge, or evidence that should have been admitted.

GRADE BOOST

You should refer to the ***ECHR*** in every question on criminal process. Relevant articles for criminal process are:

- ***Article 5 ECHR***: Right to liberty
- ***Article 6 ECHR***: Right to a fair trial.

KEY TERMINOLOGY

acquittal: the defendant has been found not guilty and will go free.

STRETCH AND CHALLENGE

Often new evidence coming to light will prompt leave for appeal to be granted based on the fact that the conviction is unsafe. This is important on the grounds of ***Article 6 ECHR***; however, the courts are not always as lenient in their interpretation of unsafe. Look at the case of **Simon Hall** who had his appeal against murder dismissed. Do you think there has been a breach of his Article 6 right to a fair trial since he alleged that new evidence could prove his innocence?

Sentencing

A sentence is the **punishment** given to a defendant who has been convicted of an offence. The type of sentence they receive will depend on the type of offence they have committed and whether they are an adult or a youth offender.

The judge is responsible for sentencing in the Crown Court and the magistrates decide the sentence in the magistrates' court. The sentencing power of each court are:

Magistrates' court	Crown Court
• £5,000 fine (but this can be unlimited for **some** Level 5 offences). • Maximum 6 months in prison (12 months for consecutive sentences). • Youth Detention and Training Order for up to two years.	• Unlimited fine. • Maximum life imprisonment.

The tariff, or length of the sentence will be determined by the court, who will look at:

- age of the offender
- seriousness of the offence
- likelihood of further offences being committed
- extent of harm likely to result from further offences.

GRADE BOOST

Section 85 Legal Aid, Sentencing and Punishment of Offenders Act 2012 is the legislation responsible for removing magistrates' upper fine limit for Level 5 offences and it came into force in 2015. Level 5 offences include selling alcohol to children and the unauthorised sale of (football) tickets.

Aims of sentencing

People often assume the one aim of sentencing is to punish individuals, but other factors need to be considered, such as the effect on the community and the long-term rehabilitation of the offender.

Section 142 Criminal Justice Act 2003 outlines five aims of sentencing:

1. Retribution (punishment)
This is the classic aim of sentencing, and is a way of punishing the defendant because it has been established that they have committed a crime and an element of blame rests with them. The punishment must fit the crime, and so the sentence given must be proportionate to the crime that has been committed.

2. Deterrence
Individual deterrence is where the individual offender is deterred from offending again. **General deterrence** aims to deterring others from committing a crime, showing society the potential consequences of committing a crime and making an example of the offender. Obviously the harsher the sentence, the more likely it is to act as a deterrent.

3. Protection of society
This is where the sentence given will protect the public from the offender. For example, a dangerous driver could be given a driving ban, or a convicted burglar could be given an electronic tag to stop them from leaving their house after dark.

4. Rehabilitation
This is where the offender is given a sentence which will help rehabilitate their behaviour and prevent them from offending again. This is particularly effective for youth offenders, as a wide belief is that a period of imprisonment is not effective in preventing reoffending. For this reason, the ***Criminal Justice Act 2003*** offers community sentencing, which can be tailored to help the offender and the community as a whole.

5. Reparation
Reparation essentially means paying back to society what you have taken away, for example in the form of compensation or through unpaid community work. For example, someone who has been convicted of criminal damage may be ordered to remove graffiti or repair any damage they have caused.

Exam Skills

If an examination question asks about the theories of sentencing, it is good practice to give examples of types of sentences that support that theory.

Sentencing of youth offenders

Offenders aged between 10 and 17 are classed as youth offenders, and are usually tried in the **youth court**, unless the case is so serious that it is tried in the Crown Court. Youths can also be tried in the Crown Court if they are being tried alongside an adult offender. The role of the youth court was consolidated in the case of ***Thompson and Venables v UK (1999)***, where the ECtHR held that it was a breach of ***Article 6 ECHR*** to have youths tried in an adult court because it was perceived as intimidating and daunting for them.

The youth court is usually located in the same building as the magistrates' court. It is not open to the public and is more informal; for example, the district judges do not wear wigs and there is only limited access for the press. Young offenders are also entitled to have an **appropriate adult** with them at all times, and this is provided for under ***s57 Police and Criminal Evidence Act 1984*** and ***Code C PACE***.

Several types of sentences are available for youths, but the primary aim of youth sentencing, according to ***s142 Criminal Justice Act 2003***, is to prevent reoffending and to rehabilitate the offender so that they change their behaviour while compensating, or 'repairing', society for the damage that has been caused.

KEY TERMINOLOGY

appropriate adult: a parent, guardian or social worker who must be present when a youth under the age of 17 is being interviewed in police custody, or on trial at the youth court. Their role is to make sure the young person understands legal terminology, is aware of their rights and is comforted and reassured.

Pre-court sentencing

The table shows disposals available in the youth justice system for those offenders who have committed a first offence or pleads guilty to an offence.

Youth restorative disposal (YRD)	Youth caution	Youth conditional caution
This is used for 10 to 17 year olds who have committed minor crimes. The offender must admit fault and there has to be the option for them to apologise or put right the harm they have caused. It aims to strike the balance between addressing the offence and providing support for young people by encouraging them not to commit further crimes or anti-social behaviour.	Youth cautions and youth conditional cautions were introduced by the ***Legal Aid, Sentencing and Punishment of Offenders Act 2012*** in April 2013, to replace police reprimands and final warnings.	This is for a more serious first offence or for a subsequent offence. It is a caution with conditions attached to it that the young person must adhere to. Young people who receive a youth conditional caution will be referred to Youth Offending Service (YOS).

Youth rehabilitation order (YRO)

These were introduced under ***s147 Criminal Justice Act 2003***. They are a type of community sentence imposed by the court, a flexible order that aims to reduce reoffending and the number of youths in custody. The order can last for a maximum of three years and can be applied to any criminal offence that has been committed by an individual under the age of 18.

The following requirements can be attached to a youth rehabilitation order:

- activity
- unpaid work
- curfew
- prohibited activity
- exclusion
- electronic monitoring
- local authority residence
- supervision
- education
- intoxicating substance
- mental health treatment
- drug testing.

Supervision of the youth will be carried out by the **youth offending team**, and the youth will be required to visit their case worker who will work out a **youth rehabilitation order plan** with them, to address their behaviour and help them move forward. If a youth offender breaches the order three times, they will have to return to court and could face a period in custody.

Youth fines

Youth fines should reflect the offender's ability to pay. If the youth is under 16, paying the fine is the responsibility of a parent or guardian, and it is their ability to pay that is taken into consideration when the level of fine is being set.

First tier sentencing

These are community sentences that are designed to act as a **deterrent** from committing further crime and provide a way in which the offender can attempt to rehabilitate and prevent reoffending in the future.

Referral order	Reparation order	Parenting order
ss16–28 Powers of Criminal Courts (Sentencing) Act 2000	***ss73–75 Powers of Criminal Courts (Sentencing) Act 2000***	***Criminal Justice Act 2003***
This is given for a first offence, when the offender pleads guilty. The young person will be referred to a youth offender panel, which will draw up a contract which will last between three and twelve months, aiming to address the causes of the offending behaviour and giving the offender an opportunity to repair the damage they have caused.	This allows the offender to take responsibility for their behaviour and express their remorse to society by repairing the harm caused by the offence. For example, they may be required to meet their victim, clean up graffiti or undertake some form of unpaid work.	These can be given to parents for up to a year. Conditions attached may be having to attend counselling sessions and the order will contain a list of things their offending child must and must not do, for example attend school or be at home between certain hours. They are intended to support the parents in dealing with their child's behaviour. If a parent breaches the order, they can be fined up to £1,000. The aim is to prevent reoffending, and the order will only be granted if the court is satisfied that it will help prevent further crime.

Discharges

Discharges are the same for adults and youth offenders, under ***ss12–15 Powers of Criminal Courts (Sentencing) Act 2000***.

- **Conditional discharge**: This sentence is rarely used, but is a way of giving the offender a 'cooling off' period. The youth will receive no punishment on the condition that they do not reoffend.
- **Absolute discharge**: an offender is released without punishment and nothing further is done.

Custody

Custody will only be granted to a youth in very serious cases.

Detention and training order ***ss100–106 Powers of Criminal Courts (Sentencing) Act 2000***	***s90 Powers of the Criminal Courts (Sentencing) Act 2000***	***s91 Powers of Criminal Courts (Sentencing) Act 2000***
This is a period in custody for a youth offender, and the length can vary between **four months** and **two years**. The first half of the sentence is served in custody, and the second half is served in the community under the supervision of the **Youth Offending Team**. During this community element, the offender will have to undertake reparation work and adhere to any targets contained in the **training and supervision plan** which will have been agreed with their youth offending team worker. These orders are only given to those youths who are a particularly high risk, or are persistent offenders, or have committed a particularly serious offence, because custody is not usually the most appropriate solution for a youth offender. Any breach of the order at any stage of the process could result in a fine or continued detention in custody.	If the conviction is for murder, the court is obliged to set a minimum term to be spent in custody, after which the youth can apply to the **Parole Board** for release. If they are successful, they will be closely supervised indefinitely. This is a sentence that can only be given by the Crown Court.	This section deals with youths who have committed offences for which an adult offender would serve at least 14 years. The length of the sentence can be anywhere up to the adult maximum, life imprisonment. The young offender can be released automatically at the halfway point, and can be released up to a maximum of 135 days early on a **home detention curfew**. The offender, once released, will also be subject to a supervisory licence until their sentence expires. This is a sentence that can only be given by the Crown Court.

R v Lavinia Woodward (2017)

*The defendant struck her partner in the leg with a bread knife in a drunken rage and was charged with unlawful wounding under **s20 Offences Against the Person Act 1861**.*

GRADE BOOST

Read the judge's sentencing report for ***R v Lavinia Woodward (2017)*** and outline the aggravating and mitigating factors in his judgement when passing a suspended sentence.

Exam Skills

When you are talking about youth sentencing, you should attempt to evaluate the theories of sentencing and the different types of sentence. For example, the youth rehabilitation order deals with reparation, rehabilitation and deterrence.

STRETCH AND CHALLENGE

The **Lammy Review** was published in September 2017 by the MP David Lammy. It reviewed the treatment of, and outcomes for, black, Asian and minority ethnic individuals in the criminal justice system. One of the key recommendations was to adopt an American principle of 'sealing' (expunging or deleting) spent criminal convictions, which enables the offender to apply to have their case heard by a judge or independent body, such as the Parole Board, to prove they have reformed. This would enable them to gain employment in the future and to have a second chance as their criminal convictions would not have to be disclosed.
Read all of Lammy's recommendations in the full report, available from www.gov.uk/government/news/lammy-publishes-historic-review.

KEY TERMINOLOGY

Parole Board: a body set up under the ***Criminal Justice Act 1967*** to hold meetings with an offender to decide whether they can be released from prison after serving a minimum sentence. They complete a risk assessment to determine whether it is safe to release the person back into the community. If they are safe to be released, they will be released on licence with conditions and close supervision.

Sentencing of adult offenders

OUT-OF-COURT DISPOSALS	**Penalty Notice for Disorder (PND) (*Criminal Justice and Police Act 2001*)**	A fixed penalty given to offenders who have committed one of 24 minor offences, such as theft from shops, minor criminal damage, dropping litter and drunkenness, as well as possession of khat or cannabis. Once the penalty notice has been served, the offender must either pay the penalty or elect to go to court within 21 days. Police community support officers (PCSOs) are able to issue PNDs.
OUT-OF-COURT DISPOSALS	**Caution**	Cautions can be given to anybody aged 10 or over for minor crimes, for example graffiti. Offenders have to agree to be cautioned, and can be arrested and charged if they don't. Although a caution is not a criminal conviction, it can be used as evidence of bad character if a defendant goes to court for another crime. Cautions can show on standard and enhanced Disclosure and Barring Service (DBS) checks.
OUT-OF-COURT DISPOSALS	**Conditional caution**	This caution has certain conditions or restrictions attached to it, such as an agreement to go for alcohol or drug rehabilitation or to fix damage caused.
COURT DISPOSALS	**Absolute discharge**	The court feels that the offender has received enough punishment by going through court and so discharges the offender with no further action.
COURT DISPOSALS	**Conditional discharge**	The offender will receive no punishment on the condition that they do not reoffend for a specified period.
COURT DISPOSALS	**Fine**	The most common sentence given to adults, mostly administered for minor offences. Magistrates can give a maximum of £5,000 and the Crown Court is not limited to what it can impose. ***s85 Legal Aid, Sentencing and Punishment of Offenders Act 2012*** removed magistrates' upper limit for Level 5 offences.
COURT DISPOSALS	**Suspended sentence order**	The offender does not go to prison, but has to comply with conditions set out by the court. The suspended period can be between 14 days and one year (or six months in the magistrates' court). Breach of the conditions can result in the offender being sent to prison for the remainder of their sentence. The court can attach any of 12 requirements to the sentence.
COURT DISPOSALS	**Community order (*s177 Criminal Justice Act 2003*)**	A court can impose a community order with any number of the requirements contained in the ***Criminal Justice Act 2003***. A community order encompasses both punishment and reparation to the community. It is usual to only have one requirement in less serious cases, but a more intensive package would be required for more serious offences. Requirements can include: • unpaid work • an activity • a programme (e.g. anger management or drug rehabilitation) • a prohibited activity • curfew • exclusion • residence • mental health treatment • drug rehabilitation • alcohol treatment • supervision • an attendance centre requirement. Following the ***Crime and Courts Act 2013***, every community sentence must contain a **punitive element** such as unpaid work or a curfew.

Custodial sentences

This is the most severe sentence and is for the most serious of offences. ***Section 152(2) Criminal Justice Act 2003*** stipulates that custodial sentences are only available for those offences 'so serious that neither a fine alone nor a community sentence can be justified for the offence'.

Determinate sentence

This is where the court fixes the amount of time an offender must stay in prison. This is the most common custodial sentence, though the length of sentence is usually a maximum as the offender will not always serve this amount of time.

For sentences of more than a year, the offender is likely to only serve half of their sentence and the other half will be served in the community on licence with conditions attached, and under supervision.

Indeterminate sentence

This is where the court will set a **minimum** period that the offender has to serve in prison before they are eligible for early release by the **Parole Board**.

Imprisonment for life

This is covered under ***s225 Criminal Justice Act 2003*** and suggests that an offender should serve a sentence of imprisonment for life, when:

- the offender is convicted of a serious offence (defined as carrying a maximum sentence of life imprisonment or at least ten years)
- in the court's opinion, the offender poses a significant risk to the public of serious harm by carrying out further specified offences
- the maximum penalty for the offence is life imprisonment
- the court considers that the seriousness of the offence, or the offence and one or more associated offences, justifies the imposition of imprisonment for life.

Imprisonment for public protection

This is also covered under ***s225 Criminal Justice Act 2003***, and is given to those offenders when:

- the offender is convicted of a serious sexual or violent offence which is punishable by imprisonment for life or a determinate period of ten years or more
- in the court's opinion, the offender poses a significant risk to the public of serious harm by committing further specified offences
- the offence is punishable with life imprisonment and the court is satisfied that the seriousness of the offence justifies such a sentence
- the offender has a previous conviction for an offence listed in ***Schedule 15A to the Criminal Justice Act 2003*** or the current offence warrants a notional minimum term of at least two years.

Mandatory life sentence

This compulsory sentence is given to those offenders who have been found guilty of murder. If they are considered for release by the Parole Board then they will be on a licence for the rest of their lives.

Whole life orders

These are extremely rare, and are given to the most serious offenders or persistent offenders. These prisoners can only be released on compassionate grounds with the permission of the Secretary of State. There are currently very few prisoners serving whole life orders in England and Wales.

Sentencing Council

The Sentencing Council was set up as part of the ***Coroners and Justice Act 2009***, and replaced the Sentencing Guidelines Council with the aim of encouraging transparency and consistency in sentencing.

When deciding what sentence to impose on an offender, several factors are taken into consideration, depending on whether the offender is an adult or a youth. These factors may be relevant in determining the **type of sentence** as well as its length. Each case is decided on the facts of the individual case.

GRADE BOOST

The Sentencing Council website (www.sentencingcouncil.org.uk) has all the information you need to know about how offenders are sentenced in England and Wales.

KEY TERMINOLOGY

aggravating factor: a factor relevant to an offence that has the effect of increasing the sentence. Examples include the defendant having previous convictions, or if a weapon was used in the offence.
mitigating factor: a factor relevant to the offence that has the effect of decreasing the sentence or reducing the charge. Examples include it being the defendant's first offence, or if the defendant pleaded guilty.

Youth offenders	Adult offenders
• The main aim of the system is to prevent reoffending. • The welfare of the child must be considered.	Sentence must reflect the five purposes of sentencing.
When deciding the appropriate sentence, the judge shall consider:	
• the offender's age and maturity • the seriousness of the offence • their family circumstances • any previous offending history • whether they admitted the offence.	• the seriousness of the offence • the offender's previous convictions • any **aggravating factors** • any **mitigating factors** • personal mitigation • whether the offender pleaded guilty • the maximum sentence available for the offence.
The judge will then look at any relevant **sentencing guidelines** relevant to the offence.	

STRETCH AND CHALLENGE

1. The government announced proposals to reduce sentences by 50 per cent for those who plead guilty. Research these proposals and discuss the implications on the prison population. Do you think this supports the sentencing theory of retribution?
2. Whole life orders are extremely controversial and have been challenged in the ECtHR by groups of defendants on the grounds that they breach ***Article 3 ECHR***. The defendants include Jeremy Bamber and Peter Moore and the full case is ***Vinter v UK (2013)***. Evaluate the outcomes of this or similar challenges.

Bail

An important pretrial matter is whether the defendant should stay in custody while awaiting trial or whether **bail** should be granted. A person can be released on bail at any point after being arrested by the police. Being given bail means a person is allowed to be at liberty until the next stage in the case, in line with ***Article 5 ECHR* (Right to liberty)**.

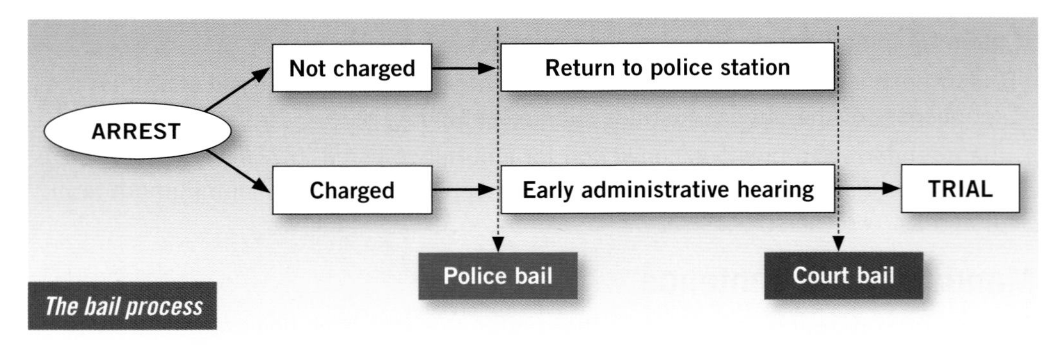

The bail process

Police bail

The police can grant bail in three circumstances:

1. When a person is released without charge on the condition that they return to the police station on a specific date. This is provided for in ***s37 Police and Criminal Evidence Act 1984***. Where a person has not been charged, the ***Policing and Crime Act 2017*** stipulates that they can be on bail for **no longer than 28 days**, starting the day after the day on which they were arrested. This is as a result of the phone hacking scandal involving the *News of the World*, where some journalists were kept on bail for up to two years. The 28 days can be extended to three months for serious fraud cases or if one of the conditions A–D in ***s47 Police and Criminal Evidence Act 1984*** are satisfied. The ***Policing and Crime Act 2017*** further stipulates that, where a person is released following their arrest, it will be without bail.
2. When a defendant has been charged with an offence until their early administrative hearing at the magistrates' court. This is provided for in ***s38 Police and Criminal Evidence Act 1984***.
3. Police can grant street bail for minor offences, without the need to take them to the police station. This is provided for by ***s4 Criminal Justice Act 2003***.

KEY TERMINOLOGY

bail: the defendant is allowed to be at liberty rather than prison before their court hearing, as long as they agree to particular conditions, such as regularly reporting to a police station.

The decision to grant bail is taken by the **custody officer**. The police can only refuse bail if:

- the suspect does not give a name and address; or
- if the name and address given is thought not to be genuine.

Therefore, bail is granted in the majority of cases and can be given to the suspect even if they have not been charged, on the agreement that they will return to the police station on a given date. This happened to Chris Jeffries, the first suspect to be arrested in the 2011 ***Joanna Yeates*** murder case.

If the police feel that they cannot grant bail, the case must be put before magistrates as soon as possible, so that they can make the decision in relation to bail.

Court bail

The court's powers to grant bail are governed by the ***Bail Act 1976***, where ***s4*** contains a presumption in favour of bail (and bearing in mind ***Article 5 ECHR***: Right to liberty), but other considerations may prevent a suspect from being granted bail. ***Schedule 1(9) Bail Act 1976*** outlines factors that need to be taken into consideration when deciding whether or not to grant bail:

- The nature and seriousness of the offence.
- The character, past record, associations and community ties of the defendant.
- The defendant's previous record of surrendering to bail.
- The strength of the evidence against them.

Bail need not be granted, if there are **substantial grounds** for believing that the suspect would:

- commit another offence while on bail
- fail to surrender to bail
- interfere with witnesses or otherwise obstruct the course of justice; or
- the suspect needs to be kept in custody for their own protection.

There is a further exception under the ***Legal Aid, Sentencing and Punishment of Offenders Act 2012***, when there are **substantial grounds** for believing that the defendant would, if released, commit an offence against an 'associated person' in a domestic violence case.

Conditional bail

The police **or** the courts can grant conditional bail under powers given to them by ***s3 Bail Act 1976*** and the ***Criminal Justice and Public Order Act 1994***. These conditions are imposed to minimise the risk of the defendant committing another offence while on bail or otherwise interfering with the investigation and, in some circumstances, for their own protection. Conditions that can be imposed include:

- curfew
- electronic tagging
- surrendering their passport
- reporting to police station at regular intervals
- residing at a **bail hostel**
- getting someone to stand **surety** for them.

The conditions that can be imposed are under the wide discretion of the police and courts, and there is no limit or restrictions on the conditions that can be imposed. Here are two high-profile examples.

- ***Dave Lee Travis (2014)*** was charged with 11 counts of indecent assault and one count of sexual assault. His conditional bail stated that he had to live at home in Bedfordshire and should not contact his alleged victims.

STRETCH AND CHALLENGE

Look at the following cases. Do you agree with the decision that was made in relation to bail?

- ***Julian Assange (2011)***
- ***Gary Weddell (2008)***
- ***Michael Donovan (2008)***

KEY TERMINOLOGY

bail hostel: a place of residence for people on bail who cannot give a fixed address, run by the Probation Service.

surety: a sum of money offered to the court by a person known to the suspect which guarantees the suspect's attendance at court when required.

STRETCH AND CHALLENGE

Research and conduct an evaluation into the effectiveness of conditions being attached to bail, particularly in light of the case of ***Weddell (2008)***.

GRADE BOOST

You should demonstrate and awareness of both court bail and police bail. It is a common mistake in examinations for candidates to omit police bail and just concentrate on court bail.

- ***Ryan Cleary (2012)*** was charged with attempting to hack the website of the Serious Organised Crime Agency. His conditional bail was extensive and stated that he should observe a curfew between 9pm and 7am every night, wear an electronic tag and only leave the house in the company of his parents. He also had to live and sleep at his home address and have no access to the Internet or possess any devices capable of Internet access.

Restrictions on bail

There have been many amendments over the years to the ***Bail Act 1976***, because of concern that bail was being given too freely, and those who were granted bail often committed further offences. The table shows the main amendments.

Amendment	Effect
s25 Criminal Justice and Public Order Act 1994	The courts were barred from granting bail in cases of murder, manslaughter and rape where the defendant had already served a custodial sentence for such an offence. However, this was held to be a breach of ***Article 5 ECHR*** in the case of ***Caballero v UK (2000)***.
s56 Crime and Disorder Act 1998	A defendant can only be granted bail in serious cases if the court is satisfied that there are exceptional circumstances.
s24 Anti-Terrorism, Crime and Security Act 2001	All bail applications from suspected international terrorists should be made to the Special Immigration Appeals Commission.
s14 Criminal Justice Act 2003	If defendant was on bail for another offence at the date of the offence, bail should be refused unless the court is satisfied that there is no significant risk that they will commit another offence.
s18 Criminal Justice Act 2003	The prosecution can appeal against the granting of bail for any imprisonable offence.
s19 Criminal Justice Act 2003	Bail will not be granted for an imprisonable offence where the defendant has tested positive for a Class A drug and where the offence is connected with Class A drugs.

Section 90 Legal Aid, Sentencing and Punishment of Offenders Act 2012 introduced the 'no real prospect test', where the court's power to refuse bail is restricted if it appears that there is no real prospect that the defendant would receive a custodial sentence if convicted.

There should be a balance in terms of upholding the defendant's human rights and protecting the public. This is especially important because at this point the suspect is still innocent until proven guilty, so should not be treated as a convicted criminal.

GRADE BOOST

Wherever possible, you need to show knowledge of the amendments to the ***Bail Act 1976*** as these are part of the factors that are taken into consideration when deciding a bail application.

STRETCH AND CHALLENGE

Discuss the way in which the courts seek to balance safeguarding a suspect's human rights with protecting the public from a potentially dangerous criminal.

Advantages and disadvantages of bail

Advantages

✓ There is a reduction in the number of defendants on remand, which means less cost to the government.

✓ The Home Office suggests that up to 20 per cent of people in prison are awaiting trial and may go on to be found innocent, or given non-custodial sentences.

✓ The defendant can maintain employment and spend time with their family during their bail period.

✓ The defendant is not restricted in the time available to prepare for trial by meeting with their legal representatives.

Disadvantages

✗ There is a risk that the defendant will interfere with witnesses or otherwise obstruct the course of justice. In the case of ***Shannon Matthews (2008)***, had the suspects been granted bail, they might have further concealed evidence and impeded the investigation.

✗ There seems to be disparity in the interpretation of the ***Bail Act 1976*** in different courts

✗ Home Office statistics state that 12 per cent of bailed suspects fail to appear at their trial, so there is a risk of them absconding or not surrendering to bail.

✗ It is thought **a third of burglaries** are committed by people who are on bail for another offence.

The Crown Prosecution Service

When a suspect is arrested, they will not automatically be prosecuted. The decision to prosecute rather than caution or drop the case lies with an independent body known as the **Crown Prosecution Service (CPS)**. Before the CPS was established in 1986, the decision to prosecute was taken by the police.

Establishment of the CPS

- **1970 Justice Report** identified problems with the police making the decision to prosecute. These were prosecution bias, potential infringement of right to a fair trial after miscarriages of justice involving police tampering with evidence, and conflict of interest, as the same body investigating and prosecuting was seen as inappropriate.
- **1978 Phillips Royal Commission** recommended the establishment of an independent agency to take charge of prosecuting suspects.
- **1985** ***Prosecution of Offences Act*** established the CPS.

Structure and aims of the CPS

The CPS is headed by the **Director of Public Prosecutions** (DPP), currently **Alison Saunders**, who is answerable to the Attorney General. The CPS generally takes control of a case as soon as the police have finished collecting evidence and conducting the investigation. It has five main roles, to:

- **advise** police on the charge that should be brought against the suspect, using the CPS Charging Standards (see page 169)
- **review** cases
- **prepare** cases for court
- **present** cases in court, as CPS lawyers have rights of audience
- **decide** whether to bring a prosecution against the suspect. (This is the CPS's main role.)

Structure of the CPS

The CPS is divided into 14 areas of England and Wales. Each area is headed by a Chief Crown Prosecutor. Each of the 14 areas is further split into branches, which usually correspond to the police forces, and each branch is headed by a Branch Crown Prosecutor. An additional 'area' is CPS Direct, which provides an out-of-hours service to the police on charging advice.

CPS Inspectorate

The CPS Inspectorate was set up under the ***Crown Prosecution Service Inspectorate Act 2000*** and is an independent body answerable to the Attorney General. Its role is to enhance the quality of justice through independent inspection and assessment of prosecution services, and, in doing so, to improve effectiveness and efficiency after a recommendation by Sir Iain Glidewell in his 1999 report. Its website is www.hmcpsi.gov.uk.

The CPS uses two key documents to outline its role, how it makes decisions and what service the public can expect.

Code for Crown prosecutors

This is the code of practice that Crown prosecutors use to determine whether to charge a suspect with an offence. The code is contained in ***s10 Prosecution of Offences Act 1985***.

The full code test is based on two aspects relating to whether the suspect will be charged:

1. **Evidential test**: Is there a realistic prospect of conviction?
2. **Public interest test**: Is it in the public interest to prosecute?

The areas of the CPS. London is split into North and South. (Source: Crown copyright)

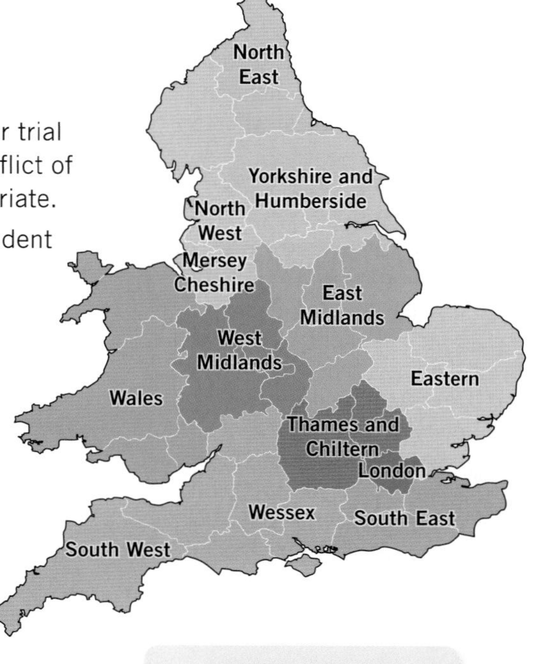

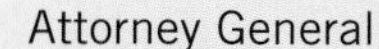

DPP

Chief Crown prosecutors e.g. Wales

Branch Crown prosecutors e.g. South Wales, Dyfed Powys, North Wales, Gwent

Lawyers and support staff

Structure of the CPS

GRADE BOOST

This background to the history and role of the CPS provides a useful introduction to an essay about the CPS.

A case has to pass the evidential test before it moves onto the public interest test; if it fails the evidential test, the case will proceed no further.

1. Evidential test

In order to pass the evidential test, the CPS must be satisfied that there is a realistic prospect of conviction: a judge or jury is more likely than not to find the suspect guilty. It is an objective test and having a lot of evidence is not enough; the evidence has to be sufficient, reliable and **admissible**.

Unreliable evidence	Reliable evidence
Blurred CCTV	DNA
Confession obtained by oppression	Eyewitness from the scene of a crime
Hearsay	Voluntary confession
Eyewitness testimony of a child	

An example is in the ***Damilola Taylor Case (2002)***, when unreliable witnesses and inadmissible evidence made the case the centre of an investigation.

If the evidential test is not passed then the case must be discontinued under ***s23 Prosecution of Offences Act 1985***. If the evidential test is passed, the case passes onto the next stage, which is the public interest test.

2. Public interest test

Prosecutors used to consider a series of factors to determine whether a suspect should be charged, but this has changed to a series of questions after a report by the former Director of Public Prosecutions (DPP), Kier Starmer ('The Public Prosecution Service – Setting the Standard', 2009). The questions are:

a. How serious is the offence committed?

b. What is the level of culpability of the suspect?

c. What are the circumstances of the crime and the harm caused to the victim?

d. Was the suspect under the age of 18 at the time of the offence?

e. What is the impact on the community?

f. Is prosecution a proportionate response?

g. Do sources of information require protecting?

These last three questions take into account the findings of the 2009 report, which emphasises a holistic approach to looking at the offence and the circumstances surrounding it. Crucially, this includes taking into account the feelings of the victims, witnesses and other affected parties.

When considering the public interest test, the prosecutor may also consider whether an **out-of-court disposal** would be more appropriate (see Sentencing of adult offenders, page 70).

The threshold test

Sometimes, the CPS decides that the full code test has failed, and there is not enough evidence to charge the suspect, but the suspect is still believed to be too much of a risk to be released. In these cases, the CPS will apply the **threshold test** relating to whether the suspect will be charged:

- Is there a reasonable suspicion that the person arrested has committed the offence in question?
- Can further evidence be gathered to provide a realistic prospect of conviction?

GRADE BOOST

When you are talking about the evidential test, give examples of reliable and unreliable evidence. When talking about the public interest test, give at least three factors for and three factors against prosecution. You should also mention the threshold test whenever you can.

KEY TERMINOLOGY

admissible: useful evidence which cannot be excluded on the basis that it is immaterial, irrelevant or violating the rules of evidence.
hearsay: second-hand evidence which is not what the witness knows personally but is something they have been told.

STRETCH AND CHALLENGE

The DPP published guidelines on shaken baby cases in February 2011 because of the difference in opinion among medical experts. Do you think it is always in the public interest to prosecute such cases because of the debate?

Casework Quality Standards

This is a document published by the CPS in October 2014, which outlines the standards that the public can expect from the CPS and are important in holding the CPS to account if it fails to provide the service outlined by the standards.
Each standard contains benchmarks of quality that the CPS must achieve:

- **Standard 1:** Victims, witnesses and communities.
- **Standard 2:** Legal decision making.
- **Standard 3:** Casework preparation.
- **Standard 4:** Presentation.

The complete document, including the benchmarks of quality, can be found at www.cps.gov.uk/publications/docs/cqs_oct_2014.pdf

Reforms of the Crown Prosecution Service

The CPS has been the subject of much criticism and reform since its establishment and it has often been accused of not achieving what it set out to do.

Narey Review (1998)

Criticism	Reform
Lack of preparation and a considerable delay in bringing the cases to court.	Caseworkers were employed and trained to review files and present straightforward guilty pleas in court, which freed up CPS lawyers to deal with more complex cases.

Glidewell Report (1999)

<table>
<tr><th>Criticism</th><th>Reform</th></tr>
<tr><td>12% of cases were being discontinued by the CPS where the police had charged.</td><td rowspan="2">The 13 areas were divided into 42 areas, to correspond with the police forces, each with a Chief Crown Prosecutor and each with the responsibility to decide to prosecute.</td></tr>
<tr><td>Charges were downgraded in an alarming number of cases.</td></tr>
<tr><td>Tense working relationships between the police and the CPS, with a hostile 'blame culture', led to inefficiency and poor preparation.</td><td rowspan="2">The CPS is now based in police stations, and 'joined up working' is encouraged, with an emphasis on the police and CPS to collaborate on shared issues. This also helps cut the delay in bringing cases to court. The introduction of Criminal Justice Units has attempted to make the working relationships more amicable.</td></tr>
<tr><td>Long delays were reported between arrest and sentence, along with a distinct lack of preparation.</td></tr>
<tr><td>Many witnesses were unreliable in court, and sometimes did not turn up at all.</td><td>A revised code for Crown prosecutors was published with detailed guidance on the application of the evidential test.</td></tr>
</table>

Macpherson Report (1999)

This was the report written after the murder of Stephen Lawrence, when the police were investigated for potential racism.

Criticism	Reform
The police were institutionally racist, and there were serious criticisms of the investigation because the victim was black.	Every police force is now under a legal obligation to publish a racial equality policy to protect victims and defendants. Regular inspections are carried out to ensure that these rules are being followed.

STRETCH AND CHALLENGE

1. www.independent.co.uk/news/uk/home-news/police-crown-prosecution-service-disclosure-lawyers-trial-a7846021.html is a 2017 article about some failings of the CPS. Do you think these findings are reflective of an improved service, or are we still seeing the problems identified by Glidewell?
2. It is not only the CPS that can charge a suspect; individuals are able to bring a private prosecution. Research the limitations on private prosecutions, paying particular attention to the case of ***Whitehouse v Lemon (1976)***.

STRETCH AND CHALLENGE

3. Look at the case involving ***Lord Janner (2015)*** where DPP, Alison Saunders, was under pressure to step down because she deemed Lord Janner, a House of Lords peer, unfit to stand trial for child sex offences because he had dementia. Even though there was enough evidence to proceed with charges, Ms Saunders decided it was not in the public interest to prosecute. Could this decision be damaging to the reputation of the CPS?
4. It is often reported that celebrities who have been accused of sex offences are usually acquitted (for example, William Roache and Michael Le Vell). Is this a misapplication of the full code test? Could these acquittals also be attributed to pressure from the media and the government?

Auld Review (2001)

This review recommended the introduction of **statutory charging**. This scheme has been running since 2006, giving the CPS the responsibility of determining the charge for a suspect in all but the most minor routine cases, for which the police still retain the charging responsibility. This ensures the correct charge is brought and that only those that are strong enough to stand trial get to court. This will reduce the number of cases that are discontinued, in line with the recommendations from Glidewell. This was later implemented in the ***Criminal Justice Act 2003***.

Abu Hamza (2006)

This case involved a Muslim cleric who was jailed for inciting murder and racial hatred. The police complained on several occasions that they had put evidence before the CPS but the CPS had continually refused to prosecute. This suggests that working relationships between the police and the CPS were still hostile.

'The Public Prosecution Service – Setting the Standard' (2009)

This is a report published by the former DPP, Keir Starmer, on his vision for the CPS. He envisaged an enhanced role for public prosecutors in engaging with their communities to inform their work and address their concerns. Broadly speaking, he set out three main aims, to:

- protect the public
- support victims and witnesses
- deliver justice.

He saw the CPS being able to achieve these aims by:

- addressing offending and using out-of-court disposals where appropriate
- deciding the charge in all but the most routine cases
- taking the views of the victims into account
- taking decisions independently of any improper influence
- recovering assets from criminals
- ensuring that witnesses can give their best evidence
- presenting their own cases in court
- helping the court to pass an appropriate sentence.

Exam Skills

If you are asked to **evaluate** or **consider the effectiveness of** the CPS, make sure that you include as much as you can from the various reports and remember to develop a balanced argument.

Summary: Criminal process

- **Sentencing powers**
  - Magistrates' court: Unlimited fine; Maximum six months' imprisonment.
  - Crown Court: Unlimited fine; Maximum life imprisonment
- **Aims of sentencing** (***s142 Criminal Justice Act 2003***):
  - Retribution
  - Deterrence (individual and general)
  - Protection of society
  - Rehabilitation
  - Reparation
- **Young offenders** are aged 10–17 and tried in the youth court
- **Youth sentencing:** Primary aim is to prevent reoffending and rehabilitate the offender.

- **Out-of-court** youth sentencing:
  - Youth restorative disposal
  - Youth caution
  - Youth conditional caution
- **Youth rehabilitation order**: A community sentence with requirements, e.g. activity, unpaid work or drug testing requirements.
- **First tier youth sentencing:**
  - Referral order
  - Reparation order
  - Parenting order
  - Conditional discharge
  - Absolute discharge
- **Youth custody**: Detention and training order; life imprisonment
- **Adult sentencing**: Primary aim is punishment and protection of society
- **Out-of-court** disposals
  - Penalty notice for disorder
  - Conditional cautions
  - Cautions
- **Court disposals**
  - Absolute discharge
  - Conditional discharge
  - Fine
  - Suspended sentence order
  - Community order
- **Custodial sentences**
  - Determinate sentences
  - Indeterminate sentences
  - Mandatory life sentences
  - Whole life orders
- **Bail**: Following arrest, either:
  - **Charged**: ***s38 Police and Criminal Evidence Act 1984***: Police bail then early administrative hearing at magistrates' court; court bail then trial
  - **Not charged** (maximum 28 days): ***s37 Police and Criminal Evidence Act 1984***: Police bail; return to police station
- Bail need not be granted if there are substantial grounds for believing that the suspect would:
  - Commit another offence whilst on bail
  - Fail to surrender to bail
  - Interfere with witnesses or otherwise obstruct the course of justice
  - Be required to stay in custody for own protection
- ***s90 Legal Aid, Sentencing and Punishment of Offenders Act 2012***: 'No real prospect test'
- Factors taken into consideration for bail: ***Schedule 1(9) Bail Act 1976***:
  - Nature and seriousness of the offence
  - Defendant's character, past record, associations and community ties of the defendant
  - Defendant's previous record of surrendering to bail
  - Strength of the evidence against defendant
- **Conditional bail**: Granted under the ***Criminal Justice and Public Order Act 1994***
- **Restrictions on bail**: Mainly contained in the ***Criminal Justice Act 2003*** to balance protecting the public and upholding the defendant's rights

Juries

Spec reference	Key content	Assessment Objectives	Where does this topic feature on each specification/exam?
WJEC AS/A Level **1.6:** Criminal process **Eduqas AS Level** **1.2.2:** Criminal process **Eduqas A Level** **1.2.2:** Criminal process	• The role of lay people: role of magistrates, jury trial including jury selection, the jury and questions of fact, majority verdicts, jury secrecy and the use of juries in the Coroner's Courts, criticisms and alternatives to the jury system	**AO1** Demonstrate knowledge and understanding of legal rules and principles **AO3** Analyse and evaluate legal rules, principles and issues	**WJEC AS/A Level:** Unit 1 Section B **Eduqas AS Level:** Component 1 Section B **Eduqas A Level:** Component 1 Section B

The history of jury trials

Trial by jury is an ancient and democratic institution within the legal system, dating back to the **Magna Carta**. It is based on the principle of 'trial by one's peers' and provides an opportunity for the lay person to participate in the administration of justice. This means that 12 members of the public, selected at random, can see for themselves that justice is being done. The jury also acts as a restraining influence on judges as it takes the decision of guilt or innocence out of the judge's hands.

A major milestone in the history of the jury was the case of **Bushell (1670)**. Before this, judges would try to bully juries into convicting the defendant but, in this case, it was established that the jury were the judges of fact, with a right to return a verdict based on their conscience. The judge can thus never direct a jury to return a guilty verdict and this point was more recently upheld in the House of Lords in the case of ***R v Wang (2005)***.

The importance of this power is that juries may acquit a defendant, even when the evidence demands a guilty verdict. This situation arose in ***R v Ponting (1985)*** and in the ***GM Crops case*** in 2000. In both cases, the jury sympathised with the defendants, believing them to have acted fairly and thereby acquitting them. This power, also known as **jury equity**, is quite controversial.

Significant milestones in the history of jury trials

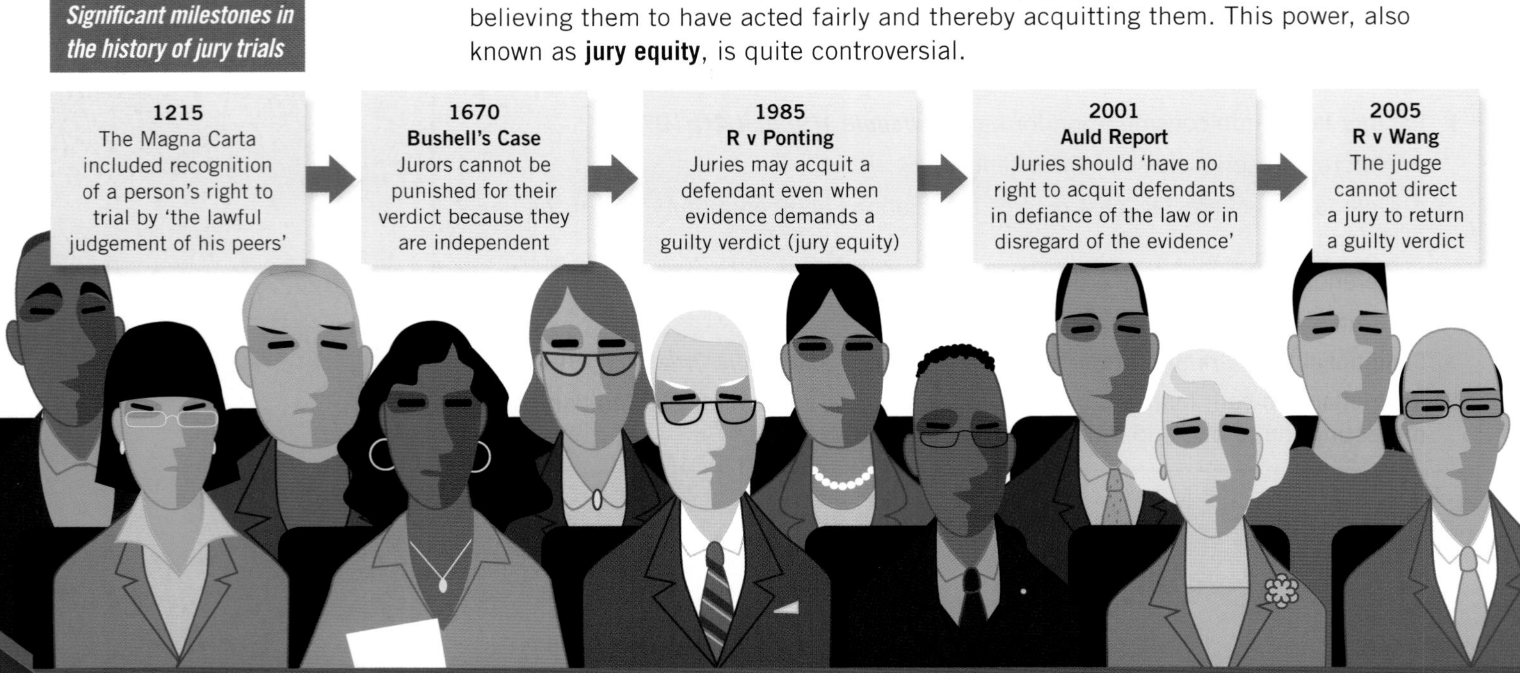

Role of the jury

Criminal cases

The jury sits in the Crown Court and listens to the evidence presented by both prosecution and defence counsel. Jury members also examine exhibits such as photographs of the crime scene and alleged weapons. They have to weigh up all the facts and decide for themselves what actually happened. They observe how each witness performs during examination and cross-examination in an effort to judge the credibility of that person.

They listen to the judge who will sum up the evidence for them and direct them on relevant points of law. They must then retire to consider their verdict. They must aim to reach a unanimous verdict but if, after a reasonable time (not less than two hours), they cannot agree, the judge can inform them that they can reach a majority verdict of 11–1 or 10–2 under the ***Juries Act 1974***. Anything less than 10–2 is known as a hung jury.

Jury members thus have a dual function in the administration of justice:

1. They consider the facts and return a verdict.
2. They represent society and symbolise democracy.

Legal authority

Juries Act 1974.

Types of cases

Criminal juries usually sit on **indictable** cases in the Crown Court. This includes cases such as murder, manslaughter and rape.

Civil cases

The jury sits in the county court or High Court and members have a dual role:

1. They decide the liability of the defendant.
2. They decide the amount of damages if they find in favour of the claimant.

Legal authority

High Court: *s69 Supreme Court Act 1981*.
County court: *s66 County Courts Act 1984*.

Types of cases

- Fraud.
- False imprisonment.
- Malicious prosecution.
- Defamation (the right to a trial by jury in defamation cases was removed by the ***Defamation Act 2013***, and use of a jury in these cases is now subject to the courts' discretion).

Coroners' court

The jury sits in the coroner's court to decide a cause of death where a death has occurred in suspicious circumstances.

Types of cases

- Deaths in police custody.
- Deaths in prison.
- Deaths caused by an industrial accident.
- Deaths where the health and safety of the public is involved.

Examples of cases

The inquests into the Hillsborough disaster and the death of Princess Diana.

STRETCH AND CHALLENGE

R v Cilliers (2017) concerned a woman who was on trial for attempting to murder her husband by tampering with his parachute. The jury in the case were discharged for failing to reach a verdict and there were also allegations of bullying among the jury.
Research this case and make a note of the problems with jury trials highlighted by this case.

Juries are required at a coroner's court when deaths have occurred in susicious or unusual circumstances

STRETCH AND CHALLENGE

Research the jury selection for the Hillsborough Inquest, when the judge outlined specific requirements for the jury. This link may help: www.bbc.co.uk/news/uk-england-merseyside-26783600. What were these criteria? Think about the impact this would have had on the random and representative nature of the jury.

Juries Act 1974
Aged 18–70

Auld Report 2001
- Jury service too easily avoided
- Pool of jurors needs to be widened to increase representation

Criminal Justice Act 2003
Aged 18–70
Deferrals only

- Serious criminal convictions
- Currently on bail
- Mental disorder

Criminal Justice and Courts Act 2015
Aged 18–75
Four new offences

Jury eligibility

The **Juries Act 1974** as amended by the **Criminal Justice Act 2003** and the **Criminal Justice and Courts Act 2015** provides that potential jurors must be:

- aged 18–75
- on the electoral register
- a UK resident for at least five years since their 13th birthday.

Many categories of person used to be considered ineligible or excused from jury service. However, following the **Auld Review** of the criminal justice system (see page 78) and the subsequent ***Criminal Justice Act 2003***, the ***Juries Act 1974*** has been amended. This is because the Auld Report advised that jury service was too easily avoided and that the jury should be far more representative. The general principle behind the ***Criminal Justice Act 2003*** is to ensure that every eligible person between 18 and 70 (now 75) should perform this public duty if called upon. the revised rules mean that anyone can now serve on a jury, including judges, police officers and members of the legal profession. However, a member of the armed forces may be excused from jury service if their commanding officer provides a statement that certifies that their absence from service would be prejudicial to the efficiency of the service. The only other persons who are disqualified from jury service are those:

- currently on bail
- with a diagnosed mental illness
- who have serious criminal convictions (and served more than five years in prison)
- who have been convicted of an offence under the ***Criminal Justice and Courts Act 2015***.

The **Jury Central Summoning Bureau** is responsible for ensuring that members of the public serve as required. It deals with requests for being excused but can only allow individuals to defer their service rather than fully excusing them from it. It is not possible to be fully excused because the Auld Report found that the same categories of people kept being excused, resulting in an unrepresentative jury pool.

Computers produce a random list of potential jurors from the electoral register. It is necessary to summon more than 12 jurors for a particular trial, and bigger courts tend to summon up to 150 people every fortnight.

Jurors receive a set of notes briefly explaining the procedure and the functions of the juror. The normal length of jury service is two weeks although it can be longer for complex cases. Jury service is compulsory and failure to attend or to be unfit because of alcohol or drugs is a criminal offence; this is known as **contempt of court**.

Recent cases have shown how controversial these reforms are.

R v Abdroikov (2007)
In two cases, serving police constables were on the jury and, in the third, a CPS solicitor. The House of Lords held that this could give an appearance of bias, contrary to the right to fair trial where police evidence is being challenged. It allowed two appeals and the convictions were quashed.

Hanif and Khan v UK (2011)
The ECtHR held that the presence of police officers on the jury could breach ***Article 6 ECHR*** *(Right to a fair trial). In this case, the police officer knew a police witness in a professional capacity.*

Contempt of court

The courts take participation in jury service very seriously, and failure to attend if a juror is called is a criminal offence known as **contempt of court**.

R v Banks (2011)

Matthew Banks was jailed for 14 days for contempt of court after missing jury service to see a musical in London. He was in the middle of a trial and the case had to be postponed for a day as a result.

R v Fraill (2011)

Joanna Fraill was jailed for eight months for contempt of court after sitting on a jury and contacting the defendant on Facebook to discuss the case.

AG v Davey and Beard (2013)

Two jurors were each jailed for two months for contempt of court.

Mr Davey posted a strongly-worded message on Facebook during the trial of a man for sex offences, suggesting he was going to find the defendant guilty. His defence was that he was just expressing shock at the type of case he was on.

Mr Beard was on a fraud trial. He researched the case on Google and gave his fellow jurors extra information about the number of victims of the alleged fraud.

The ***Criminal Justice and Courts Act 2015*** created four new offences in relation to jury deliberations and researching a case. Conviction of any of these offences can result in up to **two years** in prison.

- ***s71 (s20A Juries Act 1976 as amended)*** created an offence of 'researching' a case during the trial period. 'Researching' means intentionally seeking information that the juror knows will be relevant to the case. Means of research include asking a question, searching the Internet, visiting or inspecting a place or object, conducting an experiment or asking another person to seek information.
- ***s72 (s20B Juries Act 1976 as amended)*** created an offence for a juror to intentionally disclose information obtained under **s71** to another member of the jury.
- ***s73 (s20C Juries Act 1976 as amended)*** created an offence for a juror to engage in 'prohibited conduct', which is defined as trying the case otherwise than on the basis of the evidence presented in the proceedings.
- ***s74 (s20D Juries Act 1976 as amended)*** created an offence for a juror to intentionally disclose information about statements made, opinions expressed, arguments advanced or votes cast by members of the jury during their deliberations. The exception is for the purposes of an investigation by the court into whether an offence or contempt of court has been committed by a juror in the proceedings.

R v Smith and Deane (2016)

This case was brought under the Criminal Justice and Courts Act 2015 for what the judge deemed a 'serious' contempt of court.

Mr Smith carried out Internet research on a case he was trying. He was given a nine-month term suspended for 12 months.

Ms Deane disclosed contents of jury deliberations after her jury service. She was jailed for three months, suspended for 12 months.

R v Dallas (2012)

University lecturer Theodora Dallas was jailed for six months for researching the criminal defendant while serving on a jury. She said she had been checking the meaning of 'grievous bodily harm' on the Internet then added the word 'Luton' to a search which produced a newspaper report which mentioned that the defendant had previously faced an allegation of rape. It showed he had been acquitted of the charge but it included information not disclosed during his trial.

KEY TERMINOLOGY

contempt of court: a criminal offence punishable by up to two years' imprisonment for anyone who is disobedient or discourteous to a court of law.

Jury challenging

As members of the jury are called, and before they are sworn in, they can be challenged in several ways.

Challenge for the cause

Challenge by either defence or prosecution.

This is a request that a juror be dismissed because there is a reason to believe that they cannot be fair, unbiased or capable. This may include bias on the grounds of race, religion, political beliefs or occupation. Examples include:

- knowing someone in the case
- prior experience in a similar case
- an obvious prejudice
- ineligibility or disqualification.

R v Gough (1993)

This case held that, where a juror is challenged on the grounds of bias, the test is whether there is a 'real danger' that they are biased.

Challenge to the array

Challenge by either prosecution or defence.

This is where the whole jury panel is challenged on the grounds that the summoning officer is biased or acted improperly.

Romford Jury (1993)

Out of a panel of 12 jurors, nine came from Romford, with two of them living within 20 doors of each other in the same street.

R v Fraser (1987)

Although the defendant was from a minority ethnic background, all the jurors were white (also note the case of R v Ford (1989) below)

Stand by the Crown

Challenge by prosecution or judge.

This is rarely invoked and only in cases of national security or terrorism, and where vetting has been authorised. Where it is used, the permission of the Attorney General is needed.

Racial challenges

Despite the recent reforms to make the jury more representative and to remove the middle-class 'opt out', the jury is still not racially representative. The issue of racism in the criminal justice system has been of public concern mainly due to the murder in 1993 of the black teenager Stephen Lawrence.

Groups such as the Commission for Racial Equality have argued that where, race is an issue in a trial, the jury should contain at least three ethnic minority individuals. This had been proposed by the Runciman Royal Commission in 1993 but was rejected by the government at that time.

The same proposal was included more recently in the Auld Report (see page 78) but was again rejected by the government, on the grounds that it would undermine the random principle.

R v Ford (1989)

It was held that there is no power for a judge to order a multiracial jury.

Sander v UK (2000)

This case went before the ECtHR, and it was held that the judge should have discharged the jury and ordered a retrial when a note was sent to the judge alleging racism within the jury room.

STRETCH AND CHALLENGE

The Lammy Review (see page 69) found that juries were not generally biased in their verdicts and that they were consistent in their decision making, regardless of the ethnicity of the defendant. Judges, however, according to the review, are a different story. Read more at www.theguardian.com/public-leaders-network/2017/sep/15/racial-bias-criminal-justice-system-lammy-review-magistrates-courts-jury. What could be the implications of these findings?

R v Smith (2003)
*The defendant argued that **s1 Juries Act 1974** contravened his right to a fair trial under the **Human Rights Act 1998**. This argument was rejected by the court which held that 'personal impartiality must be presumed'.*

Jury tampering

Sometimes, friends of the defendant might try to interfere with the jury. This might be bribing jury members to bring in a not guilty verdict or making threats against jury members so that they are too afraid to find the defendant guilty. In such cases, the police may be used to try to protect the jurors but this may not be effective. It is also expensive and removes the police from their other work.

To combat this, ***s44 Criminal Justice Act 2003*** provides that, where there has already been an effort to tamper with a jury in the case, the prosecution can apply for the case to be heard by the judge alone.

R v Twomey and others (2009)
This is the first and only case where trial without a jury was approved. The defendants were charged with various offences connected to a large robbery from a warehouse at Heathrow. Three previous trials had collapsed and there had been 'a serious attempt at jury tampering' in the last of them. The prosecution applied to a single judge for the trial to take place without a jury. The judge refused but the Court of Appeal overturned this decision, ordering that the trial should take place without a jury.

Alternatives to the jury

- A single judge sitting alone would save time through not having to explain everything to a jury. This would also reduce the number of verdicts which are in defiance of the law because the judge would feel it their duty to uphold the law even if it is harsh.
- A bench of judges consisting of three or five on a panel would give a more balanced view but would be far more expensive and again would lose the element of public participation.
- A specially trained jury selected from non-lawyers would ensure that the panel was capable of fulfilling its functions. However, if they were full time, they might reflect the magistracy too closely and be only older, middle-class people.
- A mixed panel consisting of a judge and two lay members is used in Scandinavian countries. This speeds up the trial process as the judge is involved in all discussions. Community participation is retained but it could be argued that the judge might have too much influence on the lay members, who might be intimidated or defer to the experienced judge.

Jury trials remain a standard procedure, but there are many alternatives that could be used

Evaluation of the jury concept

Advantages

✓ Juries allow ordinary people to participate in the justice system and so verdicts are seen to be those of society rather than the judicial system. The verdict is more likely to be acceptable because the panel should include members of the defendant's own class and race. There is an impression that justice has not only been done but is seen to be done as seen in the Magna Carta (the right to be tried by one's peers).

✓ Juries may be less prosecution-minded than judges or magistrates, considering the mix of social backgrounds.

✓ Juries offer protection against harsh or unjust laws since they will often come to a verdict which is fair rather than legally correct.

R v Owen (1992)

The defendant's son had been killed by a lorry driver who had a long criminal record for drink driving and violence. The driver showed no remorse for killing the boy. He was convicted of a driving offence, sentenced to 15 months imprisonment and released after a year. He then resumed driving his lorry unlawfully. After contacting the authorities about getting proper justice for his son, and getting nowhere, the defendant took a shotgun and injured the lorry driver. He was charged with attempted murder but, despite the evidence against him, the jury found him not guilty.

✓ The jury is not 'case hardened' in the way that some judges might be. Jurors have not become jaded and cynical about defence arguments because, for most of them, this is the first time they have served.

✓ It is argued that 12 opinions of the jury are safer than one single judge. Also, due to ***s8 Contempt of Court Act 1981*** and the new offences introduced by the ***Criminal Justice and Courts Act 2015***, discussions within the jury room are secret and thus the jury is protected from outside influence and pressure.

✓ Juries are fully capable of making common-sense decisions based on fact, which does not require specialist legal training. They should also be impartial since they are not connected to anyone in the case. This is known as jury equity and was demonstrated in the ***Ponting Case (1985)*** where the jury refused to convict even though the judge ruled there was no defence.

✓ It is an ancient institution and our whole trial system is founded upon it. Professor Blackstone said 'it is the bulwark of our liberties' and Lord Devlin described it as 'the lamp that shows freedom lives'.

Disadvantages

✗ McCabe and Purves, in 'The Shadow Jury at Work', reported that a jury can be dominated by two or three strong-minded individuals, or be persuaded by a forceful foreperson when locked in the jury room.

✗ Compulsory jury service can cause resentment or strain which might lead to some jurors being keen to get away as soon as possible and will thus go along with the majority to bring the trial to an end.

✗ Jurors might also be too easily convinced by the manner and presentation of barristers, the courtroom becoming more of a theatre with the jury easily manipulated and distracted. Appearances and prejudicial views can also be a deciding factor.

R v Alexander and Steen (2004)
This is known as the 'amorous juror' case; the defendants appealed because a female juror had bombarded the prosecution barrister with romantic proposals.

R v Pryce (2013)
The trial collapsed in the case of Vicky Pryce, the ex-wife of MP Chris Huhne, when the judge realised that the jury was struggling to understand the basics when they asked ten questions which revealed 'fundamental deficits' in understanding.

✗ Jurors may not understand the case presented to them and are often unable to weigh evidence correctly and appreciate the significance of certain matters

✗ Media influence can also be seen as a disadvantage on the grounds of ***Article 6 ECHR***.

R v Taylor and Taylor (1993)
Two sisters were charged with murder. Some newspapers published a still video sequence which gave a false impression of what was happening. After conviction, leave of appeal was granted because of the possible influence this picture could have on the jury's verdict.

✗ Juries are very difficult to research because the ***Contempt of Court Act 1981*** and the ***Criminal Justice and Courts Act 2015*** prevent jurors from discussing the case or their reasoning. This was discussed in ***R v Mirza (2004)*** and ***R v Connor and Rollock (2002)***, where it was held that ***s8*** is compatible with ***Article 6 ECHR*** (Right to a fair trial). An exception to this was in ***R v Karakaya (2005)*** where it was discovered that a juror had conducted Internet searches at home and brought the notes into the jury room. See also more recent cases such as ***Dallas (2012)*** and ***Deane (2016)***.

Summary: Role of the jury

- **Criminal**
  - **Role:** To decide verdict of guilty or not guilty in Crown Court
  - **Types of cases:** Indictable offences where the defendant pleads not guilty and some either way offences where defendant has elected for a Crown Court trial.
  - Aims to reach a unanimous verdict (12–0) or a majority if the judge agrees (10–2, 11–1)
  - Governed by the ***Juries Act 1974*** amended by the ***Criminal Justice Act 2003***
- **Civil**
  - **Dual role**: To decide liability of defendant and to decide amount of damages
  - **Types of cases**: Fraud, false imprisonment and malicious prosecution
  - Governed by ***s67 Supreme Courts Act 1981*** and ***s66 County Courts Act 1984***
- **Coroner's court**
  - **Role**: To decide cause of death in suspicious circumstances
  - **Types of cases**: Death in prison, death in police custody, death through an industrial accident or a death where the health and safety of the public is at risk
  - **Examples:** Hillsborough Inquest, Princess Diana death
- Potential jurors **must** be:
  - aged 18–75
  - on the electoral register
  - a UK resident for at least five years since their 13th birthday

- Potential jurors **cannot** be:
  - currently on bail
  - diagnosed with a mental illness
  - convicted of a serious criminal offence (and served more than five years in prison
  - convicted of an offence under the Criminal Justice and Courts Act 2015
  - a member of the armed forces if their commanding officer has provided a statement to certify that their absence from service would be prejudicial to the efficiency of the service.
- **Jury challenging:**
  - **For cause**: A request that a juror be dismissed because there is a reason to believe that they cannot be fair, unbiased or capable: ***R v Gough (1993)***
  - **To the array**: A request that the whole jury is challenged because the summoning officer is biased or acted improperly: ***Romford Jury (1993)***
  - **Stand by the Crown**: Only used in cases of national security or terrorism, and with the permission of the Attorney-General
- **Racial challenges:**
  - There is no entitlement to a multiracial jury: ***R v Ford (1989)***
  - There is an entitlement to a jury that is not racist: ***Sander v UK (2000)***
- **Jury tampering:** Interfering with the jury: ***s44 Criminal Justice Act 2003*** provides that, if this happens, the prosecution can apply for the case to be heard by the judge alone: ***R v Twomey and others (2009)***
- **Alternatives to the jury:**
  - A single judge
  - A bench of judges
  - A specially trained jury selected from non-lawyers
  - A mixed panel of a judge and two lay members
- **Advantages of juries**
  - Allow ordinary people to participate in the justice system (the right to be tried by one's peers)
  - May not be biased towards prosecution
  - Protect against harsh or unjust laws as may prioritise fairness: ***R v Owen (1992)***
  - Less cynical than legal profession
  - 12 opinions of the jury are safer than one single judge
  - ***s8 Contempt of Court Act 1981*** and ***s69–77 CJCA 2015*** protect secret deliberations
  - Jury equity: ***Ponting (1985)***
  - Lord Blackstone:'It is the bulwark of our liberties' and Lord Devlin: 'The lamp that shows freedom lives'
- **Disadvantages of juries**
  - Can be dominated by strong-minded individuals or a forceful foreperson
  - Compulsory jury service can lead to some jurors being keen to end the trial without thorough consideration
  - Jurors might also be influenced by appearances: ***R v Alexander and Steen (2004)***
  - Lack of legal knowledge: ***R v Pryce (2013)***
  - Media influence on the grounds of ***Article 6 ECHR***: ***R v Taylor and Taylor (1993)***
  - ***Contempt of Court Act 1981*** and ***CJCA 2015*** prevent jurors from discussing the case: ***R v Mirza (2004)***, ***R v Connor and Rollock***, ***R v Karakaya (2005)***

Legal personnel: Barristers and solicitors

Spec reference	Key content	Assessment Objectives	Where does this topic feature on each specification/exam?
WJEC AS/A Level **1.7:** Legal personnel **Eduqas AS Level** **1.2.3:** Legal personnel **Eduqas A Level** **1.2.3:** Legal personnel	• Barristers and solicitors: education, training and role • Structure of the legal professions; fusion, appointment, training and social background • Role of the legal executive and paralegal personnel • Regulation of the legal professions	**AO1** Demonstrate knowledge and understanding of legal rules and principles **AO3** Analyse and evaluate legal rules, principles, concepts and issues	**WJEC AS/A Level:** Unit 1 Section B **Eduqas AS Level:** Component 1 Section B **Eduqas A Level:** Component 1 Section B

The legal profession

The legal profession in England and Wales is divided into two separate branches: barristers and solicitors. Each branch does similar work (for example, both do advocacy and legal paperwork), but they differ in the amount of time dedicated to this work, with barristers spending more of their time in court. A simple analogy is with the medical profession, by thinking of the barrister as the consultant or the specialist, and the solicitor as the general practitioner. The legal profession also includes paralegals and legal executives.

Role of solicitors

There are approximately 130,000 solicitors, with 80 per cent being in private practice. The Solicitors Regulation Authority (SRA) regulates solicitors.

What types of work do solicitors do?

Most solicitors' work and income comes from commercial, conveyancing, family or matrimonial and probate work. In 1985, solicitors lost their monopoly on conveyancing work.

Solicitors do almost all their advocacy work in the magistrates' court. Until 1999, solicitors did not have full **rights of audience** upon qualification, a right barristers have always had. However, the ***Courts and Legal Services Act 1990*** and ***Access to Justice Act 1999*** changed this, and solicitors now acquire full rights of audience when they are admitted to the roll, and solicitors can exercise this right upon completion of extra training.

Solicitors' offices range from large firms to sole practitioners. Solicitors can form business partnerships, including limited liability partnerships. Most law firms are small, with 85 per cent having four or fewer partners, and 50 per cent having only one partner.

Qualifications for a solicitor

Training to be a solicitor has several stages.

1. Law degree or, for non-law graduates, the Common Professional Exam (CPE) or Graduate Diploma in Law (GDL).
2. Legal Practice Course (one year).
3. Two-year training contract.
4. Qualification as a solicitor.
5. Continuous professional development.

Legal executives can progress to become solicitors, although it is a long process.

The solicitors' governing body is called The Law Society. In 2005 membership of The Law Society became voluntary

KEY TERMINOLOGY

rights of audience: the right to appear as an advocate in any court.

KEY TERMINOLOGY

cab rank rule: a barrister is obliged accept any work in a field in which they are competent to practice, at a court at which they normally appear and at their usual rates.
chambers: office space where barristers group together to share clerks (administrators) and operating expenses.
Inns of Court: Barristers must join Inner Temple, Middle Temple, Gray's Inn or Lincoln's Inn. The Inns provide accommodation and education and promote activities.
pupillage: a one-year apprenticeship in which a pupil works alongside a qualified barrister, who is known as the pupil master.
tenancy: a permanent place for a barrister in chambers.
Queen's Counsel (QC): an appointed senior barrister who has practised for at least 10 years. They can wear silk gowns, hence 'to take silk'.

Complaints against solicitors

- The **Solicitors Regulation Authority** deals with complaints about professional misconduct of solicitors. If there is evidence of serious misconduct, the SRA can put the case before the **Solicitors' Disciplinary Tribunal**, which can reprimand, fine, suspend or, in very serious cases, strike a solicitor off the roll. If the complainant is not happy with the decision of the SRA then they can take the matter further to the **Legal Service Ombudsman**.
- **Legal Service Ombudsman** was set up by the **Office for Legal Complaints.** The Ombudsman can, among other things, order a legal professional to apologise to a client, refund or reduce legal fees or pay compensation of up to £30,000.
- Action for negligence can go through the courts; for example, ***Arthur JS Hall and Co v Simons (2000)***.

Promotion to the judiciary

Before 1990, solicitors were only eligible to apply for junior judicial appointments (e.g. circuit judges). Since the **Courts and Legal Services Act 1990** they are eligible for appointment to the higher courts.

Role of barristers

There are approximately 13,000 barristers, known collectively as **the Bar**. The governing body of barristers is the **General Council of the Bar**. The **Bar Standards Board** is responsible for regulating the Bar.

What types of work do barristers do?

Their main role is advocacy (presenting cases in court). A great deal of their work is pretrial work, opinions (considered assessment of cases), and conferences with solicitors and clients.

A key difference to solicitors is that barristers must be self-employed and cannot form partnerships. Instead, they share offices called **chambers** with other barristers, and the sets of chambers are managed by the clerk who arranges meetings with solicitors, and negotiates barristers' fees.

Not all barristers work as advocates: some barristers work for law centres, the government and private industry.

Before 2004, members of the public were not allowed to directly contact a barrister; they had to be appointed through a solicitor. In 2004, direct access was introduced so members of the public can now contact a barrister without going through a solicitor.

Barristers work according to the **cab rank rule**. This means that a barrister is obliged accept any work in a field in which they profess themselves competent to practise, at a court at which they normally appear and at their usual rates.

The Honourable Society of Lincoln's Inn is one of four Inns of Court in London, where barristers are called to the Bar. The other three are Middle Temple, Inner Temple and Gray's Inn

Qualifications for a barrister

Training to be a barrister has several stages.

1. Law degree or, for non-law graduates, the Common Professional Exam (CPE) or Graduate Diploma in Law (GDL).
2. Join one of the four **Inns of Court**.
3. Bar Professional Training Course (one year).
4. Called to the Bar.
5. **Pupillage** (one year).
6. **Tenancy** in chambers.
7. Continuous professional development.

Barristers remain 'junior' unless made QC (**Queen's Counsel**). Barristers are eligible to become a QC after 10 years in practice and they are appointed by The General Council of the Bar and Law Society. On appointment, they 'take silk'. QCs can command higher fees for their recognised expertise and status.

Complaints against barristers

- Barristers are no longer immune from liability for negligent work in court – ***Rondel v Worsley (1969)*** overruled by ***Arthur JS Hall v Simons (2000)***.
- However, see ***Moy v Pettman Smith (2005)***. This concerned the lenient treatment of a barrister by the House of Lords compared to other professionals.
- **The Bar Standards Board** deals with disciplinary matters and also oversees the training and education of barristers. The Board can discipline any barrister who is in breach of the Code, and can refer serious matters to a disciplinary tribunal. If the complainant is unhappy with the decision of the Board, the matter can be taken to the Legal Ombudsman.

Promotion to the judiciary

Barristers are eligible for appointment to all judicial posts, provided they have the necessary experience.

Representation issues surrounding barristers and solicitors

Those in the legal profession are often accused of not representing wider society. Accusations include that they are mainly middle-class and women and ethnic minorities have traditionally been underrepresented. Access may be improving but the higher positions are still dominated by white males and there is still discrimination. For example, male assistant solicitors earn on average £13,000 per annum more than females in a similar job (1998 Law Society Statistics). In 2003, only 8 per cent of solicitors and 11 per cent of practising barristers were from ethnic minorities.

Reforms and the future of the legal profession

Should the two professions merge and become one? This is a question that has been asked for many years. Moves towards fusion include:

- 1990: ***Courts and Legal Services Act***
- 1992: Solicitor-advocates were introduced
- 1999: ***Access to Justice Act*** when all barristers and solicitors acquired full rights of audience
- 2004: **Clementi Report** advocated regulation of the profession
- 2007: ***Legal Services Act*** allowed for alternative business structures.

Clementi Report

Sir David Clementi's 2004 report, 'Review of the Regulatory Framework for Legal Services in England and Wales' was followed by a White Paper, 'The Future of Legal Services – Putting Consumers First'.

The Legal Services Act 2007

This is often called the '**Tesco law**' because it aimed to make legal work such as will writing or conveyancing as accessible for consumers as buying a can of beans from a supermarket, and enabled big companies to buy law firms. Other reforms included allowing:

- legal businesses to include lawyers and non-lawyers
- legal businesses to include barristers and solicitors
- non-lawyers to own legal businesses
- alternative business structures (ABS) (e.g. in 2012, The Co-operative Society gained a licence from the Legal Services Board to offer legal services).

GRADE BOOST

It is important that you can show the examiner that you are fully aware of all proposals and reforms to the legal profession, for example Legal Services Act 2007, alternative business structures and so on. Examination questions sometimes focus on the unmet need for legal services so ensure that you are able to discuss this fully.

Other legal personnel

Legal executives

- There are over 20,000 legal executives who perform professional work under solicitors. They tend to specialise, for example in conveyancing.
- They can go on to qualify as a solicitor.
- Their governing body is the **Institute of Legal Executives.**
- Under the ***Tribunals, Courts and Enforcement Act 2007***, legal executives were given right to apply for junior judicial appointments.

Licensed conveyancers

The Courts and Legal Services Act 1990 abolished solicitors' monopoly on conveyancing.

STRETCH AND CHALLENGE

1. Look at the Legal Ombudsman's website (www.legalombudsman.org.uk). Find a case study of a complaint, discuss it with your class and give a presentation based on what you have learned.
2. Research whether QC status is a reliable indicator of excellent and expertise.

Exam Skills

This topic could feature on Unit 1 exam, Section B of WJEC AS Law, Eduqas component 1 exam AS and A Level component 1 exam. It is likely to be examined in a similar way to the WJEC 'old' specification LA1.

Part a) questions will require you to **explain** an aspect of the topic covering AO1 knowledge and understanding.

Part b) questions require you to **analyse and evaluate** an aspect of the topic covering AO3 skills.

Summary: Legal Profession

Solicitors

- Can work in a **firm or organisation**
- Mostly do **office work, but can present cases** in the magistrates' court and County Court. They can also qualify for rights of audience in the higher courts
- To qualify, they must pass the **Legal Training Course** and do a two-year training contract
- Represented by the Law Society and regulated by the Solicitors Regulation Authority

Barristers

- Usually **self-employed** but can work for an organisation
- Mostly do court work, with **full rights of audience** upon qualification
- Must be a member of one of the four **Inns of Court**
- To qualify and practise, they must pass the **Bar Professional Training Course** and undertake a **pupillage**
- To apply for **Queen's Counsel**, barristers must have been practising for at least ten years

Legal executives

- Work in **solicitor's firms** or other legal organisations
- Carry out **straightforward** matters
- Have limited rights of audience

Legal personnel: Judiciary

Spec reference	Key content	Assessment Objectives	Where does this topic feature on each specification/exam?
WJEC AS/A Level **1.7**: Legal personnel **Eduqas AS Level** **1.2.3**: Legal personnel **Eduqas A Level** **1.2.3:** Legal personnel	• Judiciary: role, hierarchy, selection, training, composition, regulation, constitutional position and judicial independence and the rule of law	**AO1** Demonstrate knowledge and understanding of legal rules and principles **AO3** Analyse and evaluate legal rules, principles, concepts and issues	**WJEC AS/A Level:** Unit 1 Section B **Eduqas AS Level:** Component 1 Section B **Eduqas A Level:** Component 1 Section B

Role of judges

The independence of the judiciary is a fundamental principle of the rule of law. Judges have a key role in controlling the exercise of power by the state through judicial review and through the ***Human Rights Act 1998***, with the power to issue ***Section 4*** **declarations of incompatibility** (***A and X and others v Secretary of State for the Home Department (2004)***).

Hierarchy of judges

Superior judges

Head of the Judiciary is the President of the Courts of England and Wales (in practice the Lord Chief Justice) (***Constitutional Reform Act 2005***).

The most senior judges are the **Justices of the Supreme Court** and **Privy Council** (***Constitutional Reform Act 2005*** replaced the House of Lords with the Supreme Court in 2009).

Lord and Lady Justices of Appeal at the Court of Appeal. Head of Criminal Division is the **Lord Chief Justice**; Head of Civil Division is the **Master of the Rolls**.

Judges in the three divisions of the **High Court**.

Inferior judges

Circuit judges at the Crown Court and county court.

Recorders (part-time) at the Crown Court and county court.

District judges at the magistrates' court and county court.

The Lord Chancellor

The role of the Lord Chancellor has existed for over 1,400 years but recently the role has been seen to conflict with the doctrine of **separation of powers**. In 2003, the government announced the intention to abolish the role but this has not yet happened. The ***Constitutional Reform Act 2005*** has maintained the role but the powers of the Lord Chancellor have been severely curtailed.

Changes to the role of the Lord Chancellor by the Constitutional Reform Act 2005

Lord Chancellor no longer:	The Lord Chancellor is now:
sits as a judge in the House of Lords	head of the Ministry for Justice
heads the judiciary	responsible for legal aid, the Law Commission and the court system
takes a role in judicial appointments process	potentially drawn from a background other than law (***s2 Constitutional Reform Act 2005***). In 2012, Chris Grayling became the first non-lawyer to hold this post for 400 years
is required to be a member of the House of Lords	
automatically becomes Speaker of the House of Lords	

Judicial appointments process

Old procedure	New procedure
Lord Chancellor took a central role in appointments.	***Constitutional Reform Act 2005*** established Judicial Appointments Commission.
Secret soundings.	Judicial Appointments Commission (JAC): 14 members (five lay, five judges, two legal professionals, a lay magistrate and a tribunal member) appointed by the Queen on the recommendation of the Law Commission.
No advertisements for judicial appointments.	The Commission is not involved in appointing judges to the Supreme Court.
Secretive: eligibility to become a judge was based on numbers of years of rights of audience.	***Tribunals, Courts and Enforcement Act 2007***: eligibility to become a judge is based on number of years of post-qualification experience.

Other countries have different systems for appointing judges. In France, judges choose at the beginning of their career to be a judge, rather than being a lawyer first, and follow a judicial career path. In the United States, judges are appointed by two methods: appointment and election.

KEY TERMINOLOGY

secret soundings: the old appointments process whereby information on a potential judge would be gathered over time, informally, from leading barristers and judges.

Training, dismissal, termination and promotion of judges

Training

Judges receive little formal training. The training they do receive is organised by the Judicial College.

Dismissal

There are five ways a judge may leave office:

1. Dismissal (High Court judges and above: ***Act of Settlement 1700***, ***Courts Act 1971*** and ***Constitutional Reform Act 2005***).
2. Suspension from office (***Constitutional Reform Act 2005*** set up disciplinary procedures).
3. Resignation.
4. Retirement (judges usually retire at 70).
5. Removal due to infirmity.

Promotion

There is no formal system for promoting judges, as it is believed that the desire to be promoted may affect their decision making. Any promotion is dealt with in the same way as the initial appointment process, through the Judicial Appointments Commission (JAC).

Judicial independence

Judicial independence is of paramount importance: it is a necessary condition of impartiality and, therefore, of a fair trial. Judges should:

- be independent from Executive, interest groups and litigants
- have an independent pay review
- have no other paid appointment or profession or business
- not sit on a case in which they have or appear to have personal interest/bias (e.g. ***Lord Hoffmann in Re Pinochet Ugarte (1999)***).

Threats to judicial independence

Ideally, judges are independent arbitrators of the law but this is not always the case.

- Judges are subordinate to the will of Parliament.
- Judges have been to seen to show political bias (see ***McIlkenny v Chief Constable of the West Midlands(1980)***; ***R v Ponting (1985)***).
- Some cases tend to show a bias towards the right wing of the political spectrum (see ***Bromley London Borough Council v Greater London Council (1982)***; ***Council of Civil Service Union v Minister for the Civil Service (1984)***; ***Thomas v NUM (1985)***).
- Some judges' attitudes towards women is out of date and stereotypical. This is of particular concern in cases involving a sexual offence such as rape.

Criticisms of the judiciary

Judges are often criticised for mostly being white and male, and for having attended public school and/or Oxford and Cambridge universities, so they are perceived as out of touch with everyday society. They may also have limited training and lack specialisation, so approaches to cases may be inconsistent.

Crime and Courts Act 2013

Part 2 of this Act deals with courts and justice. Some of the reforms that relate to judges include:

- improving the organisation of court hours
- enabling flexible working in the High Court and above, with opportunities to work flexibly clearly highlighted in each Judicial Appointments Commission (JAC) selection process
- flexible deployment, which enables judges to more easily move between courts and tribunals, to help their career development
- new selection processes, including the introduction of an 'equal merit provision' to clarify that, where two persons are of equal merit, a candidate can be selected on the basis of improving diversity. This is to encourage the appointment of more female and ethnic minority judges.

Role of the Supreme Court and reasons for its establishment

The ***Constitutional Reform Act 2005*** established the Supreme Court, which replaced the House of Lords to completely separate the UK's senior judges, and the Upper House of Parliament, which is also called the House of Lords. This is to emphasise the independence of the Law Lords and to remove them from the legislature. The Supreme Court is highest appeal court in the UK.

In August 2009, the justices moved out of the House of Lords (where they sat as the Appellate Committee) into their own building. They sat for the first time as the Supreme Court in October 2009.

Appointing judges to the Supreme Court

Under ***s23 Constitutional Reform Act 2005***, to qualify for appointment to the Supreme Court, a judge must have held high judicial office for at least two years or been a qualifying practitioner for at least 15 years in, for example, the Court of Appeal or House of Lords.

Twelve judges are appointed to the Supreme Court by the Queen on the recommendation of the Prime Minister. The Lord Chancellor recommends these judges to the Prime Minister following a selection commission set up by the Lord Chancellor. The number of judges can be increased.

The senior Lord of Appeal is called the President of the Court.

Exam Skills

This topic could feature on Unit 1 exam, Section B of WJEC AS Law, Eduqas component 1 exam AS and A Level component 1 exam. It is likely to be examined in a similar way to the WJEC 'old' specification LA1.

Part a) questions will require you to **explain** an aspect of the topic covering AO1 knowledge and understanding.

Part b) questions require you to **analyse and evaluate** an aspect of the topic covering AO3 skills.

Summary: Judiciary

- The **role of judges differs** depending on what court they sit in, and there are different types of judges in each level of the courts
- Judges are selected by the **Judicial Appointments Commission (JAC)**, which was established by the Constitutional Reform Act 2005. JAC makes recommendations to the **Lord Chancellor**
- To ensure judicial independence and act without fear of repercussions, judges must have **security of tenure**, be **independent** in all cases, and be independent from the government

GRADE BOOST

It is a common examination error when discussing the appointment process to only discuss the old procedure.
It is vital that you can fully discuss both the old and new procedures and that you can evaluate the new procedure. You must also be able to discuss whether judges are representative of society; this is affected by factors such as their class, background and ethnicity.
A judiciary question could also focus on the independence of the judiciary, so ensure you are aware of the importance of having an independent judiciary, the threats to independence, and political implications on cases.
A judiciary question could also ask you to discuss the role of the Supreme Court and the reasons for its establishment.

STRETCH AND CHALLENGE

1. Research ways in which judges can be more representative of society, for example by looking at the Lord Chancellor's Diversity Strategy (2006).
2. Consider more reforms to the appointment process. You could start by researching the findings of the government's 2007 consultation paper, 'Constitutional Reform: A New Way of Appointing Judges'.
3. Research the ***Crime and Courts Act 2013***. Will the Act improve the efficiency, transparency and diversity of judicial appointments?

Legal personnel: Magistrates

Spec reference	Key content	Assessment Objectives	Where does this topic feature on each specification/exam?
WJEC AS/A Level **1.7**: Legal personnel **Eduqas AS Level** **1.2.3**: Legal personnel **Eduqas A Level** **1.2.3:** Legal personnel	• Magistracy and district judges in the magistrates' courts: role, selection, appointment and training	**AO1** Demonstrate knowledge and understanding of legal rules and principles **AO3** Analyse and evaluate legal rules, principles, concepts and issues	**WJEC AS/A Level:** Unit 1 Section B **Eduqas AS Level:** Component 1 Section B **Eduqas A Level:** Component 1 Section B

The role of a magistrate or **justice of the peace** was established with the ***Justices of the Peace Act 1361***. They are **lay** people who volunteer to hear cases in the magistrates' court. There are also professional judges who sit alone in magistrates courts known as **district judges** (see page 100). Volunteering as a magistrate is seen as a way of giving something back to the community and gaining valuable skills. Today, magistrates' powers and functions are governed by the ***Justices of the Peace Act 1997*** and ***Courts Act 2003***.

There are approximately 28,000 lay magistrates. They must be able to commit at least 26 half-days per year to sit in court. An employer is required by law to allow reasonable time off work for an employee's service as a magistrate. Though this time off does not have to be paid, many employers will allow paid time off. If a magistrate suffers loss of earnings they can claim a set rate for this loss. Expenses are also paid for travel and subsistence.

Cases in the magistrates' courts are usually heard by a panel of three magistrates called a **bench**, supported by a legally qualified **justices' clerk** and **legal advisor**.

Appointment of magistrates

- Appointed from the age of 18.
- Must retire at 70, though they generally won't be appointed if they are over 65.
- Since 2013, magistrates are appointed by the Lord Chief Justice on behalf of the Crown, assisted by local advisory committees who vet and recommend suitable candidates.
- Individuals can now apply to become a magistrate as well as being approached by the advisory committee. Advertisements are published inviting applications.
- Selection is based on merit.
- Applications welcome from all sections of the community regardless of gender, ethnicity, religion or sexual orientation.
- Magistrates should live within 15 miles of the bench's area.
- No legal or academic qualifications are required and full training is provided.
- Certain individuals are excluded from appointment, such as police officers and traffic wardens, and those with serious criminal convictions.

GRADE BOOST

Juries are another example of how lay people are involved in the criminal justice system. You may get a question that asks you about 'lay participation' in the law. This would require you to discuss both magistrates and juries. Remember to include both. Find out about the **youth court**. How does this court differ from the ordinary magistrates court and Crown Court?

Role of magistrates

Criminal jurisdiction

Magistrates play an important role in the criminal justice system, dealing with approximately 95% of cases. They hear summary and some **triable either way offences**. Their role is to decide the guilt or innocence of the defendant and to sentence them. They also issue warrants for arrest and decide on bail applications, and are involved in appeals to the Crown Court.

They have a limited sentencing jurisdiction. They cannot order sentences of imprisonment that exceed six months (or 12 months for consecutive sentences). The maximum fine allowed in a magistrates' court has generally been **£5,000** but, for offences committed on or after 12 March 2015, the fines in a magistrates' court are unlimited in most cases. In triable either way cases, the offender may be committed by the magistrates to the Crown Court for sentencing if a more severe sentence is thought necessary. They also try cases in the youth court if the defendants are aged 10 to 17.

KEY TERMINOLOGY

triable either way: mid-level crimes (e.g. theft, assault causing actual bodily harm) that can be tried in either the magistrates' court or Crown Court.

Civil jurisdiction

Magistrates have a limited role in civil cases. They are responsible for issuing licences to betting shops and casinos, and they also hear appeals from Local Authority decisions regarding the issuing of pub and restaurant licences.

Magistrates no longer deal with adoption and domestic matters. Since 2014, the Family Proceedings Court has jurisdiction over various family law matters such as orders for protection against violence, maintenance orders and proceedings concerning the welfare of children.

The justices' clerk

Justices' clerks assist the magistrates with the law. They are qualified lawyers with a minimum five-year magistrates' court experience. Their role is to advise and guide the magistrates on questions of law, procedure and practice, as set out in the ***Justices of the Peace Act 1979***. They have to give their advice in open court and cannot influence the magistrates' decision. This is an important role and some have recommended increasing the role of the clerk to aid the efficiency of magistrates.

Training for magistrates

As lay magistrates are rarely from a legal background, they receive mandatory training. They will also be assisted by a **justices' clerk** and **legal advisor**. Magistrates' training is based on **competences** or what a magistrate needs to know and be able to do so that they can carry out the role. The **Magisterial Committee of the Judicial College** is responsible nationally for training, and at a local level this responsibility lies with the Magistrates' Association and the Justices' Clerks' Society.

Training in the first year

- **Initial training** covers the understanding of the organisation, administration, and roles and responsibilities of those involved in the court.
- **Core training** allows new magistrates to acquire and develop legal skills, knowledge and understanding.
- **Ongoing training and development** involves activities, observations of court sittings and visits to prisons and probation offices.
- **Appraisals:** during the first two years magistrates will be mentored, and an appraisal will take place to check if the magistrate has acquired the necessary competencies.

Continuation training

Magistrates continue training throughout their magisterial career. They receive additional training for youth court work.

Background of magistrates

There is an argument that magistrates do not represent the people whom they serve. They face similar criticisms to the judiciary in that they are 'middle class, middle aged and middle minded'. There are reasons why they tend to come from professional or middle-class backgrounds, such as availability to sit as a magistrate. Similarly, they tend to be middle aged or older as a result of the impact on their career of taking time to sit as a magistrate. However, magistrates are generally evenly balanced in terms of gender, with 49% being women and 51% male, and they also represent the proportion of ethnic minorities in the population, with around 7% of magistrates being from an ethnic minority compared with 7.9% in the population.

STRETCH AND CHALLENGE

In 2012, the government issued a consultation paper called '**Swift and Sure Justice**'. One proposal was to set up local **community justice centres** and some are now being piloted. The centres seek to bring together the courts and other agencies to tackle the underlying problems of crime in a community.
Research the consultation document. Do you think these centres will be achieve the aims set out in the paper? What role will magistrates play in the centres?

District judges (magistrates court)

There are also approximately 130 professional judges who sit in the magistrates' court. They act as a sole judge and usually sit in magistrates' courts in the large cities. Since the ***Constitutional Reform Act 2005***, the Judicial Appointments Commission is involved in their appointment. They receive a salary of around £90,000.

Advantages of magistrates

✓ **Lay involvement:** an example of public participation in the justice system.

✓ **Local knowledge:** community concerns and interests are represented.

✓ **Balanced view:** a bench of three magistrates should provide a balanced view.

✓ **Cost:** as volunteers, they are relatively cheap but do take longer to make decisions than professional judges. The average direct cost of a lay magistrate is £500 per year, whereas that of a district judge is £90,000. However, see below.

GRADE BOOST

There have been calls to remove lay participation in the legal system. Investigate and discuss these main reform proposals:

- Increase the role of the justices' clerk.
- Replace lay magistrates with professional judges.
- Set up a District Division (Auld Report 2001 recommendation).
- Increase the representativeness of magistrates. How could this be achieved?

Disadvantages of magistrates

✗ **Not representative:** as with the judiciary, most magistrates are from middle class and professional backgrounds.

✗ **Inconsistent:** magistrates' courts tend to come to different decisions and sentences for the same crime.

✗ **Inefficient:** magistrates can be slow to reach a decision, often retiring to consider their verdict when a professional district judge would come to a decision straight away.

✗ **Bias towards the police:** sitting in local areas, magistrates get to know the police officers that come to give evidence and tend to be more sympathetic to them than the defendant.

✗ **Cost:** despite the low average direct cost, lay magistrates incur more indirect costs than paid judges, as they are slower, they need support from the justice's clerk and also administrative support, so in reality there is very little difference between the costs of lay magistrates and district judges.

Summary: Magistrates

- Magistrates' powers and functions are governed by ***Justices of the Peace Act 1997*** and ***Courts Act 2003***
- **Lay people** aged 18–70
- Appointed based on **merit** by the Lord Chief Justice on behalf of the Crown
- Applications welcome from **all sections of the community** regardless of gender, ethnicity, religion or sexual orientation
- **Exclusions** include police officers and traffic wardens, and those with serious criminal conviction
- **Criminal jurisdiction**
  - Hear **summary** and some **triable either way** offences
  - Decide the guilt or innocence of the defendant and to sentence them
  - Limited sentencing jurisdiction
- **Civil jurisdiction**
  - Limited role in civil cases
  - Issue licences to betting shops and casinos, and hear appeals on pub and restaurant licences
- **Justices' clerks:** Qualified lawyers who advise and guide the magistrates on questions of law, procedure and practice, give advice in open court and cannot influence decisions
- **Training:** Mandatory training based on **competences** or what they need to know and do for the role
- **Background:** 'Middle class, middle aged and middle minded' but representative of gender and ethnic backgrounds
- **District judges (magistrates court):** Professional judges who sit in city magistrates' courts
- **Advantages:** Lay involvement; local knowledge; balanced view; lower direct cost
- **Disadvantages:** Not representative; inconsistent; inefficient; biased towards the police; high indirect cost

Access to justice and funding

Spec reference	Key content	Assessment Objectives	Where does this topic feature on each specification/exam?
WJEC AS/A Level **1.8:** Access to justice and funding **Eduqas AS Level** **1.2.4:** Access to justice and funding **Eduqas A Level** **1.2.4:** Access to justice and funding	• Sources of funding: civil legal aid • Sources of funding: criminal legal aid and public defender services • Funding of civil and criminal cases, including advice schemes and role of Legal Aid Agency, merit testing, means testing, eligibility criteria and priorities for funding • Conditional fee arrangements including how they work and their advantages and disadvantages	**AO1** Demonstrate knowledge and understanding of legal rules and principles **AO3** Analyse and evaluate legal rules, principles and issues	**WJEC AS/A Level:** Unit 1 Section B **Eduqas AS Level:** Component 1 Section B **Eduqas A Level:** Component 1 Section B

Many people have an **unmet need** for legal services, which simply means that they have a problem which could be solved by going to a solicitor or a court, but they are not able to get help from the system. This could be for a number of reasons:

- People fail to see that their problem has legal implications.
- People choose not to pursue their case because of implications such as cost, or they see solicitors as unapproachable.
- People do not know of the existence of a legal service or cannot find one that could help.

It is therefore clear that most people would not be able to gain access to justice unless there was some form of state-funded scheme. Equal access to legal services is a fundamental principle of the **rule of law**, as advocated by AV Dicey (see page 11). The principle of the rule of law promotes the principle of equality before the law, equal access to justice and the right to a fair trial.

History of legal aid

1949: Welfare state

The first legal aid system was established after the Second World War as part of the welfare state. It worked by providing public funding to cover assistance with the cost of litigation and representation in court. The **Legal Aid Board** administered legal aid and people were assessed based on their means to pay and whether the case merited public funding.

1980s: Different types of legal aid

The system had developed into six different schemes, still administered by the Legal Aid Board. These were:

- legal advice and assistance scheme (the 'green form' scheme)
- assistance by way of representation (ABWOR)
- civil legal aid
- criminal legal aid
- duty solicitor – police stations
- duty solicitor – magistrates' courts.

1999: Access to Justice Act

This was introduced by the Labour government following its report, 'Modernising Justice'. The legal aid system was seen as needing a dramatic overhaul as it was not delivering access to justice. The new system had four clear aims:

1. improve quality
2. improve accessibility
3. tighter control of the budget
4. promote competition between providers. Solicitor firms had to apply for a contract for legal services, on the satisfaction of certain quality criteria.

The Legal Aid Agency was replaced by the **Legal Services Commission**, which administered two schemes: the **Community Legal Service** for civil legal aid and the **Criminal Defence Service** for criminal cases.

2011: Lord Jackson, 'Review of Civil Litigation'

This report recommended a further overhaul of the the legal aid system, and has been extensively criticised. Many of Lord Jackson's recommendations were contained in the ***Legal Aid, Sentencing and Punishment of Offenders Act 2012***, which has resulted in further austerity cuts and made access to justice further out of reach for many.

Legal Aid, Sentencing and Punishment of Offenders Act 2012

This Act came into force in April 2013 and created the publicly funded legal aid system that we use today. Its biggest criticism has been the removal of significant categories from the scope of legal aid, as well as the more stringent eligibility criteria and the reduction of the amount paid to legal professionals for undertaking legal aid work.

The system is overseen by the **Legal Aid Agency**, which replaced the Legal Services Commission, and is an executive agency sponsored by the Ministry of Justice.

The Legal Aid, Sentencing and Punishment of Offenders Act 2012 also created the statutory office of the **Director of Legal Aid Casework**, who takes decisions on the funding of individual cases.

Civil legal aid

The Legal Aid, Sentencing and Punishment of Offenders Act 2012 removes some cases from legal aid funding, and states that other cases will only qualify when they meet certain criteria. The only cases or people that qualify for legal aid under ***Schedule 1*** now are:

- clinical negligence in infants
- debt, mortgage repayment, repossession of home, orders for the sale of home and involuntary bankruptcy where the person's estate includes their home
- discrimination relating to the ***Equality Act 2010***
- special educational needs (relating to young people)
- child protection and abduction
- domestic violence
- family mediation
- forced marriage
- housing issues that are a risk to health or life and homelessness
- welfare benefits (appeals on a point of law only)
- immigration (in limited cases).

CIVIL LEGAL AID
s8
Legal Aid, Sentencing and Punishment of Offenders Act 2012

Legal Aid Agency

CRIMINAL LEGAL AID
s16
Legal Aid, Sentencing and Punishment of Offenders Act 2012

In addition, ***s10 Legal Aid, Sentencing and Punishment of Offenders Act 2012*** provides that 'exceptional funding' can be granted in exceptional circumstances, where a failure to provide funding would result in a breach of the European Convention on Human Rights.

The reforms apply across all civil litigation and the most notable omission to the eligible cases is personal injury cases, where no win, no fee arrangements, or conditional fee arrangements and damages-based agreements, are the only options available (see below). Other notable omissions include employment cases, divorce and custody cases and immigration, debt (if there is no risk to the home) and many housing issues.

Only those solicitors' firms with a contract with the Legal Aid Agency can offer civil legal aid services. This introduces competition and improves standards between firms. This is a principle that was first introduced by the ***Access to Justice Act 1999***.

A telephone gateway service was set up for clients who need debt, special educational needs and discrimination advice. They can only obtain this assistance via the phoneline, which is open from 9am to 8pm on weekdays and 9am to 12.30pm on Saturdays.

GRADE BOOST

Legal advice and funding changes all the time and, although you would not be expected to include any legal reforms from the year before your exam, it is useful to demonstrate current and up-to-date knowledge.

Means test

In order to qualify for civil legal aid, a means test and a merits test must be satisfied, found under ***s4 Legal Aid, Sentencing and Punishment of Offenders Act 2012*** and under the ***Civil Legal Aid Regulations 2013***.

1. All clients will first be subject to a capital assessment, regardless of whether they are in receipt of certain benefits. Some people are automatically eligible through the passport system, that is, if they are in receipt of income support, jobseeker's allowance, universal credit, pension credit and employment and support allowance.
2. **Income limit**: to receive legal aid, the client's gross monthly income must be less than £2,657, with a disposable income of less than £733 per month.
3. **Capital limit**: the client can have capital of no more than £8,000.

The Legal Aid Agency waives all upper eligibility limits if the client is applying for legal aid for an order for protection from domestic violence or forced marriage, though a contribution may be required.

Merits test

There are a few things for whoever is making the assessment for legal aid (usually the solicitors) to consider here.

1. **Prospects of success**: how likely it is that the person applying will obtain a successful outcome. Usually, the chance of a successful outcome needs to be more than 50 per cent.
2. **Public interest**: the case must benefit an identifiable class of individuals and be of a significant wider public interest.
3. **Proportionality test**: whether the benefit to be gained from funding the case justifies the projected costs.
4. **Likely damages**: the amount of damages the client is likely to receive if they are successful. High is more favourable because the solicitor will potentially receive more money.

Citizens Advice

Previously called the Citizens Advice Bureau, this is a national body and registered charity that provides free, easily accessed legal advice, so is an option as an alternative to legal aid. Face-to-face advice is offered at community centres, doctors' surgeries, courts and prisons, via phone and email services and online.

Civil legal aid: Evaluation of Legal Aid, Sentencing and Punishment of Offenders Act 2012

- Civil legal aid is now only available in a limited number of cases, so that the government saves money.
- Access to legal aid has dramatically fallen under the reforms, and some categories of cases are completely inaccessible for legal funding. Hazel Genn notes that these cuts will lead to an 'inevitable deterioration in effective access to justice' (Source: www.lawgazette.co.uk/analysis/dame-hazel-genn-warns-of-downgrading-of-civil-justice/48739.article).
- Lord Neuberger: 'the most vulnerable in society are going to be affected by the cuts' (Source: www.bbc.co.uk/news/uk-21665319).
- Many people have to pay privately, find charitable help, or represent themselves.
- People representing themselves will put an increased burden on the courts as the hearing will last longer.
- The telephone gateway service provision has been criticised for a lack of public awareness as well as fewer referrals than expected for face-to-face advice.
- Some solicitors' firms are going out of business because there are not enough legally aided cases.
- Two-thirds of family cases going through the family courts have at least one side with no lawyer.
- Cuts to civil legal aid mean people are encouraged to look for an alternative to court: mediation, arbitration, tribunals, out-of-court settlements etc.
- Alternative sources of funding have seen an increase in business.
- Applications to the Bar Pro Bono Unit (a charity which helps people to find free legal assistance from volunteer barristers) have doubled since 2012. This has led to a serious strain on this service and similar charitable organisations, and it is questionable how long they will be able to cope with the increased demand. Successes such as the ***Heather Ilott case (2017)*** have raised the profile of the Bar Pro Bono Unit.

'No win, no fee' arrangements

The ***Legal Aid, Sentencing and Punishment of Offenders Act 2012*** provides for two types of **'no win, no fee'** arrangements. These arrangements are particularly useful for personal injury cases, but will also provide access to justice for those who do not qualify for civil legal aid.

KEY TERMINOLOGY

no win, no fee: an agreement between a solicitor and a client whereby the client will only pay the legal fees if the case is won.

Conditional fee arrangements		Damages-based agreements
↓	↓	↓ ↓
WIN	LOSE	WIN
Legal representative gets paid the usual fee, plus an uplift, or success fee.	Legal representative does not get paid.	Legal representative gets paid a percentage of the damages recovered.

Conditional fee arrangements (CFAs)

CFAs were first introduced by the ***Courts and Legal Services Act 1990*** and then more widely in the ***Access to Justice Act 1999***. They are not part of the legal aid system and are an entirely private agreement between the legal representative and the client. They are available for personal injury cases, as these cases are no longer funded by the legal aid system.

KEY TERMINOLOGY

uplift fee/success fee: additional fee in a no win, no fee case, of up to 100 per cent of the legal representative's basic fee, which is payable if the case is won. If the case is not won, the losing party will not have to pay any fees.

A notable change made by ***s44 Legal Aid, Sentencing and Punishment of Offenders Act 2012*** was that the losing side no longer has to pay the costs of the winning party. The winning party typically pays out of the damages recovered. The legislation did provide for damages to be increased by 10 per cent to cover the additional fees that claimants face.

The **'uplift' or 'success' fee** can be up to 100 per cent of the basic fee, except in personal injury cases, where the success fee cannot exceed 25 per cent of the damages, excluding damages for future care and loss. This is designed to protect claimants' damages, and will ensure that any damages for future care and loss are protected in their entirety.

Damages-based agreements (DBAs)

DBAs work in a similar way to CFAs as legal representatives are not paid if the case is not successful but, if their case is successful, they are entitled to take a percentage of their client's damages. These agreements have only been widely available for civil cases since 1 April 2013; before this, they were mainly used only in employment tribunals.

The maximum payment that the legal representative can recover from the claimant's damages is capped at 25 per cent of the damages in personal injury cases, excluding damages for future care and loss, 35 per cent of the damages in employment tribunal cases and 50 per cent of damages in all other civil cases.

STRETCH AND CHALLENGE

In October 2017, the Justice Secretary, David Liddington, announced a review into the cuts to legal aid imposed by the ***Legal Aid, Sentencing and Punishment of Offenders Act 2012***. The consultation's focus is on whether the anticipated £450 million savings have been achieved and whether access to justice has been restricted, as critics of the reforms have suggested. Keep track of the progress of the review as it may offer key recommendations for reform.

Evaluation of CFAs and DBAs

- CFAs and DBAs provide access to justice for those who do not qualify for legal aid and for cases (e.g. personal injury) for which civil legal aid is not available.
- They are a private agreement, so do not cost the taxpayer anything.
- Preparation and performance may be improved on the part of the legal professional because there is a financial incentive to win the case.
- Only 'cast-iron' cases will be taken on and solicitors can essentially cherry-pick cases that have the highest chance of success.
- People are often subjected to high-pressure sales tactics by so-called claims farmers who use inappropriate marketing techniques and intimidating salespeople. They are known to approach people in hospital beds.
- Some people think these cases are literally 'no win, no fee', when in reality there are often hidden, unpredictable charges. In civil litigation, the loser normally pays the winner's costs, so individuals often have to take out expensive insurance premiums to cover the cost of losing and paying the other side's legal costs, which may not be affordable to everyone. In some cases, clients end up owing money.

Criminal legal aid

Similar principles apply for criminal legal aid as to civil legal aid; that is, the solicitors' firm has to have a contract to provide legal aid.

At the police station

Under ***s58 Police and Criminal Evidence Act 1984*** suspects have the right to access a **duty solicitor** at the police station.

R v Samuel (1988)

Access to a duty solicitor cannot be delayed after a suspect has been charged.

Under ***s58(8) Police and Criminal Evidence Act 1984***, the suspect's right of access to a solicitor can be delayed by a police superintendent or above if the suspect has not been charged, if there is reasonable belief that access to a solicitor will lead to the alerting of other suspects.

KEY TERMINOLOGY

duty solicitor: solicitors who work in private practice but have secured a contract with the Legal Aid Agency to provide criminal advice to people who have been arrested. The person in custody will have the assistance of whoever is on the rota for that day.

A duty solicitor is free for everyone at the police station, regardless of income. This is provided for by ***s13 Legal Aid, Sentencing and Punishment of Offenders Act 2012***.

The Legal Aid Agency oversees a number of different agencies responsible for legal aid at the police station.

Defence Solicitor Call Centre (DSCC)	All requests for publicly funded police station work must be made through the DSCC, which is manned by paralegals. The DSCC records the basic details of the alleged offence before deciding whether to pass the case to Criminal Defence Direct for telephone advice or whether to pass it to a duty solicitor, who will provide the suspect with a physical presence at the police station.
Criminal Defence Direct	Because of duty solicitors sometimes not turning up to police stations, Criminal Defence Direct was established to provide telephone advice to suspects at police stations. It is now the preferred method of contact in offences such as drink-driving offences, non-imprisonable offences, breach of bail and warrants.
Police station representative	In addition to duty solicitors, police station representatives can attend police stations to give advice and assistance to suspects. These are non-solicitors who are accredited to give legal advice and assistance to people detained at police stations. The standards that have to be met are available at www.sra.org.uk.
Public Defender Service	The Public Defender Service is a department of the Legal Aid Agency which operates alongside private providers to deliver legal services, advice and representation at the police station and magistrates' court through to advocacy in the higher courts.

At the magistrates' court

Two tests need to be satisfied to qualify for a **representation order**, which is criminal legal aid at the magistrates' court; this is provided for by ***s14 Legal Aid, Sentencing and Punishment of Offenders Act 2012***. It is a way of capping the availability of criminal legal aid to those suspects who could afford to pay for their own defence.

Means test

This is a financial test which looks at household income, capital and outgoings.

- **Initial means test**: if your calculation of household income is between £12,475 and £22,325 then a full means test is carried out.
- **Full means test**: this takes into account annual costs such as childcare, housing and maintenance, as well as essential spending on items like food, clothing and fuel. The outcome will determine whether the suspect will get the whole cost of their representation paid for.

If you are on certain benefits, you can passport your claim to be automatically granted criminal legal aid. These are the same benefits as apply to civil legal aid (see page 103).

Merits test: Interests of justice test

In general, the more serious the charge and consequences, the more likely it is the person will qualify. The test considers previous convictions, the nature of the offence and the risk of custody. The solicitor will have to consider the **Widgery Criteria**, by taking into account the suspect agreeing to one or more of these statements:

- It is likely that I will lose my liberty.
- I have been given a sentence that is suspended or noncustodial. If I break this, the court may be able to deal with me for the original offence.
- It is likely that I will lose my livelihood.
- It is likely that I will suffer serious damage to my reputation.
- A substantial question of law may be involved.
- I may not be able to understand the court proceedings or present my own case.
- I may need witnesses to be traced or interviewed on my behalf.
- The proceedings may involve expert cross-examination of a prosecution witness.
- It is in the interests of another person that I am represented.
- Any other reasons.

At the Crown Court

A financial eligibility threshold was introduced for Crown Court trials from 27 January 2014. A defendant's household disposable income must be under £37,500 in order to be granted legal aid, then a means test will be applied and the defendant may be liable for contributions towards the case. If a client is refused legal aid, they will be expected to pay privately for the cost of their defence.

Criminal legal aid: Evaluation of Legal Aid, Sentencing and Punishment of Offenders Act 2012

- Challenges in relation to criminal legal aid mean that, apart from having a duty solicitor, defendants need to pass a means and a merits test to get help to be represented in court. This has huge implications for the undermining of the rule of law.
- In 2014, solicitors challenged a government proposal to further cut criminal legal aid by 8.75 per cent and to reduce the number of contracts providing 24-hour cover at police station in local communities from 1,600 to 527. They lost their case and the cuts went ahead.
- The cuts also saw solicitors participate in strikes and walk outs, refusing to take on any more legal aid clients.

STRETCH AND CHALLENGE

Have a look at these articles, which highlight the effect that cuts to criminal legal aid had on legal professionals.

'Criminal defence call centres may work but are they justice?', *The Law Society Gazette*, 5 February 2009 (http://qrs.ly/yc5ruku)

'Criminal legal aid fee cuts for lawyers confirmed by justice secretary', *The Guardian*, 27 February 2014 (http://qrs.ly/ok5sg6r)

'Criminal barristers stop taking new Crown Court cases in legal aid protest', *The Guardian*, 27 July 2015 (http://qrs.ly/ve5sg73)

Summary: Access to justice and funding

- **1949–1999:**
  - Welfare state
  - Demand-led system led to 'unmet need for legal services'
- **1999–2012:**
  - Set budget
  - Introduction of conditional fee arrangements
  - Franchising legal services
  - Administered by Legal Services Commission
- ***Legal Aid, Sentencing and Punishment of Offenders Act 2012 (LASPO)***
- **Legal Aid Agency**: Director of Legal Aid Casework takes decisions on individual cases.
- **Civil legal aid**:
  - ***s8 LASPO Act 2012***: Means test and merits test:
    - Child protection
    - Family mediation
    - Special educational needs
    - Clinical negligence in infants
    - Welfare benefits
    - Loss of home
    - Domestic violence
  - ***s10 LASPO Act 2012***: 'exceptional funding' where a failure to provide finding would breach human rights.
  - **Contracts**: Only those with a contract with the Legal Aid Agency can offer civil legal aid (introduces competition and improves standards)
- **Criminal legal aid**:
  - ***s16 LASPO Act 2012*:** Criminal advice and representation is delivered through a mixed system, e.g. public defender service, lawyers in private practice with contracts with the Legal Aid Agency
  - ***s13 LASPO Act 2012***: Duty solicitor scheme at the police station: free for everyone, not means tested
  - ***s14 LASPO Act 2012***: Legal aid for representation in court: only available subject to means and merits (interests of justice) test

Rules and theory of the law of contract

Spec reference	Key content	Assessment Objectives	Where does this topic feature on each specification/exam?
WJEC A Level **3.6:** Rules and theory of the law of contract **Eduqas AS Level** **2.1.1:** Rules the law of contract **Eduqas A Level** **2.1.1:** Rules of the law of contract	• Origins and definition of contract law • Function of the law of contract • General awareness of the impact of judicial decisions, legislation and EU provisions relating to contract formation and discharge • Relationship between human rights and contract law • Arguments for the development of a European and/or global contract law system	**AO1** Demonstrate knowledge and understanding of legal rules and principles. **AO2** Apply legal rules and principles to given scenarios in order to present a legal argument using appropriate legal terminology. **AO3** Analyse and evaluate legal rules, principles, concepts and issues.	**WJEC A Level:** Unit 3 **WJEC A Level:** Unit 4 **Eduqas AS Level:** Component 2 and 3 **Eduqas A Level:** Component 2 and 3

Origins and definition of contract law

How many contracts have you entered into today? Have they all involved a piece of paper? Did they all require a signature?

A basic definition of a contract is **any agreement or promise that is legally binding**; it can be written or unwritten so long as it satisfies the requirements of a lawful contract.

Examples could include paying for parking in a pay-and-display car park, buying your lunch in the canteen, or getting on the bus. More traditionally, a contract is the document you sign when you buy a mobile phone, book a holiday or start a new job.

We need contract law to enable society to run freely. If agreements were not legally binding, what would happen if your employer just decided they did not need you any more, or your mobile phone operator just decided to stop offering a service? The law of contract seeks to provide safety for people who are let down by parties who fail to fulfil their promises in a contract.

Laissez-faire/freedom of contract

Modern contract law stems from the **laissez-faire** doctrine, which was first introduced in the 19th century. Laissez-faire is the idea that people can make agreements on their own terms and enter into a 'bargain' in their own interests and on their own terms. The ability to form contracts with no government restrictions is a key principle of economics and free-market libertarianism.

This freedom of contract principle can, however be limited by legislation, such as the ***Unfair Contract Terms Act 1977*** to ensure the notion of fairness is upheld.

KEY TERMINOLOGY

laissez-faire: contract law term used to indicate that a person should have freedom of contract with minimal state or judicial interference.

STRETCH AND CHALLENGE

The case of ***Shanshal v Al-Kishtaini (2001)*** is a good authority on the relationship between contract law and human rights and how a contract cannot deprive a person of their possessions except in the public interest, as contained under the First Protocol of the European Convention on Human Rights.

The Human Rights Act 1998

The relationship between contract law and the ***Human Rights Act 1998*** is important, though the obligations on the court are the same as for other areas of the law, that is to take into account ***s3***, which states that '**so far as it is possible to do so, primary legislation and subordinate legislation must be read and given effect in a way which is compatible with Convention rights**'.

As with other areas of law, if any aspect of contract legislation is found to be incompatible, the courts can issue a declaration of incompatibility under ***s4 Human Rights Act 1998***.

The relationship between contract law and the European Union (EU)

The EU has had a huge impact on contract law in the United Kingdom, because a number of directives have had to be implemented in the field of consumer law. It has to be noted that the impact of the European Union is subject to change with the UK leaving the EU, though it is thought that existing legislation is unlikely to be affected.

In 2011, the European Commission published a draft '**Common European Sales Law' (CESL)**, which was a type of codified contract system for the sale of goods across the EU, with the aim of improving cross-border trade and removing legal barriers between EU member states. This was after it was found that less than one in five consumers (18%) in the EU had made an online purchase with a retailer based in another EU country. Therefore, to encourage cross-border trade, the fear of dealing with other countries needed to be reduced.

The CESL proposal was withdrawn in 2015, and a modified proposal was introduced, with the aim of setting 'harmonised EU rules for online purchases of digital content', such as ebooks and apps, as well as the sales of physical goods, such as clothes and furniture. The rationale behind this proposal was to fully unleash the potential of ecommerce and create a **digital single market**.

The digital single market will still allow traders to rely on their national contract laws, but will also create a set of key mandatory EU contractual rights for cross-border sales, because 28 different sets of laws discourages companies from cross-border trading.

Summary: Rules and theory of the law of contract

- **Origins and definition of contract law:** any agreement or promise that is legally binding, written or unwritten
- **Laissez-faire**/freedom of contract: ability to make make agreements on own terms
- Can be limited by legislation, e.g. ***Unfair Contract Terms Act 1977*** to ensure fairness
- ***The Human Rights Act 1998***: ***Shanshal v Al-Kishtaini (2001)***
- **European Union (EU)**: draft '**Common European Sales Law (CESL)**' to improve cross-border trade and remove legal barriers between EU member states
- Modified proposal for a **digital single market**

Essential requirements of a contract

Spec reference	Key content	Assessment Objectives	Where does this topic feature on each specification/exam?
WJEC A Level 3.7: Essential requirements of a contract, including privity of contract **Eduqas AS Level 2.1.2:** Essential requirements of a contract **Eduqas A Level 2.1.2:** Essential requirements of a contract	• Offer: requirements of a valid offer, distinguishing offers from invitations to treat, communicating the offer, unilateral offers • Acceptance: rules of acceptance, communication of acceptance • Consideration: rules of consideration including performance of an existing duty, past consideration, part-payment and promissory estoppel • Intention to create legal relations: social and domestic arrangements, commercial and business agreements • Privity of contract: the basic rule, exceptions to the rule and the effects of the Contracts (Rights of Third Parties) Act 1999	**AO1** Demonstrate knowledge and understanding of legal rules and principles **AO2** Apply legal rules and principles to given scenarios in order to present a legal argument using appropriate legal terminology **AO3** Analyse and evaluate legal rules, principles, concepts and issues	**WJEC A Level:** Unit 3 **WJEC A Level:** Unit 4 **Eduqas AS Level:** Component 2 and 3 **Eduqas A Level:** Component 2 and 3

Formation of a contract

The law on contract concerns a **binding agreement** between two parties. It confers **obligations** on both parties to 'carry out their side of the bargain'. If they do not, it may be **breach of contract**.

The law of contract is mainly about the enforcement of promises, but not all promises will be legally enforceable. To **enforce** a contract, the courts look for the presence of certain elements. There may be a dispute about whether a contract actually exists. In deciding whether promises or agreements are enforceable, certain elements need to be proved and it must be established that the contract has been **formed** according to certain rules.

OFFER + ACCEPTANCE = CONTRACT

↓

INVITATION TO TREAT

The process of an agreement begins with an **offer.** For a contract to be formed, this offer must be unconditionally **accepted.** There must then be valid **communication of the offer** and the courts must also establish that there is (or was) **an intention to create legal relations** and **consideration.**

If these elements are not present, the courts will find that no contract exists between the parties. There cannot be an action for breach of a non-existent contract, as neither party will be bound by the promises they have made. It is therefore essential to determine whether a contract has been formed.

KEY TERMINOLOGY

breach of contract: to break a contract by not following its terms and conditions.
offer: in contract law, a proposition put by one person to another person made with the intention that it shall become legally binding as soon as the other person accepts it.
offeree: the person to whom an offer is being made and who will consequently accept the offer.
offeror: the person making an offer.

Offer

An offer is an expression of willingness by an **offeree** to enter into a legally binding agreement based on the terms set out in the offer made by the **offeror**. The contract is formed when these terms are accepted.

This seems straightforward. Why, then, does this stage of the contract cause confusion?

Contracts are formed while shopping

The difference between offers and invitations to treat

There is an important distinction in the law of contract between an **offer,** an **invitation to treat** and a mere **statement of price.** An invitation to treat does not constitute an offer.

An invitation to treat is an indication of willingness to deal but not an intention to be bound. A party is inviting offers to be made, which they are then free to accept or reject. A classic example is offering a newspaper for sale in a shop: customers can choose whether or not to buy it.

Example: A display of goods

Goods displayed for sale on the shelves of a supermarket are generally considered invitations to treat. When the customer picks up the goods, this is **not** acceptance but merely an offer to buy on the part of the customer. If they wish to buy the goods, the customer then takes them to the cash desk, where the sale is agreed on payment and at this point the contract is formed.

Pharmaceutical Society of Great Britain v Boots Cash Chemists Ltd (1953)
*A Boots pharmacy offered for sale on its shelves in a self-service shop certain goods that by law should only be sold by a registered pharmacist. The Pharmaceutical Society of Great Britain (the body responsible for enforcing this legislation) brought a prosecution against the shop for allowing customers to buy these products by helping themselves, but the Court of Appeal said it had no case. The customer, having selected the goods, made an offer to purchase when they took them to the cash desk, and a registered pharmacist, who had discretion about whether to accept the offer to buy when the goods were presented, supervised at the point of sale. The goods for sale on the shelves were therefore an **invitation to treat**, not an offer.*

Fisher v Bell (1961)
*A flick knife was displayed in a shop window with a ticket reading 'Ejector knife 4s'. It was an offence under the **Offensive Weapons Act 1959** to 'offer for sale' prohibited weapons. It was held that the display of the knife was not an offer for sale but rather an invitation to treat, where the customer had the choice of whether or not to go into the shop to offer to buy the knife.*

In these cases, it is evident that shopkeepers retain discretion to refuse sale to a person they don't feel comfortable selling to, and customers retain discretion to change their mind by returning the goods to the shelf before the sale.

Example: Lots at an auction

An auctioneer's calls for bids are an invitation to treat and not an offer. Consequently, the bids made by people at an auction are offers which the auctioneer can accept or reject. The acceptance is the fall of the hammer (in an auction without a reserve) and this is the point at which the contract is formed. The auctioneer is acting on behalf of the owner of the goods and the contract is formed between the highest bidder and the owner of the goods. An auction lot may be withdrawn at any time before the hammer falls.

British Car Auctions v Wright (1972)
A prosecution for offering to sell an unroadworthy vehicle at an auction failed as it was held that an auction is generally an invitation to treat, or make bids. The bidder makes the offer and this offer is only accepted when the hammer falls.

Harris v Nickerson (1873)
Harris saw an advert in an auction catalogue for some furniture he wanted to bid for. On attending the auction, he found the auctioneer had withdrawn from sale the items he had hoped to buy. Harris sued for breach of contract but failed. The court held that advertising the goods for sale was no more than an invitation to treat and that the contract, in any case, would not be formed until the auctioneer's hammer fell on acceptance of a bid.

Example: Goods or services advertised for sale in a newspaper or magazine
An advertisement for goods for sale is usually an invitation to treat but it can be an offer, depending on its wording and conditions. There is an important distinction here between a **bilateral contract** (invitations to treat) and a **unilateral contract** (offer).

Partridge v Crittenden (1968)
An advert in a magazine stated 'Bramble finch cocks and bramble finch hens 25s each'. The person who placed the advert was charged with offering for sale a wild bird, contrary to the ***Protection of Wild Birds Act 1954****. The divisional court said he must be acquitted. The advertisement was an invitation to treat, not an offer to sell; with limited stock, the advertiser could not reasonably intend to be bound to sell to all those who might accept. This would be obviously impractical.*

Carlill v Carbolic Smoke Ball Company (1893)
A business advertised smoke ball 'medicine', promising to pay £100 to any purchaser who used the smoke ball correctly and still got flu. Mrs Carlill used the smoke ball correctly but still got flu. The court upheld her claim for the £100, saying that the promise to pay £100 was indeed an offer that was subsequently accepted by anyone who used the smoke ball correctly and got flu. The wording of the advertisement clearly showed an intention to be bound to anyone accepting it, so it was held that the advertisement was a unilateral contract.

However, the form and wording of a contract may give rise to an offer in the case of a unilateral contract.

Example: A request for tenders
Public authorities are required to offer for tender for many of their services, and it is also a common practice for private businesses. For example, a company that wants to install new computers invites tenders (quotations) and various installers respond with different prices and conditions. The company is free to choose any installer they wish, even if it is not the cheapest. Where goods are advertised for sale by tender, the statement is not considered to be an offer but generally an invitation to treat. Any tender then proposed is the offer. If, however, the company has advertised that they will accept the cheapest bid then they are bound to give the work to the lowest bidder.

Harvela Investments v Royal Trust of Canada (1986)
The Royal Trust of Canada invited two parties to bid for some land on the understanding that the highest bid would be accepted. Harvela bid $2,175,000 and Sir Leonard Outerbridge bid $2,100,000 or $100,000 more than any other offer. Royal Trust of Canada accepted Sir Leonard's offer and Harvela successfully sued for breach of contract.

The wording of the invitation to tender made it an offer that could only be accepted by the highest bidder. The referential bid by Sir Leonard (the statement that he would outbid any other party by $100,000), was ineffective as it defeats the purpose of asking for highest bids. He had, thus, only bid $2,100,000 compared with Harvela's bid of $2,175,000.

Example: A statement of price
Simply indicating a price that would be found acceptable does not make an offer.

Harvey v Facey (1893)
Harvey telegraphed to Facey: 'Will you sell us 'Bumper Hall Pen? Telegraph lowest cash price.' Facey replied: 'Lowest cash price ... £900'. Harvey then telegraphed: 'We agree to buy ... for £900 asked by you. Please send us title deed.' It was held that Facey's telegram was an invitation to treat, and was not an offer, as it was merely a statement of price.

KEY TERMINOLOGY

bilateral contract: a contract between two parties where each promises to perform an act in exchange for the other party's act.
unilateral contract: an offer made in exchange for an act; for example, a reward for lost property.

Biggs v Boyd Gibbins (1971)

Mr and Mrs Biggs were negotiating with Mr Gibbins over the sale of some property they owned. In the course of the negotiations, they wrote to Mr Gibbins stating: 'For a quick sale I will accept £26,000.' Mr Gibbins replied: 'I accept your offer.' Mr and Mrs Biggs responded: 'I thank you for accepting my price of £26,000'. The Biggs' first letter was deemed to be an offer that Gibbins had accepted.

However, there are occasions where a statement of price can constitute an offer.

Rules of an offer

Communication of the offer

To be effective, an offer must be communicated. A person cannot accept an offer if they have no knowledge of it. The rationale is that, if a contract is an agreed bargain, there can be no agreement without knowledge.

Taylor v Laird (1856)

Taylor gave up his captaincy of a ship but needed passage back to the UK. He offered to do this by working as an ordinary crew member. His claim for wages was not successful, as the owner of the ship had not received communication of Taylor's offer to work in order to gain passage back to the UK. It was held that, in order for an offer to be accepted, there must be knowledge of it.

An offer can be made to one person, but can also be made to the world and, as long as they have knowledge of the offer, anyone can accept it. In ***Carlill v Carbolic Smoke Ball Company (1893)***, discussed on page 113, the advert was a unilateral contract, an offer on behalf of the Smoke Ball Company to anyone who satisfied the conditions laid out in it. The company had made the offer generally (to the 'whole world') and Mrs Carlill had accepted it by buying the smoke ball and still getting flu. A unilateral offer, such as the one in Carlill, cannot be withdrawn while it is being performed. If someone had bought the smoke ball and got flu, it would not be fair to void the contract once the series of events had begun.

Errington v Errington and Woods (1952)

A father purchased a house and mortgaged it in his own name for his son and daughter-in-law to live in on the agreement that, provided they kept up the repayments, the house would be transferred to them once the mortgage was paid off. After approximately 15 years, the father died and his widow sued for possession of the house. The court held that there was a unilateral contract and, though the son and daughter-in-law were not bound to go on paying, if they did, the father was bound to transfer the property to them in accordance with the promise.

The terms of the offer must be certain

The parties to a contract must know what they are contracting to and therefore the terms must not be too vague.

Guthing v Lynn (1831)

The buyer of a horse promised to pay the seller an extra £5 'if the horse is lucky for me'. It was held this was too vague to be enforceable

It is possible to withdraw the offer at any time before the offer is accepted

In principle, there is no legal commitment until a contract has been concluded by the acceptance of an offer and, up to that point, either party is free to change their mind and withdraw from the negotiations.

Routledge v Grant (1828)

Grant had offered his house for sale. He had a condition in the offer that it would remain open for six weeks. He took the house off the market after six weeks and the courts held that this was lawful as no-one had yet accepted the offer.

The offeror must communicate the withdrawal of the offer to the offeree

An offer remains open and cannot be considered withdrawn until the offeree has received it.

Byrne v Van Tienhoven (1880)

By 15 October, B clearly thinks a contract is in place, and the court agrees. The fact that A revoked the order is irrelevant, as B had accepted before receiving the revocation.

A timeline of actions relating to the case of Byrne v Van Tienhoven (1880)

1 October: A posts an order to B for some goods

8 October: A posts a letter revoking the order

11 October: B receives A's order

15 October: B replies, accepting the terms

20 October: B receives A's revocation

Communication of a withdrawal of offer can be by a reliable third party

If the offeror wants to withdraw the offer, communication of this need not be done by the offeror themselves but can be communicated through a reliable third party.

Dickinson v Dodds (1876)

Dodds offered to sell his house to Dickinson. The offer was to be 'left open till Friday'. On Thursday afternoon, Dickinson heard from a third party that Dodds had sold the property to someone else. On the Friday morning, Dickinson delivered a formal acceptance to Dodds, and then brought an action for specific performance against Dodds. The court held that the offer made to Dickinson had been withdrawn on the Thursday and was no longer capable of acceptance. This was acceptable as the third party was a reliable source who was shown to be a mutual acquaintance of both parties and who could be relied upon by both parties.

Termination of an offer

It is important to know for how long an offer is valid. The offeror might have tried to withdraw the offer or a long time might have elapsed before the offer was accepted. It would seem unfair and impractical that an offer remains open indefinitely or that an offer cannot be properly terminated. For these reasons, the courts have developed certain rules governing the duration of a valid offer.

The general rule is that an offer can be withdrawn at any time before it is accepted. Once validly accepted, there is a contract and it may be too late to withdraw. This was evidenced above in the case ***Routledge v Grant (1828)***.

However, there are some situations where an offer, once made, can be validly **terminated**.

Acceptance

Once accepted by a valid means, there is a contract and the offer ceases to be.

Rejection

If the offeree rejects the offer, that is the end of it.

Revocation

An offer can be withdrawn before it has been accepted, provided it is done correctly as highlighted above. The correct ways to revoke are as follows:

- An offer can be withdrawn at any time before it is accepted. Case: ***Routledge v Grant (1828)***.
- Revocation must be communicated or it is unsuccessful. Case: ***Byrne v Van Tienhoven (1880)***.
- Revocation can be communicated by a third party if they are reliable. Case: ***Dickinson v Dodds (1876)***.
- If the offeree has started to perform the unilateral contract, it cannot be withdrawn once performance has begun. Case: ***Carlill v Carbolic Smoke Ball Company (1893)***.

Also note the provisions of the ***Consumer Protection (Distance Selling) Regulations 2000***, which allows a 14-day cooling-off period for products bought online.

Counter-offer

If, on responding to an offer, the offeree tries to vary the terms of the contract or tries to introduce a new term, that communication may be classed not as acceptance of the contract but as a **counter-offer**. A contract is not formed at this stage. The original offeror is free to accept or reject the counter-offer, so a counter-offer is essentially a rejection of the original offer.

Hyde v Wrench (1840)

It was held that the 'counter-offer kills the original offer'. Wrench had offered to sell his estate to Hyde for £1,000 and Hyde had responded by offering £950. Wrench rejected this offer. Hyde then decided to offer £1,000 but Wrench refused. Hyde sued for breach of contract. It was decided that, by offering £950, Hyde had effectively rejected the original offer £1,000 and his offer to £950 was a counter-offer which Wrench had subsequently rejected. It was, however, highlighted that, had Wrench's original offer of £1,000 been accepted unconditionally, there would have been a binding contract.

GRADE BOOST

Claimants were known as plaintiffs until the ***Civil Procedure Rules 1998*** came into force on 1 April 1999. Using the word **'plaintiff'** when you give examples of older cases shows you are aware of this; however, you should also add a note to explain why you have chosen this terminology.

Courts have drawn an important distinction between a counter-offer and a mere **request for information.** Unlike a counter-offer, a request for information would not terminate the contract as it is not rejecting the original terms of the original offer. This would still mean the offer is open to acceptance by the offeree.

Stevenson v McLean (1880)

The plaintiff (the offeree) and defendant (the offeror) agreed terms of a contract to buy iron. The offeree then asked if he could stagger payment and delivery over a two-month period. On hearing nothing back from the offeror, the offeree telegraphed his acceptance to the offeror, only to discover he had sold the iron elsewhere. The plaintiff successfully sued for breach of contract. The judge held that there was no counter-offer, merely an enquiry for further information which should have been answered.

Lapse of time

In cases where the offer specifies that it will remain open for a certain duration, the offer automatically terminates after this time has passed. Where no specified time period is laid down, the offer remains open for a 'reasonable time' only. This is fair, as it is unreasonable to expect an offer to remain open indefinitely, especially where business transactions are concerned and an element of certainty is required.

Ramsgate Victoria Hotel v Montefiore (1866)

The defendants made an offer in June to buy shares in the plaintiff's company, but heard nothing as they only made an allocation of shares available in November. At that point, the plaintiffs accepted the defendants' offer, but the defendants refused to go ahead, saying too much time had lapsed. The court said that, although the offer had not been formally withdrawn, it would expire after 'a reasonable time', particularly given the fluctuating nature of shares, and the time had gone beyond what was reasonable.

Failure of conditions

Offers are normally made with certain conditions attached. If these conditions are not met then the offer cannot be accepted.

Financings Ltd v Stimson (1962)

The defendant had bought a car on hire purchase from a car dealer. The car dealer explained that the agreement would only become binding when it was signed by the finance company (Financings Ltd: the plaintiffs). The defendant took the car away and paid a first instalment but returned it two days later, claiming he had changed his mind. His agreement had not yet been signed by the finance company (a 'condition' of the offer) and so the finance company's claim against the defendant failed as the court held that one of the conditions of the offer had not been met and the defendant had returned the car in time.

Death

An offeree cannot accept an offer once the offeror has died. The decision may be different if the offeree does not know of the offeror's death and if there is no personal involvement. The courts have been divided on this issue.

Bradbury v Morgan (1862)

It was held that, if the offeree accepts in ignorance of the death of the offeror, a contract might be formed.

This case should be contrasted with ***Dickinson v Dodds (1876)***, where it was held that the death of either party to the contract terminates the agreement because there can be no formal acceptance.

The best view is probably that a party cannot accept an offer once they find out about the death of the offeror but that, in certain circumstances, the offer could be accepted if made in ignorance of the offeror's death.

Acceptance

Once an offer has been made by the offeror, the offeree is free to accept the offer. A contract cannot be formed until the offer has been unconditionally accepted. The acceptance must be an acceptance of each of the terms of the offer and must be a 'mirror image' of the offer. It has already been seen that trying to add new terms to the offer is not an acceptance but rather a counter-offer that implies the original offer is rejected. Acceptance can be established where the offeree's **words** or **conduct** give rise to an objective presumption that the offeree agrees to the offeror's terms.

Just as there were rules for the establishment of a valid offer, there are also rules for the successful communication of the acceptance.

Rules of acceptance

The acceptance must be unconditional

This is the 'mirror image' rule. It has been established that any attempt to change the terms of the offer is a **counter-offer** (as in the case ***Hyde v Wrench (1840)*** discussed above). A mere request for **further information** is not a rejection and the offer can still be accepted following the clarification of this information ***(Stevenson v McLean (1880)***, discussed above).

The acceptance must be communicated to the offeror

It must be a positive act, meaning that **silence does not amount to acceptance**.

Felthouse v Brindley (1863)

A man had negotiated the sale of his horse with his uncle. The uncle wrote to the nephew saying: 'If I hear no more from you, I shall consider the horse to be mine.' The nephew did not respond. The nephew's property went to auction but the auctioneer failed to withdraw the horse from the auction and it sold, despite the nephew's instruction that it be withdrawn. The uncle's action to sue the auctioneer failed as the nephew had never actually accepted his offer.

The offeree has to be aware of the existence of the offer

Inland Revenue Commissioners v Fry (2001)

Fry's husband sent the Inland Revenue a cheque for much less than the amount of tax they had asked for. He attached a note stating it was 'in full and final settlement to be accepted when banked'. Because of its postroom procedures of separating cheques from correspondence, the Inland Revenue was ignorant of this offer and, despite cashing the cheque which could, under a unilateral contract, be said to be an acceptance due to a prescribed course of conduct, the court held that the offeree must have knowledge of the offer in order to accept it.

Communication of the acceptance must be made by an authorised person
Generally this means the offeree but it has also been established that someone authorised by the offeree can communicate acceptance.

Powell v Lee (1908)
A man had been interviewed for a role as head teacher of a school and the managers subsequently decided he was the best candidate for the job. One of the managers, acting without the authority of the rest, told the man he had been accepted. However, the managers changed their minds and appointed someone else. On discovering this, the man sued for the breach of contract, claiming damages for loss of salary. The courts held that there was no valid contract (and thus no breach) as the intention to contract had not been communicated by an authorised person.

Acceptance can be in any form unless it is a requirement that it be in a specific form:
The acceptance can be in any form, including conduct, but if the offeror requires it to be made in a specific form then it is only a valid acceptance if made by that form.

Yates Building Co v Pulleyn Ltd (1975)
A piece of land was offered for sale, with the statement that, if purchasers wished to make an option to purchase, it had to be done in writing sent by 'registered or recorded delivery post'. The offeree sent his option by ordinary post and the courts held that the communication was not valid because it did not comply with the method of communication stated in the offer.

Battle of the forms

If Eve makes an offer on her standard terms and Zak accepts on a document containing his standard but clashing terms, no contract has been formed unless Eve acts upon Zak's communication, for example by delivering goods, which means she has impliedly accepted the communication. Zak has effectively made a counter-offer which has been accepted on the basis of Eve's conduct.

This situation is known as the 'battle of the forms'.

Butler Machine Tool v Excell-o-Corp (1979).
The plaintiff offered to sell a machine to the defendant. A term of the offer stated that any orders were accepted on the seller's terms and that these would prevail over any conflicting terms in the buyer's order. The defendants ordered the machine on different terms in their own standard form. At the bottom of this form was a tear-off slip for the plaintiff to fill in and send back, with the words: "We accept your order on the terms and conditions stated thereon.' The plaintiff signed and returned it, writing, 'Your official order ... is being entered in accordance with our revised quotation.' The buyer (defendant) won judgement as the conduct of the parties implied a valid contract had been formed.

In applying this logic, it will be found that, in most cases when there is a 'battle of forms', a contract is made as soon as the last of the forms is sent and received without any objections, especially where conduct implies acceptance.

Modern methods of communication

With increased use of instantaneous methods of communication such, as fax, email and internet order forms, the courts have seen a shift in the facts of the cases reaching the courts. The crucial factor appears to be how instantaneous is the method of communication?

Brinkibon v Stahag Stahl (1982)
A telex agreeing to terms and conditions was received out of office hours. The House of Lords accepted that 'instantaneous communications' could only be regarded as effective communication when the office reopened.

While this appears to be a sound decision, it could be argued it will not cover all situations and the intentions of the parties and good business practice must be paramount.

Entores Ltd V Miles Far East Corp (1955)
The courts held that the contract is only complete when the acceptance is received by the offeror and the contract is made at the place where the acceptance is received.

Although the principles laid down in the cases above are still likely to be followed, further issues may need to be examined and resolved; for example, the effectiveness of telephone answering services or delays between sending and receiving emails. Therefore, in implementing the ***Distance Selling EU Directive 97/7***, the UK enacted the ***Consumer Protection (Distance Selling) Regulations 2000*** to formalise this area and to offer consumers and sellers protection and clarity.

- These regulations apply to the sale of goods via modern methods of communication, such as fax, telephone, internet, email, TV shopping and mail order.
- Under ***Regulation 7***, the seller is under an obligation to provide the purchaser with minimum information; for example, a description of the goods, the price, arrangements for payment and delivery, and the right to cancel the contract within 14 days.
- Under ***Regulation 8***, written confirmation must also be given.
- If these rules are not followed, the contract is not formed.

In addition, the ***Electronic Commerce Directive 2000/31*** was implemented in the UK by the ***Electronic Commerce (EC Directive) Regulations 2002***. ***Article 11*** states: 'where a purchaser in accepting a seller's offer is required to give his consent through technological means, such as clicking on an icon, the contract is concluded when the recipient of the service has received from the service provider, electronically, an acknowledgement of receipt of the recipient's acceptance'.

The postal rule

Where the terms of an agreement state or imply the ordinary post (mail) is the normal, anticipated or agreed form of acceptance, acceptance takes effect when the letter is **posted** and not when it is **received**.

Adams v Lindsell (1818)
The defendants offered to sell some goods to the plaintiffs and requested an acceptance by post. On 5 September, the plaintiffs sent a letter of acceptance as specified. On 8 September, the defendants sold the goods to a third party. They received the plaintiffs' letter of acceptance by post on 9 September. The plaintiffs successfully sued for breach of contract and the postal rule was established. It was held that a contract was formed when the plaintiffs posted their letter of acceptance on 5 September and therefore the defendants were in breach.

The postal rule has been extended to cover situations where the letter is never received and not just delayed.

Household Fire Insurance v Grant (1879)
A letter detailing the allotment of shares was never received but it was held that there was still a valid agreement once the letter had been posted.

The rationale behind these decisions is that the parties can protect themselves by stating in the offer that it will not be a binding contract until acceptance is received.

The courts have so far refused to extend the postal rule to situations involving telex and email. With these situations, acceptance must be received, rather than merely sent, as per the guidance in the EU directives.

STRETCH AND CHALLENGE

Consider some of the problems with the postal rule, both in general and in relation to modern methods of communication.

Intention to create legal relations

People make promises with one another every day. It is not practical or fair that every promise can be enforced in the courts. The law has therefore reached a compromise and offered a distinction between two situations in which agreement may be made:

- **Commercial and business agreements:** The presumption is in favour of the intention to create legal relations.
- **Social and domestic agreements:** The presumption is against the intention to create legal relations.

There are, of course, situations where the facts of the case will result in a decision against these presumptions, making the presumption **rebuttable**.

As we have seen, an offer must be a statement made with the intention of it becoming binding on acceptance. It is also essential that all the parties intend to create legal rules through the formation of the contract. The determination of the parties to create legal rules is an **objective** test: they need to establish whether **reasonable parties** to such an agreement would have had an intention to create legal relations.

The courts are not concerned with the **subjective** test (the state of mind of the parties involved). They will look at the facts **as a whole** to determine whether intention to create legal relations exists.

Commercial and business agreements

In commercial and business agreements, courts will presume an intention to create legal rules exists unless there is evidence to the contrary.

Edwards v Skyways Ltd (1969)
An airline (the defendant) had to make some pilots redundant. One pilot, Edwards (the plaintiff), was given notice of redundancy as per the terms of his contract. After discussions with trade unions, the airline agreed to make ex gratia (voluntary rather than legally obligated) redundancy payments to pilots, but they tried to avoid paying Edwards this payment following his redundancy. The defendant tried to claim that the ex gratia payment was not intended to be binding, but the judge held that, since the agreement to pay was made in commercial dealings, it could be presumed to be an intention to create legal relations.

The courts have also held that offers to give away free gifts to promote a business fall under the same binding presumption.

Esso Petroleum Company Ltd v Commissioners of Customs and Excise (1976)
Esso was giving away a free World Cup coin with every four gallons of petrol purchased at its pumps. Millions of these coins were distributed. Customs and Excise tried to claim that the coins were being 'sold' and it could therefore claim purchase tax from the transaction. The courts held that, since Esso was trying to gain extra business from the promotion of the free coins, there was an intention to be legally bound by the agreement.

The courts have, however, said that it is possible for the agreement not to contain an intention to be legally binding if this is specifically stated.

Jones v Vernon's Pools Ltd (1938)
Vernon's Pools (a type of lottery) inserted a clause onto its coupons (tickets) stating the transaction would be binding in honour only and would not give rise to any legal relationship. The plaintiff sent in his winning coupon but it was lost. He tried to make a claim for his winnings but failed because the insertion of the clause onto the coupon prevented any claim as it negated the intention to create legal relations.

Social and domestic agreements

Generally, social and domestic agreements cover family members, friends and workmates. The courts will presume that legal relations do not exist unless there is evidence to the contrary.

Balfour v Balfour (1919)
A husband, who lived abroad, promised his wife in England an income of £30 per month. When the wife petitioned for divorce, she tried to claim an ongoing £30 income. Her claim failed on the basis that their agreement was made when their marriage was cordial and that they never intended to sue on it. There was no intention to be legally bound and it was not appropriate for the courts to interfere in situations like this. The courts also commented that, if they opened up their jurisdiction to cover such situations, they would likely be inundated by similar claims.

An agreement with a friend is classed as a social and domestic agreement

The courts have stated that there is a **rebuttable presumption** that domestic agreements are not intended to create legal relations. This means that, if the courts can find evidence of intention, they may also find that a legally binding agreement has been made.

Merritt v Merritt (1970)
The spouses were already separated and made an agreement that the husband would pay the estranged wife an income if she paid the outstanding mortgage. The courts held this agreement to have intention to create legal relations.

Where the parties have exchanged money, the courts are likely to remove the presumption of intention to create legal relations.

Simpkins v Pays (1955)
A lodger had entered a competition with two members of the household in which he lived. Although the entry was in the householder's name, they each contributed equally to the cost on the understanding that they would share any winnings. When they won, the householder refused to share the winnings. The court found the lodger and the two others to have intention to create legal relations and the householder had to share the winnings equally.

Consideration

The evidence of an agreement alone does not give rise to a legally enforceable contract. A promise without consideration is a **gift**, while one made for consideration is a **bargain**. Both parties to the contract must provide consideration if they wish to sue on the contract. Consideration means that each side must promise to give or do something for the other. In ***Dunlop v Selfridge (1915)***, consideration was defined as: 'An act or forbearance of one party, or the promise thereof, is the price for which the promise of the other is bought, and the promise thus given for value is enforceable.'

As with offer and acceptance, certain **rules** need to be examined in relation to the issue of consideration.

The rules of consideration

Consideration must be sufficient but not adequate

Here, the courts are saying that the consideration provided need not match in value what is being offered by each party, but the consideration must be sufficient to be legally enforceable. This depends on what the parties were satisfied with when they made the agreement.

Thomas v Thomas (1942)
A man had expressed his desire that his wife be allowed to remain in his property on his death for a (very small) payment of £1 per year. The executors did this for some years but later tried to dispossess her. The courts found that the £1 nominal payment was 'sufficient' consideration.

However, in a contrasting case that seems to go against this principle, items that are apparently of no worth have been classed as amounting to valuable and sufficient consideration.

Chappell v Nestlé Company (1960)

To promote its chocolate bars, Nestlé had offered a record for sale, for a sum of money plus three chocolate wrappers. The owners of the copyright to the record tried to sue to prevent the promotion as they would receive fewer royalties if the record was offered in return for chocolate wrappers. They failed and the courts held that the wrappers, despite being thrown away on receipt, were valid and sufficient consideration.

STRETCH AND CHALLENGE

Research the cases of ***Tweddle and Atkinson (1861)***, which demonstrates that consideration must move from the promise, and ***Collins v Godfrey (1831)***, which demonstrates that the existing contractual duty does not constitute consideration,.

The consideration must move from the promise (the person to whom the promise is made)

This means that only a party that has provided consideration can sue or be sued on the contract.

Existing contractual duty does not constitute consideration

A party simply doing something that they are already bound to do in the contract is not sufficient to amount to consideration.

There are some exceptions to these rules, where courts have reached a different decision. For example, this could apply where a party makes a promise to pay extra and receives an extra benefit from the other party's agreement to complete what they were already bound to do under an existing agreement.

Williams v Roffey Bros and Nicholls Contractors Ltd (1990)

Having agreed to refurbish a block of flats, the main contractors (the defendants), fearing that a sub-contractor (the claimant/plaintiff) would fail to meet deadlines and so cause penalties to be incurred on the main contract, offered him extra payments for prompt completion. When the claimant sought to enforce this promise, a unanimous Court of Appeal said that, if the defendants doubted whether the claimant sub-contractor would perform his contractual obligation, then a further promise by him to perform that contract might be consideration for the defendants' offer of extra money as long as the offer was not obtained by the claimant's fraud or economic duress. There may have been no legal benefit to the defendants, as they were just getting the work they expected done, but they secured the practical benefit of getting the work completed on time without the trouble of hiring a new sub-contractor and risking the claimant's bankruptcy if they sought to recover the costs and penalties.

Part-payment of debt is not consideration

The general rule laid down in ***Pinnel's case (1602)*** says that part-payment of a debt can never satisfy the whole debt. Any agreement to accept part-payment in full satisfaction of the debt is unenforceable as there is no consideration. The creditor could always sue for the balance owed.

D and C Builders v Rees (1965)

D and C Builders was owed £482 from Mr Rees, for whom they had carried out some work. After D and C waited several months for the payment, Mr Rees offered £300 to settle the debt. Due to the financial difficulties of the builders, they accepted this smaller settlement. The builders then successfully sued for the remainder. The courts held that they were not prevented by their agreement to accept less and could sue for the remainder. The courts also found that they were pressurised into accepting less by Mr Rees taking advantage of their known poor financial situation.

Two exceptions to this general rule have been examined in the courts over the years, where the agreement to pay less than the debt owed can be enforced.

Exception 1: Where something different is added or happens that is sufficient consideration
This could be, for example, an agreement to accept a smaller sum on an earlier date or to accept a payment other than in money, or a lesser sum plus something other than money.

The exception also occurs where part-payment has been made by a third party as in the case of ***Hirachand Punamchand v Temple (1911)***.

Hirachand Punamchand v Temple (1911)
A father paid a smaller sum to a money lender than was owed to cover his son's debts. The money lender accepted it in full settlement but later sued for the balance. It was held that the part-payment was valid consideration, and that to allow the moneylender's claim would be a fraud on the father.

This case shows that the courts will find that a promise to accept a smaller sum in full satisfaction will be binding on a creditor, where the part-payment is made by a third party, on condition that the debtor is released from the obligation to pay the full amount.

Exception 2: The doctrine of promissory estoppel
This is an **equitable** doctrine and has its origins in the *obiter dicta* of Lord Denning in the case of ***Central London Property Trust Ltd v High Trees House Ltd (1947)***. The doctrine provides a means of making a promise binding, in the absence of consideration, in various circumstances. The principle is that, if someone (the promisor) makes a promise which another person acts on, the promisor is stopped (or **estopped**) from going back on the promise, even though the other person did not provide consideration.

For the successful operation of the doctrine, **five essential requirements** need to be established:

- **The need for an existing contractual relationship between the parties:** It is generally considered that promissory estoppel exists to modify existing contractual relationships rather than to make new ones.
- **Need for reliance on the promise:** An essential requirement is that the promisee has relied on the promise. In the **High Trees House** case, the lessees had relied upon the promise not to put the rent back up while the flats were half empty.
- **A 'shield and not a sword':** Established in the case of ***Combe v Combe (1951)***, this means the doctrine can be used as a defence to a claim and not as a ground for bringing an action.
- **It must be inequitable for the promisor to go back on the promise:** The claimant must have agreed to **waive** (give up) some of their rights under that contract (normally the amount of the debt that has been unpaid). It must also be unfair for the promisor to withdraw the promise. This also covers situations where the promissee has extracted the promise by taking advantage of the promissory estoppel (as in the case of ***D and C Builders v Rees (1966)***).
- **The doctrine is generally suspensory:** This means that the promise is normally time-limited (as in the ***High Trees House*** case, when the agreement to reduce the rent by half was binding until the flats became full again).

Past consideration is no consideration

This simply means that any consideration given cannot come before the agreement but must come after it. For example, Callum gives Gabi a lift to work in his van. On arrival Gabi promises to give Callum £10 towards the fuel. Callum cannot enforce this promise as his consideration, giving Gabi a lift, is past.

This is a common-sense rule as it prevents people from being forced into contracts on the basis of them being sent goods or services which they have not ordered. It is, essentially, a promise which has not been agreed to by both parties.

Re McArdle (1951)
The plaintiff had carried out work on a house in which his brothers and sister had a beneficial interest. He asked them to contribute to the costs he had incurred in the refurbishment, which they agreed to do. The courts held that this agreement was not enforceable as the work had been completed before any agreement to pay had been made. The promise to pay was not supported by any consideration. The work was therefore 'past' consideration and not valid.

Privity of contract

The basic rule is that a contract cannot confer rights or impose obligations arising under it on any person or agent except the parties to it. This means that only the parties to a contract should be able to sue or enforce their rights. It is called **privity of contract**.

Tweddle v Atkinson (1861)
A father and a father-in-law contracted to give the plaintiff a sum of money. Because the contract was made between the father and father-in-law, the plaintiff could not enforce the contract, even though he was to benefit from the money.

This rule can leave some parties without a remedy so, over the years, the courts have developed exceptions in both the common law and statute to enable third parties to have rights to a contract, and now the privity rule has limited application.

Contracts (Rights of Third Parties) Act 1999

This Act enables third parties to enforce rights under a contract, if the contract was made after 11 May 2000. ***Section 1*** of the Act allows a third party to enforce terms of a contract in one of two situations:

- ***s1(1)(a)***: if the third party is specifically mentioned in the contract as someone authorised to enforce the term; or
- ***s1(1)(b)***: if the contract purports to confer a benefit upon them.

Section 1(2) of the Act contains an exception to the second situation: that the third party cannot enforce their rights if 'it appears that the parties did not intend the term to be enforceable by the third party'.

Nisshin Shipping v Cleaves (2003)
Cleaves was a company of brokers which negotiated for shipowners to loan their ships to charterers. Although Cleaves were not a party to any of the contracts, the charterers had agreed to pay a commission to Cleaves. The court held that, under the 1999 Act, the clauses of the contract ***purported to confer a benefit*** *on the brokers, and therefore there was a presumption that there was an intention for that term to be enforceable.*

Other statutory exceptions

Other statutory exceptions have developed over the years and these can be used as an alternative to the 1999 Act, although the 1999 Act is covers most situations.

- ***Married Women's Property Act 1982*** allows the beneficiary to life insurance to enforce the terms, even though they are not parties to the contract.
- ***Road Traffic Act 1988*** requires all drivers to take out third-party liability insurance.
- ***Law of Property Act 1925*** stipulates that privity of contract does not apply to restrictive covenants relating to land.

Common law exceptions

There are also common law exceptions to the general privity of contract rule that have been developed for convenience and flexibility.

KEY TERMINOLOGY

privity of contract: a doctrine which allows the parties to a contract to sue each other, but does not allow a third party to sue.

STRETCH AND CHALLENGE

Research the case of ***BBC v HarperCollins (2010)*** which concerned The Stig from the TV show *Top Gear*. He wanted to release an autobiography, but there was a contract to keep his identity a secret. Why was The Stig allowed to publish an autobiography?

GRADE BOOST

Have a look at the case of ***Jackson v Horizon Holidays Ltd (1975)***, where Lord Denning ruled that the plaintiff was entitled to damages after a holiday went wrong, not just for himself but also for his family because he had entered into the contract for their benefit as well.

Collateral contracts

This is a contract between one party and two others, where the court will find that a collateral contract between the two others evades the privity rule only where there is an intention to create a collateral contract.

Shanklin Pier v Detel Products Ltd (1951)

The plaintiffs had employed contractors to paint their pier. They told the contractors to buy paint made by the defendants, who had said that the paint would last for seven years. It only lasted for three months. The court decided that the plaintiffs could sue the defendants on a collateral contract. They had provided consideration for the defendants' promise by entering into an agreement with the contractors, which entailed the purchase of the defendants' paint.

Agency

This refers to a situation where someone has made a contract on behalf of someone else. The **agent** may contract on behalf of his **principal** with a **third party**, thereby bringing the third party into a contractual relationship.

Scruttons Ltd v Midland Silicones (1962)

A contract (called a bill of lading) limited the liability of a shipping company to $500 per package. The defendant was a stevedore, a company that unloaded and loaded ships at a dock. It had contracted with the shipping company to unload the plaintiff's goods on the basis that they were to be covered by the exclusion clause in the bill of lading. The plaintiffs were ignorant of the contract between the shipping company and the stevedores. Owing to the stevedore's negligence, the cargo was damaged and, when sued, they pleaded the limitation clause in the bill of lading. The House of Lords held that the stevedore could not rely on the clause as there was no privity of contract between the plaintiffs and defendants.

Trusts

A trust is an equitable obligation to hold property on behalf of another.

Les Affreteurs Reunis v Leopold Walford (1919)

A broker (C) negotiated a charter party by which the shipowner (A) promised the charterer (B) to pay the broker a commission. It was held that B was trustee of this promise for C, who could thus enforce it against A.

Privity of contract: An evaluation

Advantages

✓ **Free will**: Parties should be free to make contracts with whoever they wish and should only incur rights and obligations when they have agreed to be part of a contract.

✓ **Unjust**: It is unjust to allow a party to sue if they themselves cannot be sued.

✓ **Restrictive**: The privity rule restricts the rights of the parties to modify or terminate the contract.

✓ **Indefinite liability**: The exceptions, particularly the ***Contracts (Rights of Third Parties) Act 1999***, expose contractors to indefinite liability by unlimited third parties.

Disadvantages

✗ **Extended litigation**: The privity rule could lead to a chain of contract claims.

✗ **Intention of the parties**: The privity rule does not necessarily reflect the intentions of the parties, who may wish a third party to have rights and obligations.

✗ **Lots of exceptions**: The sheer number of statutory and common law exceptions makes it legally complex.

Summary: Essential requirements of a contract

- **Offer** has to be distinguished from an **invitation to treat**
- Offer must be **communicated**
- Terms of offer must be **certain**
- Offer can be **withdrawn** at any time before acceptance
  - Offeror must **communicate the withdrawal** of the offer to the offeree
  - Communication of withdrawal of an offer can be by a reliable **third party**
- An offer can be **terminated** by:
  - Acceptance
  - Rejection
  - Revocation
  - Death
  - Counter-offer
  - Lapse of time
  - Failure of conditions
- **Acceptance** must be unconditional
- Acceptance must be **communicated** to offeror
- Offeree must be aware of the **existence** of the offer
- Communication of acceptance must be by an **authorised person**
- Acceptance can be **in any form** unless it is a requirement that it must be in a specific form
- **Instant communication**: acceptance is valid **once received**
- **Postal rule**: Acceptance takes effect when the **letter is posted**
- **Intention to create legal relations:**
  - **Social and domestic arrangements**: There is a presumption that an intention to create legal relations **does not** exist, but can be rebutted if there is money involved
  - **Commercial and business arrangements:** There is a presumption that an intention to create legal relations **does** exist
- Both parties must give **consideration** if they wish to sue on a contract
- Consideration must be **sufficient**, but need not be **adequate**
- Consideration must **move from the person** to whom the promise is made
- Existing contractual duty does not constitute consideration
- Part-payment of a debt is not consideration
- Past consideration is not consideration
- **Privity of contract:** Idea that only the parties to a contract have rights under it: ***Tweddle v Atkinson (1861), BBC v HarperCollins (2010)***
- ***Contracts (Rights of Third Parties) Act 1999*** enables third parties to enforce rights under a contract: ***Nisshin Shipping v Cleaves (2003)***
- Other statutory exceptions are ***Married Women's Property Act 1982, Road Traffic Act 1988, Law of Property Act 1925***
- **Common law exceptions:**
  - **Collateral contracts:** ***Shanklin Pier v Detel Products Ltd (1951)***
  - **Agency:** ***Scruttons Ltd v Midland Silicones (1962)***
  - **Trusts:** ***Les Affreteurs Reunis v Leopold Walford (1919)***
- **Advantages**
  - Free will
  - Unjust
  - Restrictive
  - Indefinite liability
- **Disadvantages**
  - Extended litigation
  - Intention of the parties
  - Lots of exceptions

Discharge of a contract

Spec reference	Key content	Assessment Objectives	Where does this topic feature on each specification/exam?
WJEC A Level 3.10: Discharge of contract including breach of contract, performance and frustration **Eduqas AS Level 2.1.3:** Discharge of contract **Eduqas A Level 2.1.5:** Discharge of contract	• Discharge by agreement: bilateral agreements, unilateral agreements • Discharge by breach: actual breach, anticipatory breach • Discharge by frustration: impossibility, illegality, commercial, radical change in circumstances • Discharge by performance: including performance of an entire obligation, partial performance, the contract as a series of entire obligations, a substantial performance of obligations, failure to meet a strict standard of performance and failure to meet a reasonable standard of care	**A01** Demonstrate knowledge and understanding of legal rules and principles **A02** Apply legal rules and principles to given scenarios in order to present a legal argument using appropriate legal terminology **A03** Analyse and evaluate legal rules, principles, concepts and issues	**WJEC A Level:** Unit 3 **WJEC A Level:** Unit 4 **Eduqas AS Level:** Component 2 and 3 **Eduqas A Level:** Component 2 and 3

The most obvious way a contract is discharged is when all parties have performed their obligations, but there are other ways for a contract to be discharged.

DISCHARGE OF CONTRACT			
PERFORMANCE	BREACH	AGREEMENT	BREACH

Discharge by agreement

This is where the parties agree to terminate a contract, so that one or both parties are released from their obligations. There are two types of discharge by agreement.

Bilateral discharge

The assumption is that both parties are to gain a fresh but different benefit from a new agreement.

Unilateral discharge

The benefit is only to be gained by one party, who is therefore trying to convince the other party to let them off the obligations arising under the original agreement.

Discharge by breach

This is where a party fails to perform an obligation, performs an obligation defectively or indicates in advance that they will not be performing an agreed obligation under a contract. There are two types of discharge by breach.

Actual breach

This is where a party to a contract does not perform their obligations under the contract at all.

STRETCH AND CHALLENGE

Research these key cases relating to actual breach.

- ***Platform Funding Ltd v Bank of Scotland plc (2008)***
- ***Pilbrow v Pearless de Rougemont & Company (1999)***
- ***Modahl v British Athletic Federation Ltd (1999)***
- ***Abramova v Oxford Institute of Legal Practice (2011)***

STRETCH AND CHALLENGE

Research these key cases relating to anticipatory breach.

- ***Frost v Knight (1872)***
- ***Avery v Bowden (1855)***
- ***Fercometal Sarl v Mediterranean Shipping Company (1989)***
- ***White and Carter Ltd v McGregor (1962)***

Anticipatory breach

This is where a party to a contract indicates in advance that they will not be performing their obligations as agreed.

Discharge by performance

This is where all obligations under the contract have been met, and the obligations should match the requirements of the contract exactly. ***Cutter v Powell (1795)*** found that, if a contract requires entire performance and a party fails to perform the contract in its entirety, they are entitled to nothing from the other party under the contract.

There are ways in which this rule can be limited.

STRETCH AND CHALLENGE

Research these key cases relating to substantial performance.

- ***Dakin & Company v Lee (1916)***
- ***Hoeing v Isaacs (1952)***
- ***Bolton v Mahadeva (1972)***

Substantial performance

If a party has done substantially what was required under the contract, then the doctrine of substantial performance can apply. The party can recover the amount appropriate to what has been done under the contract.

Severable contracts

A contract is severable when payment becomes due at various stages of performance, rather than in one lump sum at the end when the performance is completed; for example when major building work is taking place. In these cases, the price for each stage can be claimed when that stage is completed.

STRETCH AND CHALLENGE

Research the key case ***Sumpter v Hedges (1898)*** in relation to acceptance of part performance.

Acceptance of part performance

Where one of the parties has performed the contract but not completely, if the other side has shown a willingness to accept the part performed, then the strict rule in ***Cutter v Powell (1795)*** will not apply. An example could be when a service has not been fully carried out or where only half a delivery has been made.

STRETCH AND CHALLENGE

Research these key cases relating to prevention of performance.

- ***Planche v Colburn (1831)***
- ***Startup v Macdonald (1843)***

Prevention of performance

If the other party prevents a party from carrying out their obligations because of some act or omission, then the rule in ***Cutter v Powell (1795)*** cannot apply.

Discharge by frustration

This is where something happens, through no fault of the parties, to make the performance of the contract impossible. The contract is said to be frustrated.

Taylor v Caldwell (1863)

An action failed because performance of the contract had become impossible when a building where a concert was due to take place burnt down.

Frustration usually occurs in three main types of circumstance.

Impossibility

Performance has become impossible. This might be because of the destruction of something essential for the contract's performance, the death of either party, the unavailability of the parts or because the method of performance becomes impossible.

Illegality

This is where a change in the law after the contract is formed has made its performance illegal. This can often happen in times of war when laws may change without notice.

Commercial sterility

This is where the commercial purpose of the contract has disappeared as a result of the intervening event. This is also sometimes known as 'pointless'.

The ***Law Reform (Frustrated Contracts) Act 1943*** outlines the legal consequences when a contract has been frustrated. ***Section 1(2)*** stipulates that:

> *'all sums paid or payable to any party in pursuance of the contract before the time when the parties were so discharged shall, in the case of sums so to be paid, be recoverable from him as money received by him ceases to be payable'.*

This means that a person can recover money paid under a contract prior to the frustrating event. ***Section 1(3)*** stipulates that:

> *'where any party to the contract has obtained a valuable benefit, other than a payment of money before the time of discharge, this shall be recoverable from him by the said other party a sum not exceeding the value of the said benefit'.*

This means that where a party has obtained a valuable benefit other than money, the party receiving the benefit can be ordered to pay a just sum in return for the benefit.

STRETCH AND CHALLENGE

Research these key cases relating to discharge by frustration.

- ***Robinson v Davidson (1871)***
- ***Nickoll and Knight v Ashton Edridge & Company (1901)***
- ***Pioneer Shipping Ltd v BTP Tioxide Ltd (1981)***
- ***Metropolitan Water Board v Dick Kerr & Company Ltd (1918)***
- ***Krell v Henry (1903)***
- ***Herne Bay Steamboat Company v Hutton (1903)***

Summary: Discharge of contract

- **Discharge by agreement:** parties agree to terminate a contract
  - **Bilateral discharge:** Parties get a different benefit from a new agreement
  - **Unilateral discharge:** Benefit is only to be gained by one party
- **Discharge by breach:** A party fails to perform an obligation or does it defectively
  - **Actual breach:** A party does not perform their obligations at all: ***Platform Funding Ltd v Bank of Scotland plc (2008)***, ***Pilbrow v Pearless de Rougemont & Company (1999)***, ***Modahl v British Athletic Federation Ltd (1999)***, ***Abramova v Oxford Institute of Legal Practice (2011)***
  - **Anticipatory breach:** A party indicates in advance that they will not be performing their obligations: ***Frost v Knight (1872)***, ***Avery v Bowden (1855)***, ***Fercometal Sarl v Mediterranean Shipping Company (1989)***, ***White and Carter Ltd v McGregor (1962)***
- **Discharge by performance:** All obligations under the contract have been met: ***Cutter v Powell (1795)***
- **Substantial performance:** If a party has done substantially what was required under the contract: ***Dakin & Company v Lee (1916)***, ***Hoeing v Isaacs (1952)***, ***Bolton v Mahadeva (1972)***
- **Severable contracts:** Payment due at various stages of performance
- **Acceptance of part performance:** One of the parties has performed the contract but not completely but other party will accept this: ***Sumpter v Hedges (1898)***
- **Prevention of performance:** One party prevents the other from carrying out their obligations: ***Planche v Colburn (1831)***, ***Startup v Macdonald (1843)***
- **Discharge by frustration**: Performance of the contract becomes impossible: ***Taylor v Caldwell (1863)***
- Three reasons for frustration:
  - Impossibility
  - Illegality
  - Commercial sterility
- ***Law Reform (Frustrated Contracts) Act 1943*** outlines the legal consequences when a contract has been frustrated

Remedies: Contract

Spec reference	Key content	Assessment Objectives	Where does this topic feature on each specification/exam?
WJEC AS/A Level 3.1 Remedies including damages and equitable remedies **Eduqas AS Level 2.1.4:** Remedies **Eduqas A Level 2.1.6:** Remedies	• Common law remedy of damages: compensatory damages, tests of causation, remoteness of damage, mitigation of loss • Equitable remedies: rescission, specific performance, rectification of document, injunctions	**A01** Demonstrate knowledge and understanding of legal rules and principles **A02** Apply legal rules and principles to given scenarios in order to present a legal argument using appropriate legal terminology **A03** Analyse and evaluate legal rules, principles, concepts and issues	**WJEC AS/A Level:** Unit 3; Unit 4 **Eduqas AS Level:** Component 2 **Eduqas A Level:** Component 2; Component 3

KEY TERMINOLOGY

remedy: an award made by a court to the innocent party in a civil case to 'right the wrong'.
damages: an award of money that aims to compensate the innocent party for the financial losses they have suffered as a result of the breach.
equitable: fair.

STRETCH AND CHALLENGE

Explain the purpose of damages in tort.

STRETCH AND CHALLENGE

Research the cases of ***Jarvis v Swans Tours Ltd (1973)*** and ***Farley v Skinner (2001)*** and explain how they relate to damages for non-pecuniary losses.

A **remedy** is a 'solution' in a civil case; it is an award made by a court to the innocent party. Two types of remedy need to be considered:

1. Common law remedy of damages
2. **Equitable** remedies.

1. Common law remedy of damages

The common law remedy of **damages** is available 'as of right' if it is established that a contract is breached. Damages in contract law are an award of money to financially compensate the injured party. The purpose of damages in contract law is to put the victim, so far as it is possible and so far as the law allows, in the same position they would have been in had the contract not been broken but had been performed in the manner and at the time intended by the parties.

When a contract is breached, a party may suffer **pecuniary** (financial) loss or **non-pecuniary** loss.

Pecuniary losses

These are the financial losses that result from a breach of contract.

Non-pecuniary losses

These are other losses, such as mental distress, disappointment, hurt feelings or humiliation. Traditionally, these have not been compensated in contract law (unlike tort) but, recently, this rule has been relaxed for contracts which are specifically for pleasure, relaxation and peace of mind.

Limitations on the awarding of damages

Tests of causation

A person will only be liable for losses **caused** by their breach of contract. The defendant's breach must be an **effective** and intervening act between the breach of contract and the loss incurred to break the chain of causation (as in the case of ***Quinn v Burch Brothers (Builders) Ltd (1966)***).

Remoteness

Some losses are considered too remote (removed) from the breach of contract to be expected to be compensated by the defendant. A defendant will only be liable for such losses as were 'reasonably foreseeable' as arising from the breach. This was demonstrated in ***Hadley v Baxendale (1854)*** and later in ***Transfield Shipping v Mercator Shipping [The Achilleas] (2008).***

Mitigation of loss

Claimants are under a duty to **mitigate their loss**; they cannot recover damages for losses which could have been avoided if they had taken reasonable steps. For example, in ***Pilkington v Wood (1953)***, the claimant (plaintiff) sued his conveyancing solicitor for not noticing that his house had a defective title, making it hard to sell at the original value. Claimants cannot just sit back and allow losses to increase. If there is something they can do to reduce the impact or loss, and there are reasonable steps they can take, then they are under an obligation to do so.

KEY TERMINOLOGY

mitigation of loss: lessening or reducing a loss.

Calculating loss

Once it has been established that the defendant is liable for the loss, the court needs to calculate the sum of damages owed by the defendant to the claimant. Claimants choose to base their claim on either **loss of expectation** or **reliance loss.** It is more common to base the claim on loss of expectation; claimants cannot claim under both.

Loss of expectation

If this is the basis for the claim, the courts will aim to put claimants in the position they would have been in had the breach not occurred. The claimant would have expected a certain result from the contract so the damages will compensate for the loss of this expectation, as in ***Golden Victory (2007)***.

Ways to quantify the loss of expectation may include the following:

1. The difference in value between the goods or services of the quality indicated in the contract and those actually delivered, where they are of inferior value.
2. The difference between the contract price and the price obtained in an 'available market' (such as for a car, as in ***Charter v Sullivan (1957)***).
3. Loss of profit.
4. Loss of a chance, for example of employment, as in ***Chaplin v Hicks (1911)***.

Reliance loss

Where this is the basis for calculating damages, the courts will seek to put the claimant in the position they were in before the contract was made, as in ***Anglia Television Ltd v Reed (1972)***.

Equitable remedies

Unlike common law remedies, which are 'as of right', equitable remedies are **discretionary.**

KEY TERMINOLOGY

discretionary: it is a choice of the court whether to award or not.

Where common law remedies are inadequate to compensate the claimant, there are, instead, equitable remedies. They are provided at the discretion of the court and take into account the behaviour of both parties and the overall justice of the case.

There are four main equitable remedies:

- injunction
- specific performance
- rescission
- rectification.

Injunction

An injunction normally compels the defendant not to do a something in particular (called a **prohibitory injunction**). In ***Warner Brothers Pictures Inc v Nelson (1937)***, an actress was initially prevented from working for any company other than Warner Brothers for two years but was eventually permitted other, non-acting, employment. However, where the action has already taken place, the court may instead order a **mandatory injunction** compelling the party to do something. This would normally be an order that the defendant take action to restore the situation to that which existed before the defendant's breach.

Specific performance

An order of specific performance compels one side of the contract to perform their obligations. This is a rarely awarded remedy and is only awarded where damages would be inadequate (***Beswick v Beswick (1968)***), the contract has been made fairly (***Walters v Morgan (1861)***) and the award of specific performance would not cause great hardship or unfairness for the defendant (***Patel v Ali (1984)***). This supports the equitable nature of specific performance as a remedy.

Rescission

This remedy places parties back in their pre-contractual position. If this is not possible, rescission is not granted. It is mainly granted as a remedy in misrepresentation cases. This is known as *restitutio in integrum*. ***Clarke v Dickson (1858)*** is the most quoted case on this.

Rectification

This is an equitable remedy under which a written document can be altered to correct a mistake. It will be granted when a written agreement contradicts the actual agreement made by the parties. ***Craddock Brothers Ltd v Hunt (1923)***.

Summary: Remedies: Contract

- **Common law remedy of damages:** 'As of right'
- **Financial compensation**: Aims to put the victim, so far as possible and the law allows, in the same position had the contract been performed
- **Pecuniary losses**: Financial losses resulting from the breach of contract
- **Non-pecuniary losses**: Not traditionally awarded but now relaxed for contracts for pleasure, relaxation and peace of mind: ***Jarvis v Swans Tours Ltd (1973)***
- **Limitations**:
  - Causation: ***Quinn v Burch Bros (Builders) Ltd (1966)***
  - Remoteness: ***Transfield Shipping v Mercator Shipping [The Achilleas] (2008)***
  - Duty to mitigate loss: ***Pilkington v Wood (1953)***
- **Calculating loss:**
  1. Loss of expectation: ***Golden Victory (2007)***
  2. Reliance loss: ***Anglia Television Ltd v Reed (1972)***
- **Equitable remedies are discretionary:**
  1. Injunctions
  2. Specific performance
  3. Rescission
  4. Rectification

LAW OF TORT

Rules of tort

Spec reference	Key content	Assessment Objectives	Where does this topic feature on each specification/exam?
WJEC AS Level **2.1:** Rules and theory of the law of tort **Eduqas AS Level** **2.2.2:** Rules and theory of the law of tort **Eduqas A Level** **2.2.1:** Rules and theory of the law of tort	• Origins of the law of tort; categories of tort; theory in the law of tort • Definition of tort • Concept of fault liability versus strict liability • Economic justification of tort; corrective justice • Retributive justice • Criticisms of the tort system	**AO1** Demonstrate knowledge and understanding of legal rules and principles **AO2** Apply legal rules and principles to given scenarios in order to present a legal argument using appropriate legal terminology **AO3** Analyse and evaluate legal rules, principles, concepts and issues	**WJEC AS Level:** Unit 2 **Eduqas AS Level:** Component 2 **Eduqas A Level:** Component 2 Section B **Eduqas A Level:** Component 3 Section B

What is a tort?

A **tort** is a **civil wrong** committed by one individual against another. There are various torts covering a wide range of situations such as claims by:

- an injured road user
- a patient injured by a negligent doctor
- someone who has suffered due to excessive noise
- someone injured when visiting a premises
- a celebrity libelled by a magazine
- a landowner whose land has been trespassed on.

The tort of **negligence** is most commonly associated with this area of law but there are several other torts.

A claimant to a tort action is normally seeking some form of **remedy**. This is usually in the form of **damages** (monetary compensation) paid by the **tortfeasor** in order to compensate for the tort. However, there are other remedies available such as well as or instead of damages, such as an **injunction**.

To win some tort cases, the victim needs to prove that the tort has caused some harm; however, some torts are actionable **per se** (in themselves). In these cases, the victim only has to prove that the relevant tort has been committed, not that any damage has been done. An example is the tort of **trespass**, where the landowner can claim damages from somebody trespassing on their land, even though no harm has been done by the **trespasser**.

GRADE BOOST

The word 'tort' is French for 'wrong'. A person who commits a tort is referred to as a **tortfeasor**.

KEY TERMINOLOGY

tort: a civil wrong committed by one individual against another, such as injury caused by negligence.
tortfeasor: someone who has committed a tort.
remedy: what the claimant is seeking to 'right the wrong'.
trespasser: a visitor who has no permission or authority to be on the occupier's land.

Competing theories surround the purpose of the remedy in the law of tort. On the one hand, **corrective** (or **restorative**) **justice** supports the view that the purpose of damages in tort is to 'right the wrong'. It provides a civil recourse to put things back as they were, as far as this is possible.

On the other hand, **retributive justice,** more commonly associated with the criminal law, can also play a role. This theory is associated with punishment, with the intention of dissuading the defendant and others from future wrongdoing. In the law of tort, the knowledge that one might be sued for a tortious act might serve as a deterrent or encourage a higher standard of care when performing certain acts. However, the fact that insurance premiums rather than the defendant's savings are, in many cases, used to pay compensation means that the deterrent value is reduced, despite the knowledge that premiums may increase.

The difference between a tort and a crime

A tort is a **private law** action committed against an individual (for example, negligence or nuisance), whereas a crime is a **public law** action committed against the state (for example, theft, grievous bodily harm or murder). The aim of a tort action is to **compensate** the victim for the harm done, whereas the aim of a criminal prosecution is to **punish** the wrongdoer.

STRETCH AND CHALLENGE

There are also differences between tort and contract law. Research what these are.

There are some areas of overlap; for example, high-level damages in tort arguably 'punish' the defendant and there are also provisions in criminal law for the wrongdoer to financially compensate the victim. In some areas, one incident may result in both a criminal prosecution and proceedings for tort; for example, where a victim suffers injury as a result of someone else's dangerous driving.

Fault-based liability and strict liability

The general principle in law is that there can be **no liability without fault.** Liability in tort is based on the idea that the defendant is, in some way, at fault. Fault has been given a wide meaning in the law of tort and includes situations like **negligence** (where a defendant's behaviour has fallen below an accepted standard), intentionally causing harm, and **trespass** (where the defendant is infringing another's rights). Fault-based liability deters others as they are aware that, if found to be at fault, they may be liable to pay compensation.

STRETCH AND CHALLENGE

Research ***Rylands v Fletcher (1868)*** and explain why it is significant in tort law.

Some torts, known as **strict liability torts,** can be committed without the defendant being at fault in any way. These have the potential to be unfair as the defendant can be liable to pay damages even though they may not have been able to prevent the harm. The case of ***Rylands v Fletcher (1868)*** is an example of a strict liability tort.

Strict liability offences also exist in criminal law and are contrary to the presumption of mens rea being required for the commission of a criminal offence. Find some case examples of these.

Justifications for tort law

- The victim can be compensated for the damage caused by the wrongdoer. They can be put back in the position they would have been in (as far as possible) had the wrong not occurred (corrective or restorative justice).
- Individuals are deterred from committing acts or omissions that might hurt others, in the knowledge that they may have to pay compensation. Tort law aims to make people and companies be more careful with their acts or omissions and therefore make society safer.

- In the absence of a tort system, people who suffer injuries would be unable to claim compensation so instead may have to claim social security benefits, at the cost of the taxpayer.
- It is supported by the concept of the rule of law. For instance, a claimant unlawfully detained by the police can bring an action for unlawful imprisonment.
- Although the law of tort is largely based on corrective justice, there are elements of retributive justice. For example, in some circumstances a court can award damages to punish the tortfeasor in the form of exemplary damages.

Criticisms of tort law

- Some people believe that tort law is creating a compensation culture.
- Claims of negligence brought against state bodies such as the NHS still cost the taxpayer money.
- There is a lack of equality in the tort system. Many potential claimants may not have the financial means to bring an action in tort, and legal aid is rarely available for tort.
- Strict liability torts, as in the case of ***Rylands v Fletcher (1868)***, have been criticised for not requiring fault on the part of the tortfeasor.
- The system may be abused by people making fraudulent claims.

SUMMARY: Rules of tort

- A **tort** is a **civil wrong** (private law action) committed by one individual against another
- The aim of a tort action is to **compensate** the victim for the harm done, not to **punish** the wrongdoer
- A person who commits a tort is a **tortfeasor**
- A claimant to a tort action normally seeks a **remedy** such as damages or an injunction
- **Corrective** or **restorative justice** provides a civil recourse to put things back as they were, as far as possible
- **Retributive justice** is more common in criminal law, when the defendant is punished, but can apply to tort, e.g. exemplary damages
- **Fault-based liability: No liability without fault**, e.g. negligence or trespass
- **Strict liability torts** can be committed without the defendant being at fault: ***Rylands v Fletcher (1868)***
- **Criticisms of tort law:**
  - May create a compensation culture
  - Claims against state bodies cost the taxpayer
  - Only those who can afford it bring action
  - Strict liability torts do not require fault
  - May encourage fraudulent claims

Liability in negligence

Spec reference	Key content	Assessment Objectives	Where does this topic feature on each specification/exam?
WJEC AS Level **2.2:** Liability in Negligence for injury to people and damage to property **Eduqas AS Level** **2.2.2:** Liability in Negligence for injury to people and damage to property **Eduqas A Level** **2.2.2:** Liability in Negligence for injury to people and damage to property	• Duty of care: people and damage to property; neighbour principle; Caparo test • Breach of duty: the reasonable man; the objective standard of care • Causation of damage: 'but for' test; legal causation; foreseeability; effect of an intervening act; remoteness of damage • Psychiatric injury: primary and secondary victims	**AO1** Demonstrate knowledge and understanding of legal rules and principles **AO2** Apply legal rules and principles to given scenarios in order to present a legal argument using appropriate legal terminology **AO3** Analyse and evaluate legal rules, principles, concepts and issues	**WJEC AS Level:** Unit 2 **Eduqas AS Level:** Component 2 **Eduqas A Level:** Component 2 Section B **Eduqas A Level:** Component 3 Section B

There are many types of negligence

The tort of negligence is the most common tort. It covers a wide range of situations including medical negligence, road traffic accidents and faulty workmanship. Someone is negligent if they act carelessly to another person to whom they are legally obliged to act carefully, and if the carelessness causes the other person to suffer some harm or loss.

Negligence essentially protects against three different types of harm:

1. personal injury
2. damage to property
3. economic loss.

The elements of negligence

For a claimant to succeed in a negligence case against a defendant, three elements need to be proved:

1. The defendant owes the claimant a **duty of care.**
2. The defendant was in **breach of that duty of care.**
3. The claimant suffered **damage** as a result of the breach and that damage was **not too remote**.

Element 1: Duty of care

Only those who are owed a duty of care by a defendant will be able to claim a remedy for negligence. The tort of negligence has developed through case law and one of the first landmark rulings on the matter was in ***Donoghue v Stevenson (1932)***.

Donoghue v Stevenson (1932)

Mrs Donoghue's friend bought her bottle of ginger beer in a café. She drank some of it but then discovered a decomposing snail in the bottle. As a result, she suffered gastroenteritis. Mrs Donoghue could not sue the café as she had not bought the drink herself; therefore, she brought an action against the manufacturer of the ginger beer for not ensuring the bottles were cleaned properly. In deciding whether the manufacturer owed Mrs Donoghue a duty of care, the House of Lords established the **neighbour principle**. *Lord Atkin said that the manufacturers owed a duty of care to 'anyone who could be affected by their actions' (their neighbours). Therefore, they did owe Mrs Donoghue a duty of care and her claim succeeded.*

Lord Atkin said: 'You must take reasonable care to avoid acts or omissions which you can reasonably foresee would be likely to injure your neighbours'. He defined 'neighbour' as 'anyone who would be so directly affected by your act that you ought reasonably to have them in your contemplation'.

The neighbour principle has since been used in situations such as a lift repairer owing a duty of care to anyone using their lift and a solicitor owing a duty of care to a client who suffers financially following the negligent drafting of a legal document.

The basic concept of the neighbour principle was redefined in the key case of ***Caparo Industries plc v Dickman (1990)***. This is known as the **Caparo test (**or **incremental approach)** and is considered to be wider than the neighbour test. The test consists of three elements. It has to be shown that:

1. the damage was **foreseeable**
2. there is a sufficiently **proximate relationship** between the claimant and defendant
3. it is **just, fair and reasonable** to impose a duty of care.

Lord Bridge, in the Caparo case, also suggested that the law of the duty of care should develop on an **incremental basis** as new situations arise rather than assuming it exists in all situations.

Each of the elements of the Caparo test will now be considered in turn.

1. Foreseeability

For a duty of care to exist, it must be reasonably foreseeable that damage or injury would be caused to the particular defendant or to a class of people to which they belong (rather than people in general).

Kent v Griffiths (2000)

A doctor called for an ambulance to take a patient suffering from a severe asthma attack to hospital immediately. The ambulance failed to arrive within a reasonable time and there was no good reason for the delay. The patient suffered a heart attack which would not have happened if the ambulance had arrived on time. It was held that it was reasonably foreseeable that the claimant would suffer some harm from this delay.

2. Proximity

Proximity means 'closeness' in terms of physical space, time or relationship. This test is quite similar to the 'neighbour' test. If there is not a sufficiently proximate relationship between the claimant and defendant, the defendant cannot reasonably be expected to have the claimant in mind since they are not likely to be affected by the defendant's acts or omissions.

GRADE BOOST

In ***Hill v Chief Constable of West Yorkshire (1988)***, The family of a victim of the serial killer, the Yorkshire Ripper, brought a claim for **negligence** against the police for failing to catch the killer quickly enough. They argued that the police had been negligent in their duty. The court held that there was no duty of care, because it would not be 'fair and reasonable' to impose one on a police force for this omission.

KEY TERMINOLOGY

foreseeable: events the defendant should be able to have predicted could happen.

proximate relationship: (in tort law) how close the defendant and victim are physically or emotionally.

STRETCH AND CHALLENGE

Look up the case of ***Haley v London Electricity Board (1965)***. What damage was reasonably foreseeable?

KEY CASE

Bourhill v Young (1943)

The claimant, a pregnant Mrs Bourhill, was descending from a bus when she heard a motor accident. She did not actually see it but later saw blood on the road and suffered shock and her baby was still-born. Although it was reasonably foreseeable that someone would suffer harm as a result of the defendant's negligent driving, injury to the specific claimant was not foreseeable as she was not in the immediate vicinity of the accident and she only heard but did not see the accident. Her action therefore failed.

STRETCH AND CHALLENGE

Look up the case of ***McLoughlin v O'Brien (1983)*** on the issue of proximity. In what other ways can there be a 'proximate' relationship?

There needs to be a sufficiently proximate relationship between the claimant and defendant to claim damages

3. It is just, fair and reasonable to impose a duty of care

This is also known as the **policy test**, as judges are able to limit the extent of the tort through judicial discretion. One of the main reasons for this is the **floodgates argument**, where there is the risk of opening up a potential claim to a huge number of claimants. An American judge, Benjamin N Cardozo, referred to this danger when he warned of 'liability in an indeterminate amount for an indeterminate time to an indeterminate class'.

Mulcahy v Ministry of Defence (1996)

The claimant was a soldier who had served in the Gulf War, where he had suffered damage to his hearing. The Court of Appeal held that, although both factors of foreseeability and proximity were present, the facts required it to consider this a policy issue. The Ministry of Defence did not, therefore, owe a duty of care to servicemen in such battlefield situations.

Alcock v Chief Constable of South Yorkshire Police (1991)

This case involved people who suffered 'nervous shock' as a result of witnessing the Hillsborough stadium disaster, when 95 people were killed as a result of a crush. It was decided that it would not be just, fair and reasonable to impose a duty of care on the police in respect of a claimant who was at the other end of the ground to the crush, in which his brother-in-law was involved.

GRADE BOOST

In ***Hill (1988)***, it was held that Part 3 of the Caparo test would not be satisfied for members of the police in respect of their function of investigating and preventing crime.
In ***Robinson v Chief Constable of West Yorkshire (2018)***, Elizabeth Robinson, an elderly woman, was knocked over and injured when she was caught up in the arrest of a suspected drug dealer. At first, her claim for negligence against the police failed because of the Hill immunity, even though the judge ruled that the police had acted negligently.
In the **Court of Appeal**, her claim failed on Parts 2 and 3 of the Caparo test.
However, the **Supreme Court** drew a distinction between positive acts and omissions of the police. Mrs Robinson won her claim on the basis that a police officer is liable in negligence where the injury results from a negligent action by a police officer, as long as that injury was a reasonably foreseeable consequence. They concluded that Part 3 of the Carparo test would be satisfied where a public body's action risks causing harm which would not otherwise have existed.

Element 2: Breach of duty of care

Once a duty of care has been established, it needs to be proved that it has been **breached**: in other words, that the defendant has not fulfilled their duty of care. The standard of care to be expected is that of the **reasonable man,** which assumes that a reasonable person is 'average', not perfect. This is generally an objective test, asking 'What would a reasonable person have foreseen in this particular situation?' rather than 'What did this particular defendant foresee in this particular situation?' However, it has been developed through case law to take account of special standards of care for defendants with a professional skill, for example (see below), and other relevant factors such as the magnitude of risk.

The reasonable man test come from ***Alderson B in Blyth v Birmingham Waterworks (1865)***, which defined it as 'the omission to do something which a reasonable man would do, or doing something which a prudent and reasonable man would not do.'

For example, in the case of ***Nettleship v Weston (1971)***, when a learner driver's passenger was injured when she crashed, it was established that a learner driver is expected to meet the same standard as a qualified and competent driver.

The courts have established various tests in determining if a defendant has breached their duty of care.

i. Degree of probability that harm will be done

If the risk is very small then it may be decided that the defendant is not in breach. Care must also be taken in respect of a risk where it is reasonably foreseeable that harm or injury may occur.

Bolton v Stone (1951)

The claimant had been hit by a cricket ball whilst standing on the road outside the cricket ground. In 35 years, a cricket ball had only been hit out of the ground on six occasions and no one had ever been injured. In addition, the wicket was 100 yards from the road and there was a 17-foot-high fence between the ground and the road. It was held that the defendant was not in breach of his duty of care.

ii. The magnitude of likely harm

In this test, the courts consider not only the risk of harm but also how serious the injury could foreseeably be.

GRADE BOOST

What would the impact be of a culture where the emergency services can be sued? Is it in the public interest for police to owe a duty of care to individuals?
Research ***Michael v Chief Constable of South Wales Police (2015)***. What was Lord Keith's position in relation to the application of tort to police officers?

Paris v Stepney Borough Council (1951)

In this case, Paris was a mechanic who was blind in one eye. His employers were aware of this, yet failed to provide him with protective goggles for his work. He was blinded in his 'good' eye by a piece of metal that went in to it during his work. His employers tried to argue that it was not usual to provide goggles for such activities but it was counter-argued that, as they were aware he was blind in one eye, they should have taken greater care of his safety than for employees without that disability. The magnitude of potential harm was greater for Paris so the greater risk to the claimant meant that more precautions than normal should have been taken. The employer was found to be liable.

iii. The cost and practicality of preventing risk

With this test, the court is looking at whether the defendant could have taken precautions against the risk. If the cost of taking such precautions to eliminate the risk is disproportionate to the extent of the risk itself, the defendant will not be held liable.

Latimer v AEC Ltd (1953)

The owner of a factory used sawdust to reduce the effects of a recent flood but the factory floor remained slippery and, as a result, an employee fell and was injured. It was held that there was no breach of duty as the only way to have avoided the risk was to close the factory altogether, which was not proportionate to the level of risk involved.

iv. Potential benefits of the risk

There are some situations where the risk has a potential benefit for society.

Daborn v Bath Tramways (1946)

The claimant was injured after being hit by a left-hand drive ambulance without indicators during wartime. The Court of Appeal held that a lower standard of care than usual applied because the ambulance driver was acting in the public good, and it would have been unreasonably expensive to have converted the ambulance to right-hand drive.

Lord Justice Asquith said: 'If all the trains in this country were restricted to a speed of five miles an hour, there would be fewer accidents, but our national life would be intolerably slowed down. The purpose to be served, if sufficiently important, justifies the assumption of abnormal risk.'

However, the nature of the work of the emergency services does not make them immune from negligence claims, as can be seen in the case of ***Armsden v Kent Police (2000)***, when a driver was killed in a collision with the defendant's police car. The police car did not have its siren on and was driving fast to attend an incident when it collided with the other car when approaching a junction with a side road. The Court of Appeal found the driver of the police car had breached of his duty of care by failing to use the siren.

STRETCH AND CHALLENGE

What did the courts say regarding the standard of care to be expected where the defendant is exercising special skill or knowledge, as in the case of ***Bolam v Friern Hospital Management Committee (1957)***?

Special characteristics of the defendant

In some situations, the standard is not a purely objective one and the courts are able to take into account certain special characteristics of the defendant. Interestingly, in the case of drivers, the standard is that of the ordinary, normal driver (ignoring their experience and years qualified). This was confirmed in the case of ***Nettleship v Weston (1971;*** see above).

Professional persons

Where the defendant has a professional skill, the court will expect them to show that they have the degree of competence usually expected of a typical skilled member of that profession. This means, for example, that a GP will only be expected to exercise the normal level of skill of a GP, not that of a senior consultant or surgeon.

A defendant with a professional skill, where relevant to the case, is expected to only demonstrate the normal level of skills for their job

Children

Where the defendant is a child, the standard of care is that of an ordinarily careful and reasonable child of the same age.

Mullin v Richards (1998)

Two 15-year-olds were fighting with plastic rulers. One ruler broke and fragments blinded one of the girls in one eye. It was held that their behaviour was reasonable for their age, so the defendant was not negligent.

Element 3: Resulting damage

There has to be some sort of damage (e.g. physical injury or damage to property) resulting from the defendant's negligence. The claimant must be able to prove both that the damage was **caused** by the defendant's breach of duty and that the damage was not too **remote**; that it was reasonably foreseeable. This can be broken down into two issues:

- causation
- remoteness of damage.

Causation

Causation is decided using the **'but for' test**: 'But for (i.e. if it wasn't for) the defendant's breach of duty, would damage or injury have occurred?'

KEY TERMINOLOGY

causation (or chain of causation): the connection of the negligent act with the corresponding result.

KEY CASE

Barnett v Chelsea & Kensington Hospital Management Committee (1968)

The claimant's husband attended the defendant's hospital, complaining of severe stomach pain and vomiting. The doctor in A&E refused to examine him and he was sent home with the advice to see his own doctor. Some hours later, he died of arsenic poisoning. The defendant (the A&E doctor) clearly owed the deceased a duty of care and was also in breach by failing to examine him. However, the doctor was held not liable because the evidence showed that, by the time he attended the hospital, the man would have died anyway and the doctor could not have done anything to save him. As the deceased would have died regardless of the breach, the hospital was held not to be the cause of his death.

Remoteness of damage

It must also be established that the damage was not too **remote:** that it is not too removed from the defendant's negligence. The test for remoteness is whether there is a direct, foreseeable causation.

Wagon Mound (No. 1) (1961)

The defendant, a ship owner, negligently discharged fuel from his ship into Sydney Harbour. The oil drifted across to a wharf where welding works were taking place. The claimants were advised that there was no risk of this heavy oil catching fire on the water and as a result carried on welding but the oil did ignite, damaging the claimants' property. On appeal, it was held that the defendants were not liable for the damage to the claimant's property because the major damage to the property caused by the ignition of the oil was too remote from the original discharge of oil.

Another issue to consider is **foreseeability of damage**. This relates to the kind, and extent, of damage suffered. For example, a defendant may still be liable even if the extent of the injury was not foreseen. This can be seen in the case of ***Smith v Leech Brain & Co (1962)*** where the defendant was found liable for the death of a man who was burned on the lip by hot metal due to the defendant's negligence. The burn caused cancer and the man died. This case also illustrates the legal principle of the **'thin skull test'**, which states that the defendant must take the victim as they find them as regards their physical characteristics. This means that the defendant will be liable where injuries to the claimant are more serious than might have been anticipated because of factors which are particular to the victim.

GRADE BOOST

The case of ***Wagon Mound (No. 1) (1961)*** overruled a previous case (***Re Polemis & Furness, Withy & Co Ltd (1921)***) in that the defendant would be liable for all damage that was a direct consequence of their breach of duty. This test was considered too wide and would have the potential for too many claims to succeed.

STRETCH AND CHALLENGE

Look up the cases of ***Hughes v Lord Advocate (1963)*** and ***Jolley v Sutton (2000)*** and explain how they illustrate the issue of foreseeability.

Intervening causes

Sometimes the law will not impose liability for negligence if there is an intervening cause that breaks the chain of causation; for example, a natural event or the actions of a third party. The phrase **'res ipsa loquitur'** (Latin for 'the facts speak for themselves') is associated with this idea.

Where, in negligence cases, it is clear that the harm could not have arisen unless the defendant was negligent, the court may be prepared to infer that the defendant was negligent without hearing detailed evidence of what was or was not done. A classic example of a res ipsa loquitur situation is leaving a train door open as it departs the station, as in ***Gee v Metropolitan Railway (1873)***.

Psychiatric injury: Primary and secondary victims

Psychiatric damage is injury to the mind rather than the body; it can also be referred to as nervous shock. To claim damages, a claimant must show, using medical evidence, that they have a recognised psychiatric injury that goes beyond normal grief or distress.

Primary victims

A primary victim has either suffered physical injury as a result of another person's negligence or suffered a psychiatric injury where it was reasonably foreseeable that they could have been physically injured as a result of another person's negligence; for example, a person who is involved in a workplace accident and is not physically injured but develops a serious psychiatric condition.

Secondary victims

A secondary victim has suffered psychiatric injury as a result of another person's negligence but was not exposed to danger. Several other conditions need to be met to be classified as a secondary victim.

A case that demonstrates the law surrounding secondary victims relates to the **Hillsborough disaster** in 1989.

Following the Hillsborough disaster, ten claimants brought a case against the South Yorkshire Police.

Alcock v Chief Constable of South Yorkshire Police (1992)

The claimants were attempting to claim for nervous shock resulting in psychiatric injury which they claimed had been caused by the experience of witnessing the disaster. To claim, they had to be classed as secondary victims. Robert Alcock, one of the claimants, was in a different stand to where the disaster unfolded but witnessed distressing scenes. On leaving the ground, he went to meet his brother-in-law, who did not arrive. Alcock then had to identify his brother-in-law's heavily bruised body in the mortuary. The other claimants had similar experiences.

It was held that the claimant must usually show a sufficiently **proximate** *relationship to the victim. This is often described as a* **'close tie of love and affection'**. *Such ties are presumed to exist between parents and children, spouses and fiancés. This means other relations, including between siblings (e.g. brothers) must prove their ties of love and affection. Robert Alcock had lost a brother-in-law and the court held that there was no evidence of particularly close ties of love of affection. It was held that it must be proved that it was reasonably foreseeable that the claimant would suffer psychiatric damage. Therefore, the case did not succeed.*

GRADE BOOST

Research the Hillsborough disaster. Where did it take place? What happened and do you think anyone was negligent in causing the disaster?

Memorial to those who died in at Hillsborough

STRETCH AND CHALLENGE

Research what happened to the other claimants in the Alcock case and what this meant for tort law.

GRADE BOOST

When applying the law to a problem question, take each element of the offence and apply to the problem question. Work your way methodically through the list of elements for liability in negligence, applying them to the scenario and remembering to use appropriate legal authority throughout. Also make sure you apply each element of a relevant test (e.g. the Caparo test).

Reasonable foreseeability depends upon establishing a sufficiently proximate relationship. The closer the tie between the plaintiff and the victim, the more likely it is that they would succeed in showing that the psychiatric damage was reasonably foreseeable.

In addition, ***Alcock v Chief Constable of South Yorkshire Police (1992)*** held that, to be a secondary victim, a claimant must witness the event with their own unaided senses, hear the event in person or view its immediate aftermath: the claimant must be in close physical proximity to the event. Therefore, those who witness such an event on television, hear it on the radio or are informed about it from a third party are unlikely to be classified as secondary victims. This applied to some of the other claimants in the case.

The House of Lords did hint that a person with no sufficiently proximate relationship may be classed as a secondary victim in exceptional circumstances. Lord Keith said:

'The case of a bystander unconnected with the victims of an accident is difficult. Psychiatric injury to him would not ordinarily, in my view, be within the range of reasonable foreseeability, but could not perhaps be entirely excluded from it if the circumstances of a catastrophe occurring very close to him were particularly horrific.'

Summary: Liability in negligence

- **Duty of care:** Neighbour test: ***Donoghue v Stevenson (1932)***
- **Duty of care:** Caparo (incremental) test: ***Caparo Industries plc v Dickman (1990)***
  - Damage foreseeable: ***Kent v Griffiths (2000)***
  - Proximity: ***Bourhill v Young (1943)***
  - Just, fair and reasonable: ***Mulcahy v Ministry of Defence (1996)***
- **Breach of duty of care:**
  - Standard of care: reasonable man: ***Nettleship v Weston (1971)***
  - Probability of harm: ***Bolton v Stone (1951)***
  - Magnitude of likely harm: ***Paris v Stepney Borough Council (1951)***
  - Cost and practicality of preventing risk: ***Latimer v AEC (1953)***
  - Potential benefits of risk: ***Daborn v Bath Tramways (1946)***
- **Special characteristics** of defendant, e.g. professional persons, children: ***Mullins v Richards (1998)***
- Resulting damage **not too remote**:
  - Causation: 'but for' test: ***Barnett v Chelsea & Kensington Hospital Management Committee (1968)***
  - Remoteness of damage: Is the loss a reasonably foreseeable consequence of the defendant's negligence? ***Wagon Mound (No.1) (1961)***
  - Foreseeability of damage: ***Smith v Leech Brain (1962***; 'thin skull test')
- Intervening causes can break the **chain of causation**
- ***Res ipsa loquitur:*** The facts speak for themselves
- **Psychiatric injury:** Nervous shock; medical evidence
  - Primary victims
  - Secondary victims: proximate relationship (close ties of love and affection); unconnected bystanders: ***Alcock v Chief Constable of South Yorkshire Police (1992)***

Occupiers' liability

Spec reference	Key content	Assessment Objectives	Where does this topic feature on each specification/exam?
WJEC AS Level **2.3:** Occupiers' liability **Eduqas AS / A Level** **2.2.3:** Occupiers' liability	• Liability in relation to lawful visitors (Occupiers' Liability Act 1957) • Liability in relation to trespassers (Occupiers' Liability Act 1984) • Special categories of visitors, especially children	**A01** Demonstrate knowledge and understanding of legal rules and principles **A02** Apply legal rules and principles to given scenarios in order to present a legal argument using appropriate legal terminology **A03** Analyse and evaluate legal rules, principles, concepts and issues	**WJEC AS Level:** Unit 2 **Eduqas AS Level:** Component 2 Section A **Eduqas A Level:** Components 2 and 3 Section B

The tort of negligence comes from the common law. However, occupier's liability comes from both statute law and the common law. This area of tort involves the liability of an occupier to both visitors and persons other than visitors on their premises. There are two key statutes:

1. The ***Occupiers' Liability Act 1957***, which covers visitors.
2. The ***Occupiers' Liability Act 1984***, which covers persons other than visitors.

Occupiers' Liability Act 1957

This Act concerns the duty owed to visitors. (A visitor is often referred is a 'lawful visitor' to distinguish them from unlawful visitors or trespassers.)

Who is an occupier?

The ***Occupiers' Liability Act 1957*** does not define who is the occupier, but ***s1(2)*** does state that the rules of common law shall apply. The test is occupational control: who has control over the premises?

In ***Wheat v Lacon & Co (1966)***, four categories of occupier were identified.

1. If a landlord lets premises then the tenant will be the occupier.
2. If a landlord who lets part of a building retains certain areas (such as an entry hall) then the landlord will be the occupier in respect of those areas.
3. If an owner licenses (allows) a person to use premises but reserves the right of entry then the owner remains the occupier.
4. If contractors are employed to carry out work on the premises, the owner will generally remain the occupier, although there may be circumstances where the contractor could be the occupier.

Who is a visitor?

Under the common law, a visitor is a person who has express or implied permission to enter the premises.

Under the Occupiers' Liability Act 1957, persons who have a right to enter premises conferred by law (e.g. fire fighters and police officers) are lawful visitors

The common duty of care

Section 2 Occupiers' Liability Act 1957 imposes a common duty of care that is owed to lawful visitors:

1. An occupier of premises owes the same duty (the common duty of care), to all their visitors, but they can extend, restrict, modify or exclude this duty to any visitor or visitors by agreement or otherwise.
2. The common duty of care is to take reasonable care in all circumstances to see that the visitor is reasonably safe when using the premises for the purposes for which they are invited or permitted by the occupier.

The ***Occupiers' Liability Act 1957*** lays down guidelines in applying the common duty of care:

- ***S2(3)(a)*** An occupier must be prepared for children to be less careful than adults.
- ***S2(3)(b)*** An occupier can expect a person, in the exercise of their calling, to appreciate and guard against any special risks ordinarily incident to it (i.e. if the person is there to perform a particular role that has particular risks, the occupier can assume they will take care).
- ***S2(4)(a)*** A warning may discharge the duty of care (i.e. it is sufficient for the occupier to warn the visitor about any dangers).
- ***S2(4)(b)*** The occupier is not liable for the fault of an independent contractor if they acted reasonably in entrusting the work to that contractor and took reasonable steps to ensure that the contractor was competent and the work was properly carried out.

There are a number of references in the ***Occupiers' Liability Act 1957*** (as there are in other Acts and in the common law) to **'reasonable'**.

GRADE BOOST

What is the meaning of 'reasonable'? Read Lord Reed's explanation of the 'reasonable man' test in ***Healthcare at Home Limited v The Common Services Agency (2014).***

STRETCH AND CHALLENGE

Research the following cases and explain how they apply to the ***Occupiers' Liability Act 1957***:

- ***Haseldine v Daw (1941)***
- ***Phipps v Rochester (1955)***
- ***Wheat v Lacon & Co (1966)***
- ***Glasgow Corporation v Taylor (1992).***

Special categories: Children

Children do not form a special category on their own, but the ***Occupiers' Liability Act 1957 s2(3)(a)*** states that occupiers must be prepared for children to be less careful than adults.

Occupiers' Liability Act 1984: Persons other than visitors

This Act concerns the duty owed to persons other than visitors. (A 'person other than a visitor' is often referred is an 'unlawful visitor' or trespasser.)

Who is an occupier?

Anybody who would be classified as an occupier under the ***Occupiers' Liability Act 1957*** is an occupier under the ***Occupiers' Liability Act 1984***.

Trespassers

The common law was very harsh towards trespassers, including children. In ***Addie v Dumbreck (1929)*** it was held that there was no duty of care owed by occupiers to trespassers to ensure that they were safe when coming onto the land. The only duty was not to inflict harm wilfully.

However, in ***British Railways Board v Herrington (1972)***, the House of Lords used its 1966 Practice Statement and departed from its precedent in ***Addie v Dumbreck (1929)*** to hold that a duty of care could be owed to trespassers. The decision in this case eventually led to Parliament introducing the ***Occupiers' Liability Act 1984***.

STRETCH AND CHALLENGE

Find out the facts of the case and the decision of the House of Lords in:

- ***Adie v Dumbreck (1929)***
- ***British Railways Board v Herrington (1972).***

The statutory duty of care

Under ***s1(3) Occupiers' Liability Act 1984*** an occupier of premises owes a statutory duty of care to an unlawful visitor if:

- they are aware of the danger or have reasonable grounds to believe that it exists; and
- they know, or have reasonable grounds to believe, that the unlawful visitor is in the vicinity of the danger concerned or that they may come into the vicinity of the danger; and
- the risk is one against which, in all the circumstances of the case, the occupier may reasonably be expected to offer the unlawful visitor some protection.

Under ***s1(4) Occupiers' Liability Act 1984*** the duty owed to persons other than visitors is to take reasonable care in all the circumstances to see that they are not injured on the premises by the danger concerned.

The table below shows the differences between the duty imposed under the ***Occupiers' Liability Act 1984*** from that imposed under the ***Occupiers' Liability Act 1957***.

Occupiers' Liability Act 1957	Occupiers' Liability Act 1984
To take such care as is reasonable to see that the **visitor** will be reasonably safe in using the premises for the purposes for which they are invited or permitted by the occupier to be there.	To take care as is reasonable to see that the **non-visitor** is not injured on the premises by the danger concerned.

GRADE BOOST

Research Lord Hoffman's judgement in ***Tomlinson v Congleton Borough Council (2003)***, described right. Was the council liable under the ***Occupiers' Liability Act 1957***? Was the council liable under the ***Occupiers' Liability Act 1984***?

Lord Hoffmann was one of the House of Lords judges in the ***Tomlinson v Congleton Borough Council (2003)*** case. He said: 'Parliament has made it clear that, in the case of a lawful visitor, one starts from the assumption that there is a duty, whereas in the case of a trespasser one starts from the assumption that there is none.'

This means that, under the ***Occupiers' Liability Act 1957***, a duty of care is owed to all visitors, whereas, under the ***Occupiers' Liability Act 1984***, a duty is owed only if certain conditions are met (such as the occupier being aware of the danger).

KEY CASE

Tomlinson v Congleton Borough Council (2003)

Tomlinson was aged 18. He visited an artificial lake which was part of a country park in Congleton in Cheshire. Canoeing and windsurfing was permitted in one area of the lake and angling in another but swimming and diving were not permitted. Tomlinson ignored warning signs not to enter the lake (which stated 'Dangerous water. No swimming') and dived into it. He hit his head on the bottom, causing him to break his neck and become tetraplegic. He brought proceedings against Congleton Borough Council claiming for loss of earnings, loss of quality of life and the cost of the care he would require as a result of his injuries.

Tomlinson may have been a visitor when he arrived at the lake but it was accepted that he was a trespasser when he entered the water as he was aware that he was not permitted to dive in the lake. The council was aware of the danger and had introduced patrols and warning signs to stop swimming and diving. The House of Lords dismissed Tomlinson's claims.

Summary: Occupier's liability

- Occupier's liability comes from statute law and the common law
- ***Occupiers' Liability Act 1957***
  - Concerns the duty of care owed to visitors
  - Does not define who is the occupier, but the rules of common law apply ***(s1(2))***. Who has control over the premises? ***Wheat v Lacon & Co (1966)***
  - A visitor is a person with express or implied permission to enter the premises
  - ***S2(3)(a)*** Be prepared for children to be less careful than adults
  - ***S2(3)(b)*** Visitors should be expected to guard against special risks associated with the reason for their visit
  - ***S2(4)(a)*** A warning may discharge the duty of care
  - ***S2(4)(b)*** The occupier is not liable for the fault of an independent contractor if they took reasonable steps to ensure that the contractor was competent and the work was properly carried out
  - **'Reasonable man'**: Lord Reed: ***Healthcare at Home Limited v The Common Services Agency (2014)***
  - ***Haseldine v Daw (1941), Phipps v Rochester (1955), Wheat v Lacon & Co (1966), Glasgow Corporation v Taylor (1992).***
- ***Occupiers' Liability Act 1984***
  - Concerns the duty of care owed to persons other than visitors (unlawful visitors or trespassers)
  - **Trespassers:** ***Addie v Dumbreck (1929)*** but ***British Railways Board v Herrington (1972)***
  - ***S1(3)*** An occupier of premises owes a statutory duty of care to an unlawful visitor if they are aware of the danger, they know that the unlawful visitor is in the vicinity of the danger and the occupier may reasonably be expected to offer some protection against the risk
  - ***S1(4)*** The occupier's duty to persons other than visitors is to take reasonable care that they are not injured
- ***Tomlinson v Congleton Borough Council (2003)***
- Lord Hoffmann: Under the ***Occupiers' Liability Act 1957***, a duty of care is owed to all visitors, but, under the ***Occupiers' Liability Act 1984***, a duty is owed only if certain conditions are met

Remedies: Tort

Spec reference	Key content	Assessment Objectives	Where does this topic feature on each specification/exam?
WJEC AS Level 2.4: Remedies **Eduqas AS Level 2.1.4:** Remedies **Eduqas A Level 2.2.7:** Remedies	• Damages including compensatory damages; mitigation of loss; injunctions	**AO1** Demonstrate knowledge and understanding of legal rules and principles **AO2** Apply legal rules and principles to given scenarios in order to present a legal argument using appropriate legal terminology **AO3** Analyse and evaluate legal rules, principles, concepts and issues	**WJEC AS Level:** Unit 2 **Eduqas AS Level:** Component 2 Section A **Eduqas A Level:** Components 2 and 3 Section B

The main remedies for tort are:

- **damages**: the aim is to put the injured party in the same position they would have been in if the tort had not occurred. Damages are the main remedy for tort
- **injunctions**: a court order instructing a party to do or refrain from doing something. In tort, injunctions are mostly used in cases of nuisance.

Damages

Mitigation of loss

A claimant who has suffered a loss as a result of a tort is entitled to damages for any losses. However, the claimant is expected to take reasonable steps to mitigate any losses.

Types of damages payable

The following are the main categories of damages payable for tort:

- general
- special
- nominal
- contemptuous
- aggravated
- exemplary.

General damages

These are damages which cannot be calculated before the trial so the court has to calculate them. Examples are damages for loss of future earnings and for pain and suffering.

Special damages

These are damages which are capable of being calculated at the time of the trial. Examples are loss of earnings and medical expenses before trial.

Nominal damages

These damages are awarded when there has been little or no harm caused and the court wishes to award a very small amount. They are only used for torts which are **actionable per se**. This means the tort does not require proof of damage to be actionable: damages are payable just because the tort has happened. Defamation and trespass are torts which are actionable per se.

GRADE BOOST

A ship called *The Barracuda* was sunk by another ship, which had negligently collided with it, causing damage. *The Barracuda* refused any offer of aid after the collision and it sank. Can *The Barracuda* make a claim against the other vessel for the sinking of their ship? If *The Barracuda*'s refusal of aid is regarded as negligent, the owners can only recover the damage caused by the collision and not the sinking of the ship.

KEY CASE

Rookes v Barnard (1964)
This case is important because, when it was heard on appeal in the House of Lords, Lord Devlin explained the purpose of exemplary damages and the circumstances when they could be awarded. He said: 'Exemplary damages are essentially different from ordinary damages. The object of damages in the usual sense of the term is to compensate. The object of exemplary damages is to punish and deter.'

STRETCH AND CHALLENGE

Some people argue that exemplary damages should not be allowed because the purpose of civil law is not to punish. Punishment, it is argued, should be the purpose of the criminal law. Do you think exemplary damages should be payable in cases of tort?

KEY CASE

Fletcher v Bealey (1884)
The judge, Pearson J, said: *'There must, if no actual damage is proved, be proof of imminent danger, and there must also be proof that the apprehended damage will, if it comes, be very substantial. I should almost say it must be proved that it will be irreparable, because, if the danger is not proved to be so imminent that no one can doubt that, if the remedy is delayed, the damage will be suffered, I think it must be shown that, if the damage does occur at any time, it will come in such a way and under such circumstances that it will be impossible for the plaintiff to protect himself against it if relief is denied to him in a quia timet.'*

Quoted in ***London Borough of Islington v Elliott and Morris (2012)*** paragraph 30.

Contemptuous damages

These damages are awarded when the level of harm has been low and the court believes that an action should not have been taken, even though the defendant has been liable under tort. These damages can be as low as one pence. Unlike nominal damages, they can be awarded for any tort.

Aggravated damages

These are damages awarded over and above that needed to put the claimant back in the position that they would have been in, had the tort not occurred. They represent an additional sum of money because the initial harm was made worse due to some aggravating factor. They are mostly awarded in cases of defamation and trespass to the person.

Exemplary damages

These are sometimes called 'punitive damages'. These are damages whose purpose is to punish the defendant for committing the tort. They are only awarded in certain circumstances.

Lord Devlin identified three circumstances when exemplary damages could be imposed:

- Oppressive, arbitrary or unconstitutional action by the servants of the government.
- Where the defendant's conduct was calculated by them to make a profit for themselves which may exceed the compensation payable to the claimant.
- Where a statute authorises the paying of exemplary damages.

Injunctions

An injunction is a court order that requires the defendant to behave in a certain way. Injunctions can take two forms:

- **Prohibitory injunctions** instruct the defendant to not behave in a certain way (i.e. to stop committing the tort).
- **Mandatory injunctions** instruct the defendant to take an action to rectify the situation created by the tort. They are rarely granted in tort actions.

Injunctions tend not to be used for torts such as negligence or occupier's liability. They are mostly used for the torts of nuisance, trespass to land and defamation.

Quia timet injunction

This is an injunction which is obtained prior to the commission of a tort. *Quia timet* is Latin for 'because he fears'. The circumstances when a *quia timet* may be granted were stated in ***Fletcher v Bealey (1884)***: the danger must be imminent, the potential damage must be substantial and the only way the claimant can protect themselves is through a *quia timet*.

Interim injunction

This is also known as an interlocutory injunction and may be granted once an action has begun but before the main court hearing. The injunction will instruct the defendant to not behave in a certain way.

The conditions for granting an interim injunction was stated in ***American Cyanamid v Ethicon (1975)***:

- There must be a serious issue to be tried.
- The 'balance of convenience' must favour the granting of the injunction. If there is no imbalance then no injunction should be issued so as to preserve the status quo.

The balance of convenience

An interim injunction is only granted if the claimant undertakes to pay damages to the defendant for any loss sustained as a result of the injunction if it is held that the claimant had not been entitled to restrain the defendant from doing what they were threatening to do. However, these damages may not be adequate compensation if the defendant is made to stop doing something. The courts must try to balance the need for the injunction against the effects on the defendant.

Lord Diplock stated that the court must weigh one need against another and determine where the balance of convenience lies.

Injunctions as an equitable remedy

Injunctions are an equitable remedy (actions that a court prescribes that should resolve a dispute). They are therefore at the discretion of the court and not a right. The maxims (general principles) of equity determine when they might not be awarded.

- **One who seeks equity must do equity**. Injunctions will not be granted if the claimant acted unfairly (e.g. if they encouraged the defendant to commit the tort).
- **Equity does nothing in vain**. The court will not award an injunction if the defendant will be unable to comply with its terms.
- **Delay defeats equity**. The court is unlikely to award an injunction where there has been an unreasonable delay in asking for an injunction.

Summary: Remedies: Tort

- **Damages**: aim to put the injured party in the same position they would have been in if the tort had not occurred
  - **Mitigation of loss:** A claimant is entitled to damages for losses but must take reasonable steps to mitigate such losses
  - **General damages:** Cannot be calculated before the trial e.g. loss of future earnings, pain and suffering
  - **Special damages:** Can be calculated at the time of the trial e.g. loss of earnings, existing medical expenses
  - **Nominal damages:** Small amounts for actionable per se cases where there was little or no harm and no proof of damage needed e.g. defamation, trespass
  - **Contemptuous damages:** Minimal damages following low level of harm and the court believes that an action should not have been taken
  - **Aggravated damages:** additional damages awarded because an aggravating factor made the initial harm worse e.g. defamation, and trespass to the person
  - **Exemplary (punitive) damages**: Punish and deter the defendant: ***Rookes v Barnard (1964)***
- **Injunctions**: a court order instructing a party to behave in a certain way; mostly used for nuisance, trespass to land and defamation
  - **Prohibitory injunctions** instruct the defendant to **not** behave in a certain way (i.e. to stop committing the tort)
  - **Mandatory injunctions** instruct the defendant to take an action to rectify the situation
  - ***Quia timet* injunction:** Obtained before the tort is committed if danger is imminent, damage would be substantial and no other protection available: ***Fletcher v Bealey (1884)***
  - **Interim (interlocutory) injunctions** instruct the defendant to not behave in a certain way and may be granted once an action has begun but before the main court hearing (balance of convenience: ***American Cyanamid v Ethicon (1975)***
  - Injunctions are an equitable remedy not a right

CRIMINAL LAW

Rules and theory of criminal law

Spec reference	Key content	Assessment Objectives	Where does this topic feature on each specification/exam?
WJEC AS / A Level **3.12:** Rules and theory of criminal law **Eduqas AS Level** **2.3.1:** Rules of criminal law **Eduqas A Level** **2.3.1:** Rules of criminal law and theory in criminal law	• Definition of crime and the purpose of criminal law • Burden and standard of proof • Codification of criminal law • Functions of the Crown Prosecution Service, including outline of the roles of the Attorney General and the Director of Public Prosecutions (see page 75) • Bail and remand in custody including police and court bail (see page 72) • The trial process, including youth justice, trial procedure and the appeal process (see page 64) • The pervasive nature of law and society, law and morality and law and justice on criminal law	**AO1** Demonstrate knowledge and understanding of legal rules and principles **AO2** Apply legal rules and principles to given scenarios in order to present a legal argument using appropriate legal terminology **AO3** Analyse and evaluate legal rules, principles, concepts and issues	**WJEC AS:** Units 3 and 4 **Eduqas AS Level:** Component 2 Section B **Eduqas A Level:** Components 2 and 3 Section C

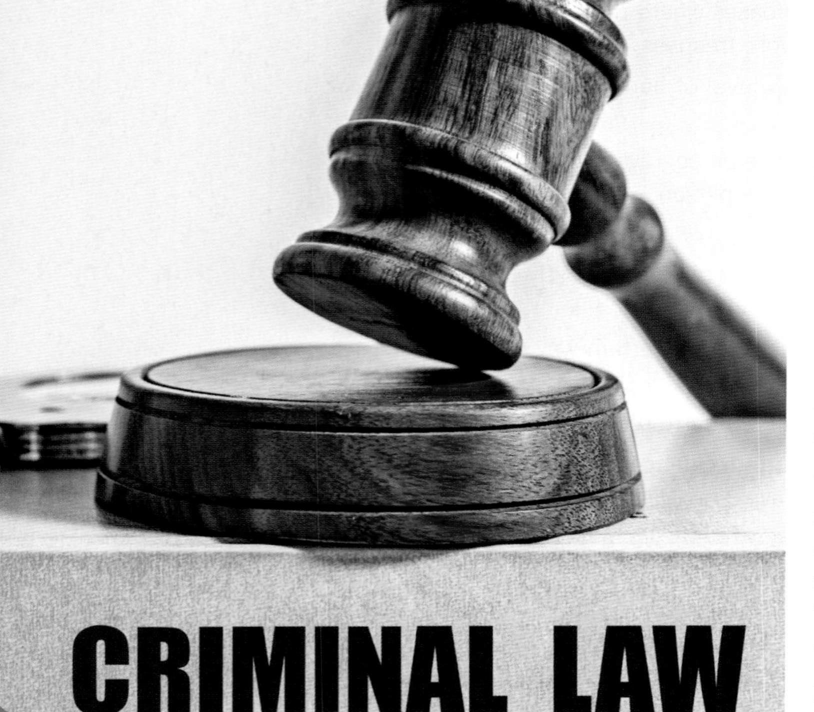

Definition of a crime

There are lots of ways to define a 'crime' but one definition is that it is a wrong against an individual, society and the state, which should be punished.

In ***Proprietary Articles Trade Association v Attorney General for Canada (1931)***, Lord Atkin stated his definition of crime:

'The criminal quality of an act cannot be discerned by intuition (made out by 'gut feeling'); nor can it be discovered by reference to any standard but one: is the act prohibited by penal consequences?'

The state (the government) develops a code of behaviour for the whole of society to adhere to, in order to maintain social control and standards in society. Those who commit crimes are prosecuted by the state (as opposed to in civil law, where actions are taken by individuals). The Crown Prosecution Service (CPS) will conduct most of these proceedings.

Most criminal law is laid down by Parliament but some criminal law offences are found in case law and common law.

Examples of common law offences

Over many years, judges have developed certain offences and may still find it necessary to do so on occasion. However, in ***Knuller v DPP (1973)***, the House of Lords stated that it did not feel it was in its remit to create offences and that this should be left to Parliament wherever possible. Parliament will step in and provide statutory guidelines when it feels it is necessary to bring the law into line with policy.

Murder

Murder is the best-known example of a common law offence. It is not defined in any statute but judges often imposed a death penalty for murder until Parliament passed the ***Murder (Abolition of the Death Penalty) Act 1965***.

Conspiracy to corrupt public morals

Shaw v DPP (1962)

The defendant published a book with the names, pictures and services offered by prostitutes and was convicted of conspiracy to corrupt public morals. There was no alternative statutory offence for the defendant to be convicted of, so the judges created this offence in this case.

Marital rape

KEY CASE

R v R (1991)

An 18th-century precedent stated that a husband could not be guilty of raping his wife. In this case, the House of Lords held that the status of women in society had changed and that they had now achieved equality with men so they should not be regarded as a form of chattel (belonging). If a wife does not consent to sex, her husband can now be found guilty of rape.

STRETCH AND CHALLENGE

Look up Sir Edward Coke's definition of murder.
How does it compare with other definitions?

Elements of a crime

For a defendant to be found guilty of a crime, two elements must be present: **actus reus** and **mens rea**. These terms come from the Latin phrase ***actus non facit reum nisi mens sit rea***: 'the act itself does not constitute guilt unless done with a guilty mind'.

Burden of proof

The prosecution has to convince the judge or jury that the defendant is criminally liable. This is a 'golden thread' that runs through the UK legal system: that a person is **presumed innocent** until proved guilty. ***Woolmington v DPP (1935)*** stressed the fact that the prosecution has to prove the case beyond reasonable doubt in any criminal trial.

'Beyond reasonable doubt' is a very high standard of proof. The judge or jury must be left with hardly a shadow of doubt in their minds that the defendant committed the crime. Otherwise, the defendant must be found not guilty.

Actus reus

The term **actus reus** has a wider meaning than 'an act'. The actus reus can be:

- a voluntary action
- an omission
- a state of affairs.

The actus reus will be different for each crime, so for murder it is unlawful killing but for theft it is the dishonest appropriation of property belonging to another. The defendant must have committed the act or omission voluntarily. If the act is done involuntarily, the defendant will not be guilty.

See page 155 for a more detailed look at the concept of actus reus.

KEY TERMINOLOGY

actus reus: 'the guilty act' that must be present for a defendant to be found guilty of a crime. It can be a voluntary action, an omission or a state of affairs.

mens rea: 'the guilty mind' that must be present for a defendant to be found guilty of a crime. It can include intention, recklessness or negligence.

An action as a result of being chased or stung by a swarm of bees may not be voluntary

A voluntary action

Hill v Baxter (1958)

The court gave examples of **involuntary** *acts, such as reflex actions after being hit on the head with a hammer or being stung by a swarm of bees. The criminal law is only concerned with fault.*

An omission

A failure to act does not usually result in someone being found criminally liable in English law. Lord Justice Stephen said: 'It is not a crime to cause death or bodily injury, even intentionally, by any omission.'

However, there are some exceptions to this rule. A person will be held criminally liable for failing to act where:

- there is a duty created by statute
- they have a contractual duty to act
- there is a duty imposed by their official position
- they have voluntarily accepted responsibility for another person
- they have created a dangerous situation
- there is a special relationship, such as with a family member.

A state of affairs

Here, the defendant has not acted voluntarily but has nonetheless been convicted of a crime. They are 'being' rather than 'doing' offences.

For someone to have committed the actus reus, in some crimes there must also be a consequence. For example, for murder someone has to end up dead. The defendant's act must have produced the unlawful killing.

STRETCH AND CHALLENGE

Research the facts of ***Larsonneur (1933)*** and ***Winzar v Chief Constable of Kent (1983)*** and discuss what the state of affairs were in these cases See page 160 for a detailed discussion on crimes of strict liability.

GRADE BOOST

Research the following cases, and discuss whether there was a duty to act in these cases:

- ***Pittwood (1902)***
- ***Dytham (1979)***
- ***Stone and Dobinson (1977)***
- ***Gibbins and Proctor (1918)***
- ***Khan (1988).***

Mens rea

Mens rea translates as 'guilty mind' . There are different levels of mens rea. From highest to lowest, they are:

- intention
- recklessness
- negligence.

The levels of mens rea are explained in more detail on page 156.

Intention

This was defined by the courts in ***R v Mohan (1975)*** as 'a decision to bring about, in so far as it lies within the accused's power, [the prohibited consequence], no matter whether the accused desired that consequence of his act or not'.

The defendant's motive is irrelevant when deciding intention. There are two types of intention:

1. **Direct intention:** the defendant wants a result and carries out an act to achieve it. Generally, this is easier to prove based on the circumstances of the crime.
2. **Indirect/oblique intention:** the defendant doesn't want the outcome but realises that, in acting as they do, that there is a possibility that it will happen.

Recklessness

A definition of recklessness is a situation where the defendant knows that there is a risk that their actions will lead to harm but goes on to take the risk regardless. This is a lower form of mens rea than intention.

Negligence

See page 158 for more information about the concept of mens rea and negligence.

STRETCH AND CHALLENGE

For the meaning of **intention**, research and discuss the following cases:

- ***Hyam v DPP (1975)***
- ***Moloney (1985)***
- ***Hancock and Shankland (1986)***
- ***Nedrick (1986)***
- ***Woollin (1998)***
- ***Matthew and Alleyne (2003).***

Codification of the criminal law

In most countries, criminal law is codified: they have a coded or written document that details each part of the criminal law. In the UK, criminal law is found in numerous statutes and in common law. It can be difficult for lawyers, let alone lay people, to find the law and keep up to date with it. But surely it is important that we should know the criminal law if we can be deprived of our liberty if we break it.

The ***Law Commission Act 1965*** established the Law Commission (see page 28), which was given the task of codifying the criminal law. However, it found the task impossible. Eventually, with help from senior academics, a draft criminal code was published in 1989 which incorporated the criminal law as well as suggestions for reform. However, Parliament has never legislated on this and it remains in draft form.

GRADE BOOST

Remember that the rules set out in this section apply to all the offences you will learn about in criminal law.

Summary: Rules and theory of criminal law

- A crime is a wrong against an individual, society and the state which should be punished by the state: ***Proprietary Articles Trade Association v Attorney General for Canada (1931)***
- The Crown Prosecution Service (CPS) will conduct most of these proceedings
- **Common law offences**: only Parliament should create offences and provide statutory guidelines: ***Knuller v DPP (1973)***
  - **Murder:** Not defined in any statute. Death penalty abolished in ***Murder (Abolition of the Death Penalty) Act 1965***
  - **Conspiracy to corrupt public morals:** ***Shaw v DPP (1962)***
  - **Marital rape:** ***R v R (1991)***
- **Actus reus**: 'the guilty act' must be present for a defendant to be found guilty of a crime
  - A voluntary action: ***Hill v Baxter (1958)***
  - An omission or failure to act is criminally liable under certain conditions. Duty to act: ***Pittwood (1902)***, ***Dytham (1979)***, ***Stone and Dobinson (1977)***, ***Gibbins and Proctor (1918)***, ***Khan (1988)***
  - A state of affairs: ***Larsonneur (1933)***, ***Winzar v Chief Constable of Kent (1983)***
- **Mens rea**: 'the guilty mind' must be present for a defendant to be found guilty of a crime
  - Direct or indirect (oblique) intention: ***Mohan (1975)***, ***Hyam v DPP (1975)***, ***Moloney (1985)***, ***Hancock and Shankland (1986)***, ***Nedrick (1986)***, ***Woollin (1998)***, ***Matthew and Alleyne (2003)***
  - Recklessness
  - Negligence
- **Burden of proof:** The prosecution has to convince the judge or jury that the defendant is criminally liable but they are **presumed innocent** until proved guilty: ***Woolmington v DPP (1935)***
- **Beyond reasonable doubt**: The judge or jury must be sure that the defendant committed the crime to be found guilty
- ***Law Commission Act 1965*** established the Law Commission to codify criminal law but 1989 criminal code remains in draft form

General elements of criminal liability

Spec reference	Key content	Assessment Objectives	Where does this topic feature on each specification/exam?
WJEC AS/A Level 3.13: General elements of liability **Eduqas AS Level 2.3.2:** General elements of liability **Eduqas A Level 2.3.2:** General elements of liability	• Burden and standard of proof • Actus reus (voluntary, involuntary conduct, consequences and omissions) • Mens rea (negligence, recklessness, intention), fault • Causation (legal and factual) • Strict liability	**AO1** Demonstrate knowledge and understanding of legal rules and principles **AO2** Apply legal rules and principles to given scenarios in order to present a legal argument using appropriate legal terminology **AO3** Analyse and evaluate legal rules, principles, concepts and issues	**WJEC AS/A Level:** Unit 3; Unit 4 **Eduqas AS Level:** Component 2 **Eduqas A Level:** Component 2; Component 3

The burden and standard of proof

In a criminal case, the burden of proving guilt is on the prosecution. The standard to which it needs to prove this guilt is **'beyond reasonable doubt'**. The standard of proof is higher in a criminal case than in a civil one, as the impact on a defendant of being found guilty of a criminal offence is much greater. It also supports the principle of **'innocent until proven guilty'** and ***Article 6 EHCR*** (right to a fair trial).

GRADE BOOST

The standard of proof in a civil case is 'on the balance of probabilities' and the burden of proof is on the claimant.

Elements of crime

There are generally two elements required for the commission of a criminal offence: **actus reus** (the guilty act) and **mens rea** (the guilty mind). The general **presumption** is that a defendant must have committed a guilty act while having a guilty state of mind. A presumption is a starting point for the courts, which presume certain facts to be true unless there is a greater dominance of evidence to the contrary that rebuts the presumption.

This supports the Latin tenet ***actus non facit reum nisi mens sit rea***, which means the act does not make a person guilty unless the mind is also guilty. There are exceptions, which are explored in the section on strict liability (see page 160). Once this is established, **causation** needs to be proved, which looks at the link between the result and the conduct of the defendant.

KEY TERMINOLOGY

causation (or 'chain of causation'): connecting the actus reus and the corresponding result. For there to be criminal liability, there must be an unbroken chain of causation. There are two types of causation: legal and factual.

This topic will consider:

- actus reus
- omission
- mens rea
- factual causation
- legal causation
- strict liability.

Actus reus

This consists of all the elements of a crime other than the mens rea. Actus reus may consist of the following elements.

Conduct

The action requires a particular conduct (behaviour) but the consequence of that behaviour is insignificant. An example is perjury, where a person lies under oath. It is irrelevant whether the lie is believed or affects the case; it is the conduct of lying that is sufficient as the actus reus.

Result

The action requires a particular end result. An example is murder, when the crime requires the result of the victim dying. It also requires causation to be proved.

State of affairs

For these crimes, the actus reus consists of 'being' rather than 'doing'; for example, 'being' in charge of a vehicle while under the influence of alcohol or drugs. There is a link with strict liability (see page 160).

R v Larsonneur (1933)

Mrs Larsonneur, a French national, was brought to the UK from Ireland in police custody, against her will: she had no desire to come to the UK. She was arrested on arrival in the UK for being an illegal alien . The fact she had not wanted to come to the UK, nor had any power over her transfer, was irrelevant as she was 'found' or 'being' illegally in the UK. She was found guilty.

Another case that demonstrates a 'state of affairs' crime is ***Winzar v CC Kent (1983)***. In this case, the defendant was found drunk in a hospital and slumped on a chair. The police were called and removed him to the street, where they charged him with being 'drunk on the highway', contrary to the ***Licensing Act 1872***. These crimes are also known as **absolute liability offences** and are considered in the section on strict liability on page 160.

Omission

This is a 'failure to act'. The general rule is that it is not an offence to fail to act unless someone is under a **duty to act.** A person could walk past a random person drowning in a fountain and be under no legal obligation to help them get out.

Duty to act

A person can only be criminally liable if they have failed to act when under a legal duty to do so and the crime is capable of being committed by omission. There are recognised situations where a person is under a duty to act.

1. Statute

If a statute requires an action, it is unlawful not to do so. For example, under ***s6 Road Traffic Act 1988***, failing to provide a breath sample or a specimen for analysis is an offence.

2. Contract

Individuals may be contracted to act in a particular way and, if they fail to act when under this contractual duty, they may be liable for an offence. The case of ***R v Pitwood (1902)*** illustrates this.

3. Duty arising out of a special relationship

Certain family relationships, such as parent-child and spouses, result in a duty to act. The case of ***R v Gibbins and Proctor (1918)*** demonstrates this.

KEY CASE

R v Pitwood (1902)

A carter was killed after Pitwood, a level-crossing keeper, failed to close the crossing gate when he went on lunch. He had a contractual duty to ensure the crossing gate was closed and his failure to act led to the death of the carter.

KEY CASE

Gibbins and Proctor (1918)

The defendant and his lover failed to feed his daughter, who was living with them. She died of starvation. The woman, despite the child not being hers, was living in the same household and had taken the defendant's money to feed the child. She was therefore under a duty to act (to feed and care for the child). They were both found guilty of murder.

KEY CASE

R v Stone and Dobinson (1977)
Stone's younger sister, Fanny, came to live with Stone and Dobinson. Fanny suffered from anorexia and, despite some weak attempts by Stone and Dobinson to get her help, she eventually died. The jury found that a duty was assumed from electing to take care of a vulnerable adult. They should have made more of an effort to get her help and were found guilty of manslaughter.

4. Duty arising out of a person assuming responsibility for another

If a person chooses to take care of another person who is infirm or incapable of taking care of themselves, they are under a duty to do so without negligence. The case of ***R v Stone and Dobinson (1977)*** illustrates this.

5. Defendant has inadvertently created a dangerous situation, becomes aware of it, but fails to take steps to rectify it

R v Miller (1983)

The defendant was squatting in a flat. He fell asleep without extinguishing his cigarette. When he awoke, he realised the mattress was alight but merely moved to the next room and went back to sleep. His failure to act and call for help caused hundreds of pounds' worth of damage. He was convicted of arson.

The difference between a positive act and an omission

It is generally not a crime to fail to act, unless someone is under a duty to do so. For example, doing nothing while somebody drowns is an omission, but holding that person's head under the water so that they drown is a positive act. In ***Airedale NHS v Bland (1993)***, the removal of a feeding tube from a patient to allow him to die naturally was held to be an omission and therefore not a criminal act. Contrast this with **euthanasia**, where an act such as administering a deliberate overdose to terminate a person's life would be classed as a positive act and therefore a criminal offence.

Mens rea

KEY TERMINOLOGY

strict liability: a group of offences, usually regulatory in nature, that only require proof of actus reus, not mens rea.

The general presumption is that a defendant must have committed a guilty act while having a guilty state of mind. Mens rea refers to the mental element of the definition of a crime. If Parliament intended mens rea in an offence, it will often include mens rea words in the statute such as '**intentionally**', '**recklessly**' and '**negligently**'. If Parliament deliberately left out a mens rea word then the offence may be considered to be one of **strict liability.**

The mens rea differs according to the crime. For example, the mens rea of **murder** is **malice aforethought**, which has come to mean an intention to kill or cause grievous bodily harm (GBH,) whereas the mens rea of assault is **intentionally or recklessly causing the victim to apprehend the application of immediate unlawful force.**

Coincidence of actus reus and mens rea

The general rule is that, to be guilty of a criminal offence requiring mens rea, an accused must possess the required mens rea when performing the actus reus, and it must relate to that particular act or omission. This is also known as the **contemporaneity rule.** For example, Bob is planning to kill his colleague tomorrow, but kills him by accident today. This does not make Bob guilty of murder. There are two ways the courts have taken a flexible approach to this question: by **continuing acts** and **single transaction of events**.

1. Continuing acts

It is not necessary for mens rea to be present at the start of the actus reus as long as, at some point in a continuous act, mens rea appears. The case of ***Fagan v Metropolitan Police Commissioner (1969)*** demonstrates this point.

Fagan v Metropolitan Police Commissioner (1969)

Fagan accidentally parked his car on a police officer's foot when asked by the officer to park the car near the curb. Fagan did not mean to drive his car on the officer's foot. However, when asked to move, he refused. It was at this point that mens rea was formed and driving onto the officer's foot and remaining there was a continuing act.

Under the doctrine of **transferred malice**, mens rea may be transferred from an intended victim to an unintended one. This is shown in the case of **Latimer (1986)**, where the defendant hit victim number one with his belt but it recoiled off him, injuring victim number two, an innocent bystander. The defendant had committed the actus reus of the offence with the necessary mens rea. The mens rea (intention to harm the person he aimed at) could be transferred to the actual victim.

2. Single transaction of events

The courts have held that, as long as there is one unbroken transaction of events, then actus reus and mens rea need not occur at the same time. For example, if Rhidian attempts to murder Trystan by beating him to death, has not succeeded but thinks he is dead, then actually kills Trystan by running him over, Rhidian will still be guilty of murder. A similar situation arose in the case of ***Thabo Meli (1954)***.

Actus resus and mens rea do not need to be simultaneous if they are part of a chain of events

Types of mens rea

There are various types of mens rea but, for the purposes of the WJEC specification, **intention, recklessness** and **negligence** will be considered here. The mens rea for a particular offence is either defined in the relevant statute, as it is with **s47 assault occasioning actual bodily harm**, or through case law, as is the case with **oblique intent**.

Intention

Intention is always **subjective**: in order to find that a defendant had intention, the court must believe that the particular defendant on trial desired the specific consequence of their action. Consider intention in relation to the offence of murder. The mens rea of murder is **malice aforethought.** Despite the term 'malice', no malice needs to be present. For example, a murder could be committed out of love or compassion, as in the case of helping a terminally ill relative to die. No 'aforethought' is required either: murder can be committed on the spur of the moment with no prior planning. According to ***Vickers (1957)***, the mens rea of murder can be implied from an intention to cause grevious bodily harm. A defendant does not need to have intended to kill. The definition has therefore been interpreted as an intention to kill or cause GBH.

There are two types of intention: **direct** and **oblique**.

- **Direct intention** is where the defendant has a clear foresight of the consequences of their action and specifically desires that consequence. For example, Megan stabs Lauren because she desires the consequence of Lauren's death.
- **Oblique** (or **indirect) intention** is less clear than direct intent. Here, the defendant may not actually desire the consequence of the action (e.g. death), but if they realise that the consequence will happen as a **virtual certainty**, they can be said to have oblique intention. This area of law has evolved through case law. The current direction on oblique intent comes from the case of ***Nedrick (1986)*** as confirmed in ***Woollin (1998)***, when the judge stated that 'the jury should be directed that they were not entitled to find the necessary intention for a conviction of murder unless they felt sure that death or serious bodily harm had been a virtual certainty (barring some unforeseen intervention) as a result of the defendant's actions and that the defendant had appreciated that such was the case, the decision being one for them to be reached on a consideration of all the evidence'.

KEY CASE

Thabo Meli (1954)

The defendants had attempted to kill the victim by beating him up but he was not dead. They then disposed of what they thought was his corpse over a cliff. The victim died as a result of the fall. The court held that there was one transaction of events and, as long as the defendants had the relevant mens rea at the beginning of the transaction, it could coincide with the actus reus when that occurred.

KEY TERMINOLOGY

subjective: an assumption relating to the individual in question (the subject).

objective: a test that considers not the particular defendant in question, but what another average, reasonable person would have done or thought if placed in the same position as the defendant.

STRETCH AND CHALLENGE

The area of oblique intent has developed through case law over the years to the current direction. Explore the following cases and consider their facts, how the law has changed and why.

- ***S8 Criminal Justice Act 1967***: 'natural and probable consequence'.
- ***R v Maloney (1985)***: 'natural consequence of the action'.
- ***Hancock and Shankland (1986)***: 'degrees of probability'.
- ***Nedrick (1986)***.
- ***Woolin (1998)***.

Recklessness

This type of mens rea concerns the taking of an unjustified risk. Following the case of ***R v G and another (2003)***, it is now almost purely a subjective concept, so that the prosecution must prove that the defendant realised they were taking a risk. The first use of the phrase 'subjective recklessness' was in the ***Cunningham (1957)*** case and is sometimes referred to as **Cunningham recklessness**, where the court asks the question: 'Was the risk in the defendant's mind at the time the crime was committed?'

STRETCH AND CHALLENGE

Explore the cases of ***Cunningham (1957)*** and ***Caldwell (1982)***. What were the facts of the case and what did they rule in relation to negligence?

KEY CASE

R v G and another (2003)

In this case, two boys aged 11 and 12 set fire to newspapers in a wheelie bin outside a shop. The fire spread to the shop and other buildings, causing significant damage. They were convicted of arson as, at the time, arson required an objective standard of recklessness (Caldwell recklessness) and the risk would have been obvious to a reasonable person, even if it was not to the young boys. On appeal, it was decided that the objective standard was not appropriate and the subjective characteristics of the boys such as their age and immaturity should be considered by the courts. Caldwell objective recklessness was overruled and replaced with subjective recklessness.

Starting a fire that could harm people is classed as recklessness

Negligence

Negligence consists of falling below the standard of the ordinary reasonable person. The test is **objective** and has traditionally been associated with civil law. It now has some relevance in criminal law with **gross negligence manslaughter**.

Causation

Causation relates to the causal relationship between conduct and result and is an important aspect of the actus reus of an offence. There needs to be an unbroken and direct **chain of causation** between the defendant's act and the consequences of that act. There must not be a ***novus actus interveniens*** that breaks the chain of causation, or there will be no criminal liability for the resulting consequence. There are two types of causation: **factual** and **legal**.

GRADE BOOST

Remember that, occasionally, some subjective characteristics of the defendant can be considered with an objective test (such as age and gender) that may have an effect on the way they reacted.

Factual causation

This is tested using the 'but for' test and the de minimis rule.

1. The 'but for' test

This test asks 'but for' the conduct of the defendant, would the victim have died as and when they did? If the answer is no then the defendant will be liable for the death.

R v White (1910)

White poisoned his mother but she died of a heart attack before the poison had a chance to take effect. He was not liable for her death.

KEY TERMINOLOGY

novus actus interveniens: an intervening act that is so independent of the original act of the defendant that it succeeds in breaking the chain of causation. There may be liability for the initial act.

KEY CASE

R v Pagett (1983)

An armed defendant was trying to resist arrest and held his girlfriend in front of him as a human shield. He shot at the police and they shot back, killing the girlfriend. It was held that 'but for' his action of holding her as a human shield, she would not have died as and when she did. This was despite the fact it was not him who shot her.

2. The de minimis rule

De minimis means insignificant, minute or trifling. This test requires that the original injury caused by the defendant's action must be more than a minimal cause of death. ***Pagett (1983)*** also illustrates this.

Legal causation

This is tested using the impact of the injury, the 'thin skull' test and novus actus interveniens.

1. The injury must be the operating and substantial cause of death

This test considers whether the original injury inflicted by the defendant is, at the time of death, still the operating and substantial cause of death.

R v Smith (1959)

A soldier had been stabbed, was dropped twice on his way to the hospital, experienced a delay in seeing a doctor and subsequently given poor medical treatment. The court held that these other factors were not enough to break the chain of causation. At the time of his death, the original wound was still the 'operating and substantial' cause of death.

R v Jordan (1956)

*This case took a different stance to the **Smith** case. The defendant stabbed the victim. While in hospital, the victim was given an antibiotic to which he was allergic and died. The defendant was acquitted of murder because, at the time of death, the original stab wound had almost healed and the death was attributable not to that injury but to the antibiotic. The courts said that negligent medical treatment could only break the chain of causation where it is **'palpably wrong'**.*

In this context, palpably wrong means seriously wrong and so independent of the original act that it is possible to break the chain of causation. In ***R v Jordan (1956)***, it was seen as a ***novus actus interveniens*** and the original stab wound was no longer the 'operating and substantial' cause of death.

2. The 'thin skull' test

A defendant has to take their victim as they find them, meaning that, if the victim dies from some unusual or unexpected physical or other condition, the defendant is still responsible for the death. For example, if during a fight the defendant hits the victim with a punch that would not normally cause anything more than soreness and bruising but, due to the victim having an unusually thin skull, they die, the defendant is still liable for the death.

R v Blaue (1975)

The defendant stabbed a woman who happened to be a Jehovah's witness. As a result of her beliefs she refused a blood transfusion which would have saved her life. The defendant argued he should not be responsible for her death as the transfusion could have saved her life and she refused it. The court disagreed and said he must take his victim as he finds them.

3. *Novus actus interveniens* (new intervening act)

For an intervening act to break the chain of causation, it must be unforeseeable and random. It is sometimes likened to an 'act of God'. The case of ***R v Jordan (1956)*** is an example of a *novus actus interveniens*.

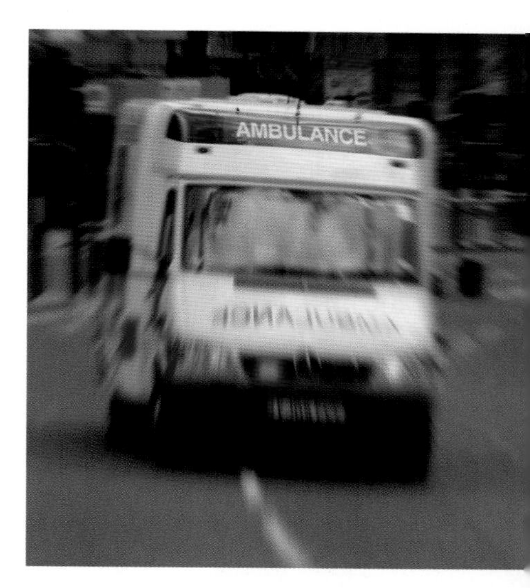

STRETCH AND CHALLENGE

A more recent case that looks at this issue is ***Cheshire (1991)***. Find out about this case and what the court said in relation to causation.

Exam Skills

When applying the law on general elements of liability to a scenario-style question, it is important to define the actus reus and mens rea of each offence using legal authority to support your definition. You then need to apply the actus reus and mens rea of each offence to the facts with supporting authority and draw a conclusion. Remember you may also have to incorporate a defence if applicable.

The concepts explored in this section will be needed for each of the offences studied at AS/A level. You will need to revisit this section when revising homicide, property offences and non-fatal offences.

Strict liability

Most crimes require both actus reus and mens rea. However, there is a group of offences known as **strict liability** where only the actus reus needs to be proved to establish liability. With these offences, there is no need to prove mens rea for at least one element of the actus reus and liability is imposed without fault on the part of the defendant. As a result, some people feel strict liability offences are unfair but, as they cover relatively minor crimes, it is generally accepted that they are needed to allow society to run smoothly. They tend to cover regulatory offences such as food hygiene, parking offences and polluting the environment. For strict liability offences, the defence of mistake is not available.

There is also a group of crimes known as **absolute liability** offences. These require proof of actus reus only but are not concerned with whether the actus reus is voluntary. (See the section about **elements of crime** on page 154, which refers to these offences as 'state of affairs' crimes and demonstrates through the cases of ***Winzar (1983)*** and ***Larsonneur (1933)*** that the actus reus need not be controlled by the defendant).

KEY TERMINOLOGY

presumption: a starting point for the courts, which presume certain facts to be true unless there is a greater balance of evidence to the contrary that disproves the presumption.

Though most strict liability offences are statutory offences, Parliament does not always make it clear whether mens rea is required. It is therefore for judges to decide whether an offence should be one of strict liability. Judges start with the **presumption** that **mens rea is always required** and no offence is strict liability. They then consider four factors to confirm or rebut this presumption.

The four Gammon factors

The case of ***Gammon (HK) Ltd v Attorney General (1985)***, where builders had failed to follow exact plans and part of the building they had constructed collapsed, confirmed that the starting point for a judge is to presume that mens rea is always required before a person can be found guilty of a criminal offence. This case laid down four **Gammon factors** the courts need to consider in determining if an offence is one of strict liability.

Judges also use statutory interpretation to interpret statutes to determine if Parliament intended the offence to be one of strict liability. Judges have to use aids of interpretation such as the literal, golden, mischief and purposive approaches to determine if an offence was intended to be one of strict liability. They also have to use rules of language and the presumption that mens rea is required.

1. Is the offence regulatory in nature or a true crime?

If the offence is regulatory in nature (meaning not criminal, minor, or with no moral issue involved) the offence is more likely to be classed as strict liability. A case that considered this question is ***Sweet v Parsley (1970)***.

Sweet v Parsley (1970)

Ms Sweet sublet her property to a group of tenants, retaining a room for herself but hardly spending any time there. The police searched the property and found cannabis. Ms Sweet was convicted under ***s5 Dangerous Drugs Act 1965*** *(now replaced), of 'being concerned in the management of premises used for the smoking of cannabis'. She appealed, alleging that she had no knowledge of the circumstances and indeed could not have reasonably been expected to have such knowledge. On appeal, her conviction was overturned, with Lord Reid acknowledging that strict liability was only appropriate for 'quasi-crimes' where no real moral issue was involved. Ms Sweet's conviction had caused her to lose her job and had damaged her reputation. It was felt that strict liability was inappropriate and the offence should be classed as a 'true crime' requiring mens rea. She did not have any mens rea so her conviction was quashed.*

2. Does the offence relate to an issue of social concern?

This is an issue of concern to general society at a given time. Issues of social concern can shift over time but tend to relate to offences such as selling alcohol or cigarettes to minors, pollution and public safety. It is felt that imposing strict liability for crimes that relate to issues of social concern will promote extra vigilance and care on the part of defendants to not commit the offence. Of course, this is only appropriate for regulatory offences and the distinction drawn in ***Sweet v Parsley (1970)*** is still applicable.

Harrow London Borough Council v Shah (1999)

The defendants were convicted of selling National Lottery tickets to a child under 16. It did not matter that they believed the child to be over 16: the offence was committed as soon as they had sold the lottery ticket to a person under 16. The courts felt this offence related to an issue of social concern.

3. Did Parliament intend to create an offence of strict liability by using certain words in a statute?

Although there is no official list of words that point towards a crime being one of strict liability, Parliament uses some words when drafting statutes that point to mens rea being required. 'Mens rea words' include **intentionally**, **recklessly** and **knowingly**. Other words have generally been interpreted by judges as pointing towards no mens rea being required. These include **possession** and **cause**.

Alphacell v Woodward (1972)

The defendants were charged with causing polluted matter to enter a river. The pumps that prevented the pollution from overflowing into the river had become clogged with leaves and, as a result, the matter leaked into the river. It was irrelevant that the defendants had no idea the pumps were clogged with leaves and had not wanted any contamination to enter the river. They had caused the polluted matter to enter the river and were therefore liable.

4. The gravity of the punishment

The more serious the criminal offence and punishment that can be imposed, the less likely it is to be one of strict liability. This reflects the fact that, with strict liability, defendants can be convicted without fault. This can be problematic as the associated small penalties do not always act as a **deterrent**. On the other hand, as in the case of ***Callow v Tillstone (1900)***, the damage to a small business's reputation can be far greater than the impact of a small fine.

Callow v Tillstone (1900)

A butcher was convicted of 'exposing unfit meat for sale'. The butcher was found guilty even though he had taken reasonable care not to commit the offence by having the carcass inspected by a vet who said it was safe to eat.

Advantages and disadvantages of strict liability

ADVANTAGES	DISADVANTAGES
Time and cost of proving mens rea: Mens rea can be difficult to prove and, if it had to be proved for every offence, the courts would be clogged with cases and some guilty individuals may escape conviction. This in turn would increase court costs.	**Possibility of injustice:** Liability is imposed without fault on the part of the defendant. Individuals may have taken all reasonable steps to avoid the behaviour and be unaware they are committing the illegal act yet still face conviction. The injustice is magnified further with absolute liability offences as in the case of ***Larsonneur (1933)***.
Protection of society by promoting a higher standard of care: As strict liability offences are easy to prove, individuals may take more care when acting in certain situations, thereby protecting society from harmful behaviour.	**Role of judges:** Judges are interpreting what they think Parliament intended in an Act. This gives judges an increased role and there is a risk of inconsistency in the imposition of strict liability.

KEY CASE

Cundy v Le Cocq (1884)

The defendant was convicted of unlawfully selling alcohol to an intoxicated person, contrary to ***s13 Licensing Act 1872***. It was held that it was not necessary to consider whether the defendant knew, should have known or should have used reasonable care to detect that the person was intoxicated. As soon as the defendant sold the alcohol to the drunken person, he was guilty of the offence.

KEY TERMINOLOGY

deterrent: something that discourages a particular action.

GRADE BOOST

Though punishments are usually small for strict liability offences, the case of ***Gammon*** is an exception. In this case the penalty was a fine of up to $250,000 or three years' imprisonment.

STRETCH AND CHALLENGE

Many of the cases in this section overlap to demonstrate more than one factor. For example, ***Alphacell v Woodward (1972)*** can be used to show how some words to indicate strict liability were intended by Parliament but it was also an issue of social concern (pollution). Think about the other cases described in this section and how they may demonstrate more than one of the factors.

ADVANTAGES	DISADVANTAGES
The ease of imposing strict liability acts as a deterrent: Individuals are deterred from carrying out the offending behaviour in the knowledge that a prosecution is likely to result in a conviction, due to only having to prove the actus reus.	**Is strict liability actually a deterrent?** As a result of the small penalties imposed for strict liability, some argue that it does not act as a deterrent. For example, large businesses may continue to carry out the offending behaviour (such as pollution), paying the small fines and not changing their practices. In addition, to act as a deterrent it is argued that a person ought to have knowledge that what they are doing is wrong so they could have taken steps to prevent it. This is not always the case with strict liability offences.
Proportionality of the punishment appropriate for strict liability: Strict liability offences tend to carry small penalties. This is appropriate as defendants may be unaware they are committing the offence or have taken all reasonable steps to avoid doing so.	**Does strict liability breach the European Convention on Human Rights?** There has been some debate over whether, according to ***Article 6(2) ECHR***, everyone should be presumed innocent until proven guilty according to law. ***R v G (2008)*** appears to allow the imposition of strict liability.

GRADE BOOST

Think of cases to demonstrate the ways that courts have protected society through the imposition of strict liability. Use these cases to provide the evaluation required for higher marks.

- Sale of unfit meat: ***Callow v Tillstone (1900)***.
- Pollution: ***Alphacell v Woodward (1972)***.
- Dangerous buildings: ***Gammon (HK) Ltd v Attorney General (1985)***.
- Food hygiene: ***Callow v Tillstone (1900)***.

STRETCH AND CHALLENGE

1. A harsh sentence is more likely to be a deterrent from committing crime. Explain how deterrence is linked to theories of punishment.
2. Explore the following cases and consider how the question of strict liability in relation to human rights was dealt with by the courts:
   - ***Hansen v Denmark (1995)***
   - ***Salabiaku v France (1988)***.

Proposal for reform

The Law Commission proposed a ***Criminal Liability (Mental Element) Bill (1977)***, where the onus would be on Parliament, if it wished to create an offence of strict liability, to make this clear in the Act of Parliament. It is Parliament's responsibility to decide the nature of criminal liability and to provide a clear indication to judges of whether it intended to create a crime with no requirement of mens rea. This would prevent some of the confusion and inconsistency of judicial decisions.

Exam Skills

Strict liability as an aspect of this topic is likely to feature as a question in its own right. It lends itself to an explanation and evaluation of the current law.

Summary: General elements of criminal liability

- A criminal case has to be proved by the prosecution **beyond reasonable doubt**
- **Actus reus** and **mens rea** needed for the commission of a criminal offence
- **Factual causation:**
  - 'But for' test: ***R v White (1910)***
  - De minimis rule: ***R v Pagett (1983)***
- **Legal causation:**
  - The injury must be the operating and substantial cause of death: ***R v Smith (1959), Jordan (1956)***
  - The thin skull test: ***R v Blaue (1975)***
  - Novus actus interveniens: ***R v Pagett (1983)***
- **Contemporaneity rule**: coincidence of actus reus and mens rea**:**
  - Continuing acts: ***Fagan v MPC (1969)***
  - Single transaction of events: ***Thabo Meli (1954)***
  - Transferred malice: ***Latimer (1986)***

- **Actus reus: Guilty act**
  - Conduct crimes: perjury
  - Result crimes: murder
  - State of affairs crimes: ***R v Larsonneur (1933)***
  - Omissions
- **Omissions:** Not a crime to fail to act unless under a **duty to act**:
  - Statute: ***Road Traffic Act 1988***: breath sample
  - Contract: ***R v Pitwood (1902)***
  - Duty arising out of a special relationship: ***R v Gibbins and Proctor (1918)***
  - Duty arising out of a person assuming responsibility for another: ***R v Stone and Dobinson (1977)***
  - Defendant has inadvertently created a dangerous situation, becomes aware of it, but fails to take steps to rectify it: ***Miller (1983)***
- **Mens rea**
  - Direct and oblique intention: virtual certainty test: ***Nedrick (1986)***, ***Woolin (1998)***
  - Recklessness: subjective: ***R v G and another (2003)***
  - Negligence
- **Strict liability** crimes do not require proof of mens rea for at least one element of the actus reus
- Tends to cover regulatory offences e.g. food hygiene, parking offences, polluting
- Offences tend to be **statutory** but require **statutory interpretation** by judges, as Parliament doesn't always make it clear whether an offence is strict liability
- Starting point for judges is **presumption** that mens rea is always required: ***Gammon (HK) Ltd v Attorney General (1985)***
- Presumption can be rebutted by considering **four Gammon factors:**
  1. Is the offence regulatory in nature or a true crime? ***Sweet v Parsley (1970)***
  2. Does the offence relate to an issue of social concern? ***Harrow London Borough Council v Shah (1999)***
  3. Did Parliament intend to create an offence of strict liability by using certain words in a statute? e.g. **intentionally**, **knowingly**. Non mens rea words include **possession**, **cause**: ***Alphacell v Woodward (1972)***, ***Cundy v Le Cocq (1884)***
  4. The gravity of the punishment: ***Callow v Tillstone (1900)***, ***Gammon (HK) Ltd v Attorney General (1985)***
- **Advantages of strict liability:**
  - Reduces time and cost of proving mens rea
  - Protection of society by promoting a higher standard of care
  - Ease of imposing strict liability acts as a deterrent
  - Proportionality of appropriate punishment
- **Disadvantages of strict liability:**
  - Possibility of injustice
  - Role of judges in interpreting statutes can lead to inconsistency
  - Small penalties may reduce deterrence
  - Does strict liability breach the European Convention on Human Rights? ***R v G (2008)***
- Proposals for reform: ***Criminal Liability (Mental Element) Bill (1977)***

Hierarchy of non-fatal offences against the person

Spec reference	Key content	Assessment Objectives	Where does this topic feature on each specification/exam?
WJEC AS/A Level 3.14: Offences against the person **Eduqas AS Level 2.3.3:** Offences against the person (non-fatal) **Eduqas A Level 2.3.3:** Offences against the person	• Non-fatal offences: Criminal Justice Act 1988: assault and battery • Non-fatal offences: Offences Against the Person Act 1861: actual bodily harm; wounding and grievous bodily harm; wounding and grievous bodily harm with intent	**AO1** Demonstrate knowledge and understanding of legal rules and principles **AO2** Apply legal rules and principles to given scenarios in order to present a legal argument using appropriate legal terminology **AO3** Analyse and evaluate legal rules, principles, concepts and issues	**WJEC AS/A Level:** Unit 3; Unit 4 **Eduqas AS Level:** Component 2 **Eduqas A Level:** Component 2; Component 3

Exam Skills

At A Level, the topic of 'Offences again the person' is split into fatal offences and non-fatal offences. These aspects of the topic are likely to feature separately on the exam. **The Eduqas AS specification only requires students to know about non-fatal offences. However, both WJEC and Eduqas A Level specifications require students to know about both non-fatal and fatal (homicide) offences.** Fatal offences are covered in Book 2 and non-fatal offences are covered in this book.

The majority of offences do not result in death. There are five non-fatal offences against the person that need to be considered. From least to most serious, these are:

1. assault
2. battery
3. s47 actual bodily harm (ABH)
4. s20 grievous bodily harm (GBH)
5. s18 grievous bodily harm (GBH) with intent.

It is important to be aware of the actus reus and mens rea of each offence with case law to support.

It is also important to appreciate the hierarchical relationship between the offences, as it will affect any **plea bargaining**. Plea bargaining is an agreement between prosecution and defence in a criminal case that the charge will be reduced if the defendant pleads guilty. For example, a defendant charged with a s20 offence will be offered the opportunity to plead guilty to the lesser s47 offence. On the face of it, this seems unfair and not in the interests of justice but the courts rely upon defendants pleading guilty.

The CPS **charging standards** (see page 169) provide guidance to prosecutors for what injuries constitute which non-fatal offence. They don't, however, have any legal significance and are merely there to guide.

KEY TERMINOLOGY

plea bargaining: the defendant pleads guilty to a lesser offence in return for a lower sentence to save court time and make the trial more predictable.

Assault

Assault is not defined in an Act of Parliament, as it is a **common law** offence.

Section 39 Criminal Justice Act 1988 provides that assault is a **summary offence** with a maximum sentence on conviction of six months' imprisonment or a fine.

Actus reus

The actus reus of assault is any act which causes the victim to apprehend the immediate infliction of violence, such as raising a fist, pointing a gun or threatening somebody. In the case of ***Logdon v DPP (1976)***, as a joke, the defendant pointed a gun at the victim. She was frightened until he told her it was a replica gun. The court held that the victim had apprehended immediate physical violence, and the defendant had been at least reckless as to whether this would occur.

Words can amount to an assault, as can silent telephone calls. In ***R v Ireland, Burstow (1997)*** the defendant made silent telephone calls to three women and these were held to be sufficient to cause the victim to apprehend the immediate infliction of unlawful force. In ***Constanza (1997)*** threatening letters were held to amount to an assault. Words can also take away liability for assault as in ***Tuberville v Savage (1669)*** where the accused put his hand on his sword and said 'If it were not assize time I would not take such language from you.' (At the time of the ***Tuberville*** case, periodic criminal courts called assizes were held across the UK where judges would travel to various areas to try cases. In this case, it meant the judges were in town.) The threat was the hand being placed on the sword, which could have amounted to an assault; however, because he coupled this with the statement that he would not use his sword as it was assize time, the words took away liability for the assault.

The threat has to be 'immediate', though this has been interpreted liberally by the courts as can be evidenced by the cases of ***Ireland***, ***Constanza*** and ***Smith***.

Smith v Chief Superintendent of Woking Police Station (1983)

The victim was in her nightdress in her downstairs window. The defendant, who had trespassed on to her property, was staring at her through the window and, even though the door was locked and she was behind the window, it was deemed to be sufficiently 'immediate' for an assault.

GRADE BOOST

It is important for the exam to be able to explain the actus reus and mens rea of each offence, appreciating the subtle differences and overlaps between them. You should support with case law and then apply each element to the facts of a problem scenario.

KEY TERMINOLOGY

common law (also case law or precedent): law developed by judges through decisions in court.
summary offence: the least serious offences, triable only in the magistrates' court.

Mens rea

The mens rea of assault, as defined in the case of ***R v Savage, Parmenter (1992)***, is that the defendant must have either intended to cause the victim to fear the infliction of immediate and unlawful force, or must have seen the risk that such fear would be created (**subjective recklessness**).

Recklessness is now generally subjective. It must be believed that the defendant in question foresaw the consequence of their action but took the risk anyway. This is also known as **Cunningham recklessness,** from the case of ***R v Cunningham (1957)***. **Caldwell recklessness (objective)** has all but been abolished following the decision in ***R v G and another (2003)***.

Pointing a gun is an actus reus of assault if it causes the victim to fear immediate unlawful violence.

Battery

As with assault, battery is not defined in an Act of Parliament; it is a **common law** offence. ***Section 39 Criminal Justice Act 1988*** provides that battery is a **summary offence** with a maximum sentence on conviction of six months' imprisonment or a fine.

Though assault and battery are two separate and distinct offences, they can sometimes be charged together as 'common assault'.

Actus reus

The actus reus of battery is the application of unlawful physical force on another. It is accepted that a certain amount of physical force happens in daily life (***Collins v Wilcock (1984)***), such as walking down a busy street where people may bump into one another. For it to be a battery, the force must be unlawful.

The application does not need to be direct, as in the case of ***Haystead v DPP (2000)***, where the defendant punched a woman, causing her to drop her child. It was held to be indirect battery of the child. Similarly, in the case of ***Fagan v Metropolitan Police Commissioner (1969)***, Fagan accidentally parked his car on a police officer's foot when asked by the officer to park the car near the curb. Fagan did not mean to drive his car on the officer's foot. However, when asked to move, he refused. The force was applied indirectly by the car driving onto the officer's foot and was unlawful when he refused to move.

The term 'physical force' implies that a high level of force needs to be applied, but this isn't the case. In the case of ***Thomas (1985)***, it was held that touching the hem of a girl's skirt while she was wearing it was akin to touching the girl herself. The victim also need not be aware that they are about to be struck; therefore, striking someone from behind will constitute battery. Contrast this with assault, where the victim must fear the application of unlawful force and so therefore must be aware of it.

Unlike assault, a battery can be committed by **omission** where there is a duty to act. In ***DPP v Santana-Bermudez (2004)***, the defendant was asked by a police officer searching him whether he had any 'needles or sharps' on him. He failed to inform her and when she searched him she pricked her finger on a hypodermic needle in his pocket. It was held that his failure to inform her of the presence of the needle was sufficient to satisfy the mens rea.

Mens rea

The mens rea of battery is intention or subjective recklessness to apply unlawful force on another, as confirmed in of ***R v Venna (1976)***.

s47 Actual bodily harm (ABH)

KEY TERMINOLOGY

occasion(ing): to bring about or to cause.

The statutory offence of actual bodily harm (ABH) is set out in ***s47 Offences Against the Person Act 1861*** which provides that it is an offence to commit an assault **occasioning** actual bodily harm.

Although the statute only refers to assault, the offence may also be committed by a battery. It is in fact far more common for offences under s47 to be committed by battery than by an assault.

ABH is a **triable either way** offence (see page 62). The maximum sentence for ABH is five years' imprisonment

Actus reus

The actus reus for ABH can be broken down into three elements:

1. assault or battery **2.** occasioning **3.** actual bodily harm.

1. Assault or battery

The first element of ABH requires proof of the actus reus of either an assault or battery as defined above.

2. Occasioning

The assault or battery must occasion actual bodily harm. The **chain of causation** therefore needs to be established between the defendant's act and the harm caused. For there to be criminal liability, there must be an unbroken chain of causation. This is usually easy to prove but in the case of ***R v Roberts (1971)*** a woman jumped from a moving car, injuring herself, and the question was whether choosing to jump from the moving car had broken the chain of causation. She jumped as the defendant was making sexual advances towards her, including touching her clothes. It was held that the defendant had committed a battery by touching the woman's clothes and that had caused her to jump out of the moving car, thereby injuring herself. It was stated that the victim's reaction (jumping from the car) did not break the chain of causation if it was reasonably foreseeable, provided it was not so 'daft or so unexpected that no reasonable man could be expected to foresee it'. If this was the case then it could constitute a **novus actus interveniens.**

3. Actual bodily harm

The definition of what constitutes ABH was clarified in the case of ***Miller (1954)*** as 'hurt or injury calculated to interfere with health or comfort'; that is, ABH can be physical or psychological harm. It can include cutting someone's hair, as in ***DPP v Smith (2006)***. The case of ***Chan Fook (1994)*** also makes the point that the injury needs to be more than 'transient or trifling'. The word 'actual' in this context means that, though the injury doesn't need to be permanent, it should not be so trivial as to be insignificant.

Mens rea

The mens rea of battery is the same as for assault or battery. There is no requirement to prove any extra mens rea for the actual bodily harm, as per ***Roberts (1971)*** and confirmed in ***R v Savage (1992)*** confirmed this.

s20 Grievous bodily harm (GBH)

The statutory offence of grievous bodily harm (GBH) is set out in ***s20 Offences Against the Person Act 1861***, which provides that it is an offence to **maliciously** inflict grievous bodily harm or wound the victim.

Grievous is defined in ***DPP v Smith (1961)*** as 'really serious harm', and confirmed in ***Saunders (1985)***. In ***R v Brown and Stratton (1998)***, injuries such as bruising, broken nose, missing teeth and concussion were held to be grievous bodily harm. GBH is a **triable either way** offence. The maximum sentence for GBH is five years' imprisonment, but this has been criticised as being the same as for the lesser offence of ABH.

Actus reus

GBH can be proved by either showing an **infliction** of grievous bodily harm or a **wounding** of the victim. It is important to choose the charge carefully as being either infliction of GBH or a wound.

GRADE BOOST

You should state what the mens rea of assault or battery actually is:

- **Assault:** Intention or subjective recklessness to cause the victim to apprehend the infliction of immediate unlawful violence.
- **Battery**: Intention or subjective recklessness to apply unlawful force on the victim.

KEY TERMINOLOGY

wounding: to break both layers of the skin, usually resulting in bleeding.

KEY CASE

R v Savage (1992)
A woman went into a bar and saw her ex-partner's new girlfriend. She went up to her and said, 'Nice to meet you, darling' and threw beer from her glass over her. While doing so, she accidentally let go of the glass, which broke and cut the other woman's wrist. She argued that she had only the mens rea of battery (throwing the beer) but the court held that this was irrelevant. No additional mens rea was required for the actual bodily harm (the glass cutting the woman's wrist). As long as she had the mens rea for battery then the mens rea of ABH was satisfied.

KEY CASES

Clarence (1888)
A husband passed a sexually transmitted disease to his wife by having intercourse with her. It was ruled that 'inflict' required an assault or battery and, as she had consented to sexual intercourse, neither of these was present. This is now considered to be bad law.

M'Loughlin (1838)
A scratch or break to the outer skin is not sufficient if the inner skin remains intact.

KEY TERMINOLOGY

maliciously: interpreted as meaning with intention or subjective recklessness.

STRETCH AND CHALLENGE

The leading case is now ***R v Savage (1992)***, while ***DPP v Parmenter (1992)*** confirmed this point. Find out more about these cases.

KEY TERMINOLOGY

indictable: the most serious offences, triable only in the Crown Court.

GRADE BOOST

S18 is a crime of **specific intent**, meaning that it can only be proved with intention as the mens rea. S47 and s20 are both **basic intent** offences as they can be proved with either intention or recklessness.

1. Infliction of GBH

The term **'inflict'** has caused difficulty in the courts over the years. In ***Clarence (1888)***, the term was given a very restrictive meaning but, more recently, in ***Dica (2004)*** the meaning was widened to include recklessly transmitting HIV to an unaware victim as being 'infliction' of GBH.

A similarly wide approach is demonstrated in ***R v Halliday (1889)***, where a husband frightened his wife to the extent that she jumped out of their bedroom window to escape. The court held that her injuries had been directly inflicted by the defendant even though she had voluntarily jumped from the window.

The case of ***R v Bollom (2003)*** established that the age and characteristics of the victim are relevant to the extent of the injuries sustained.

2. Wounding

A wound requires a breaking in the continuity of the skin, usually resulting in bleeding. In ***Moriarty v Brooks (1834)***, it was held that both the dermis and the epidermis must be broken; however, in ***JCC (A Minor) v Eisenhower (1984)***, an internal rupture of blood vessels in the victim's eye as a result of being shot with a pellet gun was not held to amount to wounding within s20.

Mens rea

The mens rea for GBH is defined by the word **maliciously.**

The case of ***Mowatt (1967)*** decided that it does not need to be established whether or not the defendant intended or was reckless as to the infliction of GBH or a wound as long as it can be proved that he intended or was reckless to cause some physical harm. This was further clarified in the case of ***DPP v A (2000)***, where it was held to be sufficient to prove the defendant intended or foresaw that some harm might occur and it was not necessary to show the defendant intended or foresaw that serious harm would occur.

s18 Grievous bodily harm (GBH) with intent

The statutory offence of grievous bodily harm with intent is set out in ***s18 Offences Against the Person Act 1861***, which provides that it is an offence to **intend** to maliciously wound or cause grievous bodily harm. Section 18 is an **indictable** offence. The maximum sentence for ***s18 Offences Against the Person Act 1861*** is life imprisonment, reflecting the gravity of s18 in comparison to s20 of the same Act.

Actus reus

Like the actus reus for s20, the actus reus for s18 is either maliciously wounding or causing grievous bodily harm. It refers to the term '**cause**' as opposed to 'inflict' and though they are not the same (***R v Ireland, Burstow (1997)***) they have been taken to mean that causation is required. The meaning of 'wound' and causing 'grievous bodily harm' are the same as for s20.

Mens rea

The key difference between s20 and s18 is that s18 can only be proved with intention (direct or oblique) whereas s20 can be established with recklessness or intention to cause some harm.

The mens rea has two aspects:

1. The defendant must 'maliciously' wound or cause grievous bodily harm.
2. The defendant must have specific intent to either cause grievous bodily harm to the victim or to resist or prevent the lawful apprehension or detainer of any person.

Section 18 is a **specific intent offence** (as required by ***R v Belfon (1976)***) and requires intention to **maliciously** cause grievous bodily harm, thus reflecting the severity of the injuries and culpability of the defendant.

STRETCH AND CHALLENGE

Have a look at the charging standards on the CPS website and make a list of the likely injuries for each of the offences mentioned in this section.

Charging standards

The CPS has issued guidelines known as **charging standards** for the offences against the person, to ensure greater consistency. It details types of injury (e.g. swelling, graze, black eye, etc.) and the charge that should follow if such injuries are present.

Exam Skills

This topic is frequently examined as a problem scenario. You will need to be able to explain and/or apply the criminal liability of the parties involved. More than one non-fatal offence is likely to feature in the exam.

You might also be required to analyse and evaluate the effectiveness of the law in this area and consider proposals for reform.

Summary: Hierarchy of non-fatal offences against the person

- **Assault**
  - **Actus reus**: apprehension of immediate infliction of unlawful violence. Common law offence: ***s39 Criminal Justice Act 1988***
  - **Mens rea**: intention or subjective recklessness to cause the victim to fear the infliction of immediate unlawful force
- **Battery**
  - **Actus reus**: application of unlawful physical force. Common law offence. ***s39 Criminal Justice Act 1988***
  - **Mens rea**: intention or subjective recklessness to apply unlawful force on another
- **ABH:** ***s47 Offences Against the Person Act 1861***
  - **Actus reus**: 1. assault or battery, 2. occasioning, 3. actual bodily harm
  - **Mens rea**: the same as for assault or battery; no additional mens rea required for the actual bodily harm
- **GBH:** ***s20 Offences Against the Person Act 1861***
  - **Actus reus**: malicious infliction of grievous bodily harm or wounding (breaking of the skin)
  - **Mens rea**: intention or subjective recklessness to inflict 'some' harm
- **GBH with intent:** ***s18 Offences Against the Person Act 1861***
  - **Actus reus**: malicious wounding or causing grievous bodily harm. Indictable offence; maximum life imprisonment
  - **Mens rea**: specific intent crime; intention to maliciously cause GBH
- **CPS charging standards**

Rules, theory and protection of human rights law

Spec reference	Key content	Assessment Objectives	Where does this topic feature on each specification/exam?
WJEC AS/A Level **3.1:** The rules and theory of human rights law **Eduqas AS Level** **2.4.1:** The rules of human rights law and theory in human rights law **2.4.2:** Protection of rights and freedoms in the UK **Eduqas A Level** **2.4.1:** The rules of human rights law and theory in human rights law **2.4.2:** Protection of rights and freedoms in the UK	• The rules of human rights law and theory in human rights law • Human rights and civil liberties and the distinction between them • The roles played by Parliament and the courts in their regulation • The debate relating to the entrenched nature of the Human Rights Act 1998 • Protection of rights and liberties within the UK constitution • The European Convention on Human Rights • The impact of the Human Rights Act 1998; a UK Bill of Rights • Criticisms of human rights; entrenched nature of the HRA in the devolutionary settlements of Wales, Scotland and Northern Ireland	**AO1** Demonstrate knowledge and understanding of legal rules and principles **AO2** Apply legal rules and principles to given scenarios in order to present a legal argument using appropriate legal terminology **AO3** Analyse and evaluate legal rules, principles, concepts and issues	**WJEC AS/A Level:** Unit 3; Unit 4 **Eduqas AS Level:** Component 2 **Eduqas A Level:** Component 2; Component 3

KEY TERMINOLOGY

entrenched: a firmly established piece of law which is difficult, or unlikely, to change (e.g. the US Bill of Rights). The UK has no laws that are entrenched.

STRETCH AND CHALLENGE

Explain some advantages and disadvantages of entrenched laws.

Citizens in the UK are fortunate in that they live in a country where human rights are protected. The UK has an 'unwritten constitution' and, presently, no **entrenched** Bill of Rights, but certain rights and freedoms have been guaranteed by the UK's membership of various international institutions such as the United Nations and the Council of Europe. This section will explore the nature of human rights protection in the UK.

Human rights theory

Human rights are often described as **inalienable, universal** and **interdependent.** They emphasise the belief that common humanity is shared across the globe. All people everywhere in the world are entitled to human rights.

- **Inalienable** means that that they cannot be taken or given away.
- **Universal** human rights theory says that they apply to everyone simply by being human.
- **Interdependent** means that each human right, in some way, contributes to a person's dignity. Each right relies on the others.

They are also described as **indivisible.** Human rights are inherent to the dignity of every human person, and cover civil, cultural, economic, political and social issues. Therefore, all human rights are considered to have equal status and are not positioned in a hierarchical order. Denying a person one right invariably hinders their enjoyment of other rights.

Civil liberties

There is a debate about the difference between human rights and civil liberties. To many people, the difference is largely semantic and the terms are often used interchangeably with some overlap between the meaning of 'rights' and 'liberties'. However, the key difference is why a person has them. Human rights arise just by being a human, whereas civil rights arise by citizens being granted that right; for example, the rights given to American citizens by the US Constitution. The UK does not have a written constitution but is a signatory to the ***Universal Declaration of Human Rights (UDHR)*** and the ***European Convention on Human Rights*** (ECHR), the latter being incorporated into domestic law via the ***Human Rights Act 1998***. However, the UK does not yet have a British Bill of Rights.

The European Convention on Human Rights (ECHR)

Following the atrocities of the Second World War, the international community came together to collectively agree to protect human rights and promote peace. They formed the **United Nations (UN)**, which subsequently adopted the ***UDHR*** in 1948. This is seen as the inception of modern human rights protection. This was followed by the formation of the **Council of Europe**, which, in turn, adopted the ECHR. This is separate to the European Union and covers more countries; its aim is to uphold peace and protect human rights within Europe. The UK has since **incorporated** most of the ECHR into domestic law via the ***Human Rights Act 1998***.

The **Council of Europe** oversees states' adherence to the ECHR. Other institutions overseeing the ECHR are the **Committee of Ministers** and the **Parliamentary Assembly.**

As society evolves, human rights also evolve and the ECHR (along with other human rights treaties) is considered to be a **living instrument**. For example, when the ECHR was written in 1950, modern technologies did not exist that today influence the interpretation of, for example, the right to privacy.

The rights and freedoms protected by the ECHR are shown in the table below.

Article	Right
2	Right to life.
3	Freedom from torture, inhuman or degrading treatment.
4	Freedom from slavery and forced labour.
5	Right to liberty and security of the person.
6	Right to a fair trial.
7	Freedom from retrospective law.
8	Right to respect for private and family life, home and correspondence.
9	Freedom of thought, conscience and religion.
10	Freedom of expression.
11	Freedom of assembly and association.
12	Right to marry and start a family.
14	Prohibition of discrimination.

The rights contained within the ECHR can be categorised as **absolute, limited** or **qualified.**

- **Absolute rights:** These are the strongest rights. The state cannot deviate from these rights and they can never legally be breached. Example: the right to a fair trial ***(Article 6)***.

GRADE BOOST

Research the role of each of the institutions overseeing the ECHR.

- **Limited rights:** The state can deviate from these rights but only in the prescribed limitations laid down in the right. Example: the right to liberty ***(Article 5)***.
- **Qualified rights:** Most human rights are qualified rights. These are the weakest rights and can be removed when 'prescribed by law, necessary and proportionate in a democratic society in order to fulfil a legitimate aim'. They may be restricted to protect the rights of others or for the public interest. Example: freedom of expression ***(Article 10)***. They often involve balancing one human right against another.

STRETCH AND CHALLENGE

Consider the difference between a 'right' and a 'liberty'.

The ECHR has been signed by 47 states, each with varied social and legal histories. It allows each state discretion to give effect to the rights in different ways, in order to reflect their distinct histories and legal frameworks. This is known as the **margin of appreciation** and it can be either wide (in most cases) or narrow, where there is a consensus across most European states (see ***Handyside v The United Kingdom (1976)***).

GRADE BOOST

The UK did not incorporate ***Article 13*** 'the right to an effective remedy'.

Proportionality is also important when considering qualified rights in particular. This gives the court the power to balance competing rights, for example, ***Article 10*** against ***Article 8***. Absolute rights do not lend themselves to proportionality as they cannot be deviated from.

Citizens' rights in the UK have traditionally been thought of as **residual**. This means that what a citizen is not allowed to do is set out by law and what they can do (rights and freedoms) is not. This is evidenced in ***Malone v Metropolitan Police Commissioner (1979)***. Residual freedoms are quite easy to remove and difficult to enforce, so protection in the UK before ***HRA 1998*** was weaker.

The European Court of Human Rights (ECtHR) is based in Strasbourg

Before the HRA, the ECHR, not being part of domestic law, was not always binding as a source of law by judges in UK courts. In ***R v Secretary of State ex parte Brind (1990)***, Lord Ackner said that, while unincorporated, the treaty 'cannot be a source of rights and obligations'. Similarly, in ***Derbyshire County Council v Times Newspapers (1993)***, the ECHR was considered useful as an **extrinsic aid.**

GRADE BOOST

An example of the UK responding to a judgement of the ECtHR is by passing the ***Contempt of Court Act 1981*** following the ruling in ***The Sunday Times v UK (1979)*** (known as the 'Thalidomide case').

The European Court of Human Rights (ECtHR)

The ECHR also established the **European Court of Human Rights (ECtHR),** which sits in Strasbourg and is the final court of appeal for individuals who feel their human rights have been violated. The ECtHR is the primary enforcement mechanism of the ECHR. The UK may be brought before the ECtHR by individuals alleging that their rights have been violated. Before the ***HRA 1998***, individuals had to use the right of **individual petition**, granted in 1966, in order to appeal to the ECtHR. All domestic remedies had to have been exhausted first, which was both time consuming and expensive. However, when the ECtHR declared the UK had illegally removed human rights, the country did usually respond positively to the judgment. While the UK was not under a **legal obligation** to amend the law, it was under a moral obligation. For example, the ***Contempt of Court Act 1981*** was passed as a result of ***Sunday Times v UK (1979)***, when the ECHtR held that the common law offence of contempt of court breached ***Article 10*** of the ECHR.

GRADE BOOST

Consider the impact of ***HRA 1998***. There are several key sections of the HRA that need to be considered. It is important to include examples and/or case law and/or evaluation to support your answer.
As well as the sections considered in the table below, residual freedoms became positive rights. The moral obligation to uphold human rights became a legal one.

An example of a case where an individual petitioned the ECtHR is ***McCann v UK (1995)*** on the matter of the UK's 'shoot to kill' policy and a breach of ***Article 2*** (the right to life).

The Human Rights Act 1998 (HRA)

The ***Human Rights Act 1998 (HRA)*** provided citizens in the UK with **positive rights** and strengthened their protection domestically. It **incorporated** the majority of the ECHR into domestic law and provided UK judges with additional powers and duties to uphold citizens' human rights.

The table shows key sections of the HRA.

Section	Detail	Case law / example / evaluative point
s7	The ECHR is now directly applicable in the UK courts; a citizen who believes that their human rights have been removed is able to take the case to a national court. Citizens can still take their cases to the ECtHR at Strasbourg on appeal.	
s2	When deciding on a case involving alleged breaches of human rights, courts in the UK must **take into account** the precedents of the ECHR. They are not binding, but they are **strongly persuasive.**	***Leeds City Council v Price (2006)*** demonstrates that UK courts can choose a UK precedent over a ECHR decision. If there is a conflicting UK precedent, then the UK precedent will be used instead. If the ECHR precedent is clear and there is no UK precedent, then the ECHR precedent should be followed (***Ullah 2004***). **Evaluative point**: Power given to unelected judges under ***ss2*** and ***3***, particularly when combined with ***s6***.
s3	When deciding a case involving human rights, judges must interpret a law **'so far as is possible to do so'** compatibly with human rights.	***R v A (2001)***: Lord Steyn said the duty under ***s3*** goes beyond the purposive approach. A 'declaration of incompatibility' should be a measure of last resort. ***Ghaidan v Godin-Mendoza (2004)*** provides the current approach for the use of ***s3***.
s4	If a statute cannot be interpreted broadly enough to ensure compatibility with ECHR rights, judges can issue a **declaration of incompatibility**.	***Bellinger v Bellinger (2003)***. ***Anderson (2003)***. ***Belmarsh detainees (A and Others (2004))***. ***R v Mental Health Tribunal ex parte H (2001)***.
s6	Individuals can sue 'public authorities' for breaches of human rights. These are bodies whose functions are 'public' or 'partly public'. Courts and tribunals are considered public authorities.	'Standard' public authorities (e.g. NHS, armed forces, prison service). 'Functional' public authorities can be classed as either public or private depending on the nature of their work and the proximity of their relationship with the state (see ***Poplar (2001)*** and ***YL v Birmingham City Council (2008)***). **Implied horizontal direct effect:** If a human rights issue is raised in a private case, the public authority (e.g. the court which hears the case) is under a duty to protect these rights (see ***Douglas and Jones v Hello! Ltd (2005)***).
s10	If a declaration of incompatibility has been issued, Parliament has the power to change this quickly using a **fast-track** procedure.	**Evaluative point**: under ***s10(2)***, Parliament can change the law using the fast track procedure if there is a 'compelling reason'. However, merely issuing a declaration of incompatibility is not necessarily a 'compelling reason'.
s19	All legislation that is passed after the ***HRA 1998*** came into force **should** have a statement of compatibility.	**Evaluative point:** Under ***s19(1)(b)*** a law can be passed without a statement of compatibility. Ministers are not saying the law is 'incompatible', just that they are unable to declare it 'compatible'. Two Bills that did not have a statement of compatibility are the ***Local Government Bill 2000*** and the ***Communications Bill 2003***. Both are now Acts of Parliament.
s8	A court may grant 'any just and appropriate remedy within its powers'.	**Evaluative point:** The UK chose not to incorporate ***Article 13*** which would have required courts to provide an 'effective remedy'.

STRETCH AND CHALLENGE

Research some further cases on declarations of incompatibility under ***s4***. Did the UK change its law?

A British Bill of Rights

There are ongoing proposals to replace the ***Human Rights Act 1998*** with a **British Bill of Rights**. The ***HRA*** is simply an Act of Parliament and could be removed at any time; it is not **entrenched** and neither is the ECHR. The UK is one of only a couple of developed Western countries without a Bill of Rights.

Some positive impacts of the ***HRA 1998*** are evidenced by the sections and case examples in the table above but there are also limitations and criticisms. One of these came following the ECtHR decision to block the deportation of the radical Muslim cleric, Abu Qatada, in the case of ***Othman (Abu Qatada) v UK (2012)***. Repealing the HRA would not necessarily mean leaving the Council of Europe and the protection of the ECHR.

A commission was established by the Conservative–LibDem coalition to consider replacing the ***HRA 1998*** with a Bill of Rights. The commission published its final report in 2012, entitled **'A UK Bill of Rights? The Choice Before Us'**. Although its findings were largely inconclusive, a majority of the commission's members supported establishing a Bill of Rights. The main reason cited was lack of public support for the HRA. The Bill of Rights issue featured in the Conservatives' 2015 election manifesto but has been suspended until Brexit is concluded.

What would be different with a British Bill of Rights?

- It would be **entrenched** and difficult to change or remove. On the other hand, this could mean that the rights are also fixed and therefore could become out of date. The current unwritten constitution allows for flexibility to adapt over time.
- The rights could be more 'British' and could include additional rights.
- It would **curb the power of the Executive** and provide a check on the government of the day. The courts would have the power to refuse to apply any law which conflicted with the Bill of Rights. This increased power of the unelected judiciary is also a criticism of such a proposal and would, arguably, weaken parliamentary sovereignty.
- It would provide clearer guidance for judges on balancing rights such as Articles 8 and 10 ECHR.
- The fast-track procedure ***(s10 HRA)*** could be removed and replaced with a requirement that amendments to incompatible legislation would have to have a full parliamentary debate.

Potential problems with a Bill of Rights

- The **Good Friday Agreement** includes reference to the HRA and repeal of this could undermine the Northern Ireland peace process.
- **Devolution** settlements (e.g. for the Scottish Parliament) include reference to the ECHR.

STRETCH AND CHALLENGE

Look up the **Sewell Convention**. What impact would the repeal of the HRA have on this?

Summary: Rules, theory and protection of human rights law

- Human rights: inalienable, universal and interdependent
- Civil liberties
- ***European Convention on Human Rights (ECHR)*** agreed following Second World War
- Council of Europe oversees States' adherence to the ECHR
- ECHR as a 'living instrument':
- Absolute, limited and qualified rights
    - Pre-***Human Rights Act (HRA) 1998*** use as an 'extrinsic aid: ***Derbyshire County Council v Times Newspapers (1993)***
    - ***R v Secretary of State ex parte Brind (1990)***: ECHR 'not domestic law'
- Margin of appreciation: ***Handyside v UK (1976)***
- Proportionality
- Residual freedoms: ***Malone v MPC (1979)***
- European Court of Human Rights (ECtHR): Right of individual petition 1966
- ***McCann v UK (1995)***
- ***HRA 1998*** incorporated the majority of ECHR into domestic law:
    - ***s7:*** Applicable in UK courts
    - ***s2:*** ECHR rulings are strongly persuasive but not binding: ***Leeds City Council v Price (2006), Ullah (2004)***
    - ***s3:*** Judges under a duty to interpret laws compatibly with human rights 'so far as possible to do so': ***Ghaidan v Godin-Mendoza (2004)***
    - ***s4:*** Declaration of incompatibility: ***Bellinger v Bellinger (2003)***
    - ***s10:*** Incompatible legislation can be changed quickly using a 'fast track' parliamentary procedure
    - ***s6:*** Individuals can sue 'public authorities' for breaches of human rights. Standard, functional and courts/tribunals. Implied horizontal direct effect: ***Douglas and Jones v Hello! Ltd (2005)***
    - ***s19:*** Statement of compatibility required: ***Communications Act 2003***
    - ***s8:*** A court may grant 'any just and appropriate remedy within its powers'
- **UK Bill of Rights** would:
    - Be entrenched
    - Curb Executive power
    - Provide clearer guidance for judges on balancing rights
    - Remove fast track procedure
    - Potentially affect devolution settlements and Good Friday agreement

Specific provisions within the ECHR

Spec reference	Key content	Assessment Objectives	Where does this topic feature on each specification/exam?
WJEC AS/A Level 3.2: Specific provisions within the ECHR **Eduqas AS Level 2.4.3:** Specific provisions within the ECHR **Eduqas A Level 2.4.3:** Specific Provisions within the ECHR	• Provisions of Article 5, right to respect for liberty and security of the person; Article 5 exceptions and restrictions • Provisions of Article 6, right to a fair trial; nature of an absolute right • Provisions of Article 8, right to respect for private and family life, home and correspondence; Article 8 exceptions; negative and positive obligations • Provisions of Article 10, right to freedom of expression. Article 10 exceptions • Provisions of Article 11, right to freedom of peaceful assembly and to freedom of association with others, including the right to form and to join trade unions. Article 11 exceptions	**AO1** Demonstrate knowledge and understanding of legal rules and principles **AO2** Apply legal rules and principles to given scenarios in order to present a legal argument using appropriate legal terminology **AO3** Analyse and evaluate legal rules, principles, concepts and issues	**WJEC AS/A Level:** Unit 3; Unit 4 **Eduqas AS Level:** Component 2 **Eduqas A Level:** Component 2; Component 3

The rights contained within the ECHR can be categorised as either **absolute, limited** or **qualified.** This section will explore ***Articles 5, 6, 8, 10*** and ***11***.

- **Absolute rights:** These are the strongest rights. The state cannot deviate from these rights and they can never legally be breached. Example: the right to a fair trial ***(Article 6)***.
- **Limited rights:** The state can deviate from these rights but only in the prescribed limitations laid down in the right. Example: the right to liberty ***(Article 5)***.
- **Qualified rights:** Most human rights are qualified rights. These are the weakest rights and can be removed when 'prescribed by law, necessary and proportionate in a democratic society in order to fulfil a legitimate aim'. They may be restricted to protect the rights of others or for the public interest. Example: freedom of expression ***(Article 10)***. They often involve balancing one human right against another.

EDUQAS A LEVEL

Article 5: The right to respect for liberty and security of the person

5(1)

Everyone has the right to liberty and security of person. No one shall be deprived of their liberty save in the following cases and in accordance with a procedure prescribed by law:

(a) the lawful detention of a person after conviction by a competent court

(b) the lawful arrest or detention of a person for non-compliance with the lawful order of a court or in order to secure the fulfilment of any obligation prescribed by law

(c) the lawful arrest or detention of a person effected for the purpose of bringing them before the competent legal authority on reasonable suspicion of having committed an offence or when it is reasonably considered necessary to prevent them committing an offence or fleeing after having done so

(d) the detention of a minor by lawful order for the purpose of educational supervision or their lawful detention for the purpose of bringing them before the competent legal authority

(e) the lawful detention of persons for the prevention of the spreading of infectious diseases, of persons of unsound mind, alcoholics or drug addicts or vagrants

(f) the lawful arrest or detention of a person to prevent them effecting an unauthorised entry into the country or of a person against whom action is being taken with a view to deportation or extradition.

5(2)

Everyone who is arrested shall be informed promptly, in a language which they understand, of the reasons for their arrest and of any charge against them.

5(3)

Everyone arrested or detained in accordance with the provisions of paragraph 1(c) of this Article shall be brought promptly before a judge or other officer authorised by law to exercise judicial power and shall be entitled to trial within a reasonable time or to release pending trial. Release may be conditioned by guarantees to appear for trial.

5(4)

Everyone who is deprived of their liberty by arrest or detention shall be entitled to take proceedings by which the lawfulness of their detention shall be decided speedily by a court and their release ordered if the detention is not lawful.

5(5)

Everyone who has been the victim of arrest or detention in contravention of the provisions of this Article shall have an enforceable right to compensation.

Summary of Article 5

In essence, ***Article 5*** states that everyone has the right to **liberty and security of person**. This is a limited right: there are prescribed limitations provided for in the Article.

Article 5(1) provides that any arrest or detention must be lawful and 'in accordance with a procedure prescribed by law'. An exhaustive list for when the right can be overridden is given in ***Article 5*** and includes things such as detention after conviction by a court, detention following lawful arrest (remand), detention of those who breach court order, detention of those with mental health issues and detention of minors.

GRADE BOOST

Article 5 links to the topic of police powers.

STRETCH AND CHALLENGE

Look up each right covered in ***Article 5*** on https://rightsinfo.org and summarise what each means in plain English. Make a note of landmark cases regarding the application of each right. Also make a note of any interesting statistics about each right.

Article 6: The right to a fair trial

6(1)

In the determination of their civil rights and obligations or of any criminal charge against them, everyone is entitled to a fair and public hearing within a reasonable time by an independent and impartial tribunal established by law.

Judgment shall be pronounced publicly but the press and public may be excluded from all or part of the trial in the interests of morals, public order or national security in a democratic society, where the interests of juveniles or the protection of the private life of the parties so require, or to the extent strictly necessary in the opinion of the court in special circumstances where publicity would prejudice the interests of justice.

6(2)

Everyone charged with a criminal offence shall be presumed innocent until proved guilty according to law.

6(3)

Everyone charged with a criminal offence has the following minimum rights:

(a) To be informed promptly, in a language which they understand, and in detail, of the nature and cause of the accusation against them.

(b) To have adequate time and facilities for the preparation of their defence.

(c) To defend themselves in person or through legal assistance of their own choosing or, if they have not sufficient means to pay for legal assistance, to be given it free when the interests of justice so require.

(d) To examine or have examined witnesses against them and to obtain the attendance and examination of witnesses on their behalf under the same conditions as witnesses against them.

(e) To have the free assistance of an interpreter if they cannot understand or speak the language used in court.

GRADE BOOST

Article 6 links with all instances where a person would face a civil hearing or criminal trial. It is not limited to situations involving human rights so would also link with topics within the other specification options: criminal, contract and tort.

Summary of Article 6

Article 6 is an absolute right and can never be deviated from by the state. It provides for the **right to a fair trial** and covers both civil and criminal situations. There are three essential components to ***Article 6***: a **fair** and **public hearing,** which should take place within a **reasonable time** and be made by an **independent and impartial tribunal** established by law.

It allows for the exclusion of the press and/or public if the case involves morals, public order or national security. This also applies if the exclusion is in the interests of juveniles, to protect the private life of the parties or in special circumstances if the court believes publicity would prejudice the interests of justice.

Articles 6(2) and ***(3)*** provide that, in any criminal case, the accused shall be considered innocent until proven guilty. They set out some minimum rights; for example, the right to be assisted by a lawyer.

Articles 8, ***10*** and ***11*** are all **qualified rights**. They are all structured similarly, with part 1 of each Article providing for the basic right, and part 2 providing that the right may be removed in some circumstances (the '**qualifications**').

Qualified rights can be removed when:

- prescribed by law
- it is necessary in a democratic society and proportionate
- it fulfils a legitimate aim; for example, the protection of the rights and freedoms of others.

Case law generally centres on whether the removal of the right is justifiable and often involves balancing one right against another.

Article 8: The right to respect for private and family life, home and correspondence

Article 8(1)

Everyone has the right to respect for their private and family life, their home and their correspondence.

8(2)

There shall be no interference by a public authority with the exercise of this right except such as is in accordance with the law and is necessary in a democratic society in the interests of national security, public safety or the economic well-being of the country, for the prevention of disorder or crime, for the protection of health or morals, or for the protection of the rights and freedoms of others.

Summary of Article 8

The parts outlined in ***Article 8(2)*** are the 'legitimate reasons' when the right can be interfered with by a public authority. The other aspects of a qualified right (prescribed by law and necessary in a democratic society and proportionate) also apply.

There are four expressly protected interests under ***Article 8***:

1. private life
2. home
3. family
4. correspondence.

Article 8 contains both **negative** and **positive obligations**. The state is under a negative obligation not to interfere with privacy rights but ***Article 8*** includes a positive obligation on the state to act in a manner which protects an individual's right to private and family life: see ***Y v the Netherlands (1985)***.

Case law suggests that an individual's right to private life extends to situations which might at first appear to be relatively public situations. The court asks whether the person has, in all the circumstances, a reasonable or legitimate expectation of privacy. There is a clear link to the topic of privacy.

GRADE BOOST

There are links with the topic of defamation, breach of confidence and interception of communication. ***Article 8*** is often balanced against ***Article 10***.

Article 10: Freedom of expression

10(1)

Everyone has the right to freedom of expression. This right shall include freedom to hold opinions and to receive and impart information and ideas without interference by public authority and regardless of frontiers. This Article shall not prevent states from requiring the licensing of broadcasting, television or cinema enterprises.

10(2)

The exercise of these freedoms, since it carries with it duties and responsibilities, may be subject to such formalities, conditions, restrictions or penalties as are prescribed by law and are necessary in a democratic society, in the interests of national security, territorial integrity or public safety, for the prevention of disorder or crime, for the protection of health or morals, for the protection of the reputation or rights of others, for preventing the disclosure of information received in confidence, or for maintaining the authority and impartiality of the judiciary.

Summary of Article 10

As with ***Article 8***, the parts outlined in ***Article 10(2)*** are the 'legitimate reasons' when the right can be interfered with by a public authority. The other aspects of a qualified right (prescribed by law and necessary in a democratic society and proportionate) also apply. This provision is frequently in the news as the 'freedom of the press' and other media is related to the courts deciding whether the media have been acting appropriately in the dissemination of certain information. There are clear issues with the regulation of information distributed via social media and the Internet, yet the right to freedom of expression is crucial in any democracy. Part of ensuring that freedom of expression and debate is possible is protection of a free press and journalistic sources.

Where freedom of expression is at risk of being taken away, ***s12 Human Rights Act 1998*** provides that the courts must have 'special regard' to the right of freedom of expression in any case where it is in issue, and the public interest in disclosure of material which has journalistic, literary or artistic merit is to be considered. It has been used in cases involving the issuing of **injunctions** and **super-injunctions.** ***Section 12*** had been considered to give 'special protection' to freedom of expression, though this has been called into question following the Supreme Court ruling in the 'Celebrity Threesome' case of ***PJS v News Group Newspapers (2012)***. They held that neither ***Article 10*** (freedom of expression) nor ***Article 8*** (privacy) has preference over the other.

The following are considered areas of law where freedom of expression is protected or taken away:

- Defamation.
- Breach of confidence.
- Contempt of court.
- Obscenity.
- Freedom of assembly (right to protest).

GRADE BOOST

There are links with the topic of defamation, breach of confidence, freedom of assembly, interception of communication and obscenity. ***Article 10*** is often balanced against ***Article 8*** and also ***Article 6*** when considering contempt of court laws.

Article 11: Freedom of assembly and association

11(1)

Everyone has the right to freedom of peaceful assembly and to freedom of association with others, including the right to form and to join trade unions for the protection of their interests.

11(2)

No restrictions shall be placed on the exercise of these rights other than such as are prescribed by law and are necessary in a democratic society in the interests of national security or public safety, for the prevention of disorder or crime, for the protection of health or morals or for the protection of the rights and freedoms of others. This Article shall not prevent the imposition of lawful restrictions on the exercise of these rights by members of the armed forces, or the police, or of the administration of the state.

Summary of Article 11

Article 11 has two elements: the right to freedom of assembly and the right to freedom of association.

The right to freedom of assembly covers peaceful protests, demonstrations and public and private meetings. Being a qualified right, it can be restricted for the legitimate reasons outlined above. There is a clear balance to be struck between ***articles 10 and 11***.

The right to freedom of association permits individuals to join with others for a particular objective; for example, the right to join a trade union or political party. Freedom of association also provides for a negative right for individuals who may not be compelled to join an association. There is also a positive obligation on the state to provide legal safeguards for those who associate with other states that are also under a positive obligation to provide legal safeguards for individuals who associate with others.

GRADE BOOST

There is a link with the topics of public order and freedom of expression. There is a clear balance to be struck between ***articles 10 and 11***.

Reform of human rights

Spec reference	Key content	Assessment Objectives	Where does this topic feature on each specification/exam?
WJEC AS/A Level 3.5: The debate relating to the protection of human rights in the UK **Eduqas AS Level 2.4.5:** Reform **Eduqas A Level 2.4.6:** Reform	• Reform of the protection of human rights in the United Kingdom • The need for a United Kingdom Bill of Rights • The role of the Equality and Human Rights Commission	**AO1** Demonstrate knowledge and understanding of legal rules and principles **AO2** Apply legal rules and principles to given scenarios in order to present a legal argument using appropriate legal terminology **AO3** Analyse and evaluate legal rules, principles, concepts and issues	**WJEC AS/A Level:** Unit 3; Unit 4 **Eduqas AS Level:** Component 2 **Eduqas A Level:** Component 2; Component 3

The debate relating to the protection of human rights in the UK

The Council of Europe drew up the ECHR. The Council of Europe was set up after World War II to achieve unity among countries in matters such as protection of fundamental human rights. The Council now has 45 members. The **European Convention on Human Rights and Fundamental Freedoms** was drafted and signed in 1950, ratified by UK in 1951 and became binding in 1953.

The ***Human Rights Act (HRA) 1998*** was passed by the Labour government following its landslide victory in 1997, based on a promise to 'bring rights home.' The Act incorporated the ECHR (and first protocol) into domestic law and came into force in October 2000. According to ***s7 HRA 1998***, the ECHR is directly applicable in UK courts, with no need to go to the European Court of Human Rights (ECtHR), although it is possible as a last resort.

In practice, the Act was the most important constitutional development for over 300 years but, since it was passed, many people have questioned whether we have now made the transition from liberties to rights or whether we still need a Bill of Rights for Britain.

Analysis of the Human Rights Act 1998

It is clear that ***HRA 1998*** is not the same as, for example, the US Bill of Rights, which entrenches rights and allows courts to strike down legislation. Instead, the HRA preserves the doctrine of parliamentary sovereignty, as Parliament alone can decide whether to repeal or amend legislation.

However, incorporation of the ECHR into domestic law is a step towards a Bill of Rights for Britain.

The HRA does have drawbacks. The government may proceed with legislation despite any incompatibility with ECHR rights. There is a wide margin of appreciation permitted under the ECHR and most Convention rights are only qualified. The courts cannot strike down or refuse to apply incompatible legislation. The Act is vulnerable to repeal. There is a clear shift in power since incorporation, with unelected judges having a greater influence over social policy than in the past. However, it could be argued that this means a clearer separation of powers and greater respect for the rule of law as a result of such increased activism by the judiciary.

The Commission for Equality and Human Rights was set up in 2007, and became fully operational in 2009. Its functions include:

- providing advice and guidance
- conducting inquiries
- bringing cases
- monitoring the ECHR in domestic law
- scrutinising new laws
- publishing regular reports.

A Bill of Rights for the UK?

Among Western democracies, only the UK and Israel do not have a Bill of Rights. America, South Africa and most of Europe do. However, a Bill of Rights is only as effective as the state that enforces it.

Advantages and disadvantages of a Bill of Rights

Advantages	Disadvantages
Controls the Executive: A Bill of Rights offers a check on the huge powers of the Executive (e.g. The government and its agencies, such as the police etc.) Courts could refuse to apply legislation that was incompatible with the Bill of Rights.	**Not needed**: Some argue that our rights are adequately protected.
Judiciary must uphold ECHR: Under ***s3 HRA***, judges must interpret all laws to be compatible with human rights BUT only so far as it is possible to do so. This means that an Act that breaches rights in the Convention still prevails but this would not be the case with a Bill of Rights.	**Inflexible**: It would be hard to change.
Entrenchment: The HRA is not entrenched therefore it can be repealed. A Bill of Rights would be entrenched.	**Could lead to uncertainty**: Many Bills of Rights have a loose drafting style.
New rights: The HRA did not bring in any new rights but a Bill of Rights would.	**Weak**: A Bill of Rights is only as effective as the government that underpins it.
	Increased power to the judiciary: Judges are not elected and power would be removed from Parliament.
	Difficult to draft: It is hard to identify what could be included.

GRADE BOOST

It is crucial when you are considering whether the UK needs a Bill of Rights to be aware of the arguments for and against the current protection of our human rights in the ***Human Rights Act 1998***.

STRETCH AND CHALLENGE

Research the case of ***Othman (Abu Qatada) v UK (2012)***. Was the UK government justified in its anger at the ECHR's decision, which it believed hindered its fight against terrorism and crime?

STRETCH AND CHALLENGE

The government published a report in 2012 called **'A UK Bill of Rights? The Choice Before Us'**. Research its findings on whether the Human Rights Act should be repealed and replaced with a British Bill of Rights.

Exam Skills

Reform of the protection of human rights in the UK is a topic that could feature in its own right. However, when addressing any specific question on the ECHR and/or HRA, you should be fully prepared to discuss reforms of the current law.

Summary: Reform of human rights

- Council of Europe drafted the **European Convention on Human Rights and Fundamental Freedoms** (1950), ratified by UK in 1951 and binding from 1953
- The ***Human Rights Act (HRA) 1998*** incorporated the ECHR into domestic law and came into force in October 2000 and is a step towards a Bill of Rights for Britain
  - ***s7 HRA 1998***: ECHR is directly applicable in UK courts
  - Drawbacks of HRA: Legislation can still be incompatible with ECHR rights; vulnerable to repeal; unelected judges can now influence social policy
- **The Commission for Equality and Human Rights** was set up in 2007, and became fully operational in 2009
- **Advantages of a UK Bill of Rights**
  - Controls the Executive
  - Judiciary must uphold ECHR
  - Entrenchment
  - New rights
- **Disdvantages of a UK Bill of Rights**
  - Not needed
  - Inflexible
  - Could lead to uncertainty
  - Ineffective if government is weak
  - Increased power to the judiciary
  - Difficult to draft
- **'A UK Bill of Rights? The Choice Before Us'**
- ***Othman (Abu Qatada) v UK (2012)***

Restrictions of the ECHR

Spec reference	Key content	Assessment Objectives	Where does this topic feature on each specification/exam?
WJEC AS/A Level **3.3:** Restrictions, including restrictions permitted by the European Convention on Human Rights **Eduqas AS Level** **2.4.4:** Restrictions, including restrictions permitted by the European Convention on Human Rights **Eduqas A Level** **2.4.4:** Restrictions, including restrictions permitted by the European Convention on Human Rights	• Public order offences: freedom to meet, gather, demonstrate and protest; relationship between maintenance of public order and legitimate expression of opinion and dissent. Control of public gatherings, meetings and protests. Offences against public order, including incitement to racial hatred and religious hatred • Police powers: the law relating to police powers of stop and search; search of premises; arrest; detention; powers relating to terrorism; rights of persons in police custody; admissibility of evidence. Remedies against the police, including for malicious prosecution and false imprisonment • Interception of communications: access to information relating to individuals; surveillance, telephone tapping • Duty of confidentiality: misuse of private information; breach of confidence; official secrets legislation; contempt of court • Obscenity: arguments for and against restriction; problems of definition; methods of control; controls over books, magazines, films, DVDs, live performances, broadcasting; reforms • Torts of defamation: protection of reputation: defamation • Torts of trespass, harassment	**AO1** Demonstrate knowledge and understanding of legal rules and principles **AO2** Apply legal rules and principles to given scenarios in order to present a legal argument using appropriate legal terminology **AO3** Analyse and evaluate legal rules, principles, concepts and issues	**WJEC AS/A Level:** Unit 3; Unit 4 **Eduqas AS Level:** Component 2 **Eduqas A Level:** Component 2; Component 3

Exam Skills

This topic includes several sub-topics that could be examined as either an essay-style question or as a problem-style question on either unit/component of the WJEC/Eduqas specifications. Essentially, this aspect of the specification can be broken down into the following topics. There is slightly different content depending on whether the WJEC or Eduqas specification is being studied. This will be made clear in the relevant section.

- Public order.
- Police powers.
- Interception of communication.
- Duty of confidentiality.
- Obscenity.
- Defamation.
- Torts of trespass and harassment.

Public order

STRETCH AND CHALLENGE

Think back to the topic on 'Specific provisions of the ECHR'. What categories of right are ***articles 8*** and ***11***? What does this mean?

Obviously, there is a close connection between freedom of expression and freedom of assembly. People may wish to come together for the purposes of expressing opinions and ideas. This means that constraints on this freedom may also be constraints on freedom of expression.

Some degree of order and control is necessary for freedom to be meaningful in any society, but a society characterised by excessive concern for order and control would stifle healthy debate and criticism, repress a freedom and probably lack imagination and dynamism. Any attempt to encourage freedom carries dangers of lawlessness and disorder. Yet, ultimately, attempts to repress are also likely to end in protest and violence. Many incidents which threaten or involve breaches of public order are associated with events and activities which have a serious purpose in society. For instance, these could be protests about major social and political issues, concerns with questions of employment, or concerns with the pursuit of alternative lifestyles which do not easily fit in with the way communities are usually organised and run. When public order is threatened by these kinds of events and activities rather than by ordinary acts of violence, disorder and vandalism, there is a need to balance the preservation of order against the need to preserve and support fundamental freedoms.

STRETCH AND CHALLENGE

Research ***Beatty v Gillbanks (1882)***. What happened in this case concerning the right to peaceful assembly?

The most effective way to maintain public order may be to prevent the trouble arising in the first place by strictly controlling or even prohibiting related activities and events. Yet there is a danger that this may be seen as the easy way out of the problem, with the result that freedom of expression and assembly are effectively repressed. The court resisted this temptation in ***Beatty v Gillbanks (1882)*** when holding that marchers behaving peacefully and lawfully should not be prohibited from marching merely because another group of marchers would oppose them and thus threaten the peace. Effectively, the authorities had to control the other group.

Nevertheless, there are now many preventive powers which may be used to restrict otherwise lawful activity.

Public Order Act 1986

Marches/processions

Section 11: **Duties of organiser.** This concerns organisers of a march, not a meeting. The police must be given six days' notice of a procession intended to show support for, or opposition to, the views or actions of a person or group, to publicise a cause or campaign, or to mark or commemorate event (the aim is to target political processions). The notice must specify the date, time and proposed route, along with the organiser's name. The notice requirement is not required if it is 'not practical' to give such notice. Otherwise it is an offence to fail to give notice, or to deviate from the details given in the notice (***s11(7)) s11(8)*** and ***(9)***). A defence for the organiser is if they can show that the march deviated and they (a) did not suspect it had occurred or (b) it was beyond their control.

Section 11 creates a criminal offence but prosecutions are rare. The ***s11*** notice requirement causes confusion as it states that notice is not required if it is not practical to give any notice. This is not to be interpreted to mean that a phone call five minutes before a spontaneous demonstration will always be sufficient, as the section does refer to written notice

Section 12: **Conditions on marches/processions.** The police are given power to impose conditions regarding time and place of a **procession** if they think that it might result in:

1. serious public disorder

2. serious damage to property

3. serious disruption to the life of the community

4. a belief in the presence of intimidation or coercion.

These four situations known as triggers. Factors taken into account include the time and place of the procession and the route. It is an offence to break the conditions imposed. The fourth trigger is a political statement: 'the intimidation of others with a view to compelling them not to do an act they have a right to do or to do an act they have a right not to do'. This might be, for example, a racist march in an Asian area, which might be regarded as intimidating but not coercive; however this would fall under the third trigger.

According to ***Reed (1987)***, the four triggers should be interpreted strictly, and the words not diluted. The defendants shouted, raised their arms and waved their fingers, which might cause discomfort but not intimidation. In ***Newsgroups Newspapers v Sogat (1982)***, abuse and shouting did not amount to a threat of violence.

The police can, however, invoke conditions as they see fit to deal with a situation. The courts may be unlikely to find police decisions unlawful in this regard, but note the effect of the ***Human Rights Act 1998***. According to ***Kent v Metropolitan Commissioner (1981)***, a challenge would only succeed if it were held to be unreasonable (e.g. no trigger existed).

Section 13: **Banning order.** On the application of the police, the local authority, with the Home Secretary's consent, can impose a 'blanket ban' on marches. A ban **must** be imposed if it is thought that it may result in serious public disorder. The ban would cover **any** march within the time and area specified, which could include a peaceful march. The ban can stay in force up to three months. ***Section 13*** is used where the police believe the powers under ***s12*** are inadequate. Anyone who organises a march knowing of a ban commits an offence and can be arrested under ***s13(10)***.

Meetings/assemblies

Section 16: **Definition of a meeting/assembly.** This is seen as an assembly of two or more persons in a public place which is wholly or partly in the open air (numbers at meetings were amended by ***Anti-Social Behaviour Act 2003*** and were previously 20 or more).

Section 14: **Powers of police to impose conditions on meetings** using the same four triggers as for ***s12***. The police are given the power to impose conditions on static assemblies, held wholly or partly in the open air, if more than two people are going to be present. As well as the power to impose conditions in advance, ***s14*** allows the police to impose conditions at the time of the assembly and then to arrest those who fail to comply. Conditions include the place it is held, its duration and the maximum number of people. An assembly is **not** subject to the notice requirement found in ***s11***.

The police tried unsuccessfully to execute their powers under ***s14*** in ***DPP v Baillie (1995)***.

DPP v Baillie (1995)

Baillie was involved in promoting festivals and social events. He had distributed free news sheets and provided a telephone information service which gave vague details of when and where events would take place. The police issued a ***s14*** *notice ordering him to comply with certain conditions regarding a particular gathering, and in due course he was convicted for failing to comply with the order. The court ruled that the police had not had the power to issue the order because they had not known about the proposed event to know whether the conditions for the exercise of* ***s14*** *had been satisfied.*

Criminal Justice and Public Order Act 1994

Section 14A–C: **Trespassory assemblies**. On the application of the police, ***s14A*** gives power to the local authority (with the Home Secretary's consent) to prohibit the holding of all trespassory assemblies for a specified period of not more than four days in the whole, or part of, the district, but not exceeding an area represented by a circle with a five-mile radius from a specified centre.

Under ***s14B***, it is an arrestable offence to organise, participate in or incite an assembly which you know breaches a banning order.

The first case interpreting ***s14A*** was ***DPP v Jones (1998)***.

DPP v Jones (1998)

*The police had obtained an order from the local authority under **s14A** prohibiting for four days all assemblies within a four-mile radius of Stonehenge. The respondents had taken part in a peaceful, non-obstructive gathering of about 20 people on the grass verge of a road running along the perimeter fence of the historical site, as part of a demonstration for access to the monument. This gathering contravened the order and the demonstrators were arrested on failing to disperse at the request of the police. They were convicted but on appeal the Crown Court stated that any assembly on the highway is lawful provided it is peaceful and non-obstructive. The DPP appealed to the Queen's Bench Division, which held that the Crown Court had misstated the law and the respondents had committed an offence by breaching the banning order. On a further appeal to the House of Lords, this was reversed, and the Crown Court judgement approved.*

In ***Windle v DPP (1996)***, it was found that an offence had been committed under ***s14B*** when the respondents had run after a hunt, intending to disrupt it when they were sufficiently close.

Section 61: At the request of an occupier, the police have power to require trespassers to leave land on which they were intending to reside if they have damaged the land or used threatening, abusive or insulting behaviour to the occupier, their family or their employees or agents, or have brought at least six vehicles on the land.

Section 63: The police have the power to break up or prevent open air gatherings of 100 or more people at which loud music is likely to cause serious distress to neighbours. (The numbers were lowered from 100 by ***Anti-Social Behaviour Act 2003***.)

Section 68: **Aggravated trespass**. The main targets for this offence were hunt saboteurs. However, it covers any trespasser who disrupts a lawful activity taking place on land.

Section 69: Police can direct trespassers whom they reasonably believe to have committed, or are about to commit, an offence under ***s68*** to leave the land.

Public order offences under the Public Order Act 1986

Section 1: **Riot**. This is defined as 12 or more people threatening or using unlawful violence, acting together for a common purpose. The conduct of the 12 must be such that would cause a person of reasonable firmness to fear for their safety.

Section 2: **Violent disorder**. This is similar to riot but only three or more people are required, and they do not have to be acting for any common purpose.

Section 3: **Affray**. A person commits affray by using or threatening unlawful violence so that someone of reasonable firmness would fear for their safety. No minimum number of people is required.

Section 4: **Fear or provocation of violence**. An offence is committed by using threatening, abusive or insulting words or behaviour towards another person, or by distributing any writing, sign or other visible representation which is threatening, abusive or insulting. There must be an intention to provoke or to cause fear of immediate unlawful violence. According to ***R v Horseferry Road Justices, ex parte Siadatan (1990)***, the threat of violence must be immediate.

Section 4A: **Intentional harassment, alarm or distress**. This offence is identical to that in ***s5*** except that the accused must intend to cause harassment, alarm or distress and must actually do so. The maximum penalties are far higher than those in ***s5***.

Section 5 is similar to ***s4*** but of a lower level. This section covers harassment, alarm or distress and disorderly behaviour taking place within the hearing or sight of a person likely to be caused harassment, alarm or distress. ***DPP v Orum (1988)*** confirmed that police officers can be victims of ***s5 Public Order Act 1986*** caused by swearing and other abusive/threatening behaviour.

DPP v Fiddler (1992)

*It was confirmed that an offence had been committed under **s5** when an anti-abortion protester shouted and talked to people attending an abortion clinic and displayed plastic models and photographs of human foetuses.*

DPP v Clarke (1992)

Holding up pictures of aborted foetuses was found to be both abusive and insulting.

Note the word **insulting** has now been removed from the definition in ***s5***.

Section 6: **Mens rea requirement.** There must be intention or awareness that they are being threatening or abusive. If not, they should be acquitted.

Incitement to racial hatred

This is defined in ***s17*** as 'hatred against any group of persons defined by reference to colour, race, nationality or ethnic or national origins'.

1. Firstly, words and behaviour must be 'threatening, abusive or insulting'.
2. Secondly, the actions of the person charged must either have been intended to stir up racial hatred or be likely to do so.

Sections 18–22 are **publication offences**.

- ***Section 18*** deals with speeches at meetings or demonstrations. It is an offence to use words or behaviour, or display written material, which fulfils the elements outlined in ***s16 and 17***.
- ***Section 19*** covers publishing or distributing written material. It can be used against racist organisations that circulate newsletters and leaflets intended or likely to stir up racial hatred.
- ***Section 20*** deals with the performance of plays.
- ***Section 21*** deals with showing or playing films, videos or records.
- ***Section 22*** deals with broadcasting and cable services.
- ***Section 23*** makes it an offence to simply possess racist material.

Proceedings for any of these sections can only be brought with the consent of the Attorney General.

The Racial and Religious Hatred Act 2006

This Act added a ***Part 3A*** to the ***Public Order Act***.

Section 29A: Religious hatred is defined as 'hatred against a group of persons defined by reference to religious belief or lack of religious belief'.

- The offences cover speech, publications, plays, recordings and broadcasts and possession of inflammatory material.
- The offences are limited to threatening behaviour.
- Prosecution has to prove that the defendant intended to stir up religious hatred.
- Comedians who joke about a particular religion should not be affected.

In 2006, a Danish newspaper published cartoons showing the Prophet Mohammed and caused offence to Muslims. According to ***s29J***, a publisher who reprinted the cartoons in England would be unlikely to commit an offence under ***Part 3A POA***.

Other offences relating to racial and religious hatred

- ***Crime and Disorder Act 1998*** increased penalties for racially aggravated offences.
- ***Anti-Terrorism, Crime and Security Act 2001*** extended previous Acts to include religious aggravation.
- ***Football (Offences) Act 1991*** introduced the offence of 'indecent or racialist chanting' at a designated football match.

Private law remedies

Apart from control by the police, private persons can seek injunctions:

Hubbard v Pitt (1976)

Protesters handed out leaflets and carried posters outside the claimant's estate agency, who claimed they were trespassing over the public footpath outside. The claimant was awarded an injunction to prevent their demonstrations. The defendants appealed but the injunction was upheld. The question of rights to use the highway was irrelevant as the court was concerned only with the private law rights of the claimant in relation to an alleged private nuisance.

Denning MR gave a dissenting judgement, saying: 'The public have a rite of passage over a highway but the soil may belong to someone else. The owner of the soil may sue if a person abuses the right of passage so as to use it for some other and unreasonable purpose, such as where a racing tout walked up and down to note the trials of the race horses (see ***Hickman v Maisey (1900)***). But those cases do not give Prebble and Co. a cause of action here, because Prebble and Co. do not own the pavement; it is a highway. The surface is vested in the local authority and they have not complained, nor could they, since no wrong has been done to them or their interest. The courts should not interfere by interlocutory injunction with the right to demonstrate and to protest any more than they interfere with the right of free speech; provided that everything is done peaceably and in good order.' and 'the right to demonstrate and the right to protest on matters of public concern ... are rights which it is in the public interest that individuals should possess' and that 'history is full of warnings against suppression of these rights.'

Serious Organised Crime and Police Act 2005 (SOCPA)

SOCPA contains a number of measures that have severely restricted the freedom to protest near Parliament and other 'sensitive' sites.

To hold a demonstration in the 'designated area' of 1km from Parliament, the law says that six days' notice must be given to the Metropolitan Commissioner (or 24 hours if six days was not 'reasonably practicable'). They must allow the demonstration but may impose conditions which can be changed without notice on the day by any senior police officer. One of the considerations covers 'disruption to the life of the community', a catch-all category that allows the police to stop almost any protest (although processions organised under the ***Public Order Act 1986*** are exempt). Loudspeakers are banned except for use by those in certain positions of authority.

Sections 128–138 SOCPA relate to restrictions on protesting at 'designated sites' (military bases and some government and royal sites) and in the 'designated area' around Parliament.

An amendment to ***s136 SOCPA*** was made in the ***Serious Crime Act 2007***, which makes people convicted of 'intentionally encouraging or assisting an offence' under ***s132 SOCPA*** (protesting without police authorisation near Parliament) liable to imprisonment for up to 51 weeks, a fine of up to £2,500, or both.

SOCPA received most publicity for its ban on unauthorised protests within 1km of Parliament. It is widely accepted to have been devised to end the five-year protest of Brian Haw opposite the Houses of Parliament.

R (on the application of Haw) v Secretary of State for the Home Department (2006)
In 2001, Brian Haw began to camp in Parliament Square as a one-man protest against war and foreign policy. He only left his makeshift campsite to attend court hearings, surviving on food brought by supporters.

He originally camped on the grass in Parliament Square but, when the Greater London Authority took legal action to remove him, he relocated to the pavement, which was administered by Westminster City Council. In 2002, Westminster City Council attempted to prosecute Haw for obstructing the pavement but the case failed as his banners did not impede movement. His continuous use of a megaphone led to objections by Members of Parliament who had offices nearby.

***Section 132–8 SOCPA** banned all unlicensed protests but, because Haw's protest was ongoing and on Parliament Square prior to the enactment of the Act, it was unclear whether the Act applied to him.*

*As preparation for implementing the new **SOCPA** began, Haw won an application for judicial review in 2005, successfully arguing that a technical defect in the Act meant it did not apply in his case. The Act states that demonstrations must have authorisation from the police 'when the demonstration starts', and Haw asserted that his demonstration had begun before the passage of the Act, which was not made retrospective. Although the commencement order to bring the Act into force had referred to demonstrations begun before the Act came into force, there was no power for the commencement order to extend the scope of the Act.*

Haw was joined in 2005 by Barbara Grace Tucker who, since Haw's death in 2011, continued her presence opposite the Houses of Parliament. She was arrested countless times, usually on a charge of 'unauthorised demonstration'.

The government appealed against the judgement, and in May 2006 the Court of Appeal allowed the appeal and declared that the Act did apply to Haw. The court found that the intent of Parliament was clearly to apply to all demonstrations in Parliament Square regardless of when they had begun.

'The only sensible conclusion to reach in these circumstances is that Parliament intended that those sections of the Act should apply to a demonstration in the designated area, whether it started before or after they came into force.'

In another example, **Maya Evans** recited the 97 names by the Cenotaph memorial to Britain's war dead in Whitehall, near Downing Street. She was the first person to be tested and found guilty under ***s132 SOCPA*** (unauthorised protests near Parliament). Evans was given a conditional discharge and ordered to pay £100. Many people claim that, under ***SOCPA***, free speech and the right to protest is being undermined. Lord Strathclyde said: 'Freedom does not die in one blow; it dies by inches in public legislation.'

Breach of the peace

In common law, the police have the power to arrest without warrant if a breach of the peace has been committed, if there is reasonable belief that a breach of the peace will be committed, or if they think it will be repeated. This was widely used during the 1984/85 miners' strike to prevent access to picket areas. This power to arrest for breach of the peace was technically abolished by ***SOCPA***, which makes **all** offences arrestable if it is necessary to arrest according to one of the necessity factors.

Moss v McLachlan (1985)
There had been violent conflict between members of different trade unions during the 1984–5 miners' strike and the police had found it difficult to maintain the peace. The defendants were four of about 60 striking miners who were intent on a mass demonstration at a nearby colliery. They were stopped by the police less than five minutes' from the nearest pit. The police feared a violent episode would occur if they went there. The men tried to push past the police and were arrested.

The miners lost their appeal. The court accepted that the police had acted correctly; a test of 'close proximity both in place and time' and a breach of the peace was held to be 'imminent and immediate'.

Foy v Chief Constable of Kent (1984)

Striking miners were held up more than 200 miles from their destination, suggesting that the requirement of proximity stated in ***Moss v McLachlan (1985)*** *was now unnecessary. In assessing whether a real risk existed, the police took into account news about disorder at previous pickets. There did not appear that there was anything about these particular miners to suggest that they might cause a breach of the peace. Therefore, the police were able to deny them their freedom of movement and assembly on no more substantial grounds than that other striking miners had caused trouble in the past.*

Note the difference in proximity of the miners between ***Moss v McLachlan (1985)***, where they were 2 to 4 miles away from the collieries they intended to picket, and ***Foy v Chief Constable of Kent (1984)***, where they were over 200 miles from their intended place of picket.

GRADE BOOST

Was there an imminent and immediate breach of the peace in ***Foy v Chief Constable of Kent (1984)?*** Were the miners in 'close proximity in both time and place'? Research ***Nicol v DPP (1996)***, ***Steel v UK (1998)***, ***Redmond-Bate (1999)*** and ***Bibby (2000)***. What do these cases tell us about the police's powers to arrest for breach of the peace?

STRETCH AND CHALLENGE

Compare ***R (Laporte) v Chief Constable of Gloucestershire (2007)*** with ***Austin and Another v Commissioner of Police of the Metropolis (2007)***.

KEY CASES

R (Laporte) v Chief Constable of Gloucestershire (2007)

In March 2003, officers from seven police forces, acting under the direction of Gloucestershire Police, stopped three coaches from London carrying 120 anti-Iraq war protesters. The protesters had been planning to join thousands of people in a demonstration at RAF Fairford. Some of the protesters, including Laporte, had purely peaceful intentions, but some items suggesting violent intent were discovered on the coaches by the police. The coaches were returned to London under police escort, without any opportunity for the passengers to get off.

Laporte sought a judicial review of the actions of the Chief Constable in preventing her from attending the protest and forcibly returning her to London. The court rejected her first complaint but upheld her second. The Court of Appeal upheld that decision. Both parties appealed. The issue was whether the Chief Constable's actions were prescribed by law and necessary in a democratic society.

The House of Lords allowed Laporte's appeal. The House of Lords found that the Chief Constable's actions were not prescribed by law; neither was there a power to take action short of arrest to prevent a breach of the peace which was not sufficiently imminent to justify arrest. The Chief Constable's actions were disproportionate because they were premature and indiscriminate. It was disproportionate to restrict Laporte's exercise of her rights of freedom of expression and the right to peaceful protest under ***Articles 10*** and ***11 ECHR*** because she was with some people who might, in the future, breach the peace.

Austin and Another v Commissioner of Police of the Metropolis (2007)

This case involved the May Day demonstrations in London, when police surrounded about 3,000 people in Oxford Circus and did not allow them to leave for seven hours to prevent the spread of violence. One claimant, who had simply been there on business and was not one of the protesters, sought damages for false imprisonment and unlawful detention.

The claimant's case failed. The court said that the police have powers to act out of necessity to defend property. It was reasonable for the police to have treated all those in Oxford Circus as demonstrators until they came forward with their personal circumstances. Less intrusive action would not have been appropriate or effective. In exceptional circumstances, it was lawful for the police to act in this way to prevent an imminent breach of the peace.

Obstruction of the highway

Under ***s137 Highways Act 1980***, it is an offence 'if a person without lawful authority or excuse in any way wilfully obstructs the free passage along a highway'. For the purposes of this crime the highway includes the pavement as well as the road. If a police officer orders a speaker, distributor, vendor or audience to move along, and they refuse to do so, they are likely to be arrested for obstruction of the highway or obstruction of a constable in the execution of their duty.

Lord Esher in ***Harrison v Duke of Rutland (1893)*** considered access to be a right to pass or repass, for any reasonable or usual mode of using the highway as a highway. In ***Arrowsmith v Jenkins (1963)***, a pacifist meeting was held in a street which linked two main roads. The meeting blocked the street and the organiser cooperated with the police in unblocking it. The road was blocked completely for five minutes, and partly for fifteen. Although the police had notice of the meeting, the organiser was arrested and convicted. In ***Nagy v Weston (1966)***, **reasonable** use of the highway constituted a lawful excuse. The test of reasonableness will consider length of obstruction, its purpose, place and whether there is actual or potential obstruction.

Obstruction of the police

Obstruction of the police is a statutory offence under ***s89 Police Act 1996***. The courts have been willing to uphold a wide use of this offence, even where its use restricts freedom of assembly. In ***Duncan v Jones (1936)***, a speaker addressing a crowd from a box on the highway was told to stop because the police feared a breach of the peace. Although the only grounds for this fear was that a disturbance had occurred in the same place a year earlier, the courts upheld the arrest of the speaker for obstruction after she refused to stop speaking.

Police powers

Police powers are considered in the context of human rights as they sometimes involve the deprivation of a suspect's liberty and invasion of their privacy.

The main Act governing police powers is the ***Police and Criminal Evidence Act 1984 (PACE)*** though others also give the police powers over citizens. Within ***PACE*** and other Acts, police are given discretion with the ways they exercise their powers and **remedies** are available for breach of these powers.

A remedy is a solution in a civil case (e.g. payment of compensation). In this context it can also refer to a claimant taking a civil action against the police or making a complaint against the police force in question that may result in disciplinary action or an apology. (You can read more about police complaints on page 199.) Codes of Practice run alongside ***PACE*** and provide guidelines for the exercise of certain powers. Breach of the codes cannot give rise to legal action but, if there is a 'serious and substantial' breach, evidence could be excluded.

The **Royal Commission on Criminal Procedure** (RCCP or Philips Commission) concluded in 1981 that a balance needed to be reached between 'the interests of the community in bringing offenders to justice and the rights and liberties of persons suspected or accused of crime'. ***PACE*** was passed following these findings and consolidated police powers into one Act.

The powers of the police can be broken down into five main sections:

1. Stop and search (persons, vehicles and premises)
2. Arrest
3. Detention and interrogation
4. Admissibility of evidence
5. Complaints against and police and remedies

GRADE BOOST

It is crucial when discussing police powers to accurately refer to the sections of ***PACE*** or other Acts that provide the police with the power to carry out a particular act or that guide their conduct. In the exam, remember with a problem-style question to **identify** and **define** the law, **apply** the law to the facts and reach a **conclusion** as to whether the power was correctly used. Even if an action has been done correctly, you still need to discuss the law that gives them that power.

STRETCH AND CHALLENGE

'Reasonableness' is tricky concept and depends on what the individual deems reasonable and acceptable. This provides the police with some measure of discretion in the exercise of their powers.

1a. Stop and search of persons and vehicles

Section 1 PACE

Police can stop and search persons or vehicles in a public place or a place to which the public has access if there are **reasonable** grounds to suspect they will find stolen or prohibited articles. This search must take place in a public place, which is defined as a place to which the public have access and is not a dwelling.

Section 23 Misuse of Drugs Act 1971

Police can stop and search any person or vehicle if they have reasonable suspicion that they will find controlled drugs.

Section 1(3) Criminal Justice Act 2003

Police have extended powers to stop and search for articles intended to be used to cause criminal damage.

Section 1(6) PACE

Police may seize any stolen or prohibited articles.

Code A paragraph 2.2

This gives guidance on 'reasonable suspicion'. There is a two-stage test:

1. The officer must have genuine suspicion that they will find the stolen or prohibited object.
2. The suspicion that the object will be found must be reasonable. This means that there must be an objective basis for that suspicion, based on facts, information and/or intelligence or some specific behaviour. Reasonable grounds for suspicion cannot be supported by personal factors alone (e.g. physical appearance), or with regard to any of the protected characteristics under the ***Equality Act 2010*** such as, age, disability, race, religion or gender. Generalisations or stereotypical images that certain groups are more likely to be involved in criminal activity will not give grounds for reasonable suspicion, and nor will a person being known to have previous convictions.

There are powers where the police do not need reasonable suspicion, such as under ***s44 Terrorism Act 2000*** and ***s60 Criminal Justice and Public Order Act 1994.***

Section 60 Criminal Justice and Public Order Act 1994 (CJPOA)

If a police officer of or above the rank of inspector reasonably believes that serious violence will take place in an area, they can authorise the stop and search of persons and vehicles in that area for up to 24 hours to look for dangerous instruments or offensive weapons.

The use of the power to conduct ***s60*** searches without reasonable suspicion was unsuccessfully challenged as breaching ***Article 8 ECHR*** (right to a private life) in ***R (Roberts) v Commissioner of the Police of the Metropolis (2015).***

Section 60AA CJPOA (1994)

This gives powers to require the removal of face coverings. However, the officer must reasonably believe that someone is wearing such an item wholly or mainly to conceal their identity.

The power in ***s44 Terrorism Act 2000*** was successfully challenged in ***Gillan and Quinton v the UK (2010).*** The European Court of Human Rights (ECtHR) ruled that the powers were an illegal breach of ***Article 8 ECHR*** as they were so broad they failed to provide safeguards against abuse. Following this decision, the government announced that it was suspending the power to stop and search a person without suspicion under ***s44***. The power was replaced with new stop and search powers in ***s47A Terrorism Act 2000*** as amended by ***s59–62 Protection of Freedoms Act 2012***.

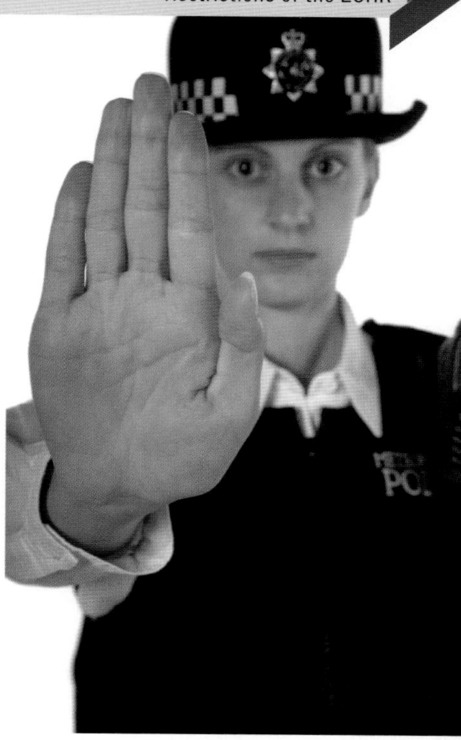

The test for authorising ***s47A*** powers is that the senior police officer giving it must:

- reasonably suspect that an act of terrorism will take place
- consider that the powers are necessary to prevent such an act.

The maximum authorisation length was cut from 28 to 14 days and should be authorised for no longer than is necessary.

Section 117 PACE

Reasonable force can be use in carrying out the stop and search. This also applies to the arrest. It is a 'floating section'.

Section 2 PACE

Before carrying out a stop and search, police officers must take reasonable steps to follow the correct procedure and bring five things to the attention of the suspect, for example, the police officer should identify themselves, the station at which they are based and the grounds for carrying out the search. In ***R v Bristol (2007)***, a failure to provide the necessary information rendered a stop and search unlawful because the PC had failed to give his name and station. Evidence found could be ruled inadmissible in court.

Section 2(3): Police officers not in uniform must provide documentary evidence of their ID.

Section 2(9): A suspect can be asked to remove their outer coat, jacket and gloves in public. Headgear and footwear can be removed but in private and in the presence of an officer of the same sex.

Section 3 PACE

After the search, the police must make a written record of the search unless this is not practicable and there are exceptional circumstances. If it is not practicable straight away, it should be done as soon as practicable. A ***s3*** record must include five items such as the person's ethnic origin, the object of the search, the grounds for making it, the date, time and place and the outcome of the search.

Section 4 PACE

An officer of the rank of superintendent or above can authorise in writing the setting up of road checks to see if the vehicle is carrying a person who has committed an offence other than a road traffic offence, a person who is a witness to such an offence, a person intending to commit such an offence or a person who is unlawfully at large.

KEY CASE

Osman v DPP (1999)
Officers failed to give their name or station, making the search unlawful.

GRADE BOOST

When studying this topic, make the connections with human rights. Many of the cases above were challenged on the basis of human rights.

1b. Search of premises

Searches of premises can be carried out with or without a warrant. Any property can be searched if a person consents to it.

Search with a warrant

The main provisions are found in ***s8 PACE***. This gives the police the power to apply to a magistrate for a search warrant. The magistrate must be satisfied that the police have reasonable grounds to believe that an indictable offence has been committed and that there is material on the premises which is likely to be of substantial value to the investigation and that the material is likely to be relevant evidence. It must be impractical for the search to be made without a warrant (because, for example, they cannot communicate with the occupier, they have not consented to entry or they need immediate entry to the premises).

Search without a warrant

There are four key sections:

- ***Section 17:*** Police may enter to make an arrest with or without a warrant, capture a person unlawfully at large or to protect people or prevent damage to property.

- ***Section 18:*** After an arrest for an indictable offence, police can search premises occupied or controlled by the suspect if they reasonably believe there is evidence of the offence or other offences on the premises.
- ***Section 32:*** After an arrest for an indictable offence, an officer can enter and search the premises where the person was arrested or where they were just before being arrested, if the officer reasonably suspects it contains evidence relating to the paticular offence.
- ***Section 19:*** Once lawfully on the premises, the police can seize and retain any relevant evidence.

Code B

This provides important guidelines for the exercise of the power to search premises. It provides that searches of premises should be carried out at a reasonable time with reasonable force and showing due consideration and courtesy towards the property and privacy of the occupier(s).

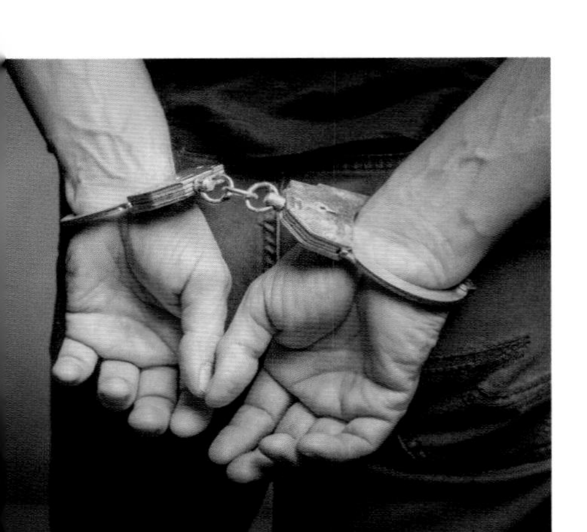

2a. Arrest with a warrant

Arrest can be carried out with and without a warrant. Police must apply to the magistrates for an arrest warrant. The name and details of the offence should be specified to the police and, once granted, provides the power to a constable to enter and search premises to make the arrest if required.

2b. Arrest without a warrant

This is covered by ***s24 PACE*** as amended by ***s110 SOCPA 2005***. An arrest without a warrant can be made if a constable has reasonable grounds to believe that a person **is** committing, **has** committed or is **about** to commit an offence or has reasonable grounds to suspect the defendant is guilty **and,** importantly, that an arrest is **necessary**.

'Necessary' to arrest

Under ***s24(5)***, a constable must have reasonable grounds for believing it is **necessary to arrest** the person for reasons given in ***s24(5)***. These grounds are:

a) to enable the name of the person in question to be ascertained (where it is not known or where the constable believes the one provided to be false)
(b) to enable the address of the person in question to be ascertained as in (a)
(c) to prevent the person in question—
(i) causing physical injury to himself or any other person
(ii) suffering physical injury
(iii) causing loss of or damage to property
(iv) committing an offence against public; or
(v) causing an unlawful obstruction of the highway
(d) to protect a child or other vulnerable person from the person in question
(e) to allow the prompt and effective investigation of the offence or of the conduct of the person in question
(f) to prevent any prosecution for the offence from being hindered by the disappearance of the person in question.

GRADE BOOST

Code A also applies to arrest. Reasonable suspicion can never be based on personal factors alone, such as race, age, sex, previous convictions and other general stereotypes. ***Article 5 ECHR*** provides that everyone has the right to liberty. Arrest interferes with this right and must be exercised lawfully.

Code of Practice G

This governs the power of arrest. In recognition of the ***Human Rights Act 1998*** and the right to liberty, the power of arrest should be fully justified and the police have to prove that it is necessary. Police officers using this power should consider whether their objectives could be met in any other way.

The ECtHR case of ***O'Hara v UK (2000)*** confirmed the two-part test for 'reasonable suspicion'. The officer must have actual suspicion (subjective) and there must be reasonable grounds for that suspicion (objective).

Section 117 PACE

Officers can use reasonable force to make the arrest.

Section 28 PACE

For an arrest to be valid, certain procedural elements must be complied with. Even if it is obvious, the suspect must be told in accessible language that they are being arrested and the grounds for the arrest.

Code C PACE

The suspect must be cautioned on arrest: *'You do not have to say anything. But it may harm your defence if you do not mention when questioned something which you later rely on in court. Anything you do say may be given in evidence.'*

Section 24A PACE as amended by SOCPA

This provides a power to a person other than a constable to arrest without a warrant anyone who is in the act of committing an indictable offence, or anyone they have reasonable grounds for suspecting are committing an indictable offence. They must have reasonable grounds for believing an arrest is necessary and that it is impracticable for an officer to make the arrest. The term **indictable** within ***SOCPA*** not only means the most serious offences but also crimes that are triable either way.

Section 32 PACE

A constable may search an **arrested** person at a place other than a police station if they have reasonable grounds for believing that the arrested person may present a danger to themselves or others, are in possession of evidence or present a danger.

3. Detention and interrogation

Section 30 PACE

The suspect must be taken to the police station as soon as possible after arrest unless they are required elsewhere.

Section 36 PACE

On arrival at the police station, the **custody officer** decides whether there is enough evidence to charge the suspect.

Section 37 PACE

If there is not sufficient evidence to charge a suspect, police will assess whether such evidence might be obtained through questioning and, if so, a suspect may be detained for these purposes. If not, the suspect should be released. If enough evidence exists to charge on arrest, the suspect should be granted bail under ***s38 PACE***.

Once detention has been authorised, the custody officer must begin a custody record for the detainee which must record the reasons for detention (***Code C*** and ***s37***).

Section 40 PACE

A person detained but not yet charged should have their detention reviewed after first six hours and then every nine hours by the custody officer.

Section 41 PACE

Police could authorise detention without charge for up to 24 hours. This was increased to 36 hours (***s42***) following the ***Criminal Justice Act 2003***.

Section 44 PACE

The maximum period of detention is 96 hours, on approval of magistrates.

Section 54 PACE

Police may conduct an **ordinary search** on an **arrested** person on arrival at the police station and seize any item they believe the suspect might use to cause physical injury to themselves or any other person, to damage property, to interfere with evidence, or to assist them to escape; or any item the constable has reasonable grounds for believing may be evidence relating to an offence.

KEY TERMINOLOGY

Custody officer: a constable of at least the rank of sergeant who is present in the custody suite of a police station and is responsible for the welfare and rights of people brought into custody. They keep a custody record.

STRETCH AND CHALLENGE

The ***Terrorism Act 2006*** allows detention to be extended to 14 days where the offence relates to terrorism.

Intimate searches and samples

Section 55: **Intimate search:** The police, on the authorisation of an inspector or higher, have the power to carry out an intimate search of a suspect's body's orifices where the superintendent has reasonable grounds for believing that the suspect has concealed something they could use to cause physical injury to themselves or others while in police detention or in the custody of a court; or that such a person may conceal a Class A drug. The search must be carried out by a registered medical professional or a registered nurse.

A search of the mouth used to be classed as an intimate search. Drug dealers would frequently hide drugs in their mouths in the knowledge that the police could not search them. This gave them time to dispose of the evidence. ***Section 65 PACE*** as amended by ***CJPOA 1994*** now provides that a search of the mouth is a non-intimate search.

Also relevant are the following sections of ***PACE:***

- ***Section 62:*** Intimate samples such as blood, saliva and semen can be taken from the suspect.
- ***Section 63:*** Non-intimate samples such as hair and nail clippings can be taken if authorised by an inspector or above.
- ***Section 64:*** DNA information can be extracted from the samples and placed indefinitely on the national DNA database. In ***S and Marper v UK (2008)*** , the ECtHR ruled that it was a breach of ***Article 8 ECHR*** to retain DNA indefinitely if there was no conviction. The ***Protection of Freedom Act 2012*** allows for the indefinite retention of DNA profiles only where a person has been convicted of a recordable offence. The DNA sample of anyone arrested but not charged or charged and later acquitted of most offences cannot be retained.
- ***Section 65:*** A person may also be identified by intimate samples as defined by ***s65*** (i.e. bodily samples, swabs and impressions).
- ***Section 61*** and ***s27***: Police can take fingerprints from suspects.
- ***Section 61A PACE*** as amended by ***SOCPA (2005)***: Impressions of footwear can be taken.

Rights and treatment of suspects during detention and interrogation

Section 60: The police must make a record of the interview and keep it on file. Interviews should be tape-recorded. However, it has been found that interviews can take place outside the police station, for example, on the way to the station. In some areas, the police also video interviews.

Section 56: The suspect has the right to have someone informed of their arrest. This right can be suspended for up to 36 hours if it is felt that the person chosen by the suspect may interfere with the investigation in some way (e.g. by alerting other suspects or destroying evidence).

Section 58: The suspect has the right to consult a solicitor privately and free of charge. Again, this right can be suspended for up to 36 hours for the reasons mentioned in ***s56***. This advice can be given over the telephone by **Criminal Defence Service Direct.**

Section 57: Vulnerable suspects (those under 17 or those who are mentally disordered or disabled) must have an **appropriate adult** with them during questioning. This right is in addition to the ***s58*** right. The absence of this person may render any confession **inadmissible** in court.

Code C: The suspect must be cautioned on arrest and before each interview. Suspects have the right to read the Codes of Practice. Code C also deals with conditions of detention. Suspects must be given adequate food, refreshment, sleep and breaks. The interview room must be adequately lit, heated and ventilated and a suspect must be allowed to sit. Interviews should not exceed two hours in length. Persons under the age of 16 should not be kept in police cells.

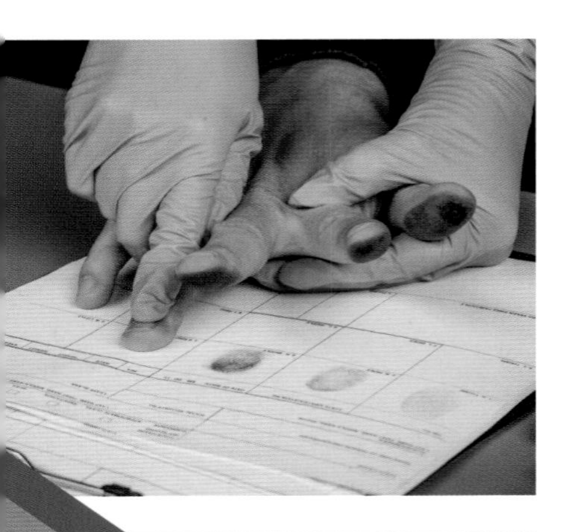

GRADE BOOST

Under ***Code of Practice E,*** interviews are tape-recorded in the case of offences triable on indictment, including those triable either way.
Note ***Article 8 ECHR:*** the right to respect for a person's private and family life, their home and their correspondence.

KEY CASES

R v Samuel (1988)
The suspect was detained and questioned for armed robbery but was refused access to solicitor on several occasions, as police felt there was a danger that other suspects could be warned. It was held that this was unjustified and, although Samuel confessed to the offence, the confession could not be used in court.

R v Grant (2005)
Interference by the police in a person's right to consult with a solicitor was held to be so serious that Grant's conviction for murder was quashed.

Admissibility of evidence

It is essential that police powers are exercised correctly for the evidence obtained to be used in court (is admissible). The courts can refuse to admit evidence that has not been properly obtained.

The following sections of ***PACE*** are relevant.

Section 76(2)(a)

Confession evidence may be excluded at trial if it is obtained by **oppression.** If this is raised, it is up to the prosecution to prove beyond reasonable doubt that the confession was not obtained by oppression. According to ***s76(8)*** oppression means torture, inhuman or degrading treatment or the use of threat or violence.

Section 76(2)(b)

Confession evidence may be excluded at trial if it was obtained in circumstances which make it unreliable. In the cases of ***R v Samuel (1988)*** and ***R v Grant (2005)***, failure to provide access to legal advice rendered the confessions inadmissible.

Section 78

Any evidence, including a confession, may be excluded on the ground that it would adversely affect the fairness of the trial. This includes situations such as not writing up the interviews straight after they had finished, as in ***R v Canale (1990)***.

Other relevant points

Breaches of the Codes of Practice must be 'serious and substantial' for the evidence obtained to be considered for exclusion.

Under ***s57*** vulnerable suspects (those under 17 and mentally disordered or disabled people) must have an appropriate adult with them during questioning. The absence of this person may render any confession inadmissible in court. Under ***s77***, the jury would be warned that a confession was made by a mentally disabled person.

The police have wide ranging powers that must be exercised with discretion. There is always the risk of misinterpretation of a situation and errors being made, but the powers are essential in order to keep the public safe. Where there have been errors, remedies may be available.

Exam Skills

When answering a question on this topic, be sure to include as many sections of relevant legislation as you can and apply them to the facts of a scenario-style question. Remember to **identify**, **define** and **apply** the law to reach a **conclusion** on that point of law before moving on to the next point. Even if the police appear to have exercised their powers correctly, it is still important to discuss this in the same way, just concluding that it was correctly done. This is a very common topic at A Level.

Complaints against and police and remedies

According to the rule of law, no one is above the law and everyone is equal under it. This also applies to the police. Even though the police have the power to lawfully infringe a person's human rights, such as the right to liberty under ***Article 5 ECHR***, they must do so within the powers they have been given and without breaking any law. They should also adhere to the ***PACE*** Codes of Practice.

Anyone can make a police complaint. The complainant does not need to be a 'victim' of police misconduct. They might, for example, have witnessed an incident which they feel should be the subject of a complaint. The complaint should be made within one year and must be against a particular officer, group of officers or civilian staff. It is therefore important for a complainant to get as many details about the officer(s) as they can to file the complaint. General complaints about police policy and practice or local police may be made to the Home Office via a local MP or the Local Police Authority.

To ensure the police act within the law, an aggrieved citizen can either make a complaint or sue through the civil courts. The police complaints procedure used to be overseen by the Police Complaints Authority (PCA) but, due to wide criticisms, it was abolished by the ***Police Reform Act 2002***, which replaced it with the Independent Police Complaints Commission (IPCC). Its role is to investigate, supervise or manage complaints against the police and make sure they are dealt with effectively. The IPCC aims to be more independent, open and accessible than the PCA, so that individuals feel more willing to make a complaint. An alternative or additional option is for the aggrieved person to take a civil action and sue the police.

This section is going to explore the procedure for making a complaint, the role of the IPCC and the possibility of taking a civil action against the police.

Complaints procedure

All complaints start with the individual (or a solicitor or MP on their behalf) making a written complaint to the police force in question. The IPCC does not have the power to record complaints and, if a complaint is made to them, it must be forwarded to the relevant police force. Usually, complaints are considered and recorded by the **Professional Standards Department** (PSD) of the police force concerned. (In the Metropolitan Police, this is the Directorate of Professional Standards.) The PSD decides whether to record the complaint and, if they do not, the complainant has the right of appeal. The PSD then decided whether the complaint should be dealt with informally (under the 'local' or 'informal' resolution procedure). The likely outcome of a local resolution is an apology with no right of appeal. If the PSD decides the complaint is suitable for formal resolution, it will be dealt with through the local investigation procedure. This will require the police to appoint an investigating officer of the same rank or above as the officer being investigated, from the same force or a different one. The police have discretion to refer a matter to the IPCC and the IPCC can decide to deal with a particular case.

There are, however, occasions where a complaint must be forwarded to the IPCC. The IPCC may decide to investigate, supervise or manage the complaint.

In the most serious cases, the IPCC will carry out an independent investigation. For slightly less serious cases, the IPCC will manage a police investigation ('managed' investigations). Usually, the police will deal with the complaint and the IPCC will supervise the investigation ('supervised' investigation) or the police will deal with the case alone ('local investigation' not to be confused with 'local resolution'). The local police must refer the following incidents to the IPCC, which can investigate even if a complaint has not been made:

- Deaths following police contact (e.g. while in custody or during an incident) or cases involving serious injury to a member of the public.
- Fatal road accidents involving a police vehicle.
- Use of a firearm by an officer on duty.
- Allegations of aggravated discriminatory behaviour.
- Allegations of assault.
- Allegations of hate crime.
- Allegations that an officer has committed a serious arrestable offence while on duty.
- Allegations of corruption.

The IPCC can also refer a case to the Crown Prosecution Service (CPS) if it believes that an officer should be prosecuted and this will be dealt with in the same way as a prosecution against a citizen.

The Independent Police Complaints Commission (IPCC)

The IPCC was established by the ***Police Reform Act 2002*** and became operational in April 2004. Its stated statutory purpose is to 'increase public confidence in the police complaints system in England and Wales'.

The IPCC replaced the PCA as the government felt a more independent, accessible and open service was needed to encourage people to come forward with complaints against the police and have confidence in the investigation. The IPCC will independently investigate some cases by over from the police, but normally the police are likely to be involved in some capacity.

The IPCC is overseen by a chair and 12 commissioners who, by law, must not have worked for the police in any capacity. The commissioners are appointed by the Home Secretary.

The IPCC has been involved in some high-profile and contentious investigations, for example, the shooting on the London Underground of Jean Charles de Menezes, who was mistakenly believed to be a suicide bomber. No criminal prosecution was taken. Other examples include the death of Ian Tomlinson at the G20 protests and the police handling of historic sex abuse cases.

STRETCH AND CHALLENGE

Look up the incidents mentioned above, and any other relevant cases investigated by the IPCC. Compile a report on what happened and the IPCC's conclusion.

Civil actions against the police

An individual may bring a civil action against the police and seek **damages** for the injuries and loss sustained. Under the IPCC and its extended powers of investigation, it is yet to be seen whether the failure of a complaint will hinder the success of any civil action. The police can be sued under various categories, such as malicious prosecution, false imprisonment, wrongful arrest, trespass, assault or negligence. It is normal practice to sue the Chief Constable of the police force in question; therefore, unlike the complaints procedure, the identities of the officers concerned need not be known. Cases are usually heard in the High Court and the decision and award of damages decided by a jury.

In a civil case, the standard of proof is 'on the balance of probabilities' and the burden lies with the claimant.

The police have been sued successfully several times. ***Goswell v Commissioner of Police for The Metropolis (1998)*** is an example of a successful claim against the police.

Goswell v Commissioner of Police for The Metropolis (1998)

Mr Goswell was waiting in his car for his girlfriend when he was approached by PC Trigg, who asked him to get out of his car without making any check upon the car. Mr Goswell began shouting, swearing and complaining that the police were unfairly troubling him and instead should have been out investigating a recent arson attack on his home. PC Trigg twice told Mr Goswell to calm down but he failed to do so. The officers then took hold of Mr Goswell and handcuffed him behind his back. PC Trigg struck Mr Goswell over the forehead with a police truncheon, causing a wound which bled profusely. Mr Goswell was put into a police car and taken to Woolwich police station. Only on arrival was he told why he had been arrested. He sued the police in the civil courts for assault and false imprisonment, and was awarded the considerable damages of £120,000 for assault, £12,000 for false imprisonment and £170,000 exemplary damages for arbitrary and oppressive behaviour. On appeal, this was reduced to £47,600.

STRETCH AND CHALLENGE

Judicial review in the High Court oversees the decisions of public bodies such as the police. An application is made by an individual who feels their rights have been infringed. If a public body breaches its powers, it may have breached individuals' rights and therefore the right to review the exercise of powers is an important remedy.
Protesters at the G20 demonstrations who complained of being beaten and unlawfully restrained by the police won a judicial review of the tactics used by the officers. Politician John Prescott also won a judicial review into the police inquiry into the phone-hacking scandal. Find out more about these cases.

The Commissioner of Police for the Metropolis v Thompson and Hsu (1997)
The Court of Appeal laid down important guidelines on the award of damages in civil cases against the police. Kenneth Hsu was originally awarded £220,000 in damages for wrongful arrest, false imprisonment and assault by the police but this was reduced on joint appeal (Thompson) to £35,000. Following these cases, the compensation awards have been limited due to concerns that the large awards given by juries diminished the budget available for policing. There is a current ceiling of £50,000 for exemplary damages for 'oppressive, arbitrary or unconstitutional behaviour' by the police.

Remedies for breach of police powers

It is important that there are adequate remedies in place to deter similar behaviour and to provide the complainant with some form of resolution. Among the outcomes of both local resolution and other types of investigation are:

- an apology by the police force
- an explanation
- a change in policy or procedure
- a referral to the CPS
- a recommendation that disciplinary action be taken
- judicial review.

Interception of communications

History of state surveillance

Agents of the state may invade privacy with the aim of promoting internal security or preventing or detecting crime. Such aims are legitimate; the question is whether the safeguards against unreasonable or arbitrary intrusion are adequate. Safeguards should include a clear remedy for the citizen, and strict control over the power of such interception, with proper authorisation for it. Proper authorisation is crucial since the citizen will not probably be aware of the surveillance.

Before 1985, there was no requirement to follow a legal procedure when authorising the tapping of telephones or the interception of mail. The conditions for issuing warrants for interception of postal or telephone communications were laid down in administrative rules, which had no legal force. Under these rules, the interception could be authorised to assist in a criminal investigation only if the crime was serious, normal methods had been tried and had failed, and there was good reason for believing that the evidence gained would lead to a conviction. If the interception related to security matters, it could only be authorised in respect of major subversion, terrorism or espionage, and the evidence obtained had to be directly useful to the security services in compiling the information it needed to carry out its function of protecting state security.

The Interception of Communications Act 1985

The ***Interception of Communications Act 1985 (ICA)*** made the use of telephone and mail intercepts subject to certain controls. It was introduced partly as a direct result of the ruling in the ECtHR in ***Malone v UK (1985)*** that the existing warrant procedure violated the ***Article 8*** guarantee of privacy.

KEY CASE

Malone v UK (1985)

In 1979, Mr Malone was on trial for receiving stolen goods. During his trial, evidence that his phone had been tapped came to light, and that the intercept had been authorised by the Home Secretary. Malone sought a declaration in the High Court that it was unlawful for anyone to intercept another's telephone conversation without consent (***Malone v MPC (1979)***). This line of argument failed, as did the argument based on ***Article 8*** that there was a right to privacy that had been violated by the tapping. The judge, Megarry, concluded that the ***ECHR*** did not give rise to any enforceable rights under English law and that therefore there was no direct right of privacy. (The ***Human Rights Act 1998*** would obviously now alter that position.) However, Megarry commented that, 'I find it impossible to see how English law could be said to satisfy the requirements of the Convention... This is not a subject on which it is possible to feel any pride in English law... Telephone tapping is a subject which cries out for legislation.'

Malone took his case to the ECtHR, arguing that ***Article 8*** had been violated. ***Article 8(2)*** reads: 'There shall be no interference by a public authority with the exercise of this right except such as in accordance with the law'. The ECtHR held that UK law did not regulate the circumstances in which telephone tapping could be carried out sufficiently clearly or provide any remedy against abuse of that power. However, the decision only required the UK government to introduce legislation to regulate the circumstances in which the power to tap could be used, rather than giving guidance on what would be acceptable limits on the individual's privacy.

The UK government responded by passing the ***Interception of Communications Act 1985***. This has now been replaced by ***Part 1 Regulation of Investigatory Powers Act 2000***, which in turn has been amended by the ***Investigatory Powers Act 2016***.

Bugging devices

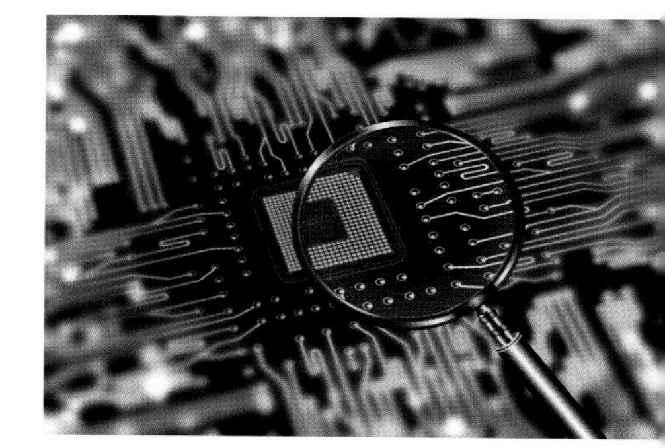

Surveillance techniques are an important way for the police and security services to maintain law and order and protect national security. However, as said in the Supreme Court of Canada, 'one can scarcely imagine a state activity more dangerous to individual privacy than electronic surveillance' (***Duarte (1990)***). Despite the development of such devices and their increased use by the state, they have continued to operate outside the control of the courts. Their use by the police was, until recently, authorised only under administrative guidelines. These guidelines failed to provide an element of independent scrutiny. The use of surveillance devices by the police has been in question in several cases, such as ***Khan (Sultan) (1996)***.

Khan (Sultan) (1996)

A bugging device had been secretly installed on the outside of a house which Khan had been visiting. Khan was suspected of involvement in importing drugs, and the tape-recording from the bug showed that he was involved. The defence argued that the tape was inadmissible as evidence because the police had no statutory authority to place bugs on private property and that therefore there had been a trespass, and the bug amounted to a breach of ***Article 8 ECHR****. The Court of Appeal held that trespass and damage to the building had occurred, and that there had been an invasion of privacy. However, the court said these were of slight significance and were outweighed by the fact that the police had largely complied with Home Office guidelines, and that the offences were serious. Khan's appeal was therefore turned down. The House of Lords recommended legislation taking into account that the regime governing the use of bugging devices was not on a statutory basis, and therefore might not comply with requirements under the ECHR.*

Police Act 1997

This Act places current practice on a statutory basis. The basis for allowing the use of bugging is very broad. An authorisation may be issued if the action is expected to be of substantial value in the prevention and detection of serious crime and the objective cannot reasonably be achieved by other means (***s93(2)***).

Serious crime is defined to include crimes of violence, those involving-financial gain and those involving many people in pursuit of a common purpose, or the crime is one for which a person of 21 or over with no previous convictions could reasonably be expected to receive a prison sentence of three years of more.

Various groups and bodies put forward pleas for exemption from the Act, including Catholic priests who were afraid their confessionals would be bugged, doctors and solicitors. However, there are no exemptions to the Act.

Under ***s93(5)***, authorisation for a warrant may be issued by the Chief Officer of Police, or, if this is not practicable, by an officer of the rank of Assistant Chief Constable. The authorisation will be given in writing, except in an emergency, where it may be given orally (***s95(1)***).

A written authorisation will last for three months, an oral one for 72 hours. Both forms can be renewed in writing for a further three months. A independent commissioner appointed under ***s91(1)*** must be notified of the authorisations as soon as they are made (***s96***) but this does not prevent the police acting on the authorisation. If the commissioner subsequently quashes the authorisation, destruction of any records may be ordered unless they are required for any pending criminal or civil proceedings.

STRETCH AND CHALLENGE

Do you think the involvement of independent commissioners provides oversight and scrutiny? Is this enough control over the actions of the police? Should the judiciary be involved in the authorisation process?

In certain circumstances, commissioners must give prior approval to the authorisation (***s97***). Such approval is needed where the property is believed to be a dwelling, a bedroom in a hotel or office premises. It is also needed where the authorising officer believes that the knowledge to be gained is likely to result in any person acquiring knowledge of confidential personal information, confidential journalistic material or matters subject to legal privilege. The involvement of commissioners, even in a limited capacity, does give some degree of independent oversight and scrutiny. No provision is made under the Act for independent review of the authorisation of bugging in the ordinary courts.

Regulation of Investigatory Powers Act 2000

This repeals the ***ICA 1985*** but is there greater regulation under this Act? All forms of surveillance are brought under it:

- ***Section 1*** makes it an offence to intentionally and without lawful authority intercept communications by a postal service or telecommunications system.
- This offence extends to voicemail messages, even after they have been accessed by the intended recipient (***R v Edmondson (2013)***).
- An interception will be lawful if done with consent (***s3***) or with a warrant (***s5***).
- Authorisation is governed by ***s5–16***.
- Power to issue a warrant lies with the Home Secretary.
- Application for a warrant must come from one of a list of people specified in ***s6***.
- The warrant is only to be issued if the Home Secretary believes it is 'necessary' for certain specified purposes set out in ***s5(3)*** and if the conduct authorised by the warrant is proportional to what is sought to be achieved by that conduct (***s5(2)***).

The specified purposes set out in ***s5(3)*** are:

a) *the interests of national security*

b) *preventing or detecting serious crime*

c) *safeguarding the economic wellbeing of the UK; or*

d) *giving effect to an international mutual assistance agreement in circumstances equivalent to those falling within (b).*

'Serious' crime as outlined in (b) is defined in ***s81(3)*** as:

a) *that the offence or one of the offences that is or would be constituted by the conduct is an offence for which a person who has attained the age of 21 and has no previous conviction could reasonably be expected to be sentenced to imprisonment for a term of three years or more*

b) *that the conduct involves the use of violence, results in substantial gain or is conduct by a large number of persons in pursuit of a common purpose.*

Section 8 deals with the contents of the warrant, which must specify the target and contain information about addresses.

Section 9 deals with the duration of the warrant. The initial period is three months from issue, but it may be renewed an unlimited number of times, provided the Home Secretary continues to believe it is necessary.

- Supervision of the warrant system is by an independent Interception of Communications Commissioner.
- The commissioner is obliged to report annually to the Prime Minister.
- The powers of the commissioner are supervisory and do not extend to taking action in relation to particular warrants.
- The only route of complaint for those dissatisfied with the system is to a tribunal established under ***s65***.

Section 67 makes it clear that the tribunal is to operate on the principles of 'judicial review'. This means that its focus is more on procedure rather than substance.

- If the tribunal finds that there has been impropriety, it has the power to quash a warrant, order the destruction of any information and to award compensation.
- There is no further appeal from the tribunal.
- In 2010, the tribunal received 164 complaints and upheld six of them.

EDUQAS A LEVEL

Covert surveillance

Covert surveillance is now regulated by ***ss26–48 RIPA***. Surveillance is defined in ***s48*** to include:

- monitoring, observing or listening to persons, their movements, their conversations or their other activities or communications
- recording anything monitored, observed or listened to in the course of surveillance
- surveillance by or with the assistance of a surveillance device.

Section 26 identifies three types of behaviour covered by the Act: directed surveillance, intrusive surveillance and the conduct and use of covert human intelligence sources.

Section 26: **Intrusive surveillance**. Intrusive surveillance occurs when a device or an individual is present on residential premises or in a vehicle, or where it is carried out in relation to such premises or vehicle. If the device is not on the premises, it is not intrusive unless the device consistently provides information of the same quality and detail as might be expected from a device actually on premises or in a vehicle.

Section s26(2) states that covert but not intrusive surveillance is directed surveillance if 'it is undertaken for the purpose of a specific investigation and in order to obtain private information about a person'.

Section s26(8) defines what is meant by a covert human intelligence source. Such a source will establish or maintain a relationship with a person for the covert purpose of using the relationship to obtain access to information, or provide access to another, or for the covert purpose of disclosing information obtained from the relationship.

STRETCH AND CHALLENGE

Research the cases of ***R v Hall (1994)*** and ***R v Stagg (1994)***. The police actions in both cases would clearly fall within the definition found in ***s26 RIPA***.

Section 26(8) is most likely to cover the actions of police informers. Authorisations are granted under ***ss28–32. Sections 28*** and ***29*** **cover directed surveillance,** which may be authorised on the same grounds as those in the ***Police Act 1997.*** A superintendent can authorise it, it must be necessary and proportionate, the grounds include national security and the economic wellbeing of the UK, and the crime to be prevented or detected does not have to be serious. ***Section 28*** also includes 'public safety', 'public health' and tax collection.

Section 32: **Authorisations for intrusive surveillance** are granted by the Secretary of State or senior authorising officers (e.g. chief constables). Requirements of necessity and proportionality apply but the grounds are limited to national security, the economic wellbeing of the UK and serious crime. Notice must be given to Surveillance Commissioner and authorisation will not take effect until it has been approved.

Evaluation of RIPA

- The procedures improve the previous situation, in that ***RIPA*** provides a statutory framework for the operation of powers which will involve infringements upon a person's privacy.
- However, the control over the exercise of surveillance power by the tribunal is vague. The exclusive jurisdiction of the tribunal means that there is no appeal to the domestic courts from its decision; however appeal to the ECtHR must be a strong possibility.
- For directed surveillance and the use of covert surveillance sources, there is no involvement of the Surveillance Commissioners so therefore there is a lack of independent supervision.
- There are also problems as to whether individuals will be aware that their rights have been infringed. How will you know if surveillance is being carried out on you?

Investigatory Powers Act (IPA) 2016

The ***IPA 2016*** brings together and updates existing powers (***RIPA 2000*** will continue until expressly repealed). The IPA introduced:

- a 'double-lock' for the most intrusive powers, so that warrants issued by a Secretary of State will also require the approval of a senior judge
- new powers and restated existing ones, for UK intelligence agencies and law enforcement to carry out targeted interception of communications, bulk collection of communications data, and bulk interception of communications
- a powerful new Investigatory Powers Commission to oversee how the powers are used
- new protections for journalistic and legally privileged material
- a requirement for judicial authorisation for acquisition of communications data that identify journalists' sources
- harsh sanctions, including the creation of new criminal offences for those misusing the powers.

Evaluation of surveillance in the UK

- Are further reforms needed or is the ***IPA 2016*** enough?
- Should surveillance evidence be admissible in court? Britain's security services fear that allowing intercept evidence to be used in a court of law would undermine its work, but globally the UK's stance on this issue is an exception. The USA, Canada, New Zealand, Ireland, Australia, Hong Kong and South Africa all allow certain kinds of intercept evidence in their courts of law. A judge and not a politician has the power to authorise telephone interception in all those countries (except Ireland).

- Why is Britain reluctant to follow what other countries do?
- England has perhaps the first instance of interception being used in a court of law when, in 1586, Mary, Queen of Scots, was convicted of treason on the basis of intercepted mail.
- There is also a loophole in the law which allows taped conversations from prison, mandatory for category A prisoners, to be used in evidence.
- Phone calls the Soham killer Ian Huntley made to Maxine Carr and his mother were used to secure a conviction in 2003.

Independent oversight and admissibility

- In Australia, the Attorney General issues warrants for intelligence purposes and judges do so for serious crime investigations. Evidence from intercepted phone calls, email and mail is admissible in court.
- In Canada, you must apply to a judge, although in an emergency police can intercept communications without a warrant. Evidence from intercepted phone calls, email and mail is admissible in court.
- In Hong Kong, a three-judge panel authorises and oversees the use of covert surveillance. Only intercepted mail evidence is admissible in court.
- In Ireland, interceptions are authorised by the Minister for Justice, reviewed by a High Court judge. Intercepted evidence from phone calls, email and mail is admissible in court.

Duty of confidentiality

Breach of confidence and privacy

Do we in English and Welsh law have a right to privacy? Lord Justice Glidewell in ***Kaye v Robertson (1991)*** stated that 'it's well known that in English law there is no right to privacy, and accordingly there is no right of action for breach of a person's privacy'. In this country, unlike in the USA, there is no overarching, all-embracing course of action for 'invasion of privacy'.

Wainwright v Home Office (2003)

The claimants, a mother and son, were strip-searched for drugs on a prison visit in 1997, in breach of the prison rules, and were humiliated and distressed. The second claimant, who was mentally impaired and suffered from cerebral palsy, developed post-traumatic stress disorder. The judge held that trespass to the person, consisting of wilfully causing them to do something to themselves which infringed their right to privacy, had been committed against both claimants and that trespass to the person, consisting of wilfully causing a person to do something calculated to cause them harm, had been committed against the second claimant in addition to a battery. They were awarded basic and aggravated damages. The Court of Appeal allowed the Home Office's appeal against the finding of trespass, dismissing the first claimant's claim and reducing the award of damages to the second claimant.

The issue in ***Wainwright v Home Office (2003)*** was whether English common law recognises a cause of action for invasion of privacy. The court held that there was no common law tort of invasion of privacy and that creation of such a tort required a detailed approach which could only be achieved by legislation.

This was the first time the House of Lords had been asked to declare whether an action for invasion of privacy exists in English law. The case confirmed the widely held view that declaration of a general right to privacy is beyond the acceptable limits of judicial development of the common law. However, protection of various aspects of privacy is a fast-developing area of the law. The decision of the Court of Appeal of New Zealand in ***Hosking v Runting (2004)*** is an example of this.

***Hosking v Runting* (2004)**
The claimants were a celebrity couple who had had twin girls in 2001, and declined to give interviews about them or allow them to be photographed. They separated in 2002. The first defendant, a photographer, was commissioned by the second defendant, a publisher, to photograph the claimants' 18-month old twins. He took the photos in a street, while they were with their mother but without her knowledge. The claimants brought proceedings to prevent publication of the photographs, on the basis that their publication would amount to a breach of the twins' privacy. Randerson J held that New Zealand courts should not recognise privacy as a distinct cause of action. The claimants appealed.

The issues in the cases were whether:

1. *there was a freestanding tort of privacy in New Zealand*
2. *any other cause of action could prevent the publication of the photographs.*

On appeal, the court held by a majority of 3–2 that there is a freestanding tort of invasion of privacy in New Zealand. It was held that the expansion of breach of confidence, as has happened in the UK courts, might lead to the same outcome, but greater clarity was achieved by analysing breaches of confidence and privacy as separate causes of action. Privacy and confidence are different concepts. There are two fundamental elements for a successful claim for interference with privacy:

1. *The existence of facts in respect of which there is a reasonable expectation of privacy.*
2. *Publicity given to those private facts that would be considered highly offensive to an objective, reasonable person.*

The New Zealand Court of Appeal revived the privacy debate in New Zealand and beyond by recognising a common law tort of privacy. The cases contain a helpful review of English and commonwealth cases. In the UK, the development of the law has been spurred by enactment of the ***Human Rights Act 1998***.

Breach of confidence

As explained in the previous section, there is no tort of invasion of privacy in England and Wales. However, legal controls can be used against the media and others. There is also competition between freedom of expression and respect for an individual's privacy. Both are vitally important rights.

What is privacy? The **Calcutt Committee (1990)** defined it as 'the right of the individual to be protected against intrusion into his personal life or affairs, or those of his family, by direct physical means or by publication of information'.

What, therefore, is breach of confidence? It is a civil remedy giving protection against the disclosure or use of information which is not generally known, and which has been entrusted in circumstances imposing an obligation not to disclose it without authorisation.

The use of the civil law of breach of confidence to protect privacy can be traced back to ***Prince Albert v Strange* (1849)**.

***Prince Albert v Strange* (1849)**
Both Queen Victoria and Prince Albert sketched as a hobby. Sometimes they showed their drawings to friends or gave them away. Strange obtained some of these sketches and arranged a public viewing of them. He also published a catalogue listing them. Prince Albert filed a claim for the return of the sketches and a surrender of the catalogue for destruction. The court awarded Prince Albert an injunction, restraining Strange from publishing a catalogue describing Prince Albert's sketches.

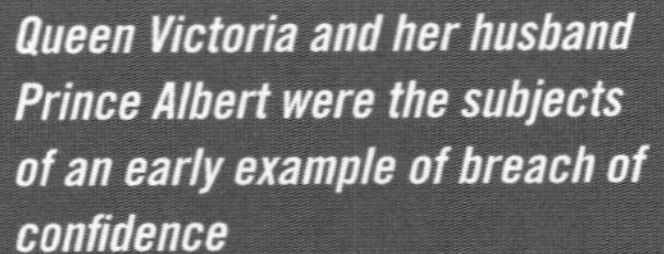
Queen Victoria and her husband Prince Albert were the subjects of an early example of breach of confidence

Another example is ***Argyll v Argyll (1967)***, where it was held that the Duchess of Argyll could obtain an injunction to prevent newspapers from revealing secrets about her marriage, which had been disclosed to the newspaper by her husband, the Duke.

The three traditional elements of breach of confidence were summarised in the key case of ***Coco v AN Clark (Engineers) Ltd (1969)***:

1. The information must have the necessary quality of confidence about it.
2. The information must have been given in circumstances importing an obligation of confidence.
3. There must be unauthorised use of that information.

What is '**information**' for the purposes of the law of confidence?

It can include information concerning an individual's sexual orientation, as in ***Stephens v Avery (1988)***, photographs, as in ***HRH Princess of Wales v MGN Newspapers Ltd (1993)*** and photos from a film set, as in ***Shelley Films Ltd v Rex Features Ltd (1993)***.

Stephens v Avery (1988)
The parties had been friends and had discussed their sex lives. The defendant took the information to a newspaper editor, who published it. The claimant sought damages, saying the conversations and disclosures had been confidential. The court held that the defendants had published knowing that the material was disclosed in confidence. Information about sexual activities could be protected under a duty of confidence, where it would be unconscionable for someone who had received information on an expressly confidential basis to disclose it.

HRH Princess of Wales v MGN Newspapers Ltd (1993)
The court had no hesitation in granting injunctions to prevent the Daily Mirror and others from publishing photographs of Princess Diana exercising in a gymnasium, taken by the gym owner without her knowledge or consent.

Shelley Films Ltd v Rex Features Ltd (1993)
The defendant was restrained by injunction from publishing photographs which had been taken on set of a forthcoming film, Frankenstein, photographs of which the producers had taken steps to keep confidential. The court held that the photographer knew that the occasion was a private one and that the taking of photographs by outsiders was not permitted.

As a very public figure, Princess Diana often tried to protect her privacy

Since ***Stephens v Avery (1988)***, the basic principle appears to be that confidentiality will be enforced if the information was received on the basis that it is confidential. The fact that information is given in confidence may be expressly communicated to the defendant, but can be implied from the circumstances surrounding the communication, as in ***Fairnie (Deceased) and Others v Reed and Another (1994)***.

Fairnie (Deceased) and Others v Reed and Another (1994)
Confidential information about the format of a board game, which the claimant wished to sell, was mentioned by him in passing during a conversation with a virtual stranger. The stranger was not told that it was given in confidence. The Court of Appeal held that the information was given in confidence due to the clear commercial value of the information.

Public interest defence

Confidential information will not be protected if the public interest outweighs the interest in preserving confidentiality. In ***AG v Guardian Newspapers Ltd (No 2) (1990)***, the interest in maintaining confidentiality was outweighed by the public interest in knowing the allegations in the book, *Spycatcher*.

STRETCH AND CHALLENGE

Research the following cases to see how the law of breach of confidence was applied in these cases:

- ***Woodward v Hutchings (1977)***
- ***Lion Laboratories v Evans and Express Newspapers (1988)***
- ***X v Y (1998)***
- ***Campbell v MGN (2004)***
- ***Douglas v Hello (2005)***
- ***Re S (A Child) (Identification on Publication) (2004)***
- ***Ash v McKennitt (2006)***

STRETCH AND CHALLENGE

- Despite ***Venables and Thompson v News Group Newspapers (2001)*** being regarded as an exceptional case justifying an exceptional order, the courts have gone on to make two further orders, in favour of two other notorious criminals, Mary Bell and Maxine Carr. Research these cases. Do you think such an order is likely to be granted to anyone who can claim that their infamy is likely to lead to someone making death threats against them?

AG v Guardian Newspapers Ltd (No 2) (1990)

A retired secret service spy sought to publish his memoirs. At the time of publication, he was living in Australia. The British government sought to restrain publication in Australia, and the defendant newspapers sought to report those proceedings, which would involve publication of the allegations made in the book. The Attorney General sought to restrain the publications.

The court held that a duty of confidence arises when confidential information comes to the knowledge of a person in circumstances where they have notice, or are held to have agreed, that the information is confidential, with the effect that it would be just in all the circumstances that they should be precluded from disclosing the information to others.

The principle of confidentiality only applies to information to the extent that it is confidential. In particular, once it has entered what is usually called the **public domain**, as it had in this case, then generally the principle of confidentiality can have no application to it.

Note that what is of interest to the public may not be in the public interest.

Breach of confidence and privacy after the Human Rights Act 1998

Article 8 ECHR (the right to privacy) is now incorporated into the ***Human Rights Act 1998***. How quickly or how far will judges move the law in the direction of the protection of privacy?

Individual privacy cannot be considered in isolation. Privacy must be weighed alongside freedom of speech and expression, which is also an important right under ***Article 10 ECHR***.

Venables and Thompson v News Group Newspapers (2001)

The claimants, the convicted murderers of a toddler, James Bulger, applied for indefinite injunctions to restrain publication of their new identities and their whereabouts. The issue was whether the court had the authority to protect an adult's identity in circumstances where there was a serious risk to physical safety. It was argued that the court should exercise its equitable jurisdiction to make the orders sought by the claimants. The claimants were notorious and at risk of serious physical harm then and in the future. The claimants' rights under ***Article 2 ECHR*** *(the right to life) demanded protection which could be provided by extension of the law of confidence. An injunction was granted restraining publication of the claimants' identities and their whereabouts.*

Associated Newspapers Ltd v Prince of Wales (2006)

The Mail on Sunday *published extracts of a diary by Prince Charles, Prince of Wales. The extracts published from the diary, titled 'The Great Chinese Takeaway', were personally embarrassing to the Prince. They had been written on a flight back from Hong Kong to the United Kingdom after the transfer of sovereignty of Hong Kong to China, and had been handed out to Prince Charles's friends. The Prince described the Hong Kong handover ceremony as an 'awful Soviet-style' performance and 'ridiculous rigmarole' and the likened Chinese officials to 'appalling old waxworks'. The Prince sought to claim confidentiality and copyright in them when The* Mail on Sunday *tried to publish them. The Prince won the case and gained an injunction which prevented The* Mail on Sunday *from publishing further extracts from the diary.*

The author JK Rowling has found the privacy of herself and her family affected by ECHR

Murray v Express Newspapers (2008)
The defendant newspaper took a photograph of the claimant, the young son of the author of the Harry Potter *books, JK Rowling, being pushed by his father in a buggy down a street with his mother walking alongside. The photograph was taken covertly using a long-range lens and was later published in* The Sunday Express. *The claimant (represented by his parents as litigation friends) issued proceedings against* The Sunday Express *for breach of privacy and confidence and under the* ***Data Protection Act 1998****. The court dismissed the claimant's claims.*

Mosley v News Group Newspapers (2008)
The defendant newspaper published a film showing the claimant involved in sex acts with prostitutes. It characterised them as 'Nazi' style. He was the son of a fascist leader, and chairman of an international sporting body. He denied any Nazi element, and claimed breach of confidence. The court had to balance the interest of protecting Mosley's private life with the interest of News Group Newspapers' right of freedom of expression. Mosley won his case. The fact that there is no clear law of privacy does not mean that people's privacy right cannot be protected when their privacy has been breached. An individual whose privacy has been interfered with can rely on the common law, breach of confidence and ***Article 8 ECHR****. This case clearly confirms that the courts are willing to protect individuals' rights to a private life when there is intrusion by the media which is not justifiable.*

Author of a Blog v Times Newspapers (2009)
The claimant, a serving police officer, was the author of the Night Jack blog, which described his police work and his opinions on a number of social and political issues relating to the police. He sought to conceal his identity by blogging under a pseudonym. A journalist for The Times had accurately identified the claimant. The claimant applied for an injunction to prevent The Times publishing his identity. He argued that the newspaper was subject to an enforceable duty of confidence not to reveal his identity and that he had a reasonable expectation of privacy in respect of the information that he was the blog's author, and there was no public interest justification for disclosing his identity. The court held that the information that the claimant was the author of the blog was not protected by breach of confidence, nor did it qualify as information in respect of which the claimant had a reasonable expectation of privacy, since blogging is a public activity. The injunction was refused.

BBC v HarperCollins Ltd (2010)
The publisher HarperCollins intended to publish the autobiography of the driver who performed the role of 'The Stig' on the BBC's Top Gear television programme from 2003 until 2010. It had been an important characteristic of The Stig that his identity was not known to the public. The BBC sought an injunction to prevent the publication of the book on the basis that the driver owed the BBC a duty not to disclose confidential information, including that he was The Stig. The court held that anyone who had an interest in knowing the identity of The Stig knew it, and the fact that the driver was The Stig was so generally accessible that the information had lost its confidential character. The BBC was not granted the injunction and HarperCollins released the book.

Hutcheson v News Group Newspapers (2011)
The businessman Christopher Hutcheson attempted to use a super-injunction to prevent The Sun newspaper from publishing the fact that he had fathered two children from an affair. The case received significant media coverage because the TV chef Gordon Ramsay was his son-in-law. Mr Hutcheson was not granted an injunction and the court held that there could be no reasonable expectation of privacy in this case.

GRADE BOOST

The decision in ***Mosley v News Group Newspapers (2008)*** attracted a lot of criticism from the media. The court was accused of bringing in a new privacy law by the back door, leading to greater restrictions on the freedom of the press to publish stories about the rich and powerful. Do you agree?

STRETCH AND CHALLENGE

Research ***Napier v Pressdram Ltd (2009)***, where an injunction was not granted to the claimant, who was trying to restrain the magazine *Private Eye* from publishing the outcome of a complaint to the Law Society. Do you agree with the decision in this case?

Terry v Persons Unknown (2010)
The Premiership footballer John Terry was not granted a super-injunction to prevent The News of the World *publishing a story about his private life. The injunction was rejected after the High Court ruled the primary purpose of the injunction was to protect commercial interests, in particular with sponsors, and not to protect his privacy.*

Ferdinand v MGN (2011)
The Sunday Mirror *published an article about an alleged affair between Rio Ferdinand and an interior designer, Ms Storey. Ferdinand described the article as a 'gross invasion of my privacy' and brought legal action in which he sought damages and a worldwide injunction against further publication. Ferdinand said that he had not seen Ms Storey for years at the time of publication, but they had exchanged text messages between that time and his becoming captain of the England football team in 2010. He claimed that there had been a misuse of private information. The Mirror Group Newspapers argued that he had been appointed captain on the basis that he was a 'reformed and responsible' character. The case centred on whether* The Sunday Mirror *had a public interest defence based on* ***Article 10 ECHR*** *(the right to freedom of expression), or whether Ferdinand was entitled to privacy in accordance with* ***Article 8 ECHR*** *(the right to respect for private and family life). The court ruled in favour of Mirror Group Newspapers, saying: 'Overall, in my judgement, the balancing exercise favours the defendant's right of freedom of expression over the claimant's right of privacy'.*

CTB v News Group Newspapers (2011)
A famous married footballer (Ryan Giggs, known in the case as CTB) successfully obtained an injunction restraining the defendants from publishing his identity and allegations of an affair. The court held that there could be no doubt that the subject of the threatened publication was matter in respect of which CTB had a reasonable expectation of privacy and which he was entitled to ***Article 8 ECHR*** *protection.*

Setting the boundaries for privacy and the European Court of Human Rights

KEY CASE

Von Hannover v Germany (No 2) (2012)
This case concerned balancing privacy with freedom of expression. In a unanimous decision, the court found that Germany had not failed in its obligation to respect the applicants' ***Article 8 ECHR*** rights when it refused to grant an injunction against the publication of a photograph taken of Princess Caroline of Monaco and her husband while on holiday at a ski resort in Switzerland.
This case follows on from ***Von Hannover v Germany (No 1)(2005)***, when the court held that Princess Caroline's ***Article 8*** rights had been infringed by the publication of photographs of her with her children.
She, with her husband, brought several cases in Germany for an injunction to prevent further publication of three photographs taken while she was on holiday with her family. The German court, relying on the first Von Hannover decision, granted an injunction coveering two of the three photographs on the basis that they were wholly in the sphere of private life. However, the first photo showed Princess Caroline and her husband walking and was accompanied by an article commenting on, among other things, the poor health of her father, Prince Rainier of Monaco. The court held that the photo had to be considered in the context of the article and that the subject matter was of general interest as an 'event in contemporary society' and therefore not protected by privacy. Princess Caroline and her husband appealed to the ECtHR, claiming a violation of their ***Article 8*** rights. They argued that none of the photos, regardless of the accompanying articles, contributed to a debate of public interest in a democratic society but were purely to satisfy the curiosity of readers.

In ***Von Hannover (No 2)*** the court unanimously held that there had not been a violation of ***Article 8***. The ECtHR, in its supervisory role, set out relevant criteria when member states are considering how to balance ***Article 8*** and ***Article 10***:

1. Whether the information contributes to a debate of general interest. What amounts to 'general interest' will depend on the circumstances of each case but the court suggested that rumoured marital difficulties of a politician or financial troubles of a famous singer are not matters of general interest.
2. How well known the person concerned is, and the subject matter of the report.
3. The prior conduct of the individual concerned.
4. Content, form and consequences of the publication. This may also include the scope of dissemination, the size of the publication and its readership.
5. The circumstances in which the photos were taken. Relevant factors include the consent of the subject, their knowledge that the photo was being taken and whether it was taken illegally.

Springer v Germany (2012)

*The Grand Chamber of the ECtHR found that the **Article 10** rights of the publisher of a German newspaper had been violated by injunctions granted by the German courts. The tabloid had been prevented from publishing articles about the arrest and conviction of a well-known television actor for possession of cocaine. The Grand Chamber found there was a violation of **Article 10**, the right to freedom of expression, and awarded the publisher damages and costs.*

STRETCH AND CHALLENGE

In the absence of a tort of invasion of privacy, the existing laws of breach of confidence have served many celebrities in their battles for the right to privacy (e.g. Catherine Zeta Jones). Do you think a privacy law is needed or does the law of breach of confidence suffice?

Duty of confidentiality

History of official secrets and the Official Secrets Acts

Exam Skills

This section, as far as 'Obscenity' on page 219, is only in the Eduqas AS and A Level specifications, not WJEC.

It is often said that the UK is more obsessed with keeping government information secret than any other Western democracy. The British government uses several methods to keep official information secret, including the doctrine of public interest immunity, the deterrent effect of criminal sanctions under the Official Secrets Acts, the civil service code and the civil action for breach of confidence.

Severe restrictions on disclosure of information are found in the ***Official Secrets Acts 1911, 1920, 1939*** and ***1989***.

During the 19th century, as government departments grew larger, the problem of confidentiality grew more acute. An 1873 treasury document urged secrecy on all members of government departments and threatened dismissal of those who disclosed any information. In 1878, a need for further safeguards was emphasised when Marvin, who worked for the foreign office, gave details of a secret treaty to a newspaper. He was prosecuted, but it was discovered that no part of the criminal law covered the situation. He had memorised the information and had not stolen any documents so no conviction could be obtained. This led to the passing of the ***Official Secrets Act 1889***. This made it an offence to wrongfully communicate information obtained as a result of being a civil servant. The state had the burden of proving both mens rea (intent) and that the disclosure was not in the interests of the state. The Act, therefore, was not strong enough so in 1911 another ***Official Secrets Act*** was passed. It has been suggested that its introduction into Parliament was misleading as it was introduced by the Secretary of State for War, not by the Home Secretary, giving the impression that it was largely an anti-espionage measure. ***Section 1*** dealt largely with espionage but ***s2*** was aimed not at enemy agents but at civil servants and other Crown employees.

The Act was passed in one afternoon, and ***s2*** received no debate at all. ***Section 2*** appeared to create a crime of strict liability and imposed a complete prohibition on the unauthorised disclosure of even trivial official information. It lacked any provision regarding the substance of the information. ***Section 2(2)*** criminalised the receiver of the information, although there did appear to be a requirement of mens rea. It did not recognise the role of the press in informing the public. There were few prosecutions under ***s2*** as it seemed to create an acceptance of secrecy in the civil service.
The demise of ***s2*** was probably due to it being seen as unacceptable in a modern democracy, and in response to the following three decisions.

Aitken (1970)

*Aitken, a reporter, disclosed that the UK government had misled the British people about the amount of aid the UK was giving Nigeria in its war against Biafra. The government said it was supplying about 15% of Nigeria's arms, whereas the true figure was 70%. Aitken disclosed the report to the press. He was prosecuted under **s2**. The judge, Mr Justice Caulfield, had little sympathy with a case brought merely to reduce government embarrassment and which had no national security interest. The facts of the report were available elsewhere. He found that mens rea was needed, and directed the jury to acquit. He also stressed the freedom of the press and that **s2** should be pensioned off. All defendants were acquitted. (Under the **1989 Act**, however, they would be guilty of making disclosures about army logistics and deployment which would be likely to jeopardise British defence interests abroad.)*

Tisdall (1984)

*Tisdall worked in the Foreign Secretary's private office. She discovered proposals to delay the announcement of a delivery of cruise missiles to Greenham Common until after it had occurred, and to make the announcement at the end of Question Time to avoid answering questions. She thought this was morally wrong and leaked it to The Guardian newspaper. She pleaded guilty under **s2** and received a six-month prison sentence but the case created adverse publicity for the government.*

Ponting (1985)

*This case ended the influence of **s2**. Ponting was a senior Ministry of Defence official who gave a Labour MP information which undermined the truth of ministerial answers to questions he had been asking in Parliament about the sinking of the Belgrano warship during the Falklands War. Ponting was prosecuted under **s2** and acquitted.*

Section 2's lack of credibility may have been a factor in the decision to bring civil as opposed to criminal proceedings against *The Guardian* and *Observer* newspapers for disclosure of allegations in *Spycatcher* (see page 209 above). Civil proceedings for breach of confidence were less risky, as they had no jury and a temporary injunction could be obtained quickly. However, the government did think that criminal law rather than civil law was in general a more appropriate response to cases such as ***Ponting (1985)***, therefore reform was needed of the ***Official Secrets Act 1911***.

Official Secrets Act 1989

The government claimed the Act would usher in a new era of openness, but it does little for freedom of information. It does narrow the wide breadth of ***s2***, although an official who makes a disclosure may face an action for breach of confidence as well as disciplinary proceedings. The Home Secretary at the time said it was 'a great liberalising measure', which must refer to other aspects of the Act. For example, features which were viewed as liberalising included the categorisation of information which makes relevant the substance, the introduction of tests for harm, the mens rea requirements of ***ss5*** and ***6*** defences, and the decriminalisation of the receiver of the information. However, the Act applies not only to Crown servants but also to journalists, it contains no defence of public interest or of prior disclosure, there is no general requirement to prove mens rea, and there is no right of access to information. What is omitted is as significant as what is included.

The Act narrows the scope of protection of official information by the criminal law to certain categories:

- Security and intelligence
- Defence
- International relations
- Crime

Security and intelligence

Section 1 covers security and intelligence information. It is a wide category and is not confined only to work done by members of the security services. It is intended to prevent members or former members of the security services, and anyone notified that they are subject to the provisions of ***s1***, from disclosing anything or appearing to relate to the operation of those services. All such members have a lifelong duty to keep silent even if their information might reveal a serious abuse of power in the security services. There is **no need to show that any harm will or may flow from disclosure**, and so **all** information, however trivial, is covered.

Section 1(3) criminalises disclosure of information relating to the security services by a former or present Crown servant, as opposed to a member of the security services. It includes a test for harm.

Section 1(4) states that a disclosure is damaging if it damages the work, or any part of, the security and intelligence services, or it is information or a document or other article whose unauthorised disclosure would be likely to cause damage, or which falls within a class of information, documents or articles which would have that effect. This test for damage may, therefore, be easily satisfied.

Defence

Section 2 covers information relating to defence. The meaning of defence is set out in ***s2(4)(a)*** , covering the size, shape organisation, logistics, order of battle, deployment, operations, state of readiness and training of the armed forces of the Crown.

Section 2(4)(b) covers the weapons, stores or other equipment of those forces and the invention, development, production and operation of such equipment and research relating to it.

Section 2(4)(c) covers defence policy and strategy and military planning and intelligence

Section 2(4)(d) covers plans and measures for the maintenance of essential supplies and services that are or would be needed in times of war.

KEY CASE

R v Shayler (2002)
This held that there is no defence of acting in the public interest.

It must be shown that a disclosure is or would likely to be **damaging** as defined under ***s2(2)*** because:

> *'(a) it damages the capability of, or any part of, the armed forces of the Crown to carry out their tasks or leads to loss of life or injury to members of these forces or serious damage to the equipment or installation of those forces; or*
>
> *(b) it endangers the interests of the UK abroad, seriously obstructs the promotion or protection by the UK of those interests or endangers the safety of British citizens abroad; or*
>
> *(c) it is of information or of a document or article which is such that its unauthorised disclosure would be likely to have those effects.'*

(a) deals with more serious harm, while (b) is much wider.

International relations

Section 3 covers information relating to international relations. The harm test under ***s3(2)*** is the same as that under ***s2(2)(b)*** and ***(c)***: '*it endangers the interests of the UK abroad and it is of information or of a document or article which is such that its unauthorised disclosure would be likely to have any of those effects.*'

This section includes disclosure of any information provided in confidence by the government to a foreign country or international organisation. This section is designed to limit media coverage of foreign policy and diplomacy.

Crime

Section 4 is concerned with crime and special investigation powers. ***Section 4(2)*** covers information which is likely to result in the commission of an offence or impede the prevention or detection of offences. There is a **harm test** relating to this information.

Section 4(3) covers information obtained using interception and security services warrants. There is **no harm test** under this category.

Section 5 makes it a specific offence for journalists and editors to publish information which they know falls into one of the protected categories, although the prosecution must prove that they had reason to believe that publication would be damaging to the security services or to the interests of the UK.

STRETCH AND CHALLENGE

Look up ***s12 OSA 1989***. Who is a Crown servant or government contractor?

If charged under ***s5***, editors can testify as to their state of mind and will be entitled to an acquittal if the jury accepts that there was no rational basis for thinking that the disclosure would damage British interests. This defence will not be available if they publish information from former or serving members of the security services (or notified persons), and are charged instead under ***s1*** with aiding and abetting or conspiring with such persons.

Section 6: It is an offence to make, without authority, a damaging disclosure of information in categories 1 to 3 that was communicated in confidence by the UK to another state or an international organisation and disclosed without the authority of that state or organisation. There are also offences relating to the retaining or failure to take care of protected documents and articles and disclosing information which facilitates unauthorised access to protected material. Mere receipt of information is no longer an offence.

Section 7: A disclosure will not lead to liability under the Act if it is authorised.

Section 8: *'Where a Crown servant or government contractor, has in their possession... any document or other article which it would be an offence under any of the foregoing provisions of the Act for them to disclose... they are guilty of an offence if:*

a) *being a Crown servant, they retain the document or article; or*

b) *being a government contractor, they fail to comply with an official direction for the return or disposal of the document or article; or*

c) *if they fail to take such care to prevent the unauthorised disclosure of the document or article.'*

Section 8(2): It is a defence for a Crown servant charged with an offence under subsection 8 to prove that, at the time of the alleged offence, they believed they were acting in accordance with their official duty.

Conclusion: Defences

- It is generally a defence for the accused to prove that they did not know that the information fell into the protected category, or that disclosure would be damaging (***1989 ss1(5), 2(3), 3(4), 4(4)(5)***).
- Under ***s5***, it is for the prosecution to prove that that the accused knew or had reasonable cause to believe that the information was protected and that disclosure would be damaging (***s5(2)(3)***).
- There is no defence that disclosure was in the public interest except in the limited situation that the information had been previously published.
- ***Section 7:*** A belief in authorisation will provide a defence.

Therefore, the defences can be summarised as follows:

1. The defendant did not know information fell into a protected category.
2. They had no reason to believe the information would cause harm.
3. They believed in lawful authorisation.

A civil action for breach of confidence could also arise.

Contempt of court

Here we are concerned with two conflicting interests: the interest in **protecting the administration of justice** and in the principle of **free speech**. The main outcome of criminal contempt is to limit the media from reporting or commenting on matters which are subject to litigation, as it may poison the minds of potential jurors or influence or intimidate potential witnesses.

The development of the common law relating to contempt of court

In deciding whether a publication amounts to a contempt of court, there is a test of whether it creates a substantial risk that justice, either in a particular case or as a continuing process, will be seriously impeded or prejudiced. The test was first formulated in the ***Contempt of Court Act 1981***, which the UK government was obliged to pass after the ECtHR held that the old contempt law was so strict that it violated the ***Article 10 ECHR*** guarantee of freedom of expression. The UK courts had banned *The Sunday Times* from conducting a campaign against Distillers, the manufacturer of the deforming drug thalidomide, and its reluctance to properly compensate victims. There were many outstanding legal actions against Distillers at the time, and the courts took the view that the newspaper campaign would prejudice issues arising during litigation and put unfair pressure on Distillers to settle for more than might otherwise have been awarded. The ECtHR rejected these arguments, saying that thalidomide was a matter of national concern, and the mere fact that litigation was in progress did not alter the right and responsibility of the media to impart information and comment about a public tragedy (see ***Sunday Times v UK (1981)***).

The ***Contempt of Court Act 1981*** therefore originated as a liberalising measure, requiring the finding of a substantial risk of serious prejudice.

Contempt of Court Act 1981

Section 1

Conduct will be contempt if it interferes with the administration of justice in particular proceedings, regardless of intent to do so. The starting point is to ask whether the article or publication relates to particular proceedings. If it appears to have a long-term effect on the course of justice generally, without affecting any particular case, it would seem to fall outside the Act.

After establishing that the publication might affect a particular case, a number of tests must be satisfied to establish the strict liability rule. It is not necessary to show that the defendant intended to prejudice proceedings, so no mens rea needs to be proven.

Section 2(3)

Was the article written during the active period? Normally, prejudicial material can only be published negligently or in ignorance of a forthcoming trial while proceedings are deemed to be 'active'.

Criminal cases become active as soon as the first formal steps in launching a conviction are taken, by arrest, issuing a warrant for arrest or issuing a summons to appear in court. Civil cases become active as soon as the case is listed as being ready for trial.

Publication of prejudicial material outside these time frames will not normally amount to contempt unless it is intended to prejudice some further trial, while publication within the active period will be in contempt if it constitutes a substantial risk of serious prejudice. A case ceases to be active when it has concluded, but it reactivates if an appeal is lodged.

Section 2(2)

Does the article create a substantial risk of serious prejudice to the trial or case? Factors that can create a substantial risk of serious prejudice include:

- words used
- proximity of article to trial
- pictures used
- profile of the person named in the article
- circulation.

Section 2(2)

Does the article create a substantial risk of serious prejudice to the trial or case? In ***AG v News Group Newspapers (1987)***, the Court of Appeal said both parts of the test must be satisfied, and showing a slight risk of serious prejudice or a substantial risk of slight prejudice would not be enough.

AG v News Group Newspapers (1987)

Allegations had been made about the cricketer, Ian Botham, who was very famous at the time. The court refused to stop the newspaper publishing allegations about his involvement in drug taking on a cricket tour of New Zealand. Botham had brought a libel action against another newspaper over these allegations, which had been published some time before, and the case was due to be tried by a jury ten months after the date of the proposed republication. The court accepted that there was a chance that a new publication in a national newspaper would influence a jury at a later date but, in view of the ten-month delay, the risk was not substantial.

STRETCH AND CHALLENGE

Compare the Ian Botham case with ***AG v Hislop and Pressdram (1991)***, where a gap of three months between the article and trial did create a substantial risk of serious prejudice.

Research ***AG v Independent TV News and Others (1985)***. What factors were relevant in this case?

Woodgate and Bowyer (2001)
The Sunday Mirror *was fined £175,000 for printing information which could have affected the trial of Leeds United footballers Jonathan Woodgate and Lee Bowyer, and which caused the whole court case to be re-run.*

Having established a substantial risk, it is necessary to ask whether there is a substantial risk that the effect of such influence will be of a prejudicial nature. It must be shown that the language used, facts disclosed or sentiments expressed would lead an objective observer to conclude that a substantial risk had been established that a person involved in the proceedings would be prejudiced, before going on to consider whether the effect could be described as serious.

Prejudice and seriousness can be established in several ways:

- An article might influence persons against or in favour of the defendant.
- An article might affect either the outcome of the proceedings or their very existence.
- Proximity of time can affect this part of the test, as can the extent to which the trial concerns a person in the public eye.

If it appears that ***s2(2)*** is established, it also needs to be established that the ***s5*** defence does not apply. ***Section 5*** contains a public interest defence, which ensures that public debate on matters of current controversy can continue even if it reflects upon matters before the courts. ***Section 5*** exonerates publications which discuss matters of general public interest in good faith if the risk of prejudice is merely incidental.

The defence was used successfully in ***AG v English (1985)***, when it was held that a newspaper article criticising the common practice of doctors allowing deformed babies to die, which was published during the trial of a doctor alleged to have committed manslaughter in these circumstances, amounted to only incidental prejudice.

Section 5 will not protect publications which directly relate to imminent or ongoing jury trials and which criticise witnesses or defendants, set out inadmissible evidence or encourage a particular outcome. The Attorney General determines whether there will be a prosecution for contempt of court.

Why have a law of contempt?

A law of contempt strikes a balance between:

- a person's right to be treated fairly in court
- a journalist's right to report what is happening in the world.

GRADE BOOST

Does the law of contempt strike a fair balance between these two conflicting interests? If not, how could it be reformed?

Obscenity

Under ***Article 10 ECHR***, a person has the right to 'freedom of expression'. This is, however, a qualified right and can be removed for a legitimate reason, such as the protection of health or morals or for the protection of the reputation or rights of others. This section covers the extent to which there is a right to shock and/or offend under English law and the ECHR.

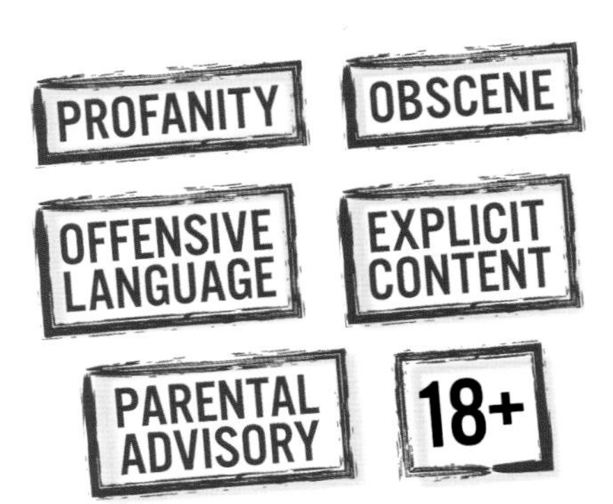

What is obscene to one person may not be to another, particularly in a more permissive society. The law has attempted to provide some clarity.

Two key statutes govern this area:

- The ***Obscene Publications Act 1959*** (as amended by the ***Obscene Publications Act 1964***).
- The ***Criminal Justice and Immigration Act 2008***.

GRADE BOOST

Remember to include in your answers when qualified rights can be taken away. These are the weakest rights and can be removed when 'prescribed by law, necessary and proportionate in a democratic society in order to fulfil a legitimate aim'.

Obscene Publications Act 1959 (OPA)

Offence

So, what is '**obscene**' according to the ***OPA***? Under ***s2(1)***, it is an offence to publish an 'obscene article for gain or not' or to have an obscene article for publication for gain.

Section 1(1) provides the definition of obscene for the purposes of the Act. It says: '*An article shall be deemed to be obscene if its effect or (where the article comprises two or more distinct items) the effect of any one of its items is, if taken as a whole, such as to tend to deprave and corrupt persons who are likely, having regard to all relevant circumstances, to read, see or hear the matter contained or embodied in it.*'

The Court of Appeal has held that 'obscenity depends on the article and not upon the author' (***Shaw v DPP (1962)***).

'**Article**' has a wide definition under ***s1(2) OPA***. It means anything '*containing or embodying matter to be read or looked at or both, any sound record, and any film or other record of a picture or pictures*' (***s1(2)***).

'**Publication**' also has a wide definition under ***s1(3) OPA***. A person 'publishes' an article who *'(a) distributes, circulates, sells, lets on hire, gives, or lends it, or who offers it for sale or for letting on hire; or (b) in the case of an article containing or embodying matter to be looked at or a record, shows, plays or projects it or, where the matter is data stored electronically, transmits that data'*. Therefore, electronically transmitting data via the internet constitutes a publication.

Difficulties have arisen in relation to internet publications. ***R v Perrin (2002)*** held that viewing a web page in England is reading a publication in this country even if the website is based in another jurisdiction. This case also concerned ***Article 10 ECHR*** and held that, under the 'margin of appreciation', 'Parliament was entitled to conclude that the prescription was necessary in a democratic society'.

Another case that had human rights implications relating to obscenity is ***Hoare v UK (1997)***, where the court held that it was a proportionate means of achieving the legitimate aim. Similarly, in ***Handyside v UK (1976)***, the ECtHR found that the ***OPA*** legitimately aims to protect morals, and that the action in question had been necessary to promote this legitimate objective. It was within the UK's 'margin of appreciation'.

Defences

There is a defence under ***s2(5) OPA 1959*** if the defendant proves there was 'no reasonable cause to suspect that the article is obscene'. ***Section 1(3)(a) OPA 1964*** provides a corresponding defence relating to a charge of 'having an obscene article for publication for gain'.

Section 4(1) provides for a 'public good' defence but can only be used where the jury has established that the article is obscene. The defendant must prove that it is for the 'public good'. It provides that a defendant will not be liable 'if it is proved that publication of the article in question is justified as being for the public good on the grounds that it is in the interests of science, literature, art or learning, or of other objects of general concern'. The 'public good' defence does not apply 'where the article in question is a moving picture film or soundtrack', but there is a comparable defence in ***s4(1A)*** in relation to a moving picture film or soundtrack where 'the publication is justified as being for the public good on the grounds that it is in the interests of drama, opera, ballet or any other art, or of literature or learning'.

The ***Obscene Publications Act 1964*** amended the 1959 Act, particularly making it an offence to have an obscene publication for gain. The 'gain' can be either for the defendant or another (***s2(1) OPA 1959*** as amended by ***OPA 1964***). 'Gain' is not defined in the statute but has been taken to cover financial gain as well as other 'gain', such as deriving pleasure from the article.

There have been calls to repeal the OPAs as there are so few prosecutions under the laws. There have also been suggestions that the CPS should review its guidance regarding the sort of content that justifies prosecution, following a failed prosecution in ***Peacock (2012)***.

Criminal Justice and Immigration Act 2008

Section 63(1) provides that it is an offence to be in possession of an 'extreme pornographic image'. The ***Criminal Justice and Immigration Act 2008*** shifts the burden from the producers and distributors of 'extreme pornography' to the viewers who merely have such images in their possession.

The definition of an 'extreme pornographic image' is multifaceted:

- Under ***s63(3)***, 'an image is 'pornographic' if it is of such a nature that it must reasonably be assumed to have been produced solely or principally for the purpose of sexual arousal'.
- Under ***s63(5A) and (6)***, an image is 'extreme' if it explicitly and realistically portrays specific matters, such as certain violence, and 'it is grossly offensive, disgusting or otherwise of an obscene character'.

Section 65 provides for some **general defences** which place the burden of proof on the defendant. There is a defence:

1. if the accused had 'a legitimate reason for being in possession of the image concerned'
2. if the defendant shows that they 'had not seen the image concerned and did not know, nor had any cause to suspect, it to be an extreme pornographic image'
3. pertaining to an unsolicited image that is not kept by the defendant 'for an unreasonable time'.

Section 66 provides for a **specific defence** for those who participate in the creation of extreme pornographic images.

KEY TERMINOLOGY

general defences: defences that can apply to any crime (with some exceptions), as opposed to 'special defences', which can only apply to certain crimes; for example diminished responsibility is only available for murder.

Defamation

Defamation is a tort where the claimant is seeking compensation for damage to their reputation.

Defamation cases require a court to balance two competing rights: the right of the claimant to protect their reputation, and the right of the defendant to freedom of expression. ***Article 10 EHCR*** provides for freedom of expression but this is a qualified right which can be removed for a legitimate reason and when necessary and proportionate.

Defamation can be divided into two parts:

- **Libel:** the defamation appears in a permanent form.
- **Slander:** the defamation appears in a non-permanent form.

The main Act for this tort is the ***Defamation Act 2013***. As this is a relatively new law, cases brought under the old law may still be relevant.

Under ***s11 Defamation Act 2013***, defamation actions are now tried without a jury unless the court orders otherwise. A judge, therefore, decides the remedy, which is usually damages but can also be an injunction.

A number of elements need to be established in order to have a successful claim:

1. The statement must be defamatory.
2. The statement must refer to the claimant or be taken to refer to the claimant.
3. The statement must have been published.
4. Publication of the statement has caused or is likely to cause serious harm to the claimant's reputation.

There are also a number of defences that might apply. Each element will now be considered further.

Defamatory statements

There is no statutory or single definition of what constitutes a '**defamatory**' statement. Case law provided the original definitions and the modern test can be found in ***Sim v Stretch (1936)***. The courts consider whether the statement would 'tend to lower the plaintiff in the estimation of right-thinking members of society generally'.

The central question in this element is: 'Has the claimant's reputation been adversely affected or put at risk by the statement?' Therefore, a statement will be considered defamatory if reading it would make an ordinary, reasonable person (not their friends and family):

- think less well of the individual referred to
- think the individual lacks the ability to do their job effectively
- avoid the individual
- treat the person as a figure of fun.

This is not concerned with how it made the person referred to feel but the impression it makes or is likely to make on those reading it. No loss or damage, financial or otherwise, needs to be proved in most cases.

What have the courts held to be 'defamatory statements'?

- In ***Byrne v Deane (1937)***, a notice implying that the claimant had informed the police about illegal gambling machines on the premises was held not to be defamatory as a 'right-thinking member of society' would likely have approve of his action of informing the police and would not think less of him as a consequence.
- In ***Jason Donovan v The Face (1998)***, the pop star successfully sued *The Face* magazine for saying he was gay when he had portrayed himself as heterosexual. It was held to be defamatory to say he had deceived the public about his sexuality as it was implying that he was a liar and hypocritical.
- In ***Berkoff v Burchill (1996)***, actor Steven Berkoff was described as 'hideous-looking' and was compared with Frankenstein's monster by journalist Julie Burchill. The court decided that the article made him an object of ridicule and he was successful in his defamation case.

STRETCH AND CHALLENGE

Think of some examples of defamatory statements, for example, falsely calling someone a paedophile.

Innuendo

A statement does not have to directly criticise the claimant. It might do so indirectly, by implication. This is known as an innuendo. In ***Tolley v JS Fry and Sons Ltd (1931)***, an amateur golfer's image was used on advertising material promoting chocolates. His amateur status meant that he should not profit from his sport, so the implication that he had been paid to advertise the chocolates was held to be defamatory. Therefore, a defamatory statement need not directly criticise the claimant. An implied criticism, known as innuendo, can be sufficient.

It is irrelevant whether a defendant intended to publish a statement that adversely affects a claimant's reputation.

Requirement of serious damage to reputation

Section 1(1) Defamation Act 2013 introduced a requirement that the defamatory statement must have caused, or be likely to cause, serious damage to the claimant's reputation. This aims to reduce the number of claims brought over trivial insults or jokes, and protects freedom of expression. Only damage to reputation is covered, not hurt feelings, and media outlets can escape liability by publishing a swift apology. This happened in ***Cooke and Another v MGN Ltd (2014)*** where a defamatory statement was published but liability was avoided by a complete apology being published in the next edition.

The statement must refer to the claimant or be taken to refer to the claimant. It must be proved by the claimant that an ordinary, reasonable reader or listener would take the statement as referring to them. There are several ways this can happen. The claimant can be named either by their actual name or a fictional name (as in ***Hulton v Jones (1910)***), the claimant's picture can be used (***Dwek v Macmillan Publishers Ltd and Others (2000)***) and the statement can refer to the claimant through context (***Hayward v Thompson (1964)***).

Defamatory statements may be made about a group of people, but overly large groups may not be able to claim, as in ***Knupffer v London Express Newspapers (1944)***, unless the claimant can be singled out. The courts have not, however, indicated a specific number of people above which a claim would fail. In ***Riches v News Group (1986)***, *The News of the World* published an article making allegations about 'Banbury CID'. No officers were mentioned by name but several of the group 'Banbury CID' successfully sued for defamation.

The statement must have been published. This covers more than just the 'traditional' newspaper, magazine or television. It means that the information has passed from the defendant to a person other than the claimant or the defendant's spouse.

STRETCH AND CHALLENGE

What has changed as a result of ***s8 Defamation Act 2013*** regarding the 'repetition rule'?

Defences to defamation

The main defences are:

1. Truth: ***s2 Defamation Act 2013.***
2. Honest opinion: ***s3 Defamation Act 2013.***
3. Responsible publication on a matter of public importance: ***s4 Defamation Act 2013.***
4. Absolute privilege.
5. Qualified privilege.
6. Offer of amends.

1. Truth

Covered by ***s2 Defamation Act 2013***, this is essentially the same as the old common law defence of 'justification' and provides for a defence to a defamation claim where the defendant can prove that the statement, however damaging to the claimant's reputation, is 'substantially' true; small inaccuracies will not prevent the defence applying. ***Gecas v Scottish Television (1992)*** will likely still apply even though it was decided under the 'old' law.

2. Honest opinion

Covered by ***s3 Defamation Act 2013***, this new defence aims to give greater protection to freedom of expression and replaces the 'old' defence known as 'fair comment' (though some of the old case law might still apply). It allows for statements of opinion (on trivial or important matters), provided that three conditions are met:

1. The statement contained a statement of opinion: ***Galloway v Telegraph Group Ltd (2004).***
2. The statement indicates, whether in general or specific terms, the basis of that opinion: ***Joseph v Spiller (2010).***
3. An honest person could have held the opinion, on the basis of:
   - any fact which existed at the time the statement was expressed
   - anything claimed to be a fact in a privileged statement that was published before the statement that is being complained about.

   This condition is a significant change from the old law and now applies an objective test.

GRADE BOOST

It is worth mentioning that the 'old' defence only applies to matters of public interest but the new defence under ***s3*** applies to a commentary on any subject. This offers greater protection for freedom of expression.

Section 3(5) states that the defence will not apply where the claimant can show that the defendant did not honestly hold the opinion they expressed (even if it was an opinion that an honest person could have come to).

3. Responsible publication on a matter of public importance

This is covered by ***s4 Defamation Act 2013***. It was previously known as the 'Reynolds' defence' from ***Reynolds v Times Newspapers (1999)*** and aims to protect the media when they responsibly report on matters of public interest (even if it turns out to be untrue).

The Act provides that it applies to statements of opinion or fact, where:

- the statement complained of was on a matter of public interest
- the defendant reasonably believed its publication was in the public interest.

'Matters of public interest' is not defined in the Act.

Reynolds v Times Newspapers (1999) set out ten factors that the court needs to consider and these were reaffirmed in ***Flood v Times (2012)***:

1. Seriousness of the allegations.
2. Nature of the information: is it a matter of public interest?
3. Source of the information: is it a reliable source?
4. Steps taken to verify the information including getting the other side of the story.
5. Status of the information: is it an old or new allegation?
6. Urgency: is the information perishable or the newspaper in competition with another?
7. Whether comment was gathered from the claimant.
8. Did the article include the gist of the claimant's opinion?
9. Tone of the article (e.g. to raise queries or call for investigations rather than creating statements of fact).
10. Does the article need to be drawn to the public's attention as quickly as possible?

Absolute privilege

Statements covered by absolute privilege cannot be defamatory. This only covers the person making the statement and not subsequent reports of the statement. The following examples are covered.

1. Parliamentary proceedings, including Hansard.
2. Fair, accurate and contemporaneous reports of court proceedings which are held in public (extended by the ***Defamation Act 2013*** to cover any court/tribunal anywhere in the world).
3. Communications between solicitor and client.
4. Statements made by one spouse to another.

Qualified privilege

Like absolute privilege, this defence applies to statements made in certain specified circumstances; it is broader than absolute privilege. It only covers statements made without malice so a claimant can sue if it can be proved the statement was made maliciously. There is a new provision in ***s6 Defamation Act 2013*** covering statements published in scientific or academic journals where the statement relates to a scientific or academic matter and, before it was published, independent subject matter 'peer review' took place.

Offer of amends

Section 2 Defamation Act 2013 provides for a procedure known as 'offer of amends', which is a written correction or apology along with the payment of compensation.

Tort of harassment

The ***Protection from Harassment Act 1997*** creates a 'statutory tort', whereby a defendant is liable to the claimant in damages if the defendant engages in a course of conduct which amounts to harassment of the claimant, and which the defendant knows, or ought to know, amounts to harassment of the claimant.

The central provision of the ***Protection from Harassment Act 1997*** is as follows:

Section1(1) *'A person must not pursue a course of conduct —*

a. *Which amounts to harassment of another, and*

b. *Which he knows or ought to know amounts to harassment of the other.'*

The prohibition in this section is enforceable by the creation of a criminal offence (in ***s2***) and by a civil remedy (in ***s3***). ***Section 3*** gives rise to the statutory tort:

Section 3(1) provides that an actual or apprehended breach of ***s1*** may be the subject of a claim in civil proceedings by the person who is or may be the victim of the course of conduct in question.

Conduct amounting to harassment, for the purposes of the 1997 Act, can arise from the defendant's spoken words, written statements, behaviour, or a combination of all three. It can be via face-to-face contact, letters, emails, phone calls, from being photographed without the claimant's consent, via radio broadcasts or via internet forums or web publications. Harassment can arise from conduct which has already occurred, or from threats to commit acts (such as publication of embarrassing material). The 1997 Act was originally aimed at preventing stalking. However, one of the most surprising elements of the 1997 Act has been to deal with workplace bullying.

What is a statutory tort?

The ***Protection from Harassment Act 1997*** creates a 'statutory tort', whereby Parliament has specified that an actionable wrong can give rise to a civil remedy, and where that wrong reflects the hallmarks of a tort (a duty, a breach, damage which is causally linked to that breach), and for which damages can be obtained in a civil court.

Summary of elements of this tort

1. A course of conduct by the defendant amounting to harassment.
2. The conduct was targeted at an individual (claimant or another person).
3. The defendant had actual or constructive knowledge of the harassment.
4. The conduct was objectively judged to be oppressive and unacceptable.
5. The defendant's harassment caused the claimant's damage.

In ***Jones and Another v Ruth and Another (2011)***, Patten LJ stated that harassment has four hallmarks. It has to be:

- persistent (the persistent tormenting or irritation of the victim)
- intentional (deliberate) conduct which its perpetrator either knows or certainly ought reasonably to be aware has this effect on the complainant)
- personal (conduct between two individuals that is intensely personal in character)
- physical or non-physical (ranging from physical force or the threat of force to more subtle but nonetheless intimidating conduct).

The harassment does not need to give rise to a recognised psychiatric injury to be actionable, mere anxiety or distress is sufficient. Where threats are alleged to be the conduct amounting to harassment, injunctive relief will be the primary remedy sought by the claimant. There is nothing in the 1997 Act which points to what gravity of harassment is necessary.

STRETCH AND CHALLENGE

Research the facts of ***Jones and Another v Ruth and Another (2011)***, where the defendant directed comments and behaviour towards the claimant which were directed at the claimant's sexuality.

STRETCH AND CHALLENGE

Research the following cases which illustrate the types of behaviour that can or cannot establish the statutory tort of harassment:

- ***Thomas v News Group Newspapers Ltd (2001)***
- ***Iqbal v Dean Manson Solicitors (2011)***
- ***Majrowski v Guy's and St Thomas's NHS Trust (2006)***
- ***WXY v Gewanter (2012)***
- ***Singh v Bhakar (2006)***
- ***AVB v TDD (2013)***
- ***Trimingham v Associated Newspapers (2012)***
- ***King v Sunday Newspapers Ltd (2012).***

The wide reach of the Act

Case law to date illustrates that a wide range of aggressive or intimidatory behaviour has been sufficient to establish the statutory tort. These include neighbourly relations, the work environment, media and paparazzi activities, and fallings-out between family members.

KEY CASE

Ting Lan Hong and KLM (a child) v XYZ (2011)
Ting Lan Hong, the claimant and mother of actor Hugh Grant's child, complained that she was regularly photographed in the street without her consent, that she received numerous phone calls telling her to tell Hugh Grant that he should 'shut up' (in relation to his appearance on the news programme, *Question Time*, regarding the phone-hacking scandal), that she was being tailed by 'a man in a black Audi', and that her friend had been told to warn her that she was being constantly followed. The court held that harassment had been proven and an injunction was granted against paparazzi photographers.

Summary – Restrictions of the ECHR

Public order

- ***Public Order Act 1986***: Riot: ***s1***; violent disorder: ***s2***; affray: ***s3***; fear or provocation of violence: ***s4***: ***R v Horseferry Road Justices, ex parte Siadatan (1990)***; harassment, alarm or distress: ***s4A***; ***s5***: ***DPP v Orum (1988)***; ***DPP v Fiddler (1992)***; ***DPP v Clarke (1992)***; mens rea requirement: ***s6***; marches/processions: ***ss11–13***; meetings/assemblies: ***s14***; ***s16***; incitement to racial hatred: ***s17***; ***s23***; publication offences: ***ss18–22***
- ***Criminal Justice Act 1994***:
  - Trespassory assemblies: ***s14A***: ***DPP vs Jones (1998)***; ***s14B***: ***Windle v DPP (1996)***; ***s14C***; ***s61***; ***s63***
  - Aggravated trespass: ***s68***; ***s69***
- Racial and religious hatred: ***Racial and Religious Hatred Act 2006: s29A***; ***Crime and Disorder Act 1998***; ***Anti-Terrorism, Crime and Security Act 2001***; ***Football (Offences) Act 1991***
- Private law remedies: ***Hubbard v Pitt (1976)***; ***Hickman v Maisey (1900)***
- ***Sections 128–138 Serious Organised Crime and Police Act 2005 (SOCPA)*** restrict the freedom to protest near Parliament and other 'sensitive' sites: ***R (on the application of Haw) v Secretary of State for the Home Department (2006)***
- Breach of the peace: ***R (Laporte) v Chief Constable of Gloucestershire (2007)***; ***Austin and Another v Commissioner of Police of the Metropolis (2007)***; ***Moss v McLachlan (1985)***; ***Foy v Chief Constable of Kent (1984)***; ***Nicol v DPP (1996)***; ***Steel v UK (1998)***; ***Redmond-Bate (1999)***; ***Bibby (2000)***
- Obstruction of the highway: ***s137 Highways Act 1980***: ***Harrison v Duke of Rutland (1893)***; ***Arrowsmith v Jenkins (1963)***; ***Nagy v Weston (1966)***
- Obstruction of the police: ***s89 Police Act 1996***: ***Duncan v Jones (1936)***

Police powers

- ***Section 1 Police and Criminal Evidence Act 1984 (PACE):*** Stop and search of persons and vehicles
- ***Code A paragraph 2.2*** two-stage test for 'reasonable suspicion'
- Reasonable force: ***s117, s2(3), s3 PACE***
- Search of premises with a warrant: ***s8 PACE***
- Search without a warrant: ***s17***: ***Osman v DPP (1999)***; ***s18; s19; s32; Code B***
- Arrest with a warrant: Police must apply to a magistrate
- Arrest without a warrant: ***s24 PACE*** as amended by ***s110 SOCPA 2005***: Reasonable grounds to believe that a person is committing, has committed or is about to commit an offence and an arrest is necessary
- Detention and interrogation: ***ss30, 36–38, 40, 41, 44, 54 PACE***
  - Fingerprinting, intimate searches and samples: ***ss27, 55,61–4 (S and Marper v UK (2008)), 65*** as amended by ***CJPOA 1994***
  - Rights and treatment of suspects during detention and interrogation: ***ss56–8, 60; Code C***
  - Admissibility of evidence: Courts can refuse to admit evidence that has not been properly obtained. ***s76(2)(a)(b)***: ***R v Samuel (1988)***; ***R v Grant (2005)***; ***s78 PACE***: ***R v Canale (1990)***;

- Complaints against and police and remedies
  - No one is above the law and everyone is equal under it, including the police
  - Complaints to the Home Office via an MP or the Local Police Authority
  - ***Police Reform Act 2002***: Independent Police Complaints Commission (IPCC) deals with serious complaints
  - Professional Standards Department (PSD) of relevant police authority deals with general complaints
  - Civil actions against the police: the standard of proof is 'on the balance of probabilities' and the burden lies with the claimant: ***Goswell v Commissioner of Police for The Metropolis (1998); The Commissioner of Police for the Metropolis v Thompson and Hsu (1997)***

Interception of communication

- ***Interception of Communications Act 1985 (ICA)***: Introduced following ***Malone v UK (1985)*** to use telephone and mail intercepts, subject to controls
- Use of bugging devices: ***Khan (Sultan) (1996)***; ***Police Act 1997***
- ***Regulation of Investigatory Powers Act 2000***: It is an offence to intentionally and without lawful authority intercept communications by a postal service or telecommunications system
- Covert surveillance: ***ss26–48 RIPA***: ***R v Hall (1994)***; ***R v Stagg (1994)***
- ***Investigatory Powers Act (IPA) 2016***: Brings together and updates existing powers (***RIPA 2000*** continues until repealed)

Duty of confidentiality

- Breach of confidence and privacy: ***Kaye v Robertson (1991)***; ***Wainwright v Home Office (2003)***; ***Hosking v Runting (2004)***
- No tort of invasion of privacy in England and Wales but legal controls can be used against the media and others: ***Prince Albert v Strange (1849)***; ***Argyll v Argyll (1967)***; ***Coco v AN Clark (Engineers) Ltd (1969)***; ***Stephens v Avery (1988)***; ***HRH Princess of Wales v MGN Newspapers Ltd (1993)***; ***Shelley Films Ltd v Rex Features Ltd (1993)***; ***Fairnie (Deceased) and Others v Reed and Another (1994)***
- Public interest defence: Confidential information will not be protected if the public interest outweighs the interest in preserving confidentiality: ***AG v Guardian Newspapers Ltd (No 2) (1990)***
- ***Article 8 ECHR*** (right to privacy) incorporated into ***Human Rights Act 1998***. Privacy must be weighed alongside freedom of speech and expression (***Article 10 ECHR***): ***Venables and Thompson v News Group Newspapers (2001)***; ***Associated Newspapers Ltd v Prince of Wales (2006)***; ***Murray v Express Newspapers (2008)***; ***Mosley v News Group Newspapers (2008)***; ***Author of a Blog v Times Newspapers (2009)***; ***BBC v HarperCollins Ltd (2010)***; ***Hutcheson v News Group Newspapers (2011)***; ***Terry v Persons Unknown (2010)***; ***Ferdinand v MGN (2011)***; ***CTB v News Group Newspapers (2011)***
- Setting the boundaries for privacy and ECtHR: ***Von Hannover v Germany (No 2) (2012); Springer v Germany (2012)***
- ***Official Secrets Acts 1911, 1920, 1939*** and ***1989***: ***Aitken (1970)***; ***Tisdall (1984)***; ***Ponting (1985)***
- ***Official Secrets Act 1989:*** Scope of protection of official information covers security and intelligence, defence, international relations, crime
- Defences to the ***Official Secrets Act 1989***: Defendant did not know information fell into a protected category; had no reason to believe the information would cause harm; believed in lawful authorisation

- A law of contempt balances a person's right to a fair trial with a journalist's right to report
- ***Contempt of Court Act 1981***: ***Sunday Times v UK (1981)***; ***AG v News Group Newspapers (1987)***; ***Woodgate and Bowyer (2001)***; ***AG v English (1985)***

Obscenity

- ***Article 10 ECHR***: Qualified right to 'freedom of expression'
- The ***Obscene Publications Act 1959*** as amended by the ***Obscene Publications Act 1964 (OPA)***: ***R v Perrin (2002)***; ***Hoare v UK (1997***; ***Handyside v UK (1976)***
- 'Obscenity depends on the article and not upon the author': ***Shaw v DPP (1962)***
- ***Criminal Justice and Immigration Act 2008*** shifts the burden from the producers and distributors of 'extreme pornography' to the viewers
- ***s11 Defamation Act 2013***: A judge decides the remedy, usually damages but can be an injunction

Defamation

- Defamatory statements: ***Sim v Stretch (1936)***; ***Byrne v Deane (1937)***; ***Jason Donovan v The Face (1998)***; ***Berkoff v Burchill (1996)***
- Innuendo: Indirect criticism by implication: ***Tolley v JS Fry and Sons Ltd (1931)***,
- Requirement of serious damage to reputation: ***s1(1) Defamation Act 2013***: ***Cooke and Another v MGN Ltd (2014)***; ***Hulton v Jones (1910)***; ***Dwek v Macmillan Publishers Ltd and Others (2000)***; ***Hayward v Thompson (1964)***; ***Knupffer v London Express Newspapers (1944)***; ***Riches v News Group (1986)***
- Defences to defamation: Truth (***s2 Defamation Act 2013***); honest opinion (***s3 Defamation Act 2013***); Responsible publication on a matter of public importance (***s4 Defamation Act 2013***); absolute privilege; qualified privilege; offer of amends

Tort of harassment

- ***Protection from Harassment Act 1997***: a statutory tort where:
  1. a course of conduct by defendant amounted to harassment
  2. conduct was targeted at an individual
  3. defendant had knowledge of the harassment
  4. conduct was oppressive and unacceptable
  5. defendant's harassment caused claimant's damage
- ***Jones and Another v Ruth and Another (2011)***: Harassment has to be persistent, intentional, personal and intimidating
- Wide reach of the Act: ***Ting Lan Hong and KLM (a child) v XYZ (2011)***

Exam practice and techniques

There is a degree of overlap between the assessments in Eduqas AS, Eduqas A Level and WJEC Law, with similar questions but variations in the wording, weighting of assessment objectives and timings. The Assessment Objectives (AOs) are the same on both the Eduqas and WJEC specifications.

- **AO1**: You must demonstrate knowledge and understanding of legal rules and principles.
- **AO2**: You must apply legal rules and principles to given scenarios in order to present a legal argument using appropriate legal terminology.
- **AO3**: You must analyse and evaluate legal rules, principles, concepts and issues.

How exam questions are set

The WJEC and Eduqas specifications in Law aim to encourage students to:

- develop and sustain their enjoyment of, and interest in, law
- develop knowledge and understanding of selected areas of law and the legal system in England and Wales
- develop an understanding of legal method and reasoning
- develop the techniques of logical thinking, and the skills necessary to analyse and solve problems by applying legal rules
- develop the ability to communicate legal arguments and conclusions with reference to appropriate legal authority
- develop a critical awareness of the changing nature of law in society
- gain a sound basis for further study
- develop knowledge of the rights and responsibilities of individuals as citizens including, where appropriate, an understanding of moral, spiritual and cultural issues
- develop, where appropriate, skills in communication, application of number and information technology
- improve, where appropriate, their own learning and performance, to facilitate work with others and solve problems in the context of their study of law.

Examination questions are written by the principal examiner responsible for the unit well in advance of the examination. A committee of experienced examiners discusses the quality of every question and changes are made to the questions until the committee agrees that they are appropriate. The questions are written to reflect the substantive content and success criteria outlined in the specification.

Exam answers are marked in relation to three AOs. The sample assessment questions for each paper on AS Eduqas Law, A Level Eduqas Law and WJEC Law explain the marks available under each AO.

Improving your exam performance

There are a few important things to remember, and common errors made by law students.

Read the instructions

There is a mixture of compulsory questions and questions where you can choose which question to answer. It is important to answer the correct number of questions and to choose your questions wisely. Rubric errors will get you no marks.

AO1: You must demonstrate knowledge and understanding of legal rules and principles

Questions where AO1 marks are available are generally testing your knowledge and understanding of a topic, and command words such as **explain**, **describe** and **outline** are all indicative of this.

AO2: You must apply legal rules and principles to given scenarios in order to present a legal argument using appropriate legal terminology

Questions where AO2 marks are available are generally testing your ability to **apply** your knowledge and understanding of a topic to a given scenario, in order to reach a conclusion. They use the command words **apply** or **advise**. Use legal authority to support your answers.

AO3: You must analyse and evaluate legal rules, principles, concepts and issues

Questions where AO3 marks are available generally require you to provide a **balanced** argument. There will always be an opportunity to look at two sides of an argument, and you should make sure that you explore both sides thoroughly. The command words are indicative of this requirement to **analyse** and **evaluate**. The examiner is looking for a reasoned, balanced argument, supported with relevant legal authority and a rounded conclusion.

Take time over your introduction

For an extended essay answer, it is good practice to write a strong introduction because it shows the examiner that you understand the topic from the start. Do not fall into the trap of writing a 'waffly' introduction; spend a couple of minutes thinking and planning before you begin to write.

Begin with a definition of the key terms contained in the question. Some examples are highlighted below:

'Explain the role of the Crown Prosecution Service.'

'Analyse and evaluate the reliability of jury trial.'

'Explain the approaches used by judges in statutory interpretation.'

Use cases to add legal authority

Use as much **legal authority** as you can remember. This is especially important when you are being tested on your skills of application (AO2) and analysis and evaluation (AO3). You also need to make sure you explain the relevance of the case.

Example: R v Young (1995)

Answer A

Another disadvantage of juries is that you do not know how the jury arrived at their verdict. This was seen in the case of **R v Young (1995)**.

Answer B

Another disadvantage of juries is that you do not know how the jury arrived at their verdict. This was seen in the case of **R v Young (1995)**, *where the jury used a Ouija board to contact the dead victim*.

The highlighted section of Answer B shows that the candidate knows and understands the relevance of the case, whereas the candidate in Answer A has just used the case to support their point and not actually progressed to showing **how**.

Where possible, try to cite the legal authority in full. An attempt at citation will be credited, but obviously it is more appropriate to learn the cases and relevant legal authority.

Answer A

Another disadvantage of the jury system is that you do not know how the jury reached their verdict as was seen in the case where the jury used a Ouija board.

Answer B

Another disadvantage of juries is that you do not know how the jury arrived at their verdict. This was seen in the case of **R v Young (1995)**, *where the jury used a Ouija board to contact the dead victim.*

It is quite clear that the candidate who wrote Answer A knows the case, but the candidate who wrote Answer B has actually cited it in full, making it clear to the examiner that there is an **excellent** or **good** knowledge, rather than just a **basic** knowledge.

Show you are aware of recent developments

Be aware of recent reforms, criticisms and current affairs in the area. Your lecturer may have made you aware of some such reports and news, but it is always good practice to keep abreast of recent developments.

Only answer the question that has been asked

Make sure you answer the question. Many candidates will have learned essays by heart and then merely repeat this answer in the examination, only to find that it does not actually answer the question at all. Read and reread the question to ensure that your planned answer is actually what is required.

Expect topics to be combined

When you are revising, be careful if you decide to omit certain topics. It is possible that a question may be asked that combines topics, and you may find that you can answer **part a** but have not done enough revision to answer **part b** as competently. Look back over past papers and see what combination of topics have been asked.

Use stimulus material with care

Where there is stimulus material, you are required to use it as a source to support what you are saying but, ultimately, you are being examined on **your** knowledge. Rewriting a table in your own words, or quoting copious amounts from the source is not going to get you any marks.

Use terminology correctly

You will be marked on your appropriate use of legal terminology and your understanding of core legal principles, yet candidates often make very simple errors. Do you know the difference between:

- CJEU and ECtHR?
- CPS and CPR?
- Guilty and liable?
- Magistrates and juries?

As obvious as these errors may seem, they are very common, so make sure you have a good grasp of definitions. It is also important to check your spelling, especially of commonly misspelt words like:

- defendant
- sentence
- precedent
- trial.

The format of the exam

If you are studying Law in Wales then you are probably entered for WJEC papers. In England, you will almost certainly be studying for the Eduqas qualification. Check with your teachers which examination you are entered for because there are differences in the papers and the expectations for each vary a great deal.

The separate examinations are known as **components** (Eduqas) or **units** (WJEC). At AS, there are two units or components in both WJEC and Eduqas papers.

WJEC papers in Law

If you are studying for a WJEC paper then your AS paper is a building block for A2. Your marks for AS will contribute to your overall examination grade. The AS papers offer slightly less challenge than A2 papers so the skills you display at A2 will be at a higher level. There may be reference to Welsh examples on examination papers and you are encouraged to use Welsh-based examples where applicable.

Below is a summary of the different papers for WJEC AS/A Level.

WJEC units for AS Law

AS Law consists of two papers: Unit 1 and Unit 2. AS Law is worth 40% of the overall A Level and can be 'cashed-in' as a distinct qualification.

UNIT 1: The Nature of Law and the Welsh and English Legal Systems

- Written examination: 1 hour 45 minutes.
- 25% of the qualification.
- 80 marks available.

This unit focuses on the structure of the Welsh and English legal systems, including their relationship with the European Union. As it is the Welsh specification, you will study the devolution settlement in Wales and its impact. You will also learn about the different sources of primary and secondary law in the Welsh and English legal systems and will consider how those laws are used by judges to make decisions. You will also develop a knowledge and understanding of the criminal justice system, civil justice system (including relevant legal personnel) and legal funding.

The examination for Unit 1 is broken into two sections.

Section A focuses on the nature of law and the various methods of law-making in the Welsh and English legal systems.

- You should spend approximately 60 minutes on this section of the exam.
- You are required to answer two compulsory questions, each worth 10 marks, and one question from a choice of two, worth 28 marks. There is a total of 48 marks available for this section of the exam.
- You should spend approximately 12½ minutes on each of the two compulsory questions (questions 1 and 2) and 35 minutes on either question 3 or 4.
- Questions 1 and 2 examine AO1 skills (knowledge and understanding).
- Questions 3 and 4 primarily examine AO2 skills (application of legal principles of and rules to a given scenario), along with AO1 skills.

Section B focuses on key features of the criminal justice system and civil justice system within the Welsh and English legal systems, including legal personnel and legal funding. It also includes the nature of law.

- You should spend approximately 45 minutes on this section of the exam.
- You are required to answer one question consisting of **part a** and a **part b** from a choice of two. The question totals 32 marks, with 8 marks for part a and 24 marks for part b.
- You should spend approximately 15 minutes on part a of your chosen question and 30 minutes on part b of your chosen question.
- **Part a** examines AO1 skills (knowledge and understanding).
- **Part b** examines AO3 skills (analysis and evaluation of legal rule, principles, concepts and ideas).

UNIT 2: The Law of Tort

- Written examination: 1 hour 30 minutes.
- 15% of the qualification.
- 60 marks available.

This unit requires you to study the rules and theory of the law of tort. You will study liability in negligence for injury to people and will be required to apply the elements of the law of negligence to hypothetical scenarios. You will also look at occupiers' liability and remedies, including damages, mitigation of loss and injunctions.

This examination consists of five compulsory questions.

- Questions 1, 2 and 3 are each worth 8 marks and examine your ability to explain the law relating to tort (AO1 skills). You should spend approximately 12 minutes on each question (1, 2 and 3).
- Question 4 is worth 18 marks and requires you to apply the law to a hypothetical scenario. This question examines your ability to apply the law (AO2 skills). You should spend approximately 27 minutes on this question.
- Question 5 is worth 18 marks and requires you to analyse and evaluate an area of tort law. This question examines your ability to analyse and evaluate (AO2 skills). You should spend approximately 27 minutes on this question.

WJEC units for A Level Law

A Level Law with WJEC builds upon the skills developed at AS. It consists of a further two papers, Unit 3 and Unit 4, and is worth 60% of the overall A Level.

UNIT 3: The Practice of Substantive Law

- Written examination: 1 hour 45 minutes.
- 30% of qualification.
- 100 marks available.

This unit requires you to learn about **two areas** of substantive law. You will need to ensure you answer the questions only on the areas you have studied. The options are:

- human rights law (Section A)
- the law of contract (Section B)
- criminal law (Section C).

The Unit 3 exam will test your knowledge and understanding of legal rules and principles in relation to the two areas of substantive law you have studied. Unit 3 examines your ability to explain the law (AO1 skills) and apply that law to a given hypothetical scenario (AO2 skills).

- The examination offers a choice of two questions per section. You therefore need to answer a total of two questions, one per section, based on the areas of law you have studied. For example, you could answer one question from Section A (human rights law) and one question from Section C (criminal law).
- Each question is worth 50 marks and you should spend approximately 52½ minutes on each question.
- Each question examines your knowledge and understanding (AO1 skills) and your ability to apply the law (AO2 skills).

UNIT 4: Substantive Law Perspectives

- Written examination: 2 hours.
- 30% of qualification.
- 100 marks available.

This unit requires you to learn about **the same two areas** of substantive law as you did for Unit 3. You will need to ensure you answer only the questions about the areas you have studied. The options are:

- human rights law (Section A)
- the law of contract (Section B)
- criminal law (Section C).

The Unit 4 exam will test your knowledge and understanding of legal rules and principles in relation to the two areas of substantive law you have studied. Unit 4 examines your ability to explain the law (AO1 skills) and analyse and evaluate the law (AO3 skills).

- The examination offers a choice of two questions per section. You therefore need to answer a total of two questions, one per section, based on the areas of law you have studied. For example, you could answer one question from Section A (human rights law) and one question from Section C (criminal law).
- Each question is worth 50 marks and you should spend approximately one hour on each question.
- Each question examines your knowledge and understanding (AO1 skills) and your ability to analyse and evaluate the law (AO3 skills).

WJEC assessment weightings for AS and A Level

Assessment objective weightings are shown below as a percentage of the full A Level, with AS weightings in brackets.

	AO1	AO2	AO3	Total
AS Unit 1	10% (25%)	7.5% (18.75%)	7.5% (18.75%)	25% (62.5%)
AS Unit 2	6% (15%)	4.5% (11.25%)	4.5% (11.25%)	15% (37.5%)
A Level Unit 3	12%	18%	–	30%
A Level Unit 4	12%	–	18%	30%
Overall weighting	**40%**	**30%**	**30%**	**100%**

Eduqas components for AS and A level Law

If you are studying for an Eduqas paper, AS is an entirely separate qualification from A Level. You will study for half the content of a full A Level but will show the same degree of skill as for a full A Level.

The separate examinations are known as components. At AS, there are two components. For the full A Level, there are three components. The content differs between the components at AS and A Level; they also have slightly different names and therefore will be considered separately in this guide. It is important that you are aware of which option you are studying and whether it is AS or A Level law.

Below is a summary of the different papers for Eduqas AS/A Level.

Eduqas AS Law

The components are:

COMPONENT 1: The Nature of Law and the English Legal System

- Written examination: 1 hour 30 minutes.
- 50% of the AS Law qualification.
- 60 marks available.

This component focuses on the structure of the English legal system, including its relationship with the European Union. You will also learn about the different sources of primary and secondary law in the English legal system and will consider how those laws are used by judges to make decisions. You will also develop a knowledge and understanding of the criminal justice system, civil justice system (including relevant legal personnel) and legal funding.

This component also includes a study of the nature of law: the distinction between enforceable legal rules and principles and other rules and norms of behaviour; criminal and civil law; and the different sources of law (including custom, statutory law and common law). The nature of law is widespread throughout this component and reference should be made to it, where appropriate, in your examination responses.

The examination for Unit 1 is broken down into two sections.

Section A focuses on the nature of law and the various methods of law-making in the English legal system, including its relationship with the European Union.

- You should spend approximately 54 minutes on this section of the exam.
- You are required to answer two compulsory questions, each worth 6 marks and one question from a choice of two, consisting of a **part a**, worth 6 marks, and a **part b**, worth 18 marks.

- You should spend approximately 9 minutes on each of the two compulsory questions (questions 1 and 2) and 36 minutes on **either** question 3 **or** 4. You should spend approximately 9 minutes on part a of this question and approximately 27 minutes on part b.
- **Questions 1** and **2** examine your knowledge and understanding (AO1 skills).
- **Questions 3** and **4** examine knowledge and understanding (AO1 skills) in part a and application of legal principles of and rules to a given scenario (AO2 skills) in part b.

Section B focuses on key features of the criminal and civil justice systems within the English legal system, including legal personnel and legal funding. It also includes the nature of law.

- You should spend approximately 36 minutes on this section of the exam.
- You are required to answer one question consisting of a **part a** and a **part b** from a choice of two. The question totals 24 marks, with 6 marks for part a and 18 marks for part b.
- You should spend approximately 9 minutes on part a and approximately 27 minutes on part b of your chosen question.
- Part a examines your knowledge and understanding (AO1 skills).
- Part b examines your analysis and evaluation of legal rule, principles and concepts (AO3 skills).

COMPONENT 2: Understanding Substantive Law

- Written examination: 1 hour 30 minutes.
- 50% of the AS Law qualification.
- 60 marks available.

This component requires you to answer two questions: one on **private** law in Section A (either **contract** or **tort**) and one on **public** law in Section B (either **criminal** law or **human rights** law). It is important that you only answer questions on the area of private and public law that you have studied.

Each of your chosen examination questions consists of four compulsory sub-part questions which test skills across all three AOs.

- You should spend approximately 45 minutes per section.
- **Questions a** and **b** on each section are each worth 6 marks and examine your ability to explain the law relating to your studies of private and public law (AO1 skills). You should spend approximately 9 minutes on each question a and b per section.
- **Question c** is worth 9 marks and requires you to analyse and evaluate an area of private or public law. This question examines analysis and evaluation (AO3 skills though the command word **assess** may be used.). You should spend approximately 13½ minutes on this question per section.
- **Question d** is worth 9 marks and requires you to apply the law to a given hypothetical scenario. This question examines your application of the law (AO2 skills). You should spend approximately 13 ½ minutes on this question per section.

Eduqas assessment weightings for AS law

	AO1	AO2	AO3	Total
Component 1	20%	15%	15%	50%
Component 2	20%	15%	15%	50%
Overall weighting	**40%**	**30%**	**30%**	**100%**

Eduqas A Level Law

COMPONENT 1: The Nature of Law and the English Legal System

- Written examination: 1 hour 30 minutes.
- 25% of the A Level law qualification.
- 50 marks available.

This component focuses on the structure of the English legal system, including its relationship with the European Union. You will also learn about the different sources of primary and secondary law in the English legal system and will consider how those laws are used by judges to make decisions. You will also develop a knowledge and understanding of the criminal justice system, civil justice system (including relevant legal personnel) and legal funding.

This component also includes a study of the nature of law: the distinction between enforceable legal rules and principles and other rules and norms of behaviour; criminal and civil law; and the different sources of law (including custom, statutory law and common law). The nature of law is widespread throughout this component and reference should be made to it, where appropriate, in your examination responses. The nature of law includes law and society, law and morality, and law and justice.

The examination for Unit 1 is broken down into two sections.

Section A focuses on the nature of law and the various methods of law-making in the English legal system, including its relationship with the European Union.

- You should spend approximately 45 minutes on this section of the exam.
- You are required to answer two compulsory questions, each worth 5 marks, and one question from a choice of two, worth 15 marks.
- You should spend approximately 9 minutes on each of the two compulsory questions (questions 1 and 2) and 27 minutes on **either** question 3 **or** 4.
- **Questions 1** and **2** examine your knowledge and understanding (AO1 skills).
- **Questions 3** and **4** examine application of legal principles of and rules to a given scenario (AO2 skills).

Section B focuses on key features of the criminal and civil justice systems within the English legal system, including legal personnel and legal funding. It also includes the nature of law.

- You should spend approximately 45 minutes on this section of the exam.
- You are required to answer one question consisting of a **part a** and a **part b** from a choice of two. The question totals 25 marks, with 10 marks for part a and 15 marks for part b.
- You should spend approximately 18 minutes on part a and approximately 27 minutes on part b of your chosen question.
- Part a examines your knowledge and understanding (AO1 skills).
- Part b examines your analysis and evaluation of legal rule, principles, concepts and issues, and the nature of law (AO3 skills).

COMPONENT 2: Substantive Law in Practice

- Written examination: 2 hours 15 minutes.
- 37.5% of the A Level Law qualification.
- 75 marks available.

This component requires you to study **three areas of substantive law (including at least one public law area and at least one private law area)**. There are four sections and you need to answer three questions in total, each from a different section. They are all scenario-style questions.

It is important that you only answer questions on the areas of private or public law that you have studied and that you answer questions on the same areas in the exams for both Component 2 and Component 3. The options are:

- **Section A**: Law of contract (private law)
- **Section B**: Law of tort (private law)
- **Section C**: Criminal law (public law)
- **Section D**: Human rights law (public law).

Each of your chosen examination questions consists of one question testing both AO1 (knowledge and understanding) and AO2 skills (application of legal rules and principles to the scenario).

Each question is worth 25 marks and you should spend approximately 45 minutes on each of the three answers.

COMPONENT 3: Perspectives of Substantive Law

- Written examination: 2 hours 15 minutes.
- 37.5% of the A Level Law qualification.
- 75 marks available.

This unit requires you to study **three areas of substantive law (including at least one public law area and at least one private law area)**. There are four sections and you need to answer three questions in total, each from a different section. They are all essay-style questions.

It is important that you only answer questions on the areas of private or public law that you have that you answer questions on the same areas in the exams for both Component 2 and Component 3. The options are:

- Section A: Law of contract (private law)
- Section B: Law of tort (private law)
- Section C: Criminal law (public law)
- Section D: Human rights law (public law).

Each of your chosen examination questions consists of one question testing both AO1 (knowledge and understanding) and AO3 skills (analyse and evaluate legal rules, principles, concepts and issues).

Each question is worth 25 marks and you should spend approximately 45 minutes on each of the three answers.

Eduqas assessment weightings for A Level Law

	AO1	AO2	AO3	Total
Component 1	10%	7.5%	7.5%	25%
Component 2	15%	22.5%	-	37.5%
Component 3	15%	-	22.5%	37.5%
Overall weighting	**40%**	**30%**	**30%**	**100%**

Sample practice questions and answers

This section uses sample questions from the specimen assessment materials (SAMs) published by the WJEC/Eduqas. They represent the different questions that can feature on each paper of the WJEC/Eduqas specifications. **The question numbers reflect those in the SAMs so do not follow a logical order within this book.**

Sample answers are supplied for each question: a stronger response and a weaker one. You can refer to the mark schemes in the SAMs while you work through these sample answers.

The responses are not the work of students but have been written by the authors of this book to provide a framework for the commentary. The commentary reflects the opinions of the authors alone and has not been produced by the examination board.

WJEC AS Law: Unit 1 Section A

Unit 1 Section A papers begin with two compulsory questions, each worth 10 marks. They are examining **AO1 Knowledge and understanding**.

Question 1

Explain the stages a Bill must go through to become an Act of Parliament. [10]

The command word **explain** requires you write in simple terms how something works.

Question 1 stronger response

All Acts of Parliament start out as Bills. A Bill is a draft proposed law which can be started in either the House of Lords or the House of Commons. Public Bills change the law of the whole country but there are also Private Bills and Private Members' Bills.

This is a good opener as it mentions the three main types of Bill. No further detail is needed as time is limited in this question and the focus is on the Parliamentary process and not the types of Bill.

For a Public Bill that starts in the House of Commons, the first stage is called the first reading. This is where the short title of the proposed law is read out. Next is the second reading. This is where the MPs in the House of Commons have their first opportunity to debate the proposed law. At the end of the second reading, the Commons votes on whether the Bill should proceed to the next stage.

The candidate makes it clear which procedure they are going to consider. This is the most popular procedure.

Once the second reading is complete, the Bill moves on to the committee stage. This involves a more detailed discussion of each clause of the Bill. Amendments to the Bill are also proposed, debated and agreed. The committee can consult experts and interest groups from outside Parliament.

Once the committee stage is finished, the Bill returns to the floor of the House of Commons for its report stage, where the amended Bill can be debated and further amendments proposed. Following the report stage, the Bill proceeds to the third reading. This is where the final vote on the Bill takes place. If it passes this stage, it proceeds to the House of Lords.

In the House of Lords, the Bill will go through the same five stages as above. If the House of Lords make any amendments to the Bill, it must go back to the House of Commons for them to consider those amendments. They will also decide whether to accept those amendments. If they do not, the Bill returns to the Lords. This process is called 'ping pong' as the Bill continues to be passed back and forth between the two Houses until they reach agreement.

The House of Commons has the power to bypass the House of Lords if they cannot reach agreement on a Bill, as the Commons is the elected House. This power is given in the **Parliament Acts 1911** and **1949**, though it is rarely used. The last time was with the **Hunting Act 2004**.

The final stage is for the Bill to receive Royal Assent. This is where the monarch gives consent to the legislation and the Bill becomes an Act of Parliament. This is merely a formality nowadays. The last time this was refused was when Queen Anne refused the Scottish Militia Bill in 1707.

Following Royal Assent, the Act will either come into force at midnight on that day or on the commencement date set. An example of an Act of Parliament is the **Theft Act 1968**.

This candidate has explained what happens at each stage rather than just listing the stages. This demonstrates excellent, detailed knowledge and understanding, and distinguishes this answer from a weaker one. It merits a level 4 mark.

It is good practice in law to provide an example to substantiate your response. The question is about laws made by Parliament and the candidate has included an example of an Act of Parliament.

Question 1 weaker response

Bills have to pass through different stages in the House of Commons in order to become an Act of Parliament. These are: first reading, second reading, committee stage, report stage and third reading where the MPs vote on the law. The law then passes to the House of Lords who also debate it. It can ping pong between the House of Commons and the House of Lords until they reach agreement. An example is the **Hunting Act 2014**. Finally, the Queen must sign the Bill, called Royal Assent.

This is clearly a weaker response and would attract a level 2 mark. The candidate has not explained each stage and the language is more informal. However, there is an example and all stages are correctly listed in the correct order. Therefore, a mark at the higher end of level 2 would be warranted.

Question 4

Read the fictitious statute and the scenario below and answer the question that follows.

Environmental Protection (Fictitious) Act 2016

Section 1:
'Any person who leaves anything whatsoever for the purposes of prostitution in such circumstances as to cause or contribute to or tend to lead to the defacement of any place to which this section applies shall be guilty of an offence.'

One of the categories to which this section applies is a public open place, which is defined in section 2.

Section 2:
'Public open space means a place in the open air to which the public is entitled or permitted to have access without payment. Any covered place open to the air on at least one side and available for public use shall be treated as a public open place.'

Jemima pinned cards advertising 'special services' on the free advertising board at her local supermarket, which was located outside, under a covered entrance. Jemima is being prosecuted under the Act.

Using the rules of statutory interpretation, advise Jemima as to whether an offence has been committed in this situation. [28]

After the two compulsory questions on Unit 1 Section A, you must answer one question from a choice of two. This question is worth 28 marks and is examining **AO1 Knowledge and understanding** for a maximum of 4 marks and **AO2 Application of legal rules and principles** for a maximum of 24 marks.

The command word **advise** requires you to briefly explain a legal concept and then apply it to the scenario in order to provide advice.

Question 4 stronger response

It is always good practice to try to identify what you think the intention of Parliament was when it passed the Act. You will not be marked down for getting it wrong. Rather, you will be credited for attempting to find the intention.

When in court, judges can follow four main rules: the literal rule, the golden rule, the mischief rule and the purposive approach. These rules help judges interpret the law that Parliament passed in order to try and establish and solve the problem that Parliament was aiming to rectify. The Environmental Protection (Fictitious) Act 2016 was, presumably, put into place to stop people being exposed to offensive items in public places and to protect the environment. In Jemima's case, there are several issues that need to be considered to determine if she has committed an offence.

If judges applied the literal rule, which is when judges follow the exact wording in the Act, as seen in the case of Whiteley v Chappel (1968), Jemima would be found guilty under Section 1 of the Act as she has left something 'for the purpose of prostitution' in a public place. Public place is defined in Section 2 of the Act and would include the advertising board outside the supermarket as this is a 'place in the open air to which the public are entitled or permitted to have access without payment' and 'any covered place open to the air on at least one side and available for public use'. However, we would need more information about the item left and whether 'special services' is literally for the purposes of prostitution. The judge could use an extrinsic aid, like a dictionary, to look this up.

The literal rule is useful because it means judges cannot abuse their powers of interpretation and it respects the sovereignty of Parliament. The judges could also apply the golden rule, which is where the judges have applied the literal rule, but it leads to an absurd result so the judge can substitute a more reasonable meaning in light of the statute as a whole. This can be seen in the case of Adler v George (1964) where a defendant who had committed an offence under the **Official Secrets Act 1981** could have escaped prosecution if the judge had used the literal rule. In the present case, Jemima might argue that the 'special services' advert did not, in fact relate to prostitution and so it was absurd to convict her under the literal rule, but this is not likely. The golden rule should only be used where the literal rule causes an absurd result.

The mischief rule, laid down in Heydon's case, considers three questions: 'What was the law before the statute?' 'What was the mischief Parliament was trying to overcome?' and 'What was the remedy Parliament was trying to put in place?' If we apply these questions to Jemima's scenario, it can be assumed that there was no law on this matter before this Act. The 'mischief' Parliament was trying to overcome was to ban material relating to prostitution from being displayed in public and the remedy Parliament was trying to put in place was to make it an offence to leave material relating to prostitution in a public place. Jemima would, therefore be guilty of an offence as she has done what Parliament was trying to overcome. The judge could also use an extrinsic aid like Hansard to look at what Parliament debated during the passing of the Environmental Protection (Fictitious) Act 2016. The short title (intrinsic aid) tells us that the Act relates to the protection of the environment.

As well as showing an excellent application of the rules, the candidate has also considered where some intrinsic and extrinsic aids might apply.

The purposive approach can also be followed by judges. This is where they look at the Act and decide what Parliament intended. This is an advantage as it does not result in injustice and means that errors in old law can be changed. The disadvantage is that judges are effectively making the law, which is not democratically acceptable as judges are not elected. This rule was used in the case of Magor & St Mellons Rural District Council v Newport Corporation (1950). The purposive approach is considered a more effective way to interpret the law as it lets judges apply what Parliament wanted from the Act. This would result in the same conclusion in Jemima's case as the mischief rule. I would use the purposive approach as it gives judges more discretion to apply Parliament's intention.

This is excellent application of the law to the scenario. The conclusion is not important – what matters is that you show the examiner that you can apply the rule to the scenario. For every rule, you should:

- give a definition of the rule
- cite a supporting case for that rule
- apply the rule to the scenario i.e. would the defendant be guilty or not guilty if the judge applied that rule?

Supporting rules with relevant cases is absolutely crucial, and this candidate has done well here to do that while applying the rule to the scenario.

This is an excellent answer, with all the key features that examiners are looking for in this type of question: 1. Explanation of the rules 2. Supporting cases 3. Application to the scenario. You will not get the marks available f you do not discuss ALL of the rules, and do not use supporting cases when you are applying the law. It is not necessarily to get absolutely correct application, but you need to show evidence that you can apply the rule and come to a sensible conclusion. This would warrant a level 4 mark for both AO1 and AO2.

Question 4 weaker response

Statutory interpretation means the methods which judges use to interpret statutes and make sense of the words of an Act of Parliament. Under the literal rule, Jemima would be guilty, as taking the literal words of the Act means that Jemima has left the 'special services' advertising card on the board in the open air outside the supermarket. This would be a 'public place', as covered by Section 2. There would be no charge brought under the golden rule, as the literal rule is not absurd.

Under the mischief rule, however, as there is ambiguity as to what 'special services' are, we need to look at Parliament's reason for passing the Act. Parliament was trying to limit material that could be offensive being left in public places. So, under this rule, Jemima might be guilty. There are also intrinsic and extrinsic aids which may be relevant here, such as Hansard.

Even though all rules are applied here, this candidate has made the classic mistake of not explaining the rules and not using case law to support their application. There is a useful 'formula' for answering these questions: explain the rule, give a case, apply it, repeat with the next rule. Candidates should also bring in extrinsic and intrinsic aids to support their answer. This candidate has left out the purposive approach.
The AO2 component tests your application as well as your use of authorities, so it is critical to provide a detailed critique. This response would warrant a low level 2 or even level 1 mark for AO1 and AO2.

WJEC AS Law: Unit 1 Section B

In this section, you need to answer one question from a choice of two. **Part a** questions cover **AO1 Knowledge and understanding** and are worth 8 marks. **Part b** questions cover **AO3 Analysis and evaluation** and are worth 24 marks.

Question 5(a)

Explain the role of the jury in criminal trials in Wales and England. [8]

The command word **explain** requires you write in simple terms about how something works.

Question 5(a) stronger response

Juries have been used to try people ever since the introduction of the Magna Carta, which stated that individuals had a right to be tried by their peers. Lord Devlin described the jury as 'the lamp that shows that freedom lives'. The jury should be independent as established in Bushell's case.

In criminal cases, the role of a jury is to decide the facts and to determine a verdict based on these facts, which is guilty or not guilty beyond reasonable doubt. The judge's role is to decide on matters of law.

The most common types of cases that juries try are indictable offences in the Crown Court such as murder or rape. A total of 12 jurors will serve during the trial and the reasoning for this is believed to have come from the religious principle that there were 12 disciples.

The jury has two hours to deliberate the arguments presented by the prosecution and defence in the secrecy of the jury room and, if they cannot reach a unanimous verdict, s17 of the **Juries Act 1974** allows a majority verdict to be given of either 11–1 or 10–2. This ensures that guilt is being established beyond reasonable doubt.

The **Criminal Justice Act 2003** allows for trial by a judge alone in the Crown Court where there is evidence of or a risk of jury tampering. This is rarely used but was used in the 'Heathrow Gang' case R v Twomey.

In conclusion, the role of the jury varies in different courts but in their most common role in the Crown Court where they are the deciders of fact.

It's good to see some brief context here setting out the importance of jury independence.

The candidate has also done well to mention the role of the jury as trier of fact and the verdict, and to bring in judge as trier of law as a comparison. There is a good mention of the standard of proof.

This paragraph is well focused on the question and the candidate has recognised the role of the jury in the Crown Court. They could also have commented on the proportion of cases in the magistrates' (95%) and Crown courts and why a jury is only present in around 2% of criminal cases (e.g. no need for a jury where defendant pleads guilty). They included some examples of indictable offences such as murder and rape.

The candidate has demonstrated excellent, detailed knowledge and understanding here to bring in the majority and unanimous verdicts and the link with the standard of proof.

The response makes an important point about trial by judge alone, which takes this answer into level 3. There's a good citation of a case example.

Overall, this is a level 3 answer. It is well focused on the question in the time available. The candidate has included some legal authority to support their response.

Question 5(a) weaker response

Juries have been used to try people ever since the introduction of the Magna Carta, which stated that individuals had a right to be tried by their peers. In criminal cases, the role of a jury is to be deciders of the facts and to determine a verdict based on these facts, guilty or not guilty.

The most common types of cases that juries are used to try are offences in the Crown Court. 12 jurors will serve throughout the duration of the trial.

The jury has two hours to deliberate in the secrecy of the jury room and if they cannot reach a unanimous verdict, the **Juries Act 1974** allows a majority verdict to be given of either 11–1 or 10–2.

Trial by jury is also used in the county court and High Court to listen to cases regarding malicious prosecution, false imprisonment, defamation and fraud. Usually eight jurors serve on such cases and their role is to determine liability and, if appropriate, to decide the amount that should be awarded to the claimant in damages.

Overall, this is a reasonable answer that does deal with the role of the jury in the Crown Court. There are several important omissions but the answer would achieve a level 2 mark.

The candidate has done well to recognise the role of the jury in the Crown Court. They could also have commented on the proportion of cases in the magistrates' (95%) and Crown courts and why a jury is only present in around 2% of criminal cases (e.g. no need for a jury where defendant pleads guilty).
The student could also have provided some examples of indictable offences such as murder or rape.

The candidate has done well here to bring in the majority and unanimous verdicts. They could also provide some evaluation by linking to the standard of proof e.g. by requiring either 10–2 or 11–1 jurors to agree on the verdict, it ensures that guilt is proved 'beyond reasonable doubt'.

Question 5(b)

Analyse and evaluate whether trial by jury is reliable. [24]

The command words **analyse** and **evaluate** require you to critically evaluate legal issues by identifying different perspectives, supporting the identification of the strongest viewpoint and demonstrating your ability to counter alternative viewpoints. Legal authorities should be used to support your arguments.

Question 5(b) stronger response

Juries play an important part in the legal system and therefore their decisions should be reliable. Trial by jury is a feature of an open and transparent legal system and was mentioned as far back as the Magna Carta.

> An introduction like this is important for longer, evaluation-style questions.

Firstly, those eligible to serve as a juror has changed throughout time. Prior to the **Juries Act 1974**, only property owners were allowed to serve as jurors and this was mainly middle-aged, white males. A report by the Morris Committee showed that 95% of women were ineligible.

> A logical place to start considering representation of the jury. There is a good discussion of this important report. The focus of this question is 'reliability' and, whilst 'representativeness' is not the main issue, it is relevant.

The **Juries Act 1974** widened the range of people eligible to serve, in an attempt to make them more representative of society. It stated that those aged 18–70, those registered on the electoral role and those that had been a UK resident for 5 years since the age of 13 were eligible, providing that they do not count as disqualified, mentally disordered or lacking in capacity. This increased the reliability of the jury because, prior to the Act, wealthy property owners would possibly be more inclined in favour of defendants of their social class, thus making them unreliable.

> The candidate has linked in their example on eligibility to the reliability of juries. They show a good understanding of the previous selection criteria.

The **Criminal Justice Act 2003** allowed even more people to be eligible to serve as a juror. It removed the categories of ineligibility, which meant judges, magistrates, prison officers and police could now serve as jurors. This, it can be argued, increased the reliability of the jury because they would make decisions that incorporated their view and the law and some might argue that professional people make more calculated judgements.

> The candidate has progressed to the important changes made as a result of the CJA 2003. They have also linked this in to the main issue of the question – the reliability of the jury – and evaluated it well.

On the other hand, jurors are supposed to be representative of society and the general presumption is that they are 'lay', otherwise a judge could determine a verdict. Some might argue that a jury consisting of legal personnel is not reliable because they might be more likely to convict in accordance with the law and be biased against defendants. The cases of **R v Abdroikof** and **R v Khan** have questioned whether this increased eligibility, which might include police officers, CPS lawyers and judges, is appropriate.

> There's a good balanced argument here. It is important to consider both sides. The candidate has brought in key case law to support their argument.

A range of advantages and disadvantages of the jury affect its reliability. The deliberations in the jury room are secret and so it could be argued that a jury trial is not reliable because they could decide a verdict by any means. For example, they could methodically consider the evidence or guess whether or not the defendant is guilty, or they could use an unconventional and unreliable method to determine guilt or innocence. In the case of **Young**, the jury were found to have used a Ouija board to contact the deceased victim and ask him who had killed him. Clearly, this is unreliable and is a risk of the deliberations remaining secret. On the other hand, this secrecy of the jury room could also be considered an advantage (therefore increasing their reliability) as jurors may feel freer in their discussions. Evidence suggests that jurors may feel less willing to serve on the jury if their discussions could be made public.

> The candidate is moving away from 'representativeness' now and is, correctly, proceeding to consider the advantages and disadvantages. They are focusing well on the question with the use of the question phrasing.

> The candidate is discussing a wide range of relevant issues and has done well here to back up their answer with reference to an appropriate case.

In addition, the jury are free to make any decision they like, even if directed otherwise by the judge. As Lord Devlin said, they are 'the lamp that shows that freedom lives'. This can sometimes lead to a 'perverse verdict', which is a decision that goes against the evidence presented. A case to show this is **R v Owen** where a lorry driver killed a man's son. The man shot the lorry driver but didn't kill him. The jury refused to find the man guilty despite him having shot the lorry driver. This was known as a perverse verdict as they should have found the man guilty but went against the evidence. Alternatively, some consider this to be an advantage, known as 'jury equity'. This means that jurors are making their decisions on the basis of 'fairness' rather than strict rules of the law. The case mentioned above is also an example of jury equity, along with the case of **Ponting**.

A good paragraph where the candidate has initially put it in context with reference to Lord Devlin's quote. They then draw in perverse verdicts and cite a relevant case to substantiate.

Jury trials have been limited by the **Criminal Justice Act 2003,** where there is a risk of jury tampering or where they would not understand the evidence in a complex fraud case. This should increase the reliability of the jury, though there are concerns that this decreases public participation. One of the advantages of the jury is public participation and an open system of justice so if this is reduced there could be potential bias.

A good discussion of a recent reform and again linked in to the question.

Another advantage is that the jury should be impartial, as no juror should be connected to anyone in the case. A jury is also not case-hardened like a judge risks being.

On the other hand, there are some further disadvantages. Jurors are told not to look at the internet for information about a case but this can be difficult to control. A study by Cheryl Thomas in 2010 concluded that around 12% of jurors looked online. This may be prejudicial to the defendant's right to a fair trial and decrease the reliability of jury trial. The **Criminal Justice and Courts Act 2015** has made it an offence for jurors to search the internet for information about their case or to inform another juror of what they have found.

The candidate uses connective words effectively to move between advantages and disadvantages. This is good practice when answering a question that requires evaluation.

Good use of evidence to support the arguments.

Furthermore, some juries have shown signs of racial bias **(Sander v UK)**. This decreases the reliability of the jury. In addition, some jurors are influenced by the media's portrayal of a crime or event. This might lead the jury to be prejudiced against a defendant.

Finally, jurors are generally lay people and therefore there is a risk that they do not understand the issues raised in a case. This is particularly true for complex fraud cases.

The candidate has included a relatively balanced view of the advantages and disadvantages of the jury. There is a good focus on the issue of 'reliability' throughout.

To conclude, juries are used in thousands of cases per year and play an important role but their decisions are not always reliable. There are suggestions of allowing a judge to try cases alone or to have lay members sit with judges to improve reliability but, for the time being, juries remain.

The candidate has included a focused conclusion here that incorporate the suggestion about judges sitting alone to try cases or with lay members. They demonstrate a good range and understanding.

Overall, this is a very good answer. The candidate has provided a well structured and detailed answer, supported by a good range of correct and appropriate legal authority. The candidate continuously linked their evaluation back to the question posed and discussed a range of relevant issues, including proposals for reform. Though not a 'perfect' answer, they would achieve a high level 4 mark.

Question 5(b) weaker response

Trial by jury was perceived to be the new more open and fairer way in which to try a case. However, there have been some criticisms of juries in the past.

Firstly, the selection process for juries does not obtain a fair representative selection of the public. While this has improved recently, with the previous selection process being anyone who owned property would be eligible to sit on a jury, it is still ripe for criticism. The current selection process is still based on citizenship, so anybody who is registered to vote is eligible to be selected to sit on a jury. This immediately excludes anyone who is homeless, anyone who is young and anyone who has lived in this country less than 5 years. It also excludes anyone who chooses not to vote.

In addition to this, there are excusals whereby anyone within a set criteria may be excused from jury service. Such people can be members of the armed forces, medical staff or anyone with illness (severe). Again, narrowing down our selection and making the jury less reliable. Although these people may simply be deferred as opposed to excused.

While the jury has been decided there are still potential risks such as jury nobbling. This was a major issue when juries were required to obtain a unanimous vote, so the majority vote has been put in place to prevent this.

In previous cases, such as Fraser (1988) where the defendant was black and the jurors were all white, there is a concern that the lack of representation may create a biased result.

There is also the possibility of a perverse verdict if there is an inadmissible piece of evidence submitted.

In summary, trial by jury is not always reliable. Our alternatives would be to allow single-judge trials, much like the civil courts, have a panel of judges or have a judge and lay magistrates to sit as a 'mini' jury. Ultimately, if we lose juries, we risk case-hardened judges deciding on these cases.

The candidate provides a limited introduction.

The candidate has done well here to mention the selection of juries and how representative they are. This is one of the reasons why they are reliable (or not). However, the answer is quite general in terms of evaluating how the changes made with the Criminal Justice Act 2003 have improved selection. This would certainly have enhanced the answer. The candidate would also have benefited from citing this legal authority.

The candidate touches upon selection criteria here but needs to expand more specifically on who is eligible to sit on a jury as per the Juries Act 1974 as amended by the Criminal Justice Act 2003. In addition, the candidate needs to be careful with their use of key terms ('excusal' and 'deferral') and to explain these more clearly. They connect these issues with 'reliability' as per the question.

A good mention here of the risk of jury nobbling and link to the verdict. The candidate could also bring in the standards of proof to evaluate how a jury verdict is reliable based on how convinced they need to be of guilt (in a criminal trial) before delivering a guilty verdict.

Good mention of relevant case law here. This adds legal weight to the answer. The candidate has also done well to focus this example on the issue of reliability and representation.

Good mention of perverse verdicts here but the end of the sentence is unclear. In addition, they should have given a case example to illustrate the problem of perverse verdicts, e.g. Young, R v Owen, Kronlid.

An example should be used to support this assertion.

It's good to see a focused conclusion here, where the candidate brings in some alternatives to the current system to evaluate. It is a good final sentence.

This is a 'satisfactory' answer in level 2 which touches on some of the main areas but the lack of explanation or legal authority to support earlier points means that the candidate would not achieve more than this level. The candidate did well later on to mention a key case but other areas also demanded some authority. However, they did use a logical structure and give an introduction, albeit brief, and a conclusion.

WJEC AS Law: Unit 2

This paper consists of just one question and all sub-parts within it are compulsory. They test all three assessment objectives: questions 1, 2 and 3 are each worth 8 marks and cover **AO1 Knowledge and understanding**, question 4 is worth 18 marks and covers **AO2 Application of the law** and question 5 is worth 18 marks and covers **AO3 Analysis and evaluation**.

Question 1

Explain how the law decides whether a duty of care is owed in negligence. [8]

The command word **explain** requires you write in simple terms how something works.

Question 1 stronger response

'Duty of care' refers to the circumstances and relationships which the law recognises as giving rise to a legal duty to take care. A failure to take such care can result in the defendant being liable to pay damages to a party who is injured or suffers loss as a result of a breach of duty of care. Therefore, it is necessary for the claimant to establish that the defendant owed them a duty of care. The existence of a duty of care depends on the type of loss and different legal tests apply to different losses.

A very good open paragraph clearly defining what is meant by duty of care.

The existence of a duty of care for personal injury and property damage was originally decided by Lord Atkin's neighbour test from Donoghue v Stevenson (1932): 'Who then in law is my neighbour?' The answer seems to be persons who are so closely and directly affected by the defendant's acts that the defendant ought reasonably to have them in their contemplation. The neighbour test for establishing a duty of care can be broken down in to two requirements – reasonable foresight of harm and relationship of proximity.

The candidate shows good knowledge of the neighbour test in Donoghue v Stevenson (1932). The answer would have been enhanced further with some illustrative examples such as the duty of care owed by drivers to pedestrians and other road users.

The test in Donoghue v Stevenson has been redefined in Caparo v Dickman (1990) and the question of whether there is a duty of care is now subject to the Caparo test. Under the Caparo test,the claimant must establish that harm was reasonably foreseeable, that there was a relationship of proximity and that it is fair, just and reasonable to impose a duty of care.

It is very good to explain how the test has been redefined in the key case of Caparo.

Overall, this answer would achieve a level 3 mark.

Question 1 weaker response

The history of the test for duty of care comes from the case of Donoghue v Stevenson. A person must take reasonable care to avoid acts which could be reasonably foreseen to be likely to injure a neighbour. Who in this situation is a 'neighbour'? This is persons who are so closely and directly affected by the defendant's act that the defendant should have thought about them.

While the introduction highlights the neighbour test in Donoghue v Stevenson, there is no definition of duty of care, and the mention of the test is brief.

Several cases have tried to amend this test and it has recently been rewritten in a case to include that certain elements must be proved, e.g. it must be reasonably foreseeable that a person in the claimant's position would be injured, there was proximity between the parties, and it is fair to impose liability on the defendant.

It is vital that for an answer such as this that the candidate cites the case that redefined the test in Donoghue (i.e. Caparo v Dickman). Overall, the answer lacks in development and supporting case law.

Overall, this answer would achieve a low level 2 mark.

Question 4

Johnny is driving his car and remembers he needs to text his mother to tell her he will not be coming home for tea that day. He manages to text his mother by holding his mobile telephone in his left hand while using his right hand to steer the car. As he turns the corner he sees Alan coming towards him in a van. Johnny drops his mobile telephone and breaks hard but the car skids into Alan's van, severely damaging the fronts of both vehicles. Alan suffers serious head injuries.

Advise Johnny as to whether he is liable for Alan's injuries. [18]

The command word **advise** requires you to briefly explain a legal concept and then apply it to the scenario in order to provide advice.

Question 4 stronger response

For Alan to succeed in a negligence action against Johnny, it must first be established that Johnny owed Alan a duty of care. The basis of whether a duty of care is owed is determined on a three-part test as laid out in Caparo Industries plc v Dickman.

> Good introduction, though it would have been further enhanced if duty of care had been defined. The candidate shows clear knowledge of the case where the test is found.

Johnny does not owe a duty to the whole world but only to those persons who could be reasonably foreseen to be affected by his actions or omissions, as determined in Donoghue v Stevenson. It could reasonably be foreseen that Johnny's decision to use his mobile phone while driving around a corner could lead to other persons being affected. If it is established that a degree of foreseeability exists, then the proximity of the parties involved must be considered. Proximity is determined on the basis of the relationship of the parties involved. There is a clear proximity of relationship between Johnny and other road users such as Alan. The courts will also consider if it is reasonable to impose a duty of care on Johnny on the basis of fairness or policy. It is both fair and in the interests of public policy to impose a duty of care on drivers who drive while using their mobile phones.

> Whilst this is good, the neighbour principle in this case could have been explained in more detail.

> There is a good application of the tests here to Alan's situation but this would have been further enhanced with supporting case law concerning duty of care and road users.

Alan has suffered damage as a result of the breach of Johnny's duty of care. There was no evidence of *novus actus interveniens* that could negate Johnny's liability for the accident and responsibility for the injuries suffered by Alan.

> Again, the candidate shows good knowledge but it would have been good practice to define the key term here. Overall, this answer would achieve a level 3 mark.

Question 4 weaker response

Firstly, it must be determined if Johnny owed Alan a duty of care. The basis of whether a duty of care is owed is based on a three-part test. Johnny only owes a duty of care to those persons who could be reasonably foreseen to be affected by his actions. In this situation, it could be argued that Johnny's decision to use his mobile phone while driving around a corner could lead to other persons being affected, and he should have been able to foresee that this could happen. The next test that needs to be proved is the proximity of the parties involved – how close the relationship between Johnny and Alan is. In this case, we also need to work out whether the courts would think it is fair to impose a duty of care on Johnny. I think in this situation they would, as drivers should not be using their mobile phones when driving, and it is because of this that Alan has suffered his injuries.

> A definition of duty of care would have been preferable here in the opening paragraph.

> While this answer does show knowledge of the test in Caparo, key cases such as Caparo and Donoghue v Stevenson are not cited, nor any other supporting case law to illustrate duty of care. The answer is lacking in development, and each point should be in a separate paragraph.

> Overall, this answer would achieve a level 2 mark.

Question 5

Analyse and evaluate the different types of damages in the law of negligence. [18]

The command words **analyse** and **evaluate** require you to critically evaluate legal issues by identifying different perspectives, supporting the identification of the strongest viewpoint and demonstrating your ability to offer and respond to alternative viewpoints. Legal authorities should be used to support your arguments.

Question 5 stronger response

The principle governing the award of damages in tort is to put the claimant in the same position they would have been in if the tort had not been committed (Livingstone v Raywards Coal Company). In some cases, the claimant will have suffered several kinds of loss. These types fall into different categories.

Firstly, the damages awarded may be classified as special damages, where there can be a precise mathematical calculation of the amount to be awarded. An example is loss of earnings, which can be worked out simply by calculating the net earnings for the claimant, including any bonuses or overtime. Special damages include other things that can be given an exact figure, for example medical expenses and prescriptions.

There are also general damages. Here, the amount can still be expressed in monetary terms but there's no precise mathematical calculation. They are worked out using a formula as the amount awarded cannot possibly be precisely calculated. General damages include compensating for pain, suffering and loss of amenity. These are non-pecuniary expenses. One of the main problems here is that damages for pain and suffering are awarded subjectively so, for example, if the claimant has been in a coma for five years, they won't receive damages for pain and suffering for this period as they would not have been aware of it (Wise v Kaye). Loss of amenity involves compensation for loss of enjoyment of life, for example, loss of a limb. Clearly, the claimant cannot be put back in the position they would have been in had the tort not occurred, and so the aim of such damages is to compensate for the injury sustained, but does it ever really make up for the loss suffered? Losses mean different things to different people. One advantage, however, is that the court can also award interest on damages.

General damages also includes loss of future earnings. The process of assessing future loss of earnings involves taking the claimant's net annual salary and multiplying it using a multiplier to reach a figure based on the length a claimant is likely to suffer loss (which could be their life expectancy if they won't work again) which is then converted into a figure.

However, when assessing damages for serious injuries, damages for future losses (such as loss of earning capacity and the cost of ongoing medical and other care) will probably make up the largest part of an award. These losses can be difficult to assess accurately, as it cannot be known what will happen in the future or what would have happened if the accident hadn't happened, especially where the claimant is a child (see the case of Giambrone v JMC Holidays (2002)).

Further problems are that the claimant could be over compensated, for example, if they make a partial recovery and can then work or enjoy a better standard of living than anticipated. Also medical or other expenses may be lower than predicted, or the claimant could profit if they invest wisely. Is it really fair for the claimant to profit in this way?

Furthermore, the opposite may occur in that a claimant who survives beyond the anticipated life expectancy may have to spend their life relying on social security when the damages are used up. Also, even where damages have been adequate, it's assumed the defendant will spend them or invest them wisely and not spend them extravagantly but this may not be the case. To get around these potential problems, compensation can be paid by regular instalments rather than in a single lump sum.

A good opening paragraph, clearly identifying the purpose of damages in tort, with case law to support it.

Good identification of the different types of damages. Some evaluation here would have further enhanced the answer, as would a little more on special damages (e.g. the claimant has to prove the special damages).

A good discussion in this paragraph of general damages and the advantages and disadvantages. The candidate makes a real attempt at evaluation here.

The candidate shows a good knowledge of how damages are calculated.

There's a good evaluation here, with a case to support it.

Again, here is a good attempt at evaluating. The candidate has considered a number of potential problems with an award of damages.

Again, a good evaluation here, looking at the opposing points of view. It is also encouraging to see the candidate offer a solution to the problems, in the form of structured settlements. The ending is a little abrupt but, overall, a strong attempt to answer the question and it would achieve a level 4 mark.

Question 5 weaker response

There are different types of damages in a negligence case. Their purpose is to compensate the claimant and to put them in the position they would have been in had the negligent event not occurred. Actual losses and future losses can be compensated, and mitigation of loss must also be considered.

Good introduction. Some key terms have been identified but not explained (e.g. mitigation of loss).

There are two types of damages. Special damages is compensation for the financial losses incurred up to the date of the trial. There are also things that can be given an exact figure, for example medical expenses, prescriptions and loss of earnings.

There are also general damages. These are to compensate for pain, suffering and loss. Examples of general damages also include compensation for loss of promotion in a job or other opportunities, and future loss of earnings. The general aim of an award of damages in tort is to put the injured party in the same position as they would have been in if the tort had not occurred. Damages in tort aim to restore the claimant to their pre-incident position. However, with general damages, it can be difficult to put a final figure on the losses.

This shows a clear understanding of general damages but there is limited evaluation and no detail on how they are calculated.

The other type of damages is special damages. This is compensation for money you have had to pay out and have lost because of the accident, injury or illness, and which you can put a figure on. Examples are money spent on travel, prescription fees and medical expenses. A court will have to decide an amount of compensation for these sorts of losses, and also take into account loss of future earnings

Key information missing here (i.e that special damages must be proved by the party claiming, and are not assumed by a court). There is also a lack of evaluation of special damages and how they are calculated. The overall answer is mainly descriptive, and lacks focus on assessment objective A03.

Overall, this answer would achieve a level 2 mark.

Eduqas AS Exam AS Law: Component 1 Section A

Component 1 Section A papers begin with two compulsory questions each worth 6 marks. They are examining AO1 – knowledge and understanding.

Question 2

Explain the techniques used by judges to avoid an awkward precedent. [6]

The command word **explain** requires you write in simple terms about how something works.

Question 2 stronger response

The doctrine of judicial precedent is based on stare decisis. That is the standing by of previous decisions. Once a point of law has been decided in a particular case, that law must be applied in all future cases that contain the same facts.

A good introduction. The candidate has defined precedent and makes it clear to the examiner that they know what the topic is about.

In order for the doctrine of judicial precedent to work, it is necessary to be able to determine what a point of law is. In the course of delivering a judgement, judges will set out their reasons for reaching a decision. The reasons which are necessary for them to reach their decision amount to the ratio decidendi of the case. The ratio decidendi forms the legal principle which is the binding precedent, meaning it must be followed in future cases that contain the same facts. It is important to separate the ratio decidendi from the obiter dicta. The obiter dicta is things stated in the course of a judgement which are not necessary for the decision and are not binding.

This is a good second paragraph, where the candidate has defined key terms. It could be cut down slightly as the question is only worth 6 marks, and the candidate has not yet started to look at the techniques a judge can use to avoid awkward precedents.

Judicial precedent works within the hierarchy of the courts. The basic rule is that a court must follow the precedents from a higher court, but they are not bound to follow decisions from courts lower in the hierarchy. For example, Supreme Court decisions bind all courts beneath them.

However, judges do have ways of avoiding precedent. They can overrule, reverse and distinguish. Overruling is where a court higher in the hierarchy departs from a decision made in a lower court. The previous decision is no longer binding. An example of overruling can be seen in R v R (1991). Overruling can also occur in a court at the same level. Reversing is where a higher court departs from the decision of the lower court on appeal, for example in the Gillick case (1986). Distinguishing is where the facts of the case are deemed sufficiently different that the previous case is no longer binding, for example Balfour v Balfour (1919) and Merritt v Merritt.

It is excellent practice to support each point with a case example of overruling, reversing or distinguishing. The candidate is not required to state the facts of the cases, because, firstly, the question is only worth six marks and, secondly, supporting a point with the correct case shows they understand how it works.

Since the 1966 Practice Statement, the Supreme Court (then the House of Lords), can now depart from its own previous decisions when it feels it is right to do so. An example of the House of Lords doing this is when Anderton v Ryan was overruled in R v Shivpuri.

It is excellent to include the practice statement with an example.

Question 2 weaker response

A judge can avoid following a precedent in a number of ways – overruling, reversing or distinguishing. Overruling is used when a higher court overrules the decisions of a lower court in an earlier case. The House of Lords and the Court of Appeal have overruled previous decisions.

Reversing is when a higher court reverses the earlier decision in the same case of a lower court, for example a decision is reversed on appeal.

Distinguishing occurs when the facts of the case before the court are different to an earlier precedent, so then judge can distinguish it.

Examples of cases are needed here to support this point.

This answer would have been enhanced if the candidate had given a brief definition of precedent at the start to show the examiner that they know how precedent works. The answer would have been enhanced further with the inclusion of the House of Lords and the Practice Statement of 1966, and the Court of Appeal and Young v Bristol Aeroplane case.

This answer is just a brief explanation of overruling, reversing and distinguishing. Although the question is only worth six marks, the candidate does need to briefly include how precedent works in the court hierarchy and give examples of cases where judges have overruled and distinguished.

Eduqas AS Exam AS Law: Eduqas Component 1 Section A

After the two compulsory questions on Component 1 Section A, you must answer one question from a choice of two. This question is broken down into two parts. **Part a** questions are worth 6 marks and are examining **AO1 Knowledge and understanding**. **Part b** questions are worth 18 marks and are examining **AO2 Application of legal rules and principles**.

Question 4(a)

Read the text below and answer part (a).

'The making and passing of legislation is central to the law reform enterprise. Only the state can make legislation and the making of it is critical to the framework of any legal system. While not every activity of a Law Commission requires legislation, the achievement of its fundamental purpose does. Who makes legislation, how they make it and where a Law Commission fits into the legislative system becomes a critical issue in charting the future.'

Sir Geoffrey Palmer, Scarman Lecture, 24 March 2015

(a) Using the text above and your own knowledge, explain the purpose of the Law Commission in promoting law reform. [6]

The command word **explain** requires you write in simple terms about how something works.

Question 4(a) stronger response

It is essential that the law does not stand still but evolves in such a way that makes it accessible and manageable for the modern day. In the UK, Parliament is able to make whatever laws it chooses under the principle of parliamentary sovereignty. As a result, successive governments have created, amended and repealed legislation, which can lead to the law becoming confused and liable to misinterpretation.

Therefore, the Law Commission was set up by the Law Commission Act 1965, with further powers added in the Law Commission Act 2009, specifically to simplify and modernise the law and with the primary purpose of promoting law reform. Under Section 3 of the 1965 Act, their key roles are to codify the law, consolidate the law, remove and repeal obsolete laws, simplify laws and propose new laws. The Commission is an independent body consisting of judges, researchers and civil servants.

The Law Commission promotes law reform, researches areas of law that require amending, publish consultation documents and draft proposals that are sent to Parliament for discussion. An example of recent work which shows its purpose in promoting law reform is the Criminal Justice and Courts Act 2015.

Since the Law Commission Act 2009 the Commission can now compel the government to give reasons why it has not implemented any proposal of the Law Commission and to produce a report for Parliament every year.

Good discussion of the important principle of parliamentary sovereignty. This links to law reform and the position of the Law Commission in relation to Parliament.

There's a good mention of the key statutes here, and a good summary incorporating key terms and demonstrating knowledge of the role of the Law Commission. There's also a clear summary of how the Law Commission researches and proposes an area of law for reform.
It is good practice to include a recent example of where this has happened. Further examples would have enhanced the answer.

The candidate shows a good knowledge of the increased role under the 2009 Act.

Question 4(a) weaker response

The Law Commission is a full time and independent law reform body. It is made up of five members of judicial people and legal academics and legal professors. However, they are only appointed for five years at a time before a new group is elected.

The purpose of the Law Commission in promoting law reform is to keep under review all law, to codify, to simplify, to modernise and to repeal. The powers of the Law Commission in promoting law reform have recently been enhanced. Under the 2009 Act, the Commission can hold ministers to account, as the Lord Chancellor tells Parliament which Law Commission Bills have been implemented, and if not, why not.

The role of the Law Commission, therefore, is to promote reform of the law. They have had some success in doing this, but not as much as they would have liked.

This is a nice introduction, outlining the composition of the Law Commission.

This answer lacks examples and statutory authority. It would have been enhanced with examples of where the Law Commission has repealed, codified and consolidated. Key statutes missing such as s3 Law Commission Act 1965.

Examples are needed here of where the Law Commission has been successful in promoting law reform.

Question 4(b)

Read the scenario below and answer part (b).

Tom, a young man, was being taken to hospital for minor injuries he sustained while playing rugby. On the way, the ambulance doors flew open and he fell out. He suffered major head injuries and went into a deep coma. At the hospital, he underwent two life-saving operations to relieve the pressure on his brain but the operations left him with severe irreversible brain damage. His mother, Nicola, is convinced that Tom will never recover and that the only way to end his suffering would be to end his life. Nicola is aware that euthanasia is against the law but wishes to campaign for reform to the law.

(b) Using the scenario above and applying your understanding of law reform, advise Nicola on the ways, apart from the Law Commission, in which she could try to promote reform of the law on euthanasia in England and Wales. [18]

The command word **advise** requires you to briefly explain a legal concept and then apply it to the scenario in order to provide advice.

Question 4(b) stronger response

In advising Nicola on other ways of reforming the law, apart from the Law Commission. Firstly, she could set up a pressure group to bring about reform of the law. There are many and varied pressure groups, which may be multi-caused such as union bodies or professional bodies, or single-caused, such as 'Save the White Tiger', but all pressure groups use similar processes in an attempt to influence the political process, and many pressure groups have had a great deal of success in getting a change in the law. Examples are Greenpeace, Fathers 4 Justice and Amnesty International.

This is a very good introduction, and the answer is clearly advising Nicola. There are some good examples here of different types of pressure groups.

If Nicola sets up a pressure group, she could try to influence Parliament by lobbying ministers and members of Parliament to campaign for her and support her cause. Nicola could do this by writing letters to her local MP and to other ministers, or by sending a petition to the Prime Minister. The key challenge for Nicola is to get a minister involved. Mary Whitehouse was a famous campaigner who championed many changes to the pornography industry and censorship laws by lobbying ministers and Parliament. If Nicola can get a minister or her MP involved, the likelihood of the law evolving is greater through debate in Parliament and public awareness.

Again, there's a real focus on advising Nicola, with the answer tailored to her and not a general answer on the different ways of reforming the law. It is good to include an example here to show areas of law that have been reformed by pressure groups.

I would advise Nicola of the role that Parliament and her MP can play in reforming the law of euthanasia. The majority of law reform is carried out by Parliament through repealing, creating, consolidating and codifying. Nicola may be able to get the support of her local MP to bring about a change in the law on euthanasia through the introduction of a Private Member's Bill on euthanasia, though very few Private Member's Bills succeed. However, the law on abortion was reformed through a Private Member's Bill, which resulted in the passing of the Abortion Act 1967.

This shows a good detailed knowledge and application here of how Nicola could try and get her local MP to support a Private Member's Bill on euthanasia, with an example here to support this.

Apart from Parliament, there are other ways Nicola could try to bring about a change in the law, for example through judicial change. Judges can reform the law on euthanasia by creating original precedent so Nicola may wish to begin a legal action. However, this is not common, as judges need to be mindful of their constitutional position in that Parliament is the supreme law maker. There have been several cases where people have unsuccessfully brought cases in an attempt to change the law on euthanasia, for example the cases of Diane Pretty, Debbie Purdy and Daniel James.

The candidate has identified another way that Nicola could try to bring about a change in the law, with case examples to support it.

Nicola could use the media as a vehicle. The media take up causes and can be very influential on Parliament. If a newspaper gets behind Nicola's campaign of law reform, this could gain Parliament's attention; for example, the passing of 'Sarah's Law' came about as a result of a campaign by the *News of the World* calling for the public to have access to the sex offender's register. Also, the intervention of the media in the Stephen Lawrence murder led to the case being reinvestigated and ultimately successful convictions.

Another way to try to reform the law has been identified, along with examples of where this has been successful

If Nicola has a successful campaign, either through media support or through setting up a pressure group, this may help to establish a Royal Commission on euthanasia which could ultimately lead to the law being reformed in this area.

The candidate has made an excellent attempt throughout the answer to advise Nicola and to not simply describe and explain the different methods of law reform.

Question 4(b) weaker response

Pressure groups are groups of people who are interested in particular subjects like Nicola, and use different ways to make Parliament listen to the changes they think should happen. They can be very persuasive and passionate and sometimes their tactics can be very extreme.

This is a limited opening statement merely indicating the role of pressure groups.

Pressure groups try to influence a change in the law by sometimes using illegal methods. An example of this is Fathers 4 Justice, members of which dressed up as Batman and Spiderman and climbed up Buckingham palace to draw an attention to the plight of fathers who are denied access to their children. However, as the tactic was illegal, this probably wasn't the best tactic to use to convince a court to allow them to see their children, so Nicola should be careful what tactics she uses to try to change the law.

There's a good relevant example here, highlighting some of the illegal methods they used.

Other examples of pressure groups include Greenpeace, which has also used some illegal methods to pressurise governments into changing laws. There are also trade unions, which are legally recognised bodies that can try to pressurise the government into changing the law but can also use legal tactics such as striking.

Another two good examples. However, it would have been preferable to not answer the question entirely through examples. This answer lacks information on pressure groups, their methods and their relationship with Parliament. This is also a general answer with very limited advice being given to Nicola on the ways she can reform the law on euthanasia.

There are other methods that Nicola could use. She could speak to her local MP to see if they have influence in Parliament, she could also do a petition and get people to sign it, or she could contact the press. However, these methods are not guaranteed to work.

There's a brief mention here of some of the other methods Nicola could use, though it is underdeveloped and lacking in examples to support .

Eduqas AS Exam AS Law: Component 1 Section B

In this section, you need to answer one question from a choice of two. **Part a** questions cover **AO1 Knowledge and understanding** and are worth 6 marks. Part b questions cover **AO3 Analysis and evaluation** and are worth 18 marks.

Question 5(a)

(a) Explain the factors which are taken into account by the police in the decision to grant or refuse bail after charge. [6]

The command word **explain** requires you write in simple terms about how something works.

Question 5(a) stronger response

Bail is the temporary release of a suspect before the next stage of a case or investigation. If bail is refused, a suspect is remanded in custody. Both the police and courts have the power to grant bail but this answer will focus only on police bail. The police can grant bail in three circumstances.

First, street bail under **s4 Criminal Justice Act 2003**. This gives the police the power to grant bail at the place of arrest without taking the suspect to the police station. A form is filled in on the street and entered into police records later. The suspect must then attend the police station at a later date.

Second is bail before charge under **sections 34 and 37** of the **Police and Criminal Evidence Act 1984**. This is where the police may release a suspect on bail while they make further inquiries due to insufficient evidence, for example. The suspect is released from police custody on the condition that they return to the police station on a specific date. An example is Christopher Jefferies. The **Policing and Crime Act 2017** has limited police bail to 28 days.

Third is bail after charge (by the custody officer) under **s38 PACE 1984**. The defendant is bailed to appear at the local magistrates' court on a set date. The custody officer can refuse bail if the name and address aren't known or they are unsure if they are correct, if they reasonably believe the suspect will not attend court, if it is necessary to prevent the suspect from committing further offences, interfering with the administration of justice or with the investigation of offences, for the suspect's own protection or if the charge is murder (**Coroners and Justice Act 2009**).

The police can impose conditions such as reporting to the police station and surrendering their passport.

A concise and effective opening statement giving a definition of bail. This addresses the nature of law element.

Good to identify the focus as there is not the time to consider both options. With these questions, focusing on the specific issue is key.

This is a clear summary with legal authority to support.

This candidate has covered, concisely, all three types of police bail and has included the correct factors for bail after charge. Each type of bail is supported with reference to legal authority. There is up-to-date law with mentions of the Policing and Crime Act 2017 and the Coroners and Justice Act 2009.

This additional point about conditions enhances this excellent answer. This candidate has demonstrated excellent knowledge and understanding of the English legal system and legal rules and principles relating to the law governing the decision to grant police bail after charge. The response is clear, detailed and fully developed.

Question 5(a) weaker response

This candidate has done well here to provide a basic definition of bail as a brief introduction. However, the answer should have been substantiated with reference to Acts. This is a weak opening paragraph.

After a person has been arrested, sometimes questioned and had all their details taken, they can be granted bail. This means they are free to leave and return to their lives before their trial. The police may also have to carry out further investigation.

The powers available to grant bail can come from the police themselves on most occasions or, if the police refuse to grant bail, which is in their power, the defendant can appeal to the courts, which also have the power to grant bail.

The candidate has superficially identified the two types of bail. The question only asks about police bail and, given the limited time available, this needs to be the focus of the answer. The candidate needs to reference street bail (s4 Criminal Justice Act 2003), bail before charge (PACE 1984) and bail after charge (s38 PACE 1984).

Police may refuse bail if the crime is more serious, for example drug dealing or rape. They may also refuse bail if they fear the person may skip bail or break the conditions of bail. Also, if the person is seen to be any threat to themselves or others.

It's good to see factors included but the candidate needs to be more precise in summarising the factors.

Bail can hold different terms and conditions, you may be forbidden from contacting certain people or may be given a curfew. If these are broken, your bail can be revoked or you may have the conditions made more strict. As long as a person is not seen as a threat and has a clean or good record of sticking to their bail, they are likely to be granted it.

Some relevant conditions are mentioned.

This answer would achieve around half the marks available. There are some errors of expression and the candidate doesn't always convey points clearly or in a sophisticated way. There is a general lack of legal authority, with only one case mentioned.

Question 5(b)

(b) Analyse and evaluate the advantages and disadvantages of bail. [18]

The command words **analyse** and **evaluate** require you to critically evaluate legal issues by identifying different perspectives, supporting the identification of the strongest viewpoint and demonstrating your ability to counter alternative viewpoints. Legal authorities should be used to support your arguments.

Question 5(b) stronger response

Bail at its core is a promise to return and it is deemed necessary for the protection of individual human rights, such as the right to liberty under Article 5 of the European Convention on Human Rights and the right to a fair trial under Article 6. There is also a balance to be struck between protecting a suspect's right and protecting the wider society. Reforms to bail have attempted to address this balance. This essay will analyse and evaluate the advantages and disadvantages of bail.

> This is a good introduction. The candidate has put the answer in context but has also referred to two key human rights in relation to bail.

Bail can be granted by either the police or the courts. Both have the power to impose conditions on bail which affect a person's liberty. If bail is refused, the suspect is remanded in custody. If it is refused by the police, the suspect has the right to ask the magistrates for bail at the earliest opportunity. Police bail was recently amended under the **Policing and Crime Act 2017** to be a maximum of 28 days. Previously, the police could grant bail before charge indefinitely (as in the case of Dave Lee Travis) which meant a criminal investigation hanging over the suspect for a long time. There may have also been restrictions on the person by way of bail conditions. This was unfair and so the law has been reformed.

> It's good to see this recent reform to bail included. The candidate has done more than just explain the change – they have linked it to the question about advantages and disadvantages of bail. There is accurate citation of legal authority.
> It's good to see the two authorities who can grant bail included. As the question does not specify, both are needed.

There are a number of advantages and disadvantages to bail and some reforms to bail will also be considered. A disadvantage of bail is that many offenders reoffend while on bail. A survey found that up to 16% of burglaries are committed by people on bail for another offence. Also, 1 in 10 murderers kill while on bail. Jonathan Vass killed Jane Clough while on bail for another offence. The prosecution did not want him to get bail but their pleas were ignored. As a result of this case and a campaign by Jane's parents, the law was changed and the **Legal Aid, Sentencing and Punishment of Offenders Act 2013** now gives the prosecution a right of appeal against a bail decision.

> This is an effective paragraph, where the candidate has started to consider some of the disadvantages of bail. Statistics and accurate citation of authority support the answer.

Some of these issues have been addressed by reforms. For example, bail for a murder charge can now only be granted by a Crown Court judge (**Coroners and Justice Act 2009**). Also, repeat serious offenders can only get bail in 'exceptional circumstances' following the ECtHR ruling in the case of **Caballero**. In cases of domestic violence, suspects should only be granted bail if there is no risk of them committing further acts of domestic violence. Furthermore, for offences committed while on bail, under **s14 of the Criminal Justice Act 2003**, if the defendant was on bail for another offence at the date of the offence, bail should be refused unless the court is satisfied that there is no significant risk they will commit another offence.

> This is an effective paragraph, where the candidate has started to consider some of the disadvantages of bail. Statistics and accurate citation of authority support the answer.

Another disadvantage of bail is that some suspects abscond when on bail. These 'bail bandits' should not be getting bail if there is a risk that they abscond.

Bail hostels are also a disadvantage of bail. They are communal houses where defendants awaiting trial or prisoners on early release from prison live. Unfortunately, they are often staffed by inexperienced people and there is loose supervision of the suspects.

Prisons are overcrowded and, therefore, more suspects are being given bail. This means that some dangerous suspects and those who go on to abscond are free on the streets.

The candidate has considered a range of disadvantages of bail and has explained them clearly, with examples to support their argument.

Another disadvantage is that the law on bail has developed in a piecemeal way with many Acts of Parliament addressing various aspects of bail. As a result, the law has become complex and difficult to find. Parliament should consolidate the law on bail.

This connective phrase transitions the answer to the other side of the argument.

On the other hand, bail does have advantages. It shows respect for a suspect's human rights, such as the right to liberty under Article 5 and the right to a fair trial under Article 6 (ECHR). People should be considered 'innocent until proven guilty' and bail is a way to achieve this. There is no compensation payable for a suspect who is remanded but then found not guilty or given a non-custodial sentence.

These are effective arguments drawing on human rights.

Bail allows people to continue with their lives. 60% of people on remand are either acquitted or given a non-custodial sentence. These people are not entitled to compensation despite perhaps losing their job or their home. So, even if the suspect is later found guilty, bail allows them some time with their friends and family before facing their punishment.

The candidate has explained this advantage well and has supported with a statistic (though a source is preferable).

Bail has also been shown to prevent suicide, as there is quite a high incidence of this amongst remand prisoners. The reforms to the 'no real prospect' test following the **LASPO Act 2012** have helped as, if there is 'no real prospect' a suspect will face imprisonment for an offence, they should receive bail and not be remanded.

This is a sophisticated connection between the argument and the reform that has addressed the issue.

Finally, bail eases prison overcrowding. Prison, even remand, is incredibly expensive for the state and so giving bail is a more effective use of public funds (when balanced with the need to protect the public).

To conclude, the award of bail involves a delicate balancing act between the rights of an unconvicted suspect and public safety. The numerous reforms to bail have caused the law to become quite unwieldy and consolidation is needed.

The conclusion ties together some of the preceding points. The candidate has also offered a judgement on the need for reform and consolidation.

Overall, this answer offers an excellent analysis of legal rules, principles and concepts relevant to the question. Analysis is detailed, with an appropriate range of supporting evidence which draws together knowledge, skills and understanding.
The candidate has included a valid and substantiated judgement and has included an excellent range of accurately cited legal authorities.

Question 5(b) weaker response

This answer does not really offer any context. The candidate just jumps straight in and doesn't offer an insight into the balancing act that bail entails.

There are advantages and disadvantages to bail. The first advantage is that bail prevents people on remand from committing suicide. This is because when they are on bail they can continue to get support from friends and family, whereas in prison they are lonely and scared. Also, bail allows people who are not yet guilty to carry on with their job. They can earn money and pay for bills and their family. Bail respects human rights such as liberty and a fair trial. Also, bail is cheaper for the government, as remanding someone can cost about £40,000 per prisoner per year. The suspect might not be guilty so this can be a waste of money.

This candidate has included a few advantages but has not really elaborated on them. The arguments need to be more developed and sophisticated. There is no citation of legal authority and the answer is largely unsubstantiated. It reads a little like a list of advantages and disadvantages. To effectively analyse and evaluate, the candidate should have added something to each statement and offered a more detailed insight into each.

The first disadvantage is that bail means that potentially dangerous individuals are able to roam the streets and put the public in danger. This has been made more difficult for murder suspects as now bail can only be granted by a Crown Court judge. There is also evidence that people offend and commit more offences when on bail for another offence and some suspects do not turn up to court, meaning that they have absconded.

Again, the candidate has listed a range of accurate disadvantages but the response is not developed and, though an example is alluded to, legal authority is required.

To conclude, bail offers both advantages and disadvantages.

This conclusion is a token gesture and doesn't add anything of value. Overall, this is a low 'adequate' response.

Eduqas AS Exam AS Law: Component 2

This paper requires you to answer two questions – one from Section A (Private law) and one from Section B (Public law), reflecting the areas of law you have studied. Each question consists of four compulsory sub-parts, testing all three assessment objectives. **Parts a and b** are each worth 6 marks and cover **AO1 Knowledge and understanding**, **part c** questions are worth 9 marks and cover **AO3 Analysis and evaluation** and part d questions are worth 9 marks and cover **AO2 Application of the law**.

Question 1(a)

(a) Explain how an invitation to treat differs from an offer. [6]

The command word **explain** requires you to write in simple terms about how something works.

Question 1(a) stronger response

An offer is a key requirement for a valid contract, along with acceptance, consideration and an intention to create legal relations. An offer is a communication which outlines the terms on which the offeror is prepared to make a contract, and gives an indication that there is an intention to be legally bound if accepted. An offer can be made to one specific person, or unilaterally to the whole world as seen in Carlill v Carbolic Smoke Ball Co (1893).

An invitation to treat is not an offer but merely an invitation for someone to make an offer. It is seen as another step in the process and does not show an intention to be legally bound. Examples of invitations to treat include advertisements in newspapers and magazines, such as in Partridge v Crittenden, goods displayed on shelves such as in Pharmaceutical Society of GB v Boots the Chemist (1953), and goods on display in a shop window such as the flick knives on display in Fisher v Bell (1961).

This is a good introduction that immediately defines the key terms in the question and convinces the examiner that the candidate knows key subject terminology.

It is pleasing to see supporting case law. With an 'explain' question, the use of case law can be used as a means of supporting key definitions.

As the question is only worth 6 marks, it is not necessary to go into detail about the facts of the cases if it is obvious what the case is about.

Question 1(a) weaker response

An offer is a requirement of contract law which shows that a person wants to enter into a contract with another person.

An invitation to treat is different from an offer because it is not a legal offer. Examples of invitations to treat are adverts in newspapers or a statement of price. Sometimes an offer can be made to everyone and not one person. This is called a unilateral offer and was seen in the case where compensation of £100 was offered for people who contracted the flu even after using their smokeballs.

The glaring omission here is the lack of case law to support examples. Not using legal authorities or appropriate subject-specific terminology will not convince the examiner that the candidate has anything more than a satisfactory knowledge at best.

It is bad practice not to name the case. Where possible, it should be cited in full, even though it is clear from the description what case is being referred to.

Question 1(c)

(c) Assess the extent to which the performance of an existing duty can constitute adequate consideration. [9]

The command word **assess** requires you to consider several options or arguments and weigh them up so that you come to a conclusion about their effectiveness or validity. Legal authorities should be used to support your arguments.

Question 1(c) stronger response

Consideration is the benefit that both parties gain when taking part in a contract. For example, if you agreed to buy a car, the consideration offered to you is the benefit of the car, and the benefit to the person selling it is getting rid of the car and the money. There are certain rules of consideration, such as the consideration need not be adequate but must be sufficient, as seen in the case of Chappell v Nestle, when it was held that old sweet wrappers were enough consideration for the benefit of a prize, in this case, a record.

Another traditional rule of consideration is that performance of an existing duty cannot constitute consideration. This was held in Collins v Godefroy where the legal obligation to give evidence in court in return for money was not considered consideration because it was his legal duty and so he could not claim the money. This rule was slightly relaxed in Ward v Byham, where a statutory duty was classed as consideration because it went above and beyond the minimum expectations.

However, the situation is no longer clear since the case of Williams v Roffey, where the court said that the performance of an existing contractual duty can constitute consideration where it results in an additional practical benefit to the other party.

The candidate shows good practice here, immediately defining key concepts from the question as an opening introduction, in this case the definition of consideration and the usual legal rules that apply to consideration.

This is good use of case law to illustrate the issue at the heart of the question.

The 'Assess' element of the question is being addressed because the candidate outlines the law and then looks at the contrasting view of the argument.

Question 1(c) weaker response

Consideration is when someone gets something in return for doing their part of the contract. The rules of consideration are:

- consideration need not be adequate, but must be sufficient
- past consideration is no consideration
- the consideration must come from the promisee
- performing an existing duty cannot be consideration for a new promise.

Therefore, it is not possible for an existing duty to be consideration. The case that said this was Collins v Godefroy. There can be exceptions for some duties where there is a benefit for the other party.

Bullet points are not usually an accepted format for examination answers.

This is the only case citation in the answer, which does not show a convincing knowledge of the topic area.

Question 1(d)

Harold is an inventor. He has designed and produced a range of different inventions which he tries to sell in his shop. He has recently made a machine called the 'Cold Buster', which he claims will stop anyone who is using it from catching a cold. He places the machine in his shop window with a price tag of £20 and a sign which states that he will give £1,000 to anyone who buys the machine and catches a cold while using it. Sally passes the shop one day and sees the machine and sign. She goes into the shop and decides to buy the machine because she sometimes gets very wet when walking her dog in the rain. Three days after beginning to use the machine, Sally catches a heavy cold after getting very wet in the park while looking for her dog who had run away. Sally contacts Harold and tries to claim the £1,000. Harold refuses. Sally is upset over Harold's refusal to pay her the money.

Advise Sally as to whether she is entitled to claim the £1000 from Harold. [9]

The command word **advise** requires you to briefly explain a legal concept and then apply it to the scenario in order to provide advice.

Question 1(d) stronger response

In order for Sally to be able to claim the £1,000 from Harold, all the required elements of a contract have to be present – a valid offer, acceptance, consideration and an intention to create legal relations. Offers have to be distinguished from invitations to treat, and as seen in the case of Fisher v Bell, goods on display in a shop or a mere statement of price would usually be considered as invitations to treat, and therefore not offers. Therefore, Harold's 'Cold Buster' machines on display in his window are not offers. However, Sally could still have a claim because Harold has made a unilateral offer – that is an offer to the whole world because Harold has indicated a course of action in return for which he makes a promise to provide consideration. This was seen in the case of Carlill v Carbolic Smoke Ball Co where an offer of £100 was made to anyone who caught the flu after using one of their smokeballs. The court in that case said that the offer to the world at large was an offer and was accepted when Mrs Carlill used the smokeball and contracted the flu. Therefore, Harold is bound by his promise and should pay Sally the £1,000. Sally could seek specific performance to make Harold pay the money, or alternatively she could seek damages.

Good use of case law, showing good application skills. It is important in all problem scenarios to state what the law is before it is applied to the scenario.

This is the key case for a scenario such as this, and its inclusion is likely to be vital for the higher bands.

Question 1(d) weaker response

Sally can claim the £1,000 from Harold because Harold has made an offer to the whole world. The same thing happened in a case where a woman contracted flu after using a smokeball when the company said that it was supposed to cure the flu. If Harold's 'Cold Buster' didn't work, then Sally had accepted Harold's offer by purchasing it and so had entered a contract that Harold had to uphold.

There is no introduction about what constitutes a valid contract or the difference between an offer and an invitation to treat, which could be crucial to the outcome of this case.

Not citing the case directly can adversely affect the mark, especially when the case is so pivotal to the scenario.

Whilst this is all legally accurate, the lack of legal authority and the lack of explanation is not enough for 9 marks.

Eduqas A Level Law: Component 1 Section A compulsory questions

Component 1 Section A papers begin with two compulsory questions, each worth 5 marks. They are examining **AO1 Knowledge and understanding**.

Question 1

Explain what is meant by the ratio decidendi and obiter dicta of a judgement. (5)

The command word **explain** requires you write in simple terms about how something works.

Question 1 stronger response

These two terms relate to the operation of judicial precedent. When a judge produces a judgement at the end of a case, this can be divided into ratio decidendi and obiter dicta comments. The ratio decidendi is the 'reason for the decision' – this is where the judge explains why they have reached their decision and the legal principles behind their decision. This part of the judgement forms a binding precedent for future cases.

The rest of the judgement is known as the obiter dicta and is not binding on future cases. This is translated as 'other things said' or things said 'by the way'. This can sometimes be where the judge speculates on what their decision might have been if the facts had been different. Obiter dicta forms persuasive precedent but not binding.

This answer would be in level 3. The candidate has fully explained each key term and the response is clear and detailed. The candidate demonstrates excellent knowledge and understanding.

Question 1 weaker response

The ratio decidendi is the reason for the decision and the obiter dicta is other things said. Ratio is binding precedent but obiter is only persuasive.

This is a brief response, though both terms are accurately defined. To get a level 2 or 3 mark, the candidate needs to offer more than just a definition.

Eduqas A Level Law: Component 1 Section A chosen questions

After the two compulsory questions on Unit 1 Section A, you must then answer one question from a choice of two. This question is worth 15 marks and is examining **AO2 Application of legal rules and principles.**

Question 3

Read the scenario below and answer the question that follows.

Sarah is a passionate protester against war and she is regularly involved in protests around Parliament Square in London, even staying overnight on occasions in a tent. The government has recently been concerned by the growing number of protesters and, to stop the protesters, the government has sought to use enabling powers under the Crime and Order (Fictitious) Act 2016 to ban existing, future and continuing demonstrations in and around Parliament Square. Sarah wishes to challenge this delegated legislation and is seeking your advice on how she can go about it.

Advise Sarah as to the ways in which she can challenge delegated legislation. In your answer you should include consideration of law and society. [15]

The command word **advise** requires you to briefly explain a legal concept and then apply it to the scenario in order to provide advice.

Question 3 stronger response

Delegated legislation is also known as secondary legislation. It is made under the authority of an enabling Act passed by Parliament and allows Parliament to make changes to the law and to pass the volume of law needed to deal with various situations. In this case, the enabling Act is the **Crime and Order (Fictitious) Act 2016**.

This is a good opening paragraph as it provides some context for the rest of the answer. The candidate has demonstrated an understanding of delegated legislation, and applies the answer to the scenario as the candidate has identified the Crime and Order (Fictitious) Act 2016 as the enabling Act. This application is essential with a question of this type.

With delegated legislation, Parliament is giving away the authority to make law to another person or body. Therefore, as Parliament is sovereign and has been elected to make law for the people, when it gives away this power it needs to retain some control over it. This also supports the principle of the rule of law. It needs to be able to check that the power is not being abused and laws aren't being made that are 'ultra vires' (beyond the powers). In this case, Sarah would have the power to challenge the enabling powers in the **Crime and Order (Fictitious) Act 2016,** which could see a secondary law passed banning future and continuing demonstrations around Parliament Square.

The candidate has demonstrated their knowledge of why control is needed. There is appropriate use of key terms.

Firstly, challenges are made in Parliament before the delegated legislation is made. These are less relevant here as Sarah is not in Parliament and so she could only challenge it in the courts after it comes into being. However, to briefly mention them, the challenges in Parliament are the enabling Act itself, affirmative, negative and super-affirmative resolution procedures and the Scrutiny Committees. These would not apply to Sarah's case.

It is important to mention both parliamentary controls and controls that take place in court. The candidate has applied this section to the scenario.

If delegated legislation was passed under the authority of the **Crime and Order (Fictitious) Act 2016**, Sarah would be able to challenge this in the High Court, using a procedure known as judicial review. This also supports the rule of law. Sarah would be seeking a ruling that the government is acting within its powers (intra vires). This confirms that the government is not above the law and both Parliament and the courts, if required under judicial review, can enforce the rule of law. The judiciary is separate from the Executive and legislature and therefore has a role in ensuring judges do not exceed their powers. The law also has to balance competing interests such as the right of the protesters to freedom of expression against the rights of the public to be safe.

As required by the specification, the candidate refers to the nature of law, and law and society.

There are two types of ultra vires – procedural and substantive. Procedural ultra vires is where the procedure for passing the delegated legislation has not been properly followed. For example, if the enabling Act required there to be consultation with interested parties and this was not carried out, or if the enabling Act required the affirmative resolution procedure to be used and the negative resolution procedure was used instead. We would need more information on the procedure used if the delegated legislation was passed. An example of where this challenge was used is the case of **Aylesbury Mushrooms**.

Good clear summary of this challenge. It is applied to the scenario and the candidate references a case to support their answer. This is essential in law.

Substantive ultra vires is where the delegated legislation is being challenged, as it possibly exceeds the power that was delegated. We would need more information to see if Sarah could use this challenge and whether the ban on demonstrations around Parliament Square goes beyond the powers in the enabling Act. A case example where this challenge was used is **R v Home Secretary ex parte Fire Brigades Union**.

There is a third challenge in the courts. This is where Sarah could say that the delegated legislation is unreasonable. This is also known as **Wednesbury** unreasonableness as it was established in this case.

Good clear summary of these two further challenges. Good citation of legal authority. There is application to the scenario.

To conclude, we need more information on the method by which the delegated legislation was passed before making a judgement on which challenge in court would be most suitable. There are challenges in Parliament that could be made prior to the delegated legislation being passed.

This is an effective conclusion and there is again reference to the scenario, which is essential for a question of this type.

Overall, this answer demonstrates a strong knowledge of delegated legislation challenges and there is thoughtful application of legal rules and principles to the situation.
There is excellent presentation of a legal argument, using appropriate legal terminology, case law and other legal authorities. The legal argument is detailed, fully developed and persuasive. This would achieve a level 4 mark.

Question 3 weaker response

There's some useful context here and the candidate mentions the main forms of delegated legislation, though these are not strictly needed for this question. With a question in this section, you must refer to the scenario. Here, for example, the candidate could have identified the enabling Act in the scenario – the Crime and Order (Fictitious) Act 2016.

The candidate has correctly (albeit briefly) explained why control is needed.

This is a brief summary with limited application of the law to the facts, which is essential for a question of this type. The candidate needs to show that they understand the law and are able to apply it.

The candidate has correctly identified the two main forms of ultra vires challenge but the answer is not developed and there is no reference to applicable case law. The candidate has failed to consider unreasonableness.

The candidate needs to explain why they feel that these don't apply. It is not necessary, with application of the law questions, to get a perfectly correct answer. The examiner is looking for an understanding of how the law could be applied. It is important, therefore, to fully explain your reasoning. Marks are available even if you don't include the correct application.

Delegated legislation is of a lower status than an Act of Parliament. It is made by someone other than Parliament but Parliament passes on the power to do this. This is called an enabling Act. There are various types of delegated legislation – orders in council, by laws and Statutory Instruments.

As Parliament is giving away some of its law-making power, it is important that this power is controlled. Sarah could challenge the delegated legislation in court in two ways – procedural and substantive ultra vires.

First, procedural ultra vires. This is where she would try and say that the correct procedure for making the delegated legislation has not been followed. We do not know, in this case, if it has or has not been followed as it doesn't say.

Second, substantive ultra vires. This is where the delegated legislation has gone beyond the powers actually delegated by Parliament. Again, we don't know if the delegated legislation that Sarah wants to challenge went beyond the powers given.

There is also control by Parliament before the delegated legislation becomes law. This is in the form of scrutiny committees and affirmative and negative resolutions. There is also the enabling Act which sets out what power is being given away and who then has the power to make delegated legislation. These don't apply to this case.

Overall, this is a weak response. Though the candidate does understand what delegated legislation is and why it needs to be controlled, the explanation behind each challenge is not developed and is too brief. There is limited application to the scenario and no reference to legal authority. This would achieve a mark within level 2.

Eduqas A Level Law: Component 1 Section B

In this section, you need to answer one question from a choice of two. **Part a** questions cover **AO1 Knowledge and understanding** and are worth 10 marks. **Part b** questions cover **AO3 Analysis and evaluation** and are worth 15 marks.

Question 5(a)

Explain the role of tribunals in the English legal system. [10]

The command word **explain** requires you write in simple terms about how something works.

Question 5(a) stronger response

Tribunals are an important part of our legal system and is a specialised court. Tribunals were recommended by the Franks Committee to be an example of 'openness, fairness and impartiality'. A tribunal will involve a legally qualified chairperson and two lay persons. They were originally set up to give the public a means of settling disputes regarding their social rights. Currently, there are three types – administrative (involving social and welfare rights), domestic (settling disputes within a private body e.g. Law Society) and employment tribunals, which deal with disputes between employers and employees. In the case of Peach Grey & Co v Sommers, the High Court held that tribunals were inferior to the courts.

> This is a detailed introduction which puts the answer into context and shows the examiner that the candidate knows about the types of tribunal. It is good exam practice to start an answer by defining the key terms in the question.

After a report by Sir Andrew Leggatt ('Tribunals for Users: One System, One Service'), several recommendations were made and implemented in the **Tribunals, Courts and Enforcement Act 2007**. This was a large reform to the tribunal system, prior to which the Act had been really complicated with over 70 different tribunals, all with different procedures. Part 1 of the Act established the Tribunal Service, which recommended that similar tribunals are grouped together and a two-tier approach has been adopted under one Tribunal Service. The First Tier tribunal consists of seven chambers, for example the Housing Chamber and the Social Care Chamber, and the Upper Tribunal consists of four tribunals, for example the Administrative Appeals Chamber. There is a right to appeal from the First Tier tribunals to the Upper Tier tribunal and then a further appeal to the Court of Appeal. The Administrative Justice and Tribunals Council keeps the tribunal system under control and ensures that all procedures are being adhered to. All tribunal judges are now appointed by the Judicial Appointments Commission which is the same body that appoints judges, so it gives tribunals a stronger reputation.

> These are two key pieces of legal authority in any tribunals answer.

> There is evidence of the candidate's excellent understanding of the legislative background to the tribunal system, and they can therefore go on to explain its workings with confidence.

There are numerous advantages with tribunals, most notably the cost, which is significantly less than a court battle as parties are encouraged not to use legal representation. Also, there is an element of expertise as the judge will have a great deal of knowledge in the relevant area. The procedures are considerably more flexible which is much more informal and relaxed than a full court battle. Speed is significant too, with tribunal judges taking an active role in case management, in line with the **Civil Procedure Rules 1998** and keeping to a strict timetable as cases are often heard within a day. They are much more independent too as the tribunal judge will have been appointed by the Judicial Appointments Commission.

> There is no requirement in part a for an evaluation, so this paragraph is unnecessary. It would be better to include some recent examples of tribunals or some newsworthy issues in relation to tribunals and their role. For example, there is no mention in this answer of employment tribunals, and this would be a useful addition for an excellent answer.

Question 5(a) weaker response

Tribunals are known as specialist courts or often as another form of ADR. An example of a tribunal is an administrative tribunal, which involve social and welfare rights, and employment tribunals, which deal with cases such as unfair dismissals and discrimination. The current tribunal system is as a result of the Leggatt Report, which suggested that there were too many tribunals and that they needed to be cut down, so now there is a First Tier tribunal and an Upper Tier tribunal. Tribunals usually have one legally qualified person and one person from each side of the argument, for example someone from a trade union.

Some examples of the chambers and the types of cases that are heard in them would be useful here.

ADR is encouraged by the **Civil Procedure Rules**, where all parties have to attempt ADR before going to court. If you are not happy with the decision of the First Tier tribunal, you can appeal to an Upper Tier tribunal and then go to court.

Again, ADR is not relevant here – the candidate can seem confused when ADR and tribunals are terms used interchangeably.
There is also no use of legal authority anywhere in this answer, which will reduce the mark and show little more than a satisfactory knowledge.

Question 5(b)

Analyse and evaluate the importance of magistrates in the criminal justice system. In your answer you should include a consideration of law and justice. [15]

The command words **analyse** and **evaluate** require you to critically evaluate legal issues by identifying different perspectives, supporting the identification of the strongest viewpoint and demonstrating your ability to counter alternative viewpoints. Legal authorities should be used to support your arguments.

Question 5(b) stronger response

The role of magistrates is to deal with criminals but they also have some civil functions. The history of lay magistrates dates back to the ***Justice of the Peace Act 1361****. There are over 28,000 magistrates, who deal with 98% of criminal cases in the magistrates' court and also summary trials. Magistrates also hear bail applications, early administrative hearings and requests for search and arrest warrants. They can also sit in the Crown Court to hear appeals. Magistrates can receive special training to sit in the youth court for youth offenders aged 10–17, and they have a limited civil jurisdiction for appeals against betting and alcohol licences and issues in the family proceedings court.*

A good introduction here with some decent reference to legal authority and an immediate link to the question in terms of defining key concepts.

Magistrates do not receive a salary but they do receive expenses and an allowance for travel and financial loss. Magistrates are appointed by the senior presiding judge on the advice of the Local Advisory Committee. A potential magistrate must be aged between 18 and 65 and must be able to commit to half a day a week in court. There are no formal legal qualifications needed but magistrates must possess the six key qualities as outlined by the Lord Chancellor in 1998. These are good character, understanding and communication, social awareness, maturity and sound temperament, sound judgement and commitment and reliability. People who are ineligible to become magistrates include traffic wardens, members of the armed forces, undischarged bankrupts and those with criminal convictions.

The average age of a magistrate is 52 years old, and so magistrates are not very representative. Most magistrates come from professional or middle-class backgrounds, although there is an even split of males and females, which is quite representative. Lay magistrates are assisted by a justice clerk who has to have been a qualified solicitor or barrister for at least 5 years. The justice clerk is not permitted to assist the magistrates in their decision making and can only advise the magistrates on issues of law.

Some recent statistics would be useful to illustrate these key evaluative points.

An advantage of magistrates is the cost, as magistrates are unpaid volunteers. Another advantage is the Bench provides a balanced view as there are usually three of them, and they are usually from the local area so have a local knowledge. In November 1998, the first blind magistrate was appointed so this shows greater diversity in the magistracy.

There's some good evaluation here, and it is all legally and factually correct, but this answer would be enhanced by referring to some recent statistics in relation to diversity, or some current affairs or issues that are relevant to the magistracy.

However, there is the theory that magistrates are prosecution-biased and are more willing to take the side of the police. Also, statistics show that there are inconsistencies in sentencing between different Benches. It is also a well-documented opinion that magistrates are 'middle-aged, middle-class and middle-minded' although this is improving slightly with a recent recruitment drive to appeal to mainstream volunteers, with adverts on local television, radio and buses. Another disadvantage is that magistrates are not legally qualified so may not be able to make the correct legal decision. Training is delivered through the Judicial College and does include some legal training and judicial aptitude but critics say this may be insufficient for the level of responsibility expected of them.

Therefore, although magistrates are very important, there are lots of disadvantages, which make them a heavily criticised aspect of the legal system. Having a lay element in the legal system, more representative of the local community than the judiciary means that this may be reflected in the justice that they are seen to serve.

Question 5(b) weaker response

The candidate shows some good knowledge on appointment of magistrates but does not really provide an analysis or evaluation.

More could be made about the role of the magistrate, to include some subject-specific terminology such as summary offences, early administrative hearings or bail applications.

Lay magistrates are not legally qualified people but they play a big role in the legal system. In order to be a lay magistrate, it is important that the person has six key qualities, which include understanding and communication, sound temperament, sound judgement, the ability to make a decision and social awareness. The person must be aged between 18 and 65 and have no criminal convictions, nor be a member of a profession that could interfere with being a magistrate, such as a police officer or a traffic warden. The Local Advisory Committee puts forward the names of potential magistrates after they have been through a two-stage interview. The first stage will check the candidate has the six key qualities and the second stage is where the magistrate is tested for judicial qualities. Magistrates can hear criminal cases, such as driving offences and minor assault, and civil cases such as the non-payment of council tax. Magistrates can also sit in the youth court to hear cases where young offenders have been accused of crimes.

The training for magistrates is split into three parts – introductory training, core training, consolidation training and then yearly appraisals. The training is overseen by the Judicial College. In court, magistrates are assisted by a justice clerk, who does not interfere with the decision but can help the magistrates with issues of law.

Providing no evaluation will seriously affect the mark, as the question specifically asks for an analysis and evaluation. There is plenty of content for marks in AO1 Knowledge and Understanding but not enough content for AO3 marks, which is the focus of this question.

Glossary

acquittal: the defendant has been found not guilty and will go free.

Act of Parliament (statute): a source of primary legislation that comes from the UK legislature.

actus reus: 'the guilty act' that must be present for a defendant to be found guilty of a crime. It can be a voluntary action, an omission or a state of affairs.

admissible: useful evidence which cannot be excluded on the basis that it is immaterial, irrelevant or violating the rules of evidence.

aggravating factor: a factor relevant to an offence that has the effect of increasing the sentence. Examples include the defendant having previous convictions, or if a weapon was used in the offence.

appropriate adult: a parent, guardian or social worker who must be present when a youth under the age of 17 is being interviewed in police custody, or on trial at the youth court. Their role is to make sure the young person understands legal terminology, is aware of their rights and is comforted and reassured.

bail: the defendant is allowed to be at liberty rather than prison before their court hearing, as long as they agree to particular conditions, such as regularly reporting to a police station.

bail hostel: a place of residence for people on bail who cannot give a fixed address, run by the Probation Service.

bilateral contract: a contract between two parties where each promises to perform an act in exchange for the other party's act.

binding precedent: a previous decision that has to be followed.

breach of contract: to break a contract by not following its terms and conditions.

Brexit: the common name given to Britain's exit from the European Union and is widely used by the media when referring to issues surrounding the negotiations.

cab rank rule: a barrister is obliged accept any work in a field in which they are competent to practice, at a court at which they normally appear and at their usual rates.

case stated: appeals on the grounds that there has been an error of law or the magistrates have acted out of their jurisdiction. Can be used by both the prosecution and defence.

causation (or **chain of causation):** connecting the actus reus and the corresponding result. For there to be criminal liability, there must be an unbroken chain of causation. There are two types of causation: legal and factual.

chambers: office space where barristers group together to share clerks (administrators) and operating expenses.

charge: the decision that a suspect should stand trial for an alleged offence.

claimant: the person bringing the action. Before 1 April 1999, this person was known as the plaintiff.

common law (also **case law** or **precedent):** law developed by judges through decisions in court.

contempt of court: a criminal offence punishable by up to two years' imprisonment for anyone who is disobedient or discourteous to a court of law.

conviction: the defendant has been found guilty and the case will proceed to the sentencing stage.

cross-examination: questioning of a witness in court by the opposing counsel.

custom: rules of behaviour which develop in a community without being deliberately invented.

damages: an award of money that aims to compensate the innocent party for the financial losses they have suffered as a result of the breach.

declaration of incompatibility: issued under s4 Human Rights Act 1998, this gives senior judges the power to question the compatibility of legislation with human rights. The declaration is sent to Parliament. It does not allow judges to strike out laws.

defendant: the person defending the action (e.g. the person accused of a crime).

delegated legislation (secondary or subordinate legislation): law created by a body other than Parliament but with the authority of Parliament, as laid down in primary legislation.

deterrent: something that discourages a particular action.

devolution: the transference of power from central government to regional or local government (e.g. the formation of the Welsh Government, the Northern Ireland Assembly and the Scottish Parliament).

direct applicability: when a piece of EU legislation is automatically binding and becomes part of a member state's law as soon as it is passed by the EU.

direct effect: allows individuals from EU member states to rely upon EU law in their own national courts, without having to take the case to the European courts.

disclosure: the obligation on both defence and prosecution to disclose all relevant evidence to the other side.

discretionary: it is a choice of the court whether to award or not.

duty solicitor: solicitors who work in private practice but have secured a contract with the Legal Aid Agency to provide criminal advice to people who have been arrested. The person in custody will have the assistance of whoever is on the rota for that day.

early administrative hearing: the first appearance at magistrates' court for all defendants suspected of a summary or indictable offence. This hearing considers legal funding, bail and legal representation.

entrenched: a firmly established piece of law which is difficult, or unlikely, to change (e.g. the US Bill of Rights). The UK has no laws that are entrenched.

equitable: fair.

examination in chief: the defence or prosecution questioning a witness in court by their own counsel.

first instance (trial court)**:** a court in which the first hearing of a case takes place. It is distinguished from an appellate court, which hears appeal cases.

Executive: the government.

First Tier Tribunal: part of the legal system that aims to settle the 'first instance' stage of legal disputes. It is split into seven chambers or specialist areas.

foreseeable: events the defendant should be able to have predicted could happen.

general defences: defences that can apply to any crime (with some exceptions), as opposed to 'special defences', which can only apply to certain crimes; for example diminished responsibility is only available for murder.

hearsay: second-hand evidence which is not what the witness knows personally but is something they have been told.

held: decided; the decision of the court.

House of Lords: the name of the Upper House in Parliament, which is the legislative chamber. Confusion arose before the establishment of the Supreme Court, as the highest appeal court was also called the House of Lords.

indictable: the most serious offences, triable only in the Crown Court.

Inns of Court: Barristers must join Inner Temple, Middle Temple, Gray's Inn or Lincoln's Inn. The Inns provide accommodation and education and promote activities.

institutional racism: a public or private body's operation or policies and procedure are deemed to be racist.

judicial precedent (case law): a source of law where past judges' decisions create law for future judges to follow.

judicial review: the process of challenging the legality of a decision, action or failure to act by a public body such as a government department or court.

laissez-faire: contract law term used to indicate that a person should have freedom of contract with minimal state or judicial interference.

lay (person): someone who is not legally qualified.

legislative reform order: a Statutory Instrument which can amend an Act of Parliament without the need for a parliamentary Bill.

maliciously: interpreted as meaning with intention or subjective recklessness.

mens rea: 'the guilty mind' that must be present for a defendant to be found guilty of a crime. It can include intention, recklessness or negligence.

mitigating factor: a factor relevant to the offence that has the effect of decreasing the sentence or reducing the charge. Examples include it being the defendant's first offence, or if the defendant pleaded guilty.

mitigation of loss: lessening or reducing a loss.

no win, no fee: an agreement between a solicitor and a client whereby the client will only pay the legal fees if the case is won.

novus actus interveniens: an intervening act that is so independent of the original act of the defendant that it succeeds in breaking the chain of causation. There may be liability for the initial act.

***obiter dicta*:** 'things said by the way'. This is not binding and is only persuasive.

objective: a test that considers not the particular defendant in question, but what another average, reasonable person would have done or thought if placed in the same position as the defendant.

occasion(ing): to bring about or to cause.

offer: in contract law, a proposition put by one person to another person made with the intention that it shall become legally binding as soon as the other person accepts it.

offeree: the person to whom an offer is being made and who will consequently accept the offer.

offeror: the person making an offer.

original precedent: a decision in a case where there is no previous legal decision or law for the judge to use.

parliamentary sovereignty: Dicey's principle that Parliament has absolute and unlimited power, and that an Act of Parliament overrules any other source of law.

Parole Board: a body set up under the Criminal Justice Act 1967 to hold meetings with an offender to decide whether they can be released from prison after serving a minimum sentence. They complete a risk assessment to determine whether it is safe to release the person back into the community. If they are safe to be released, they will be released on licence with conditions and close supervision.

***per incuriam*:** 'made by mistake'. Before the 1966 Practice Statement this was the only situation in which the House of Lords could depart from its previous decisions.

persuasive precedent: previous decision that does not have to be followed.

plea bargaining: the defendant pleads guilty to a lesser offence in return for a lower sentence to save court time and make the trial more predictable.

pre-sentence report: a report that helps the court to decide whether there are any factors in the defendant's history which may affect the sentencing.

presumption: a starting point for the courts, which presume certain facts to be true unless there is a greater balance of evidence to the contrary that disproves the presumption.

primary legislation: law made by the legislature, which in the UK is Parliament. Acts of Parliament are primary legislation.

privity of contract: a doctrine which allows the parties to a contract to sue each other, but does not allow a third party to sue.

Privy Council: the final appeal court for most Commonwealth countries.

procedural ultra vires: where the procedures laid down in an enabling Act for making a Statutory Instrument have not been followed (e.g. consultation was required but not carried out). Literal meaning: 'beyond the powers'.

proximate relationship: (in tort law) how close the defendant and victim are physically or emotionally.

pupillage: a one-year apprenticeship in which a pupil works alongside a qualified barrister, who is known as the pupil master.

Queen's Counsel (QC): an appointed senior barrister who has practised for at least 10 years. They can wear silk gowns, hence 'to take silk'.

***ratio decidendi*:** 'the reason for the decision'. This is the binding element of precedent, which must be followed.

remedy: an award made by a court to the innocent party in a civil case to 'right the wrong'.

retrospective effect: laws that operate affecting acts done before they were passed.

rights of audience: the right to appear as an advocate in any court.

rule of law: the state should govern its citizens in accordance with rules that have been agreed upon.

secret soundings: the old appointments process whereby information on a potential judge would be gathered over time, informally, from leading barristers and judges.

sentence: the punishment given to someone who has been convicted of an offence. It can be imprisonment, a community sentence or a suspended sentence or discharge.

separation of powers: state power is separated into three types, Executive, judicial and legislative, with each type exercised by different bodies or people.

***stare decisis*:** to stand by the previous decisions.

strict liability: a group of offences, usually regulatory in nature, that only require proof of actus reus, not mens rea.

subjective: an assumption relating to the individual in question (the subject).

substantive ultra vires: where delegated legislation goes beyond what Parliament intended.

summary offence: the least serious offences, triable only in the magistrates' court.

surety: a sum of money offered to the court by a person known to the suspect which guarantees the suspect's attendance at court when required.

tenancy: a permanent place for a barrister in chambers.

tort: a civil wrong committed by one individual against another, such as injury caused by negligence.

tortfeasor: someone who has committed a tort.

trespasser: a visitor who has no permission or authority to be on the occupier's land.

triable either way offence: mid-level crimes (e.g. theft, assault causing actual bodily harm) that can be tried in either the magistrates' court or Crown Court.

unilateral contract: an offer made in exchange for an act; for example, a reward for lost property.

uplift fee/success fee: additional fee in a no win, no fee case, of up to 100 per cent of the legal representative's basic fee, which is payable if the case is won. If the case is not won, the losing party will not have to pay any fees.

Upper Tribunal: hears appeals from the First Tier Tribunal, and in some complex cases will act within a first instance jurisdiction.

wounding: to break both layers of the skin, usually resulting in bleeding.

Index

Case index

Legislation index

Acknowledgements

p12 (top right) Standard Studio / Shutterstock.com; p12 (left) 271 EAG Moto / Shutterstock.com; p14 Paul Nicholas / Shutterstock.com; p15 Nerthuz / Shutterstock.com; p21 GrAl / Shutterstock.com; p25 (top) Minerva Studio / Shutterstock.com; p25 (bottom) Chris Bain / Shutterstock.com; p27 Lucian Milisan / Shutterstock.com; p33 Matthew Dixon / Shutterstock.com; p34 lazyllama / Shutterstock.com; p36 klublu / Shutterstock.com; p38 Victor Moussa / Shutterstock.com; p39 (top) ByEmo / Shutterstock.com; p39 (bottom) Araya Jirasatitsin / Shutterstock.com; p41 Photo Melon / Shutterstock.com; p44 Zerbor / Shutterstock.com; p45 ESB Professional / Shutterstock.com; p48 Africa Studio / Shutterstock.com; p55 Iconic Bestiary / Shutterstock.com; p56 (top to bottom) KZenon / Bacho / Rawpixel.com / Portrait Images Asia by Nonwarit / Shutterstock.com; p59 Andrey_Popov / Shutterstock.com; p64 Tupungato / Shutterstock.com; p80 Aleutie / Shutterstock.com; p81 kenny1 / Shutterstock.com; p85 Adam Gregor / Shutterstock.com; p86 sirtravelalot / Shutterstock.com; p89 Spiroview Inc / Shutterstock.com; p90 Angelina Dimitrova / Shutterstock.com; p91 SpeedKingz / Shutterstock.com; p92 Uber Images / Shutterstock.com; p96 hafakot / Shutterstock.com; p112 Everilda / Shutterstock.com; p114 AVA Bitter / Shutterstock.com; p118 NothingIsEverything / Shutterstock.com; p119 (top) vasabii / Shutterstock.com; p119 (bottom) Natcha29 / Shutterstock.com; p121 F8 Studio / Shutterstock.com; p125 Suphaksorn Thongwongboot / Shutterstock.com; p131 Sergey Dudyrev / Shutterstock.com; p132 hafakot / Shutterstock.com; p136 AnnIris / Shutterstock.com; p137 Andy Dean / Shutterstock.com; p138 Brian A Jackson / Shutterstock.com; p139 javi_indy / Shutterstock.com; p141 Giancarlo Liguori / Shutterstock.com; p143 (top) Doraemaon9572 / Shutterstock.com; p143 (bottom) Yustus / Shutterstock.com; p145 BravoKiloVideo / Shutterstock.com; p147 BlueRingMedia / Shutterstock.com; p149 Scott Maxwell LuMaxArt / Shutterstock.com; p150 FabrikaSimf / Shutterstock.com; p152 jkcDesign / Shutterstock.com; p153 docstockmedia / Shutterstock.com; p157 Andrei Nekrassov / Shutterstock.com; p158 TFrancis / Shutterstock.com; p159 Yorkman / Shutterstock.com; p160 Best Vector Elements / Shutterstock.com; p165 plantic / Shutterstock.com; p166 pryzmat / Shutterstock.com; p167 Duplass / Shutterstock.com; p170 art4all / Shutterstock.com; p172 Elenarts / Shutterstock.com; p174 hidesy / Shutterstock.com; p176 Branislav Cerven / Shutterstock.com; p177 Billion Photos / Shutterstock.com; p179 (top) HQuality / Shutterstock.com; p179 (bottom) alexskopje / Shutterstock.com; p180 pcruciatti / Shutterstock.com; p182 (top) David Carillet / Shutterstock.com; p182 (bottom) magic pictures / Shutterstock.com; p183 Charles Haire / Shutterstock.com; p186 Koca Vehbi /Shutterstock.com; p188 (top) pinkjellybeans / Shutterstock.com; p188 (bottom) 1000 Words / Shutterstock.com; p190 (top) melis / Shutterstock.com; p190 (bottom) 1000 Words / Shutterstock.com; p192 (top) pisaphotography / Shutterstock.com; p192 (bottom) 1000 Words / Shutterstock.com; p195 Solid Web Designs / Shutterstock.com; p196 BortN66 / Shutterstock.com; p197 Photographee.eu / Shutterstock.com; p198 PRESSLAB / Shutterstock.com; p202 Titikul_B / Shutterstock.com; p203 Robert Lucian Crusitu / Shutterstock.com; p205 Andrey_Popov / Shutterstock.com; p208 Everett Historical / Shutterstock.com; p209 mark reinstein / Shutterstock.com; p211 s_bukley / Shutterstock.com; p219 pikepicture / Shutterstock.com; p222 Adam Gregor / Shutterstock.com; p226 Denis Makarenko / Shutterstock.com